MARKET THEORY AND
THE PRICE SYSTEM

THE COLLECTED WORKS OF ISRAEL M. KIRZNER

ISRAEL M. KIRZNER

Market Theory and the Price System

Edited and with an Introduction by

PETER J. BOETTKE and FRÉDÉRIC SAUTET

LIBERTY FUND Indianapolis

Introduction and index © 2011 by Liberty Fund, Inc.

Market Theory and the Price System was first published by D. Van Nostrand in 1963.

All rights reserved

Printed in the United States of America

C 10 9 8 7 6 5 4 3 2 1
P 10 9 8 7 6 5 4 3 2 1

Library of Congress Cataloging-in-Publication Data
Kirzner, Israel M.

Market theory and the price system / Israel M. Kirzner; edited and with an introduction by Peter J. Boettke and Frédéric Sautet.

p. cm. — (The collected works of Israel M. Kirzner)

Includes bibliographical references and index.

ISBN 978-0-86597-759-4 (hardcover: alk. paper) —
ISBN 978-0-86597-760-0 (pbk.: alk. paper)

1. Marketing. 2. Prices. I. Boettke, Peter J. II. Sautet, Frédéric E.
III. Title.

HF5415 .K57 2011
338.5'21—dc22   2010044209

LIBERTY FUND, INC.
8335 Allison Pointe Trail, Suite 300
Indianapolis, Indiana 46250-1684

CONTENTS

INTRODUCTION TO
THE LIBERTY FUND EDITION

Market Theory and the Price System was published in 1963 as Professor Israel M. Kirzner's first (and only) textbook. It was also his second book publication after that of *The Economic Point of View,* three years earlier. *Market Theory and the Price System* tackles the common subject of price theory, which was part of the training of young economists at the time (and still is). While Professor Kirzner's textbook filled a gap in the market by presenting an integrated view of Austrian price theory in contrast to the Chicago approach, the book never became a commercial success, which is not surprising considering the intellectual atmosphere when it was published.

Israel Kirzner has described his graduate education in economics at New York University (NYU) as one of confusion. One night a week he learned standard price theory through George Stigler's *Theory of Price* (1946), and on another night of the week he learned about the market process from Ludwig von Mises and his classic work *Human Action* (1949).[1] Both approaches were diametrically opposed to the macroeconomics of Keynesianism, which was also taught at the time; thus, by virtue of that opposition alone, the two works seemed to be intellectually aligned. However, there were also subtle differences in emphasis and especially style of presentation that gave Kirzner food for thought.

According to Kirzner himself, he started out his career as a theorist only to learn that in the eyes of his colleagues he was a historian of economic thought. Kirzner was (and remained to the end of his teaching career at NYU) an economic theorist. He specialized in market theory and the price system. As his work matured, he came to focus primarily on the role that the entrepreneur played in the market economy. *Market Theory and the Price System* was his first systemic attempt to examine how the logic of action enables us to understand the workings of the market economy.

---

1. In fact, Kirzner has stated on more than one occasion in lectures that the first words he heard Mises speak were "the market is a process." He describes the experience as intellectually jarring: He understood what it meant to say "the market was a place," but what could it possibly mean to say that "the market is a process"? Answering that question would drive Kirzner throughout his career.

The book, originally published in 1963 (with no subsequent editions), had been part of a series of works by the Volker Fund to make sure that economic teaching did not come completely under the sway of Keynesianism.[2] Published one year earlier, in 1962, Murray Rothbard's *Man, Economy, and State* provided a systemic treatise on the principles of economics. In contrast, Kirzner's work was more or less an intermediate-to graduate-level textbook in price theory. Thus, read in tandem, these books represented an Austrian school of economics alternative to the approach of both the Chicago School of Milton Friedman and George Stigler and the Massachusetts Institute of Technology–Harvard economics of Paul Samuelson. The fate of both books in the marketplace of economics texts in the 1960s is indicative of the state of economic research and teaching at the time. The technical nuances of the approach of Rothbard and Kirzner were missed.[3]

However, even within the Austrian camp, some disagreement arose over the way to present price theory. In a memorandum to the Volker Fund dated December 1961, Rothbard raised critical objections to Kirzner's book.[4] Rothbard argued that "What Prof. Kirzner had done is, so to speak,

2. For a discussion of the role of the Volker Fund in economic research and education from the 1940s through the 1960s, see James Piereson (2005), "Funding a Movement," *The Insider.*

3. The well-known Old Institutional School economist C. E. Ayers (1963), in reviewing Kirzner's book in the *American Economic Review,* argues that the book fails in its task as a manual of technical price theory but perhaps succeeds as an ideological tract intended to instill in its readers a high esteem for the free market economy. Ayers missed the subtle *economic* argument concerning the adjustment processes of the market economy that were emerging from Kirzner's work. A lesser professional figure, Victor Heck (1963), reviewed Rothbard's *Man, Economy, and State* in the *American Economic Review* and dismissed the book as dogmatic and behind the times technically. In both reviews, it should be pointed out, the reviewers went out of their way to highlight the intellectual inspiration both Kirzner and Rothbard drew from Ludwig von Mises. It is as if mentioning Mises was almost enough circa 1960 to discredit an economic thinker. To get a good sense of this professional consensus of the times, see David Winch's (1964, 480, 482) review of *Man, Economy, and State* from the *Economic Journal.* "As befits a disciple of Ludwig von Mises," Winch writes, "Professor Rothbard has written a book that is both nostalgic and tendentious." Winch describes the book as a dogmatic apology for the free market that is "more akin to systematic theology than to economics."

4. "Comments on Israel M. Kirzner's MS: *Market Theory and the Price System,*" Rothbard Archives, Ludwig von Mises Institute, Auburn, Alabama.

to carry water on both shoulders." *Market Theory and the Price System*, by Rothbard's reading, was fundamentally a Stiglerian work in the refinements of price theory infused here and there with Austrian insights and obligatory qualifications. Rothbard failed to see the subtle argument that was emerging from Kirzner's analysis of the market system.

Kirzner's textbook sought to communicate the basic insights from Philip Wicksteed and the founders of the Austrian School of Economics to a new generation of economic students. As he puts it in the preface: "Whatever the author may have learned from Marshall, Edgeworth, and J. B. Clark, this book probably will reveal that he has learned more from Menger, Böhm-Bawerk and Wicksteed" (1963, vii). The basic idea of the book was to utilize the tools of economics reasoning to explain the market process. Kirzner states his intent clearly:

> The approach adopted in this book views the market as a process of adjustment. In this process individual market participants are being forced continually to adjust their activities according to patterns imposed by the activities of others. Market theory then consists essentially in the analysis of these step-by-step adjustments and of the way the information required for these adjustments is communicated. Equilibrium positions are not, as in other books, treated as important in themselves. They are rather seen as merely limiting cases where the market process has nothing further to do, all activities being already mutually adjusted to the fullest extent. (1963, vii)

This is what Rothbard ironically misunderstood in his "water on both shoulders" comment.[5] The equilibrium properties of markets as discussed in Stigler (and also Kirzner) are not logically wrong. However, they hold only when the mutual adjustments through exchange have been fully realized and the plans of the different agents in an economy are perfectly coordinated. Still, this knowledge of the limit theorems of the

---

5. We say "ironically" because it is mainly through Rothbard's writings that we learned that economics is not a science of exact prediction, but one of tendencies and directions. The propositions of the "evenly rotating economy" in Rothbard's *Man, Economy, and State* serve the same intellectual purpose as the Stiglerian propositions of optimality in consumer choice and producer decision do in Kirzner's *Market Theory and the Price System*. In both books, the modern reader in economics can see how this emphasis on process would later be refined into a fuller understanding of the market as a dynamic process of adjustment through entrepreneurial competition.

market system is vital to understanding the tendencies and direction of the processes of adjustment. However, the bulk of economic explanation must be on the continual adjustment of market activity that is guided by relative price movements and the lure of pure economic profit and the penalty of loss. The market economy is defined in Kirzner's system not by a state of affairs, but instead by an intricate matrix of human interdependencies in the realm of exchange relations and production decisions.

Central to *Market Theory and the Price System* is coordination—the critical question of any economic system. It is not just a matter of the allocation of scarce resources, but the coordination of activities such that the most willing demanders and the most willing suppliers have their plans dovetail through mutually beneficial adjustments through exchange. The unique framework Kirzner develops for microeconomic analysis, following Mises and Hayek, opens up for examination error in decision making, entrepreneurial profit, and competition as a process of discovery and learning. As Kirzner explained in an interview in 2006, in the book he was trying to bridge a gap between the neoclassical view of the market and what he understood Mises as saying about the market process. No one at the time really grasped Mises's view of entrepreneurship or what Hayek meant regarding the role of knowledge.

For the reader of *Market Theory and the Price System* familiar with Kirzner's later writings, the critical chapters to study carefully are 7 and 11 (especially 7). In both of these chapters we see the seeds of his more mature argument about the disequilibrium foundations of equilibrium economics and the anticipation of his theory of the competitive entrepreneurial market process. Chapter 7 attempts to describe the market as a learning process and to provide an explanation for equilibration. Price theory did not explain the causation of price changes, it just assumed it. Kirzner endeavored, along Hayekian lines, to make Mises's insights on entrepreneurship and the market process available to the modern reader of microeconomic theory. One must realize the magnitude of this endeavor—something that even Rothbard failed to see.

ACKNOWLEDGMENTS

We would first like to thank wholeheartedly Israel Kirzner for his unparalleled contribution to economic science. Kirzner's research program has deeply enriched the discipline and has shed light on some of economics' most difficult puzzles. Economists owe him an immense intellectual debt.

The publication of the Collected Works of Israel M. Kirzner would not be a reality without the participation of Liberty Fund, Inc. We are extremely grateful to Liberty Fund, and especially Emilio Pacheco, for making this project possible. To republish Kirzner's unique oeuvre has been on our minds since our time spent at New York University in the 1990s—where one of us was a professor (Peter) and the other a postdoc student (Frederic). We are thrilled at the idea that current and future generations of economists and other scholars will have easy access to Kirzner's works.

Finally, we wish to thank Rosemarie Fike for her invaluable help in the publication of this volume.

Peter J. Boettke and Frédéric Sautet

BIBLIOGRAPHY OF WORKS CITED IN THE INTRODUCTION

Ayers, C. E. (1963) "Review of Israel Kirzner, *Market Theory and the Price System*," *American Economic Review*, 53 (September): 755–756.

Heck, V. (1963) "Review of Murray Rothbard, *Man, Economy, and State*," *American Economic Review*, 53 (June): 460–461.

Mises, L. (1949) *Human Action*. New Haven, Connecticut: Yale University Press.

Piereson, J. (2005) "Funding a Movement," *The Insider*, Summer, http://www .heartland.org/custom/semod_policybot/pdf/18502.pdf.

Rothbard, M. (1961) "Comments on Israel M. Kirzner's MS: *Market Theory and the Price System*," December, memorandum to the Volker Fund, Rothbard Archives, Ludwig von Mises Institute, Auburn, Alabama.

Rothbard, M. (1962) *Man, Economy, and State*, 2 vols. Princeton, New Jersey: Van Nostrand.

Stigler, G. (1946) *The Theory of Price*. New York: Macmillan.

Winch, D. (1964) "Review of Murray Rothbard, *Man, Economy, and State*," *Economic Journal*, 74 (June): 480–482.

PREFACE

During the past few years a number of competently written textbooks on price theory have appeared. The author's excuse for adding yet another book to the elementary literature in this field is that his approach, while in no sense original, presents the subject in an entirely different light.

The approach adopted in this book views the market as a *process of adjustment*. In this process individual market participants are being forced continually to adjust their activities according to the patterns imposed by the activities of others. Market theory then consists essentially in the analysis of these step-by-step adjustments and of the way the information required for these adjustments is communicated. Equilibrium positions are not, as in other books, treated as important in themselves. They are rather seen as merely limiting cases where the market process has nothing further to do, all activities being already mutually adjusted to the fullest extent.

Despite the importance attached to the implications of the approach adopted here, users of this book will find relatively few major substantive departures from price theory as it is usually presented. The principal areas where major differences will be found arise out of the drastically reduced attention paid to perfect competition. Presuming the basic course in general economics, this book is designed for an undergraduate course in intermediate price theory.

For the rest, an author can hardly hope to have escaped revealing his own proclivities, biases, and predilections. Determined efforts have been made to subordinate geometry to economic reasoning. Whatever the author may have learned from Marshall, Edgeworth, and J. B. Clark, this book probably will reveal that he has learned more from Menger, Böhm-Bawerk, and Wicksteed.

Besides his indebtedness to the literature, the author must acknowledge much kind help received from several persons during the preparation of this book. To his teacher Ludwig von Mises, above all, he owes his appreciation of the market process. In addition to reading the finished manuscript, Professor Mises offered many helpful suggestions during its completion. It is with deep pleasure that the author dedicated this volume to him upon the attainment of his eightieth year.

The author is grateful to his colleagues at New York University, as well as to his students, for stimulating discussions on a number of points. To Professor L. M. Lachmann of the University of Witwatersrand, South Africa, he is indebted for several valuable insights that were made use of in exposition. The author's wife has patiently and cheerfully endured, aided, and encouraged throughout the book's preparation. To all these he is grateful; none of them is to be held responsible for all that remains unsatisfactory.

Israel M. Kirzner

MARKET THEORY AND
THE PRICE SYSTEM

This book is devoted to the study of the theory of the market system. In this first chapter we attempt to obtain a clear notion of what is meant by a *market;* what is meant by a *market system;* and how economic theory can throw light on the nature of *market processes.* Our discussion will clarify the relationship between market theory and other branches of economics. Moreover, it will indicate the importance of the economic theory of the market for an adequate understanding of the world we live in.

THE INDIVIDUAL AND THE MARKET

Society consists of *individual human beings.* Each human being is eager to act to improve his position, whenever this appears possible. In order to satisfy his desires, a man may act on his own (as, for example, when he paints his house by himself), or he may fulfill his ends indirectly through exchange (as when he pays another man to do the painting). Where an exchange transaction takes place freely, the two individuals involved have *both* acted to fulfill separately their respective goals.

In a predominantly free society, individuals are in most respects at liberty to act as they choose. That is, in such a society an individual is generally at liberty to take advantage of any opportunity (as *he* perceives the existence of such an opportunity) in order to improve his position (as *he* understands the idea of improving his position). He is free to act in isolation, and he is free to engage in acts of exchange with other individuals (whenever he and some other individuals both perceive the opportunity of mutual benefit through trade). As we shall find, such opportunities for mutually advantageous exchange arise constantly in society. Moreover, the exploitation by individuals of these opportunities opens up yet further opportunities of the same kind, both to the individuals themselves and to others in the society. A *market* exists whenever the individual members of a society are in sufficiently close contact to one another to be aware of numerous such opportunities for exchange and, in addition, are free to take advantage of them. A *market economy* exists wherever the ramifications of the market become so widespread and the opportunities it offers so numerous and attractive that most individuals find it advantageous to carry on their economic activities predominantly through the market rather than on their own.

The market economy is thus to be distinguished, on the one hand, from the *autarkic* economy, where individuals carry on their economic activity isolated from one another, being unaware or unwilling to take advantage of opportunities for exchange. On the other hand, it is to be distinguished from the *centrally controlled* economy where economic activity of individuals is directed by a central authority so that, although transfers of goods among individuals may be ordered by the central authority, individuals are not free to take advantage of exchange opportunities which they themselves may perceive. It is unlikely that any one of these three types of economies will exist historically in its theoretically purest form. To some extent, limited market activity is likely to arise even in the most primitive and autarkic of societies, whereas even the most rigid of centrally controlled economies leaves room, legally or illegally, for some market-type activity between individuals. Finally, even the most fully developed market economy is incapable of making it advantageous for individuals to seek the satisfaction of *all* their wants exclusively through the market. (Most men, for example, turn to the market for a haircut but not for a shave.)

In the developed market economy, the conditions of production have become adjusted to the market requirements. Over a period of time, individuals acting through the market have succeeded in setting up an organization of production and exchange which, in turn, has widened the market until it has embraced the bulk of all economic activity in the society. In such a system, as in any system where the individual is relatively free to act as he pleases, men seek to improve their positions with the means at their disposal. But, whereas the isolated individual can improve his position only by adjusting himself to, and manipulating, the conditions imposed by *nature*, in the market economy the individual acts to take advantage also of the conditions and opportunities made available by the market.

The salient fact that emerges from this discussion is that any description of market activity means the description of *individual* activity, but also that the activity of *each* participating individual in the market is conditioned by the actions of other participating individuals (either in the past or as anticipated in the future). It is this insight, we will discover, that is the basis for the economic analysis of the market system and of the processes that take place in the market.

THE MARKET SYSTEM

To the casual observer, market activity seems to be a bewildering and uncoordinated mass of transactions. Each individual in the market society is free to buy what and when he pleases, to sell what and when he pleases, to produce or to consume what he pleases, or to refrain altogether from any or all of these activities. Transactions may involve any of innumerable commodities or services, they may involve any of a wide range of quantities and qualities, and they may be concluded at any of a wide variety of prices.

Economic analysis reveals that this seeming chaos in the activity of market participants is only apparent. In fact, analysis shows that the exchanges that take place are subject to definite forces at work in the market. These *market forces* guide the individuals participating in the market in their decisions. Each market decision is made under the stress of market forces set up by the decisions, past or expected, of all the market participants. During any given period, therefore, the decisions made by individual market participants constitute an interlocking system embracing the entire scope of the market. This network of decisions constitutes the *market system*. The end results of all these decisions make up the achievements of the market system; and the tasks which society may seek to fulfill by permitting a market economy are the assigned *functions* of the market system.

The importance of the market system and of its analysis is not simply the discovery that decisions are made under constraints set up by other decisions. Market system analysis, we will discover, reveals a remarkable feature in the operation of these constraints, and it is chiefly this feature that invests market theory with its importance. The real significance of the market system lies in the fact that the mutual interplay of these constraints makes up a unique *process* through which the *decisions of different individuals* (who may be quite unknown to one another) tend to be *brought progressively into greater consistency with each other.*

Consistency and correspondence between the decisions made by different market participants are of the first importance in any successful execution by the market of its functions. If all potential members of the labor force decided to train themselves as skilled watchmakers, a catastrophic aberration of individual decisions would exist. After all, a decision to become a watchmaker depends on the confident assumption that *some* other people will be barbers, tailors, etc.

The free interplay of individual decisions in the marketplace constantly generates new forces modifying and shaping the delicate, sensitive, and interlocking decision network that makes up the system. It is the task of market theory to trace the consequences of these market forces, paying particular attention to the degree in which they constrain independently made decisions into mutually corresponding and concordant systems.

THE FOUNDATIONS OF MARKET THEORY

The construction by economists of the body of propositions that make up market theory is founded upon their consciousness of the existence and the nature of economic law. The recognition of "laws" in economic affairs implies the understanding that apparent *chains of causation* prevail in social events, just as in the physical world. Acts of individuals in the market are perceived as taken *in consequence* of definite acts, prior or anticipated, of other individuals. What goes on in the market at any one time is to be ascribed to what has gone on in the past, or to past anticipations as to what will go on in the future. Market phenomena do not emerge haphazardly in a vacuum; they are understood to be uniquely "determined" by market forces. →kind of a tautology?

While the essential concept of a law of economics is thus quite parallel to that of a law of physical nature, the two kinds of law have little further in common. Laws of physical nature are inferred from the observation of sequences of physical events. Economic laws, as we shall see, are founded on our *understanding* of the influence that a given event will have upon the actions of individuals.

To be sure, the laws of physical nature are also operative in the spheres of human activities. A heater raises room temperature, and ice lowers the temperature in the ice box; human beings are more comfortable at some temperatures than at others, and food keeps better at some temperatures than at others. These physical, physiological, or biological laws must be considered in any attempt to "explain" why men buy heaters or ice. The recognition of economic law involves the insight that, even *after* the physical, physiological, and psychological sciences have been utilized to the utmost in tracing the influences that have helped determine an economic "event," there still remain significant elements that have not been traced back to prior causes. These elements, in the absence of an economic theory, would have to be considered as undetermined by any causal forces. The recognition of economic law means the perception of determinate causal chains constraining the course of events insofar as these are left undetermined by physical, physiological, or psychological laws.

Consider, for example, the consequences upon the price of ice of a sudden sharp reduction in the quantity available for sale. The most complete application of the physical sciences (while it might throw a great deal of light on why such a reduction in the supply has occurred, or upon the possible alternative ways consumers might be able to do without ice) can in itself tell us nothing about why subsequent ice purchases are carried out at higher prices. Our explanation of the higher prices being the consequence of the reduced supply thus invokes the concept of *economic* laws, which we *understand* as explaining the result of the particular change that has occurred when other aspects of the situation have remained unchanged.

The nature and existence of economic law, and its manifestation in the interplay of market forces, must now be briefly traced back to the actions of the individual human being.

THE INDIVIDUAL AND ECONOMIC BEHAVIOR

The possibility of perceiving chains of cause and effect uniquely economic is due to the presence in human action of categories that have no parallel in the realm of physical laws. And because the mind of the individual investigating causation in economic affairs is capable of directly understanding these categories (since, as we shall see, they are self-evident to the human mind), he is capable of directly grasping the existence of economic laws. The human mind is immediately conscious of the fundamental and all-pervasive category embedded in the web of all conscious human action. This category is *purpose*. Actions are undertaken for specific purposes. We are aware of the purposive character of our own actions, and we understand that the conscious actions of other human beings also are purposive. However much we may either despise or fail to understand the particular purposes behind the actions of our fellows, we do not doubt that their actions aim at securing for themselves some situation that they prefer over what they expect to prevail in the absence of their actions.

Moreover, because we assume all action to be purposive, and because we live in a world which offers at each instant the possibility of many different kinds of action, we are immediately aware, too, that every human action must be the embodiment of a *choice among alternatives*. At each instant man must choose between the courses of action (including inaction) that are open to him. Any such adopted course, we understand, has been adopted as preferable to the rejected courses of action.

Thus, human action involves the categories of purpose, of alternatives, of choice among these alternatives, of the preferred (that is, the adopted) alternative, and of the rejected alternatives. These categories suffuse all transactions of men, both in isolation and in the market. They are the categories upon which economic theory depends for its very existence.

Economic theory approaches complex social and market phenomena by searching for the individual actions from which these phenomena arise. Any such individual action is understood as having involved the adoption of one alternative and the rejection of others. The adopted alternative is understood as having been compared with, and preferred over, the other alternatives; that is, it was considered as being either the means to the attainment of the most cherished possible purpose or the most efficient of the available means to the attainment of a specific purpose. Economic theory understands that each action inevitably involved a cost. The adopted alternative has been adopted at the expense of the rejected alternatives. The rejected alternatives, which in themselves may have been highly desirable, have been renounced for the sake of the adopted alternative. Economic theory "explains" individual actions, therefore, by tracing them to the circumstances that made them "profitable"; that is, to the circumstances that made the "costs" worthwhile. *Changes in* the patterns of human action are traced in this way either to changes in the terms on which alternatives are available relative to each other, or to changes in the framework of purposes within which the worthwhileness of the relevant costs are valued.

Market phenomena lend themselves readily to analysis in this way as soon as it is realized that the terms on which alternatives are offered to an individual are, in a market economy, determined in large part by the actions of other individuals rather than merely by natural events. It becomes illuminatingly possible to view every transaction in the market as, on the one hand, a consequence of the particular complex of alternatives presented to the individual by the market before the action was undertaken, and, on the other hand, as in some way affecting the complex of alternatives that will be subsequently faced by the individual market participants. Even the most intricately entangled web of market phenomena can be reduced to the elementary actions that they consist of. Systematic analysis of market phenomena in this way is able to yield propositions linking changing patterns in prices, qualities and quantities of output, of consumption, and the like, to logically prior changes in the "data." These logically prior changes may be either in the circumstances (arising both inside and outside the market) affecting the alternative opportunities open to individuals pursuing their purposes, or in the structure of purposes with reference to which individuals appraise the relative usefulness of opportunities open to them.

To revert to an example mentioned several pages previously, a sharp decrease in the quantity of ice supplied to the market can easily be linked, by this kind of reasoning, to a subsequent price rise. As ice purchasers find the availability of ice sharply reduced (other things being unchanged), they find it necessary to restrict the obtainable limited quantities of ice to only the most important of the uses to which the previously larger quantity of ice had been put. Thus, any additional ice block that they contemplate to purchase after the decrease in supply involves the potential fulfillment of a purpose held more important than the purpose whose fulfillment, before the decrease in supply, depended on the purchase of an additional ice block. It follows that some of the alternatives that, before the decrease in supply, were more important than an additional ice block may now be less important than an additional ice block. An alternative whose sacrifice for the sake of an additional ice block had hitherto been considered as not worthwhile will now be considered, perhaps, as highly "profitable." In other words, the cost that individuals will be prepared to incur (that is, the price that they will be willing to offer) for an additional block of ice, has risen. Further examination of the machinery of a competitive market would then readily explain the subsequent higher market prices for ice.

The simple causal chain shown thus to link a decrease in supply with a subsequent price rise has been adduced merely as an illustration of the concatenation of decisions that make up any period of market history, and of the kind of reasoning that can reveal the operation of economic law in this way. The theory of the market that we study in this book applies this kind of reasoning to the isolation of the principal types of causal chains that express themselves through market forces and that make up the skeleton of the market system of economic organization.

ECONOMIC THEORY AND ECONOMIC REALITY

Our ice block illustration, at the same time, is able to clarify the relationship between the world of economic theory and the world of economic reality. This relationship must be kept firmly in mind throughout what might otherwise appear as the unrealistic or abstract chapters that make up the bulk of this book.

Our theory of ice prices, it will be observed, did not depend upon the particular physical properties of ice. Although we may know what physical properties of ice make it an economic good, all that is required for our "ice price" theory is simply the fact that ice *is* an economic good—simply, that more of it is preferred to less of it. In fact, everything which we were able to conclude concerning the price of ice can be asserted with equal validity concerning economic goods in general.

Thus, *abstractness* and *generality* are the twin aspects of economic theory that emerge from our illustration. Economic theory is *abstract,* in the sense that the reasoning does not depend on the numerous particular properties of the data we are theorizing about. Economic reasoning throws light, for example, on situations that human beings associate with specific *sensations.* The demand for food has to do with feelings of hunger or of satiety; the demand for reading material has to do with the thrills of exploration, suspense, or learning; the supply of labor has to do with feelings of weariness and fatigue. It is emphasized that economic theory does *not* refer to these *specific* sensations. Economic theory abstracts the element of *preference*— bare and colorless—that emerges in each of these situations. In geometry a proposition may throw light on properties of rectangular objects, including restaurant tables, milk cartons, and billboards. Geometry, however, has nothing essentially to do with eating in restaurants, drinking milk, or advertising. Economic theory is in similar case: it abstracts from actual situations those elements to which it is relevant.

Economic theory is, as a consequence, *general,* in that its conclusions have validity for sets of data that may be widely different from each other in every particular aspect other than the economic. (To relieve the abstractness of the reasoning, numerous concrete examples are given of situations that may be quite general; these examples will serve only as illustrations of general propositions.) In the theory of the market economy, our propositions will relate to such entities as "goods that consumers desire more urgently," or "resources that are in relatively short supply," or "production processes that are relatively more efficient." Any such proposition may apply to many different situations.

Our "ice block" illustration demonstrates, in addition, the possibility of deducing economic propositions whose validity does not depend upon the accuracy or completeness of any empirical observations. Since our theory of ice prices did not depend on any particular physical properties of ice, nor upon any particular psychological attitudes toward ice (except that it be considered an economic good), our theory required no laboratory experiments upon ice nor any psychological observations of behavior. Our theory depended only on the logic of choice; that is, it required only that we understand what human beings will do when they find that the use that can be made today of a block of ice is more important than the use that could have been made of it yesterday. We are able to develop propositions of this kind *because we are acting human beings.* We know, without empirical observations, how a change in the attractiveness of the terms on which a human being is free to choose will tend to affect the choice of any being whose behavior is guided by reason similar to our own. Economic theory is founded on this kind of knowledge that we possess. We can analyze the effects of changes upon human action, in the abstract, because we are immediately aware of the logic that governs all human action. The logic that governs human action is the same logic that the economic theorist applies in analyzing this action. If molecules had preferences and acted purposefully to achieve them, then the physicist would have a source of knowledge concerning the behavior of physical matter quite independent of any empirical findings that he might make. This source would be his own immediate understanding of how purposeful beings tend to behave under changing patterns of alternatives. The economic theorist finds himself in precisely such a favored position.

Now, the logical validity of a proposition of economic theory does not mean that the real world presents any instances of the truth of the proposition. In mathematics, for example, it does not follow from the geometrical proposition that states that the base angles of an isosceles triangle are equal, that we will ever be able to find such a triangle. Similarly a proposition linking a restriction in the supply of ice or of any economic good (other things being unchanged) to a subsequent rise in its price does not, in itself, mean that in the real world there has been or will ever be such a restriction in supply (and it certainly does not mean that with any such a restriction in supply, the "other things" will remain unchanged). All that a proposition can assert is that, *if* given changes occurred under given conditions, then certain consequences would follow.

It is clear, then, that if the economic theorist is to be of any assistance in understanding the real world, he must develop theorems concerning situations that do occur. The economist who analyzes concrete economic problems applies propositions of far-reaching generality to particular situations in which he recognizes the dominance of conditions similar to those governing the relevant propositions. The application of economic theory in this way certainly cannot be done without careful, accurate, and complete factual and statistical descriptions of the real world situations in which it is proposed to detect the operation of the economic laws that are expounded by theory.

Therefore, the work of the "practical" economist, who aims at explaining what has happened in the real world or at predicting the likely consequences in the future of some proposed or adopted policy, must of necessity include close attention to "facts." Important and indeed indispensable as the examination of the "facts" of economic history—remote or current—may be for these purposes, this task is clearly *distinguished from that of constructing theories.* The theorist makes assumptions and uses his reasoning to develop the consequences implied in his assumptions. He may take his assumptions from wherever he pleases, including the real world. Economic theory refers to the reasoning out of consequences from assumptions, *not* to the task of selecting assumptions.

Economic theory emerges then as a *tool* that can be used in understanding the external world. The tool itself is "abstract," to be judged for its *truth* not for its *realism.* A proposition of economic theory is, to repeat, very much like a theorem in geometry: we prove its truth, and then we *may* be able to discover in the real world a situation that illustrates its truth. The economist applying theory to real world situations will clothe the abstract propositions of theory with "actual" data. His final pronouncements will "explain" one set of historical events by relating them to other historical events. These pronouncements on the chains of causation, which he claims to have detected in the real market, may certainly be properly judged for their *realism.* If a decrease in the supply of one good was found to have been followed by a rise in the price of a second good, the economist, applying theory, may perhaps explain the chain of events by saying that the second good is a close substitute of the first. The theory on which he bases his explanation is unquestionably true: the restriction of the supply of one good, other things being unchanged, leads to a rise in the price of substitutes. But whether the economist's explanation is realistic and relevant depends on whether the second good is or is not a substitute for the first; whether other things were unchanged; and so on.

In carrying out his task of explaining what has happened in the real world, or in predicting the likely consequences in the real world of a particular event, the economist thus combines theory with empirical fact. For these purposes it is frequently quite unnecessary to analyze his final report into its theoretical component on the one hand, and its factual component on the other hand. The skillful economic commentator will combine keen observation of events with statements revealing the theoretical interdependency of these events. A particular case of local unemployment may be linked to a shift in consumer tastes or to the emergence of new, cheaper resource markets elsewhere; an outflow of gold may be linked to particular governmental monetary policies; a particular pattern of industrial organization may be traced back to the tax structure, and so on. It would not be necessary, nor even helpful, in these cases, to separate economic theory from economic fact.

In studying a book such as this one, however, it is imperative that the distinction between theory and fact be kept clear. This book deals essentially with *theory*. It presents the kinds of logical procedures that must be used to understand the operation of a market economy. It presents the basic tools that the trained economist will use repeatedly in interpreting events in the real world. If these tools are to be used with success, they must first of all be forged as ends in their own right. Economic theory must first be recognized for what it is in and of itself: a body of abstract propositions deduced from hypothetical assumptions.

MARKET THEORY, ECONOMIC THEORY, AND ECONOMICS

We are now in a position to state how the subject matter of this book relates to economic theory as a whole and, even more generally, to the entire discipline of economics.

The theory that we study in this book makes up the core of economic theory, but by no means exhausts it. We investigate here the structure and operation of a market economy in its broadest theoretical outline; and it is within this general body of theory that most other branches of economic theory find their place. We are provisionally able to refrain from paying attention to these other branches of theory only by drastically simplifying the hypothetical market economy we deal with. Once the theory of the simplified market process has been mastered, then more complex and particular market situations can be dealt with by logical extensions of the theory.

In our study, for example, we ignore the possibility of trade between two separate market economies; we therefore do not study the *theory of international trade* with its impact on the market process within each country. Again, in our study, we almost completely ignore the special role played by the government as an economic agent; we therefore do not study the *theory of public finance* and the modifications brought about in the market process by governmental taxation, expenditures, or debt. We do not consider, in our study, the numerous complexities that are introduced into the market process by the various possible institutions connected with money; we therefore do not study *monetary theory*. In the same way (and partly as a result of these simplifications) we do not consider the possibility that market forces might arise that can disrupt periodically the smooth operation of the market process; in other words we ignore the necessity to construct a *theory of the trade cycle;* and so on.

In our study, therefore, we construct the theoretical *framework* within which all aspects of the economic theory of a market economy must be set. We follow through the fundamental market forces upon which and through which the impact of any special, additional economic forces will be felt. The theoretical attack upon any particular economic problem in the market must then be carried out against the background of this general and widely accepted theory of the market.

Economic theory thus embraces a range of theorems covering many more problems than are treated in this book. Moreover, as we have seen, the subject *economics* in turn customarily involves much besides economic theory. The study of an economic problem will typically involve much more than theory, and even for the purely theoretical aspect of such a study, the propositions of general market theory will be only partially satisfactory. The skilled economist must scan the data, using his theoretical competence to suggest or to detect matters requiring further explanation. In seeking such explanation he must apply his theoretical tools to the masses of data he believes to be relevant. It is not the task of market theory to set forth the methods by which the economist can most successfully use the empirical data at his disposal or the methods by which he can most skillfully apply theoretical tools to such data.

Market theory provides the basic tools required for even the most preliminary approach to economic problems. More specialized tools, in the form of the propositions of particular branches of economic theory, may be required to analyze specific problems. These tools, too, depend on the availability and quality of the basic tools we are about to assemble. The scope of market theory, within economic theory generally and within economics as a whole, is indeed narrow. Despite its narrowness, however, it is market theory that nourishes these wider fields. And in this lies its paramount importance.

SUMMARY

Chapter I clarifies the relationship between the theory of the market and other branches of economics.

Society consists of *individuals* seeking to act to improve their positions. A *market* exists where the individuals are in close enough contact with one another to be aware of mutually profitable opportunities for exchange. A *market system* exists where the individuals in a society conduct their economic activities predominantly through the market.

Economic analysis reveals chains of cause and effect linking together and coordinating the mass of transactions taking place in the market. *Market theory* investigates these chains of cause and effect. Market theory is made possible by the unique properties of human actions. These properties are embodied in the act of *choice* among alternatives, an act that the observing mind of the economist can "understand." Complex market phenomena may then be "understood" by relating them to individual acts of choice.

Economic theory is *abstract,* selecting only the key features of an economic situation for use in subsequent reasoning. Economic theory is *general;* its conclusions have validity for a wide range of possible real situations. Market theory provides the general framework for the analysis of a market system. Within this broad framework the various specialized branches of economic theory deal with more complex special cases. The theory in this book thus proceeds by drastic simplification.

SUGGESTED READINGS

Robbins, L., *An Essay on the Nature and Significance of Economic Science,* The Macmillan Co., London, 1935.

Hayek, F. A., "The Facts of the Social Sciences," in *Individualism and Economic Order,* Routledge and Kegan Paul Ltd., London, 1949.

Mises, L. v., *Human Action,* Yale University Press, New Haven, Connecticut, 1949, pp. 1–71.

Stigler, G. J., *The Theory of Competitive Price,* The Macmillan Co., New York, 1942, Ch. 1.

In this chapter and in the next, we survey the market, its overall operations and achievements. Later we will analyze, separately, the different functional sectors that compose the market, and how these various sectors interact within the market. Here, we will contemplate the forest in its entirety, before scrutinizing the separate trees, and then examine the consequences for the other trees of the existence and growth of each separate tree.

THE CONDITIONS UNDER WHICH THE MARKET OPERATES

We are considering the theoretical operation of a market system. The model of the market we will be working with can be characterized by the set of ideal conditions governing the model, which we construct for the purpose.

In a market system each member of the society is free to act, within very wide limits, as he sees fit. Moreover, the system operates within a framework of law which recognizes individual rights to private property. This means that each individual is free at each moment to employ the means available to him for the purpose of furthering his own ends, providing only that this should not invade the property rights of others. At the same time each individual can plan his activities with the assurance provided by the law, first that the means available to him at any one time are secure against appropriation by others, and, then, that he will not be prevented by others from enjoying the fruits of his productive activities.

The system recognizes the rights of individuals to enter into arrangements with one another which they believe will be of mutual benefit. Individuals may act cooperatively either by pooling their resources to produce jointly, or by each agreeing to specialize in one kind of production and to exchange parts of their production, or by the one agreeing to furnish productive services to the other in return for finished products or their equivalent. Our ideal system may be thought of as, in one way or another, ensuring the smooth fulfillment of such cooperative arrangements. Contracts are made in good faith, and contractual obligations are fulfilled to the letter.

Members of the system, being human beings, at any one time have likes, dislikes, and preferences; each follows his own moral standards.

Each member acts to fulfill "his own" purposes: but these purposes are not necessarily "selfish" ones and they may be directed toward alleviating the pain of others; and so on. Each member has more or less imperfect knowledge of the facts surrounding his field of action; each, in some degree, possesses curiosity, intelligence, determination; each has potential or actual talent for some or other activities, depending on his (natural or acquired) physical and other qualities.

Members of the system need not be aware of the entire scope of the market system or of the theory of its operation, but we may assume them to be generally content to seek to achieve their purposes within the framework of the system as they find it. In other words, while we make no other assumptions concerning the nature of the actions of individual members, we are assuming that no activity is expended with the sole purpose of replacing the market system by some system of societal organization governed by conditions substantially different from those outlined here. The system is thus consistent with the existence of the political and coercive apparatus associated with government, only to the extent necessary to ensure the maintenance of the conditions of a market system.

A society based on these conditions, starting from a previous state of individual autarky, without any specialization or exchange, can be seen as rapidly developing into an intricate exchange system. For such a successful development to occur it is however necessary that some commodity emerge in the market which is a generally accepted *medium of exchange*. With exchange confined to direct barter of goods or services for other goods or services, there can be only a limited scope for market activity. It can be confidently assumed however that the existence of market activity, even if limited, will create numerous opportunities for individuals to improve their positions by engaging in *indirect* exchange. An individual would give goods or services in return for goods that he does not himself desire, in hope of being able to exchange these goods later on for others that he does desire (but that cannot be had in exchange for his original goods or services). Widespread activity involving such indirect exchange can in turn aid the emergence of a commodity generally accepted as a medium of exchange.

Individuals will readily accept this commodity (money) in exchange for their goods or services, having complete confidence in their ability to use this commodity whenever they wish, to buy other goods or services at prices (in terms of the money commodity) more or less definitely known in advance.

For the purposes of the market system analysis undertaken in this book, we may assume that the system's history includes the evolution of a fully developed monetary machinery. The market has become completely adjusted to a system of money; all economic calculation is carried out in terms of money values, all prices are money prices, and all market transactions are exchanges of goods or services against money. (Nevertheless, for our purposes, we assume that the market operates exactly as it would operate without the existence of a money supply, but simply enjoys freedom from the inconveniences connected with direct barter. In other words money is assumed to succeed in lubricating the wheels of exchange, without itself actively directing exchange activity into channels other than those that would in principle be used in the absence of money.)[1]

MARKET ROLES

With the conditions governing the market system firmly in mind, we may turn to observe the different *roles* within the market process that can be filled by individual market participants.

Classification of roles as carried out by the economic theorist is quite different from classifications carried out from other points of view. A difference between two individuals is significant for the theorist only as it corresponds to a difference in *market function*. Market theory is organized within a conceptual framework that recognizes distinctly several such market functions.

1. *Consumers.* At the root of the whole matter lies the concept of action. Human beings act, we have seen, to improve their positions, so far as they believe themselves able to do so. Individuals participate in the market only with this final goal of improving their positions. An individual may find it necessary to undertake many different activities within the market, but the ultimate purpose of all these activities will always be to

---

1. It must be emphasized that in a real world, money can *never* be "neutral." The introduction of a medium of exchange into an economic system necessarily alters the actions of market participants because a medium of exchange is always *more* than just a medium of exchange. (In particular, people may seek to hold money as a particularly desirable form of asset under conditions of uncertainty.) It is the task of monetary theory to investigate these complications arising from the use of money in a market system. In this book we abstract from these complications.

purchase (or obtain the power to purchase) goods and services whose possession enables him to enjoy *directly* an "improvement in his position." Such goods and services are spoken of as being purchased for consumption. The primary role of *every* participant in the market, is thus that of *consumer*.

The consumer enters the market with money to purchase goods and services for consumption. This money has come into his possession as a result of his activities in the market (in some other role). In his role of consumer, each individual *chooses* between alternative patterns of consumption spending. He finds numerous opportunities to buy different kinds and quantities of consumer goods and services, each at its announced price. His means are clearly insufficient to make it possible to take advantage of more than a few of these opportunities. As a consumer, he must choose between the alternatives available to him. In analyzing the market behavior of men in their roles of consumers, market theory primarily focuses attention on the way consumers react to different possible patterns of available alternatives.

2. *Resource Owners.* Consumption goods and services, as a rule, are not directly available in nature for the taking. They must be produced from available resources. Raw materials may have to be transformed. Different materials may have to be combined. Goods may have to be transported to where they are to be consumed. All these productive activities are in general necessary; all such activities have something in common. They invariably involve the planned combination of the *productive services* of many different resources. The various possible ways of classifying resources will be considered in a later chapter.[2] Here it is sufficient to notice that in order to produce it is necessary to combine, say, the services of raw materials, manmade tools and equipment, physical space, human labor of a number of different varieties, and so on. In a system based on private property, it is likely that most, if not all, productive resources are the private property or are under the control of individual members of the system. These individuals are *resource owners*.

They are owners of raw materials, men with labor services to sell, and so on. Resource owners have an obvious role in the market system. All productive activity must begin with the purchase of the services of the

2. See Ch. 8, p. 161.

necessary productive resources. These purchases are made from resource owners. Market theory analyzes the way resource owners respond to the alternative opportunities of resource sale presented to them by the market and to changes in these opportunities.

3. *Entrepreneurs.* Under the heading "resources," we have included *everything* whose services are necessary to obtain products. There is no productive service necessary for the production of any desired good or service that can be purchased from anyone other than the proper resource owner. And yet there still remains one further role in the market system, without whose successful fulfillment production would be hopelessly inefficient. This is the role of the *entrepreneur.* The entrepreneur's role is to decide what resources should be used, and/or what goods and services should be produced; he makes the ultimate production decisions. These decisions must involve speculation concerning an uncertain future, since in its pure form an entrepreneurial decision is an act of purchase followed by a subsequent act of sale of what was previously purchased.

Among market roles, the entrepreneurial role is the least simple to grasp. The source of its elusiveness lies in the fact that some element of the entrepreneur's speculative function is exercised *whenever* human beings act. In fact we must recognize that in theorizing about the making of decisions, we may be concerned with two analytically distinct kinds of decisions. First, there is the decision between *definite* alternatives. Here the adoption of any one definitely known objective is accompanied by the sacrifice of a no less precisely known set of alternative potential objectives. This kind of decision making is clearly never possible in the real world of uncertainty (in which we wish our market system to have its setting). In a world of uncertainty men must invariably make a second kind of decision, one choosing between courses of action whose outcomes are quite uncertain, being susceptible to numerous possible unforeseeable modifications by external events. Although we can never expect to find actual instances of the first kind of decision, we may sometimes theorize concerning decisions of the second kind by temporarily reasoning *as if* the outcomes were not clouded by uncertainty. In reasoning in such a way the economist is abstracting from the speculative or "entrepreneurial" element in the making of the particular decision.

In speaking, however, of a distinct entrepreneurial role to be filled by hypothetical agents to whom we assign the name *entrepreneurs,* we are drawing attention to a unique class of decisions that it is essential for market theory to distinguish. In a system where specialization and division of labor have been carried to a fairly advanced stage, there is room for a class of decisions for which *uncertainty is of the essence* (thus to speak about such decisions as if they were made in a world without uncertainty would be self-contradictory). In such a specialized market system, it is possible to purchase *all* the productive services necessary for the production of a proposed good, at a definite total money cost. Similarly, when the good has been produced, it too can be sold in the market for a definite sum of money. By itself, a decision simply to buy a group of resources, or their productive services, involves no essentially speculative element; neither does a decision to sell a finished product, once it has been produced. But the decision to buy a bundle of productive resources at one price in order to resell "them" (that is, the finished product for whose production these productive services suffice completely) later at a higher price, is *essentially* speculative. In a market there is constant opportunity for this kind of decision to be made, and we distinguish the "pure" function of making this kind of decision by referring to it as the role of the entrepreneur. The entrepreneur must simultaneously make the decisions concerning which good he will produce and which resources he will use in its production, under the condition that he can expect only an uncertain price for the product when it will be sold. The entrepreneur makes one such speculative decision out of innumerable possible speculative decisions.

Of course, we must immediately point out that in a market system any one person is likely to fulfill more than one of these three "market roles." All resource owners and entrepreneurs are also consumers. We have already noticed, too, that a decision by an individual in his role of consumer or resource owner invariably involves an entrepreneurial element. Similarly, an individual whose activities are primarily entrepreneurial is likely to combine with them activities belonging to one or both of the other possible market roles. A producer may be contributing his own capital, and will quite probably be directly supplying supervisory labor services to the production process. In this way, he is acting in part as a resource owner. A producer may engage in entrepreneurial speculation not only in order to secure profits, but also because he obtains a peculiar thrill from taking bold risks. In this way, he is acting in part as a consumer. The resolution by the theorist of the integrated activities of a market participant into the three general, distinct functions is purely a matter of analytical expedience. We understand the market process more fully, we will find, because we understand that individuals perform a variety of functions that are susceptible to a separate theoretical "explanation."

THE STRUCTURE OF THE MARKET SYSTEM:
VERTICAL RELATIONSHIPS

The analytical isolation of the various possible market roles leads directly to the perception of a unique *structure* of human actions within the market system. The recognition of market structure is in turn the indispensable step toward the understanding of market *operation*.

In asserting that there is a structure in the decisions made in the marketplace, we mean simply that the decisions belonging to each of the various market roles are linked in a stable pattern of relationships. Decisions of resource owners, for example, are conditioned on the one hand by the urge to gain money income, and on the other hand by the different alternatives offered by various entrepreneurs. The decisions of consumers are conditioned on the one hand by their own tastes and income, and on the other hand by the different alternatives offered to them by various entrepreneurs. The decisions of the entrepreneur, in turn, are conditioned by a simultaneous appraisal of the various alternatives offered to him by those he is able to buy from, and of the various alternatives offered to him by those he may be able to sell to; and so on.

In this section we notice, first of all, markets related to each other "vertically." A vertical relationship can be said to exist between two markets when goods or services bought in one of the markets are sold (either alone or in combination with other goods or services) in the other market. The simplest possible notion of vertical structure within the market system may perhaps be obtained from Figure 2-1. The figure shows here that the market system consists of *two* markets; a market for products (in which entrepreneurs are the sellers and consumers are the buyers), and a market for productive services (in which resource owners are the sellers, and entrepreneurs are the buyers).[3] The structural relationship between the markets is seen, for example, by noticing that the prices consumers are willing to pay for particular products in the product market will determine the prices entrepreneurs can offer for particular resources in the market for productive services (also termed the resource market or the factor market).

3. Later in this chapter, the legitimacy of speaking of separate "markets" within the market system is discussed. In reality, of course, there is only *one* market where all participants meet.

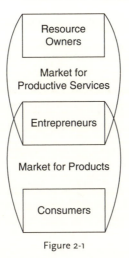

Figure 2-1

A more realistic view of the vertical structure of a typical market system would recognize that the activities of the entrepreneur may result in the production not only of goods for the consumer, but also of produced goods that can provide productive services with which other producers may produce goods or services for the consumers. The Austrian economist Menger introduced the concept of the "order" of a good to express this kind of complexity. A good demanded for consumption is a good of "lowest order." The goods required for the production of goods of lowest order are goods of second order, those required for the production of second order goods are the third order goods, and so on. The point is that entrepreneurial activity will be possible wherever there are two "vertically adjacent" markets; one market for a particular good, and another market in the goods of higher order with which the particular good can be produced. The complex vertical structure of a developed market system can now be glimpsed more fully. There are not merely the two markets whose relationship is indicated in Figure 2-1; there are likely to be numberless markets related vertically to each other in such a way. Between each pair of adjacent markets, there will be entrepreneurial activity. The entrepreneur will buy in the one market, produce, and sell in the market "below" it. (Here again, incidentally, the entrepreneurial role is closely integrated with that of resource owner. The initial decision to buy and sell in the different markets is an entrepreneurial one; but once the entrepreneurial decision has been made, and the good of higher order has been produced, the entrepreneur finds himself selling in the "lower" market just as any other resource owner.)

Moreover, although the vertical relationship between two markets may appear to stamp one of them as being "higher" than the other, there may be some other equally valid point of view from which the order of relationship is reversed. For example, iron ore is used in the production of steel which in turn is used in the production of equipment which plays a part in the mining of iron ore. The decisions of entrepreneurs buying iron ore in order to produce steel will be influenced in part by the decisions of those to whom they sell; that is, the entrepreneurs engaged in the production of mining equipment. But these latter decisions will clearly be partly influenced by the decisions of those buying this equipment—the miners of iron ore.

There are certainly strands of a vertical relationship existing between the market for iron ore, and the market for mining equipment, where the latter market is the higher; but there are, no less clearly, other strands of a vertical relationship between the two markets where the market for iron ore is the higher.

THE STRUCTURE OF THE MARKET SYSTEM:
HORIZONTAL RELATIONSHIPS

Two markets may be said to bear a horizontal relationship with one another, *either* when the goods or services sold in each of the separate markets were both bought, in part (directly or indirectly), in the same "higher" market, *or* when the goods or services bought in each of the separate markets are to be sold (in combination with other resources) in the same "lower" market. Thus the market where washing machines are bought and sold is related horizontally to that where automobiles are bought and sold, since the entrepreneurs in either of these markets will be bidding against one another in the same higher market—that for steel. Similarly, the labor market is related horizontally to the market where labor-saving machinery is bought and sold, since buyers in each of these markets are likely to be selling their products in the same lower market. Or again, the market in skilled labor for the production of automobiles is related horizontally to that for steel, because the resources sold in both these markets are combined and sold jointly in the automobile market; and so on.

Clearly, the decisions of buyers or sellers in any such markets will have to be between alternatives that are conditioned, not only by the decisions of competing buyers or sellers in the same market, but also, in part, by the decisions of buyers or sellers in the horizontally related markets. The price of steel to producers of washing machines will be determined partly by the strength of the demand for automobiles; the price that a skilled automobile worker can obtain for his labor will be determined in part by conditions in the steel market; and so on.

It should be clear from our discussion of the complexity of vertical market relationships that horizontal relationships, too, may be far from straightforward. Two markets may be related by different strands of connectedness, some of which may be vertical, others horizontal, in character. For example, sellers in the iron-ore market and sellers in the steel market may both buy the services of unskilled labor in the same labor market.

Several points of great importance ought to be made at this stage concerning the division of the market system into separate "markets." It must be recognized that any such division is quite arbitrary and is made by the market theorist only as a matter of convenience. Moreover, there are significant problems where the theorist finds it convenient to stress the *lack* of such watertight divisions. The fact is that in the most important sense, the entire market system is *one* market. Each market participant is a potential customer for each good offered for sale and a potential entrepreneur in the production of every conceivable product. There is interconnectedness between every single market decision and every other single market decision made in the system. The price paid for a shoeshine at one end of the country is connected, however tenuously, with the prices paid for the rental of high-speed computers at the other end of the country, so long as both points are within a single market system. Nevertheless, there are clearly various *degrees* of connectedness. The price of computer rentals is obviously more directly sensitive to changes in the attitudes of buyers and sellers of computers than to changes in the tastes or incomes of customers for shoeshines. Thus, the theorist finds it convenient to mark off arbitrarily different "markets" within which the connectedness of decisions is more direct than is the case between decisions in different markets. In pointing to various structural patterns between the markets that make up the market system, the theorist is indicating the less direct, more subtle—but over the long run no less powerful—influences that different markets exercise over one another.

THE ANALYSIS OF HUMAN ACTION IN THE MARKET:
THE CONCEPT OF EQUILIBRIUM

With the mutual influences that may be operative *between* markets well understood, it is desirable to consider what goes on *inside* a market. This is, after all, the kernel of market theory—the logical tracing through of the consequences within a market of given sets of data that impinge upon it.

A market process can be defined as what goes on when potential buyers and potential sellers are in mutual contact. We have seen that the market system as a whole can be treated as a single market, or that it may be treated for convenience as consisting of a number of interconnected markets. Within any market, however conceived, the theorist recognizes that at any one time each participant has definite attitudes concerning what is being bought and sold. At a given point in time, each participant has a particular eagerness to buy or to sell; for each participant there is on his "scale of values" a unique position assigned to each quantity of the commodity to be bought or sold. When a large number of such potential market participants come into contact with one another, many find opportunities for gainful action. Some buy at the going price, others sell; some find it gainful to bid prices higher than those currently quoted; some find it gainful to offer prices lower than the current prices.

The theorist usually attacks the problem of market analysis in the following way. He takes the attitudes of the various market participants, as they are assumed for any one date, and imagines that these attitudes are *maintained continuously* over an indefinite period of time. He may then describe a pattern of actions for the various participants *that, if actually adopted, would not have to be revised.* For example, the theorist may suppose that milk suppliers come daily to market with a continuous and constant supply of milk (concerning which their selling attitude is assumed to continue unchanged), and that prospective milk consumers similarly maintain, from day to day, an unchanged degree of eagerness concerning the purchasing of milk. The theorist may then describe terms on which suppliers might sell and consumers buy milk, that, if actually put into practice, would leave no opportunity for any market participant to improve his position in the future through a change in his actions. This fictional construction of the economic theorist is known as the state of *equilibrium.* The prices the milk is sold at, and the quantities of milk bought at these prices, are equilibrium prices and quantities.

Should the market participants (whose attitudes are assumed to be maintained without change) take actions that do *not* correspond to those that characterize the equilibrium market, then pressures will emerge on the participants that will lead them to *alter* their actions. Should, for example, the sellers of milk offer their milk at a price higher than the equilibrium price, then some sellers will find that milk sales are so low that it would be profitable for them to undercut the existing price. The non-equilibrium price would generate economic forces that would ensure that subsequent prices are different; and so on.

The state of equilibrium should be looked upon as an imaginary situation where there is a *complete dovetailing of the decisions* made by all the participating individuals. Every single supplier of milk, for example, who has decided that he values twenty-five cents more highly than a bottle of milk (and offers milk to the market at this price), is successful in discovering some consumer who happens to prefer a bottle of milk over twenty-five cents (and is willing to buy milk at this equilibrium price). A market that is not in equilibrium should be looked upon as reflecting a *discordancy* between the various decisions being made. Some of these discordant decisions cannot be successfully consummated in market action; they do not mesh. If sellers of milk charge too high a price, they will not find sufficient buyers. Decisions will have to be revised until a compatibility is attained between decisions that is the condition of a market in equilibrium.

The theorist who fastens his attention on a particular market upon a particular date is well aware that the decisions being made are different from the decisions that would be made in a market that had attained equilibrium. Whatever the current buying and selling attitudes of the market participants might be, they are likely to be somewhat different than on previous dates. Thus, even if previous market activity had succeeded in achieving equilibrium, from the point of view of the previous market attitudes, the situation is no longer one of equilibrium with respect to the new attitudes of buyers and sellers. But the theorist knows that the *very fact of disequilibrium itself* sets into motion forces that tend to bring about equilibrium (with respect to current market attitudes). If current attitudes were maintained unchanged (and the theorist is of course well aware that they will do nothing of the kind), then the initial state of *dis*equilibrium would itself tend to bring about an eventual equilibrium. The very fact that some of the decisions and plans currently being made are incompatible with others, so that some individuals must be disappointed, will force market participants to revise their plans in the direction of closer harmony with the other plans being made in the market. If current attitudes, to repeat, were to continue unchanged, then one might expect the plans of market participants to reach eventual full compatibility. Until then, decisions would be continually revised and adjusted. When equilibrium would have been attained, all plans would be carried out successfully and would be therefore maintained without alteration for as long as the basic attitudes continue unchanged.

The market theorist distinguishes, therefore, (a) a process of *adjustment* during which the market is in agitation, and (b) a state of equilibrium (the imaginary situation that would be achieved if the adjustments set in motion by the current market attitudes would be permitted to work themselves out fully; that is, if current market attitudes continue without change). In his analysis, the theorist may determine the conditions that would prevail on a market where equilibrium had been attained; he may do this by describing the actions that will be taken in a given *disequilibrium* market, tracing the tendency of such actions toward the attainment of equilibrium.

COMPLETE AND INCOMPLETE EQUILIBRIUM

Some further attention to these various analytical approaches is in order, and will help us, incidentally, toward a clearer grasp of the market process. A market process, we have seen, is essentially a process of *adjustment*. In this process, individuals adjust their actions to take advantage of the opportunities offered by the market; that is, they adjust their actions to "fit" the actions of other market participants. So long as unexploited opportunities exist that can be grasped through a change of action, the process of adjustment is not yet complete; somebody's plans must go unfulfilled—equilibrium has not yet been attained. Until the attainment of equilibrium, there will be unspent forces at work in the market. These forces will impel men, sooner or later, to produce *different* quantities or qualities of goods, to try to buy or to sell at *different* prices, to *move* in or out of industries, and so on. All these forces, it will be borne in mind, are set in motion by the simultaneous existence of *two* sets of factors: *first,* a given set of basic buying and selling attitudes (imagined by the theorist to be continuously maintained); and *second,* a set of prevailing decisions by market participants that have not yet been "shaken down" through the market process into a harmoniously fitting, self-renewing pattern.

Now, it must be emphasized that the twin notions of adjustment and equilibrium, while seeming to pertain only to a world of *unchanging* basic attitudes, are in fact the tools with which the theorist analyzes the effects of *change*. A new tax is imposed, a new oil field discovered, a wave of immigration is expected, a revolution in tastes is considered—the theorist explains the consequences of these changes by means of the analysis of adjustment and the description of equilibrium. In all these problems the theorist imagines a market that, before the occurrence of the change, had been in equilibrium; he imagines the state of disequilibrium such a market would be thrown into by the postulated change; he traces through the process of adjustment that would be touched off by this disequilibrium; and he finally describes the new state of equilibrium that can be attained when all the forces of adjustment have worked themselves out, imagining, of course, that throughout the adjustment period no other change in basic attitudes has occurred.

In his analysis of the consequences of such a change in the basic data, the theorist frequently finds that ripples of market forces set off by the change do not completely spend themselves until adjustments have been made in market actions far removed from the initial change. The discovery of a new oil field not only affects the price and sale of oil, but eventually affects numerous other industries; and so on. If the theorist ignores any of the adjustments—however remote—that must sooner or later be made, his system will, of course, not be one of full equilibrium. Nevertheless, economists frequently are content to trace out the market consequences of a particular event only insofar as it *directly* entails adjustments. The theorist may mark out either a time range, or a market area, within which he is especially concerned to discover the course of adjustment. When the forces which change the actions of market participants can be held to have spent themselves *within this selected range*—even though further adjustments will eventually have to be made beyond it—the theorist, loosely, may describe his selected range of the market as having attained equilibrium. Such an "equilibrium" obviously is quite incomplete; there are still market decisions (outside the "range") that will be disappointed and will have to be revised.[4] Nevertheless, it may clearly be expedient for the analyst to concentrate his attention on particular waves of adjustment, and the concept of "incomplete equilibrium"—although self-contradictory—may be of considerable usefulness.

Two kinds of incomplete equilibrium may be distinguished, depending on the criterion by which the theorist selects his "range."

1. The theorist may discover that certain market forces work themselves out fully within a relatively short period of *time*, while other such forces are felt generally only after a longer interval. He may confine his attention to the first group of forces. When these have spent themselves, he may

---

4. Moreover, revisions in decisions made outside the range may bring about secondary repercussions, in turn, upon decisions within the range.

describe his system as being in equilibrium—as it may be, in fact, for the duration of the selected time period.[5] The incompleteness of this kind of "equilibrium" is indicated by referring to it as *short-run equilibrium*—it being understood, of course, that the nature of the problem under consideration will dictate the "shortness" of the selected period, and also that a number of different such periods may be possible with corresponding equilibrium positions of different degrees of incompleteness.

2. The theorist may mark off, secondly, certain *kinds of activity* on the part of market participants that he believes to be more likely affected by the initial change in market data. He may believe, for example, that the discovery of a new oil field is likely to cause a more marked alteration in the willingness of oil producers to sell oil at given prices, than in the willingness of landlords to purchase new oil burners. The theorist might then confine his attention to the market activities of those buying and selling oil. When the decisions governing these activities are mutually compatible, then "the oil market" may be described as in equilibrium. The incompleteness of this kind of "equilibrium" is indicated by referring to it as *partial equilibrium;* that is, an equilibrium existing only in one selected "pocket" of the entire market system.[6] The possibility, discussed in earlier sections of this chapter, of distinguishing separate "markets" between which definite interrelationships exist, arises, of course, out of the kind of analysis described here. The term "general equilibrium" is reserved for the condition where *all* adjustments have been carried through to completion, so that no decisions made in the entire system, however remote from the initial change, are found to be disappointed.[7]

THE PATTERN OF MARKET ADJUSTMENT

We have seen that a market system may be divided by the theorist into more or less distinct areas of activity where market forces bring about

5. It should be realized, however, that long-run forces may start to operate well before shorter-run forces have worked themselves out. See Ch. 10, pp. 235–240.

6. Of course, the changes brought about in the "oil-burner market" as a result of changes in the "oil market" may simply *take a longer time to work themselves out.* In this sense "partial" equilibrium may be "short-run" equilibrium.

7. In the later chapters in this book, the various separate markets within a market system are frequently called "partial markets" to emphasize the partial character of analysis confined exclusively to such a separate market. On the other hand, when, as in Ch. 11, we analyze the complete market process as it embraces all the separate "markets," the market as a whole is called the "general market."

adjustments with especial speed and directness. In considering the particular course of economic forces within such a distinct area of activity, the area is referred to as a "market"—in the same way as the economy as a whole is called a market (when we are interested in the ripples of economic forces as felt throughout the system). The simplest form of market where the forces set up by human action can be analyzed is that marked out by considering only the activities of those buying and selling the same good or service.

We speak—and will be doing so frequently in this book—of a market for shoes, wheat, a particular kind of labor, and so on. We bear in mind at all times that any equilibrium achieved in such a market may be quite incomplete from the standpoint of the entire market system. It is the especial directness with which changes in the data in one part of such a market make their impact on actions through this market that justifies our undertaking this kind of separate analysis.

In the actions taking place in the market for any one commodity, such as wheat, there is always, we find, the same market process at work. In any such market there is a general tendency on the part of potential buyers and sellers to continually revise their bids and offers, until all bids and offers are successfully accepted in the market. This general tendency expresses itself in *three* specific ways. *First,* so long as there is a discrepancy in the prices offered by different would-be buyers, or in the prices asked by different would-be sellers, there will be disappointments and subsequent revisions in bids or offers.[8] *Second,* so long as the quantity of the commodity *offered for sale* at any one price (or below it) *exceeds* the quantity that prospective buyers are prepared *to buy* at this price (or above it), some of the would-be sellers will be disappointed and will be induced to revise their offers. *Third,* so long as the quantity of the commodity offered for sale at any one price (or below it) *falls short* of the quantity that prospective buyers are prepared to buy at this price (or above it), some of the would-be buyers will be disappointed and will be induced to revise their bids.

Thus, the agitation of the market proceeds under the impulse of very definite market forces. Prices offered and bid would be continually changing—even with constancy assumed in the basic production and consumption attitudes of the market participants—as would-be buyers or

8. In Ch. 7 and subsequent chapters, where the process outlined here is worked out in greater detail, it will be shown that these initial discrepancies in prices offered or asked, are the result of imperfect *knowledge.*

sellers find themselves forced to offer more attractive terms to the market. A would-be buyer might offer a higher price than before because his previous offer did not fit in with the plans of any prospective seller. Apparently all sellers aware of this previous offer found more attractive alternative ways of disposing of their commodities. A seller would be forced to lower his price because buyers found more attractive uses for their money— either elsewhere in this market, or in some other market altogether.

The general direction toward which agitation in the market is tending should be clear. If unlimited time were allowed for a market to reach its own equilibrium position—that is, if we assumed no change to occur indefinitely either in consumer valuation of the commodity or in producers' assessment of the difficulty of its production—it is easy to imagine what would finally emerge. There would be a single price prevailing in the market; all sales would be effected at this price. Individuals would offer to sell the commodity at this price, and the quantity that they offer for sale would be exactly sufficient to satisfy those other individuals who are offering to buy the commodity at the prevailing price. No would-be buyer is disappointed in his plans to buy, and no would-be seller in his plans to sell.[9]

THE CHANGING MARKET

Much of our discussion thus far has concerned the attitudes of individuals at a given point in time, or over a period during which these attitudes are assumed not to change. The analysis of the market under these artificial conditions makes it possible, in addition, to grasp the course of the market process as it would operate in the absence of these restrictive assumptions. Let us consider again the pattern of adjustment discussed in the previous section.

If we permit *change* to occur in the urgency with which prospective buyers are anxious to acquire the commodity sold in the market, or if we permit change to occur in the conditions governing the production and supply of the commodity to the market, a number of new elements enter into the situation. It is clear, first of all, that with respect to the attitudes of buyers and sellers toward the commodity *as of each moment*, a *different* equilibrium situation occurs toward which the market would tend *if the attitudes of that moment were maintained indefinitely.* Since attitudes are

---

9. It may be observed that in this case (as in all others in economics) a state of equilibrium is *not* the same thing as a state of perfect happiness. All that exists is a state in which no one is misled into making plans that cannot be executed.

permitted to change, it follows that the market process, the ceaseless agitation of the market, is being continually pulled toward a different equilibrium position. Would-be buyers and sellers who were disappointed in their past market activity—or who, even if not disappointed in the past, do not wish to be disappointed in the future—must revise their bids or offers to make them more attractive to the *current* market. A quite different importance is now attached to the skill of *anticipating* future market conditions. Disappointment of plans made by would-be sellers will spur them to undertake production only by their assessment of future demand conditions.

But the basic pattern of market adjustment is applicable in this changing market as well. The disappointments engendered at any one time by the existing absence of equilibrium will help to guide subsequent plans to anticipate the correct future conditions. Since the changes in market data can be expected to proceed only gradually, the success or failure of past plans can provide a fairly reliable indicator of how these plans must be revised in the future. Thus, market forces are still able to direct the agitation of the market *in the direction* of a uniform market price, and of a correspondence between the quantities offered and demanded in the market at given prices.

Where a considerable change in the basic market attitudes has occurred with abruptness, the consequences are not difficult to understand. The change will make itself felt initially by severely disappointing the plans of buyers and sellers who had been unable to foresee the change. If, for example, the supply of the commodity has been abruptly halted by the sudden unavailability of a vital raw material, then many buyers will find that the price they had confidently expected to obtain the commodity at is no longer in effect. If, to take a different possibility, the emergence of some new product abruptly reduces the dependency of consumers upon the commodity we are considering, then sellers will find that their offers to sell will no longer be accepted at the old prices. In short, any kind of abrupt change will immediately increase the degree of disequilibrium existing in the market, and will therefore initiate fairly rapid and extensive adjustments in the plans of buyers and sellers in the direction of the state of equilibrium corresponding to the new state of affairs.

THE MARKET SYSTEM AS A WHOLE

Our discussion of the pattern of adjustment in the market for a single commodity serves to clarify the nature of the market process as it governs activity throughout the entire market economy. We have seen that it is permissible to consider the market system as a whole, as being made up of many separate markets that have definite and powerful strands of relationship. For the market system as a whole to be in equilibrium, it is necessary for equilibrium to exist within each separate market. Within the market for each commodity, buying and selling plans must dovetail so that no disappointment occurs in the execution of any plan made throughout the system.

So long as the market system as a whole is not yet in equilibrium—that is, so long as "general equilibrium" has not yet been attained—some plans are being disappointed. The disappointed buyers or sellers may revise their plans in several ways. They may offer better terms in the same markets, or they may decide to cease (or reduce) activity in these markets and increase activity in fresh markets altogether. Disequilibrium in any one of the separate markets will thus cause adjustments in the plans made first of all by participants in that market, and then secondarily in the plans made by participants in related markets—whether horizontally or vertically related.

In any event the course of the market process is fairly clear, assuming for the moment that consumer tastes and basic production possibilities are maintained unchanged. As each separate market adjusts to bring correspondence in the buying and selling plans directly affecting it, the ripples of disappointed plans spread gradually into the related markets. Each separate market thus adjusts to disappointments in plans due to both its own initial disequilibrium, as well as to the impact of changes in plans brought about by the adjustments being made in related markets.

In the process of adjustment within each separate market, and between the separate markets making up the entire system, a principal role is played by the entrepreneur. Conditions may exist in separate markets so that adjustments can take place to improve the positions of all concerned. The entrepreneur becomes aware of this situation and undertakes the risk of attempting to make the necessary adjustment. It is through his activity that the relationships between separate markets transmit ripples of change. If, for example, on the market for a finished product, its price is in excess of the sum of the prices of *all* the resources necessary for its production, as prevailing in the separate resource markets, it is entrepreneurial activity that is at once set into motion by the inconsistency, constitutes itself the condition of disequilibrium, and is responsible for the tendency to bring about ultimate equilibrium in the market.

An important change that occurs at any point in the market system as a whole brings about direct alterations in its immediate market vicinity. Entrepreneurial activity transmits the consequences of these changes to related markets. Through the impersonal medium of altered prices, participants in other, possibly remote, parts of the market system are forced to adjust their plans to the changed conditions. The ceaseless agitation that is characteristic of a market economy becomes now for the market theorist a determinate process that is set into motion in a very definite way in response to fundamental changes in the basic data with which the market grapples. Movements of prices; growth of new industries; expansion or contraction of existing firms; the adoption of new methods of production; the search for new resources, techniques, and products; all become explainable for the theorist in terms of the totality of the market process of which they are a part.

In the next chapter we review briefly what the market process achieves. In the later chapters we turn back to examine in greater detail how market forces are transmitted, make themselves felt, and initiate adjustments. In addition we will see more specifically how each participant in the market economy plays a definite role in the whole process.

SUMMARY

Chapter 2 surveys the overall operation of a market system.

A market system is characterized by a framework of law that broadly recognizes individual freedom, responsibility, and private property rights. Market theory assumes the use of a medium of exchange.

In a market system individuals may fill the roles of *consumer, resource owner,* and/or *entrepreneur.* The chains of cause and effect that are expressed through market forces operate through the typical *structural* interdependence existing between the decisions made by consumers, resource owners, and entrepreneurs. *Vertical* relationships between market decisions exist when goods and services are bought for later sale; for example, when resources are bought by entrepreneurs from resource owners to be used in production and sold in the form of the product to consumers. *Horizontal* relationships exist, for example, when two different products require the use of the same resource in their production; or where a product may be produced with either of two resources that are substitutes for one another.

A market is in equilibrium when all decisions dovetail with each other. Disequilibrium exists when some decisions cannot be executed because they have been planned on the basis of mistaken assumptions concerning the decisions of others. The market *process* consists in the *adjustments* that are enforced upon individual decisions by the disappointments experienced in a disequilibrium market. The economic theorist may confine his attention to a *limited* series of adjustments that may be wrought out within the market system. He will recognize that the situation where all these limited series of adjustments have fully worked themselves out is one of only *partial* equilibrium. For the entire market system to be in equilibrium—that is, for a *general equilibrium* to prevail—each of the separate sectors of the market must be in harmony with each of the others. Market theory recognizes the existence of chains of cause and effect *between* all the market sectors as well as within each of them. The general market process comprises all the adjustments enforced upon the market activities of resource owners, consumers, and entrepreneurs throughout the system by an initial failure of all their decisions to dovetail perfectly with each other.

SUGGESTED READINGS

Menger, C., *Principles of Economics*, Free Press, Glencoe, Illinois, 1950, Chs. 1, 2.

Stackelberg, H. v., *The Theory of the Market Economy*, Oxford University Press, New York, 1952, Chs. 1, 2.

Hayek, F. A., "Economics and Knowledge," in *Individualism and Economic Order*, Routledge and Kegan Paul Ltd., London, 1949.

3 EFFICIENCY, COORDINATION, AND THE MARKET ECONOMY

In this chapter we complete our broad preliminary survey of the theory of the market system, its operation and achievements. Chapter 2 attempted to provide a bird's-eye view of the way the market transmits economic forces through the system, tending to make the actions of all market participants dovetail more closely in the system. The present chapter demonstrates how these interactions in the market economy enable it to fulfill the basic functions of any system of organization. We are not concerned here with what the market process is or with the patterns of relationships the process consists of, but *with how it accomplishes what it is supposed to accomplish*. Some remarks are necessary to make clear, at the very outset, the point of view from which such an appraisal can be undertaken.

THE ECONOMIC PROBLEM

Social phenomena can be examined from *two* distinct points of view. First of all, they can be examined merely *positively*. Chains of cause and effect can be proved to exist; the likely effects of particular changes can be foretold; the probable responsibility of particular prior events for definite current phenomena can be explained. Social phenomena, however, can be examined in addition from a *normative* point of view. The way prior causes bring about subsequent events can be *judged* by the success with which the process fulfills definite *goals* (believed by the investigator to be cherished by someone concerned with the usefulness of the process). A breakdown in a commuter bus service may be seen *positively* as responsible for highways swarming with an unusual number of private cars. It may be "blamed"—*normatively*—for the inconvenience experienced by those who use the bus service for a convenient means of transportation.

The economic theorist, too, is able to view his subject matter from both these perspectives. He may simply trace through the operation of market forces. Or he may, in addition, appraise the market from the perspective of one or other aspects of the "economic problem." Although the concept of an economic problem is most frequently discussed with respect to an entire society, the idea is fundamentally one relating to the individual. For an individual, the economic problem consists in ensuring that the resources at his disposal be utilized in the most effective manner possible—from the point of view of the goals which he has set up. Successful solution of this economic problem requires that the individual apportion resources to promote his various adopted goals in a pattern that will faithfully reflect the hierarchy of importance to him of the various goals. If he desires goal A more urgently than goal B, and the available resources are insufficient for both goals, a "correct" solution of the economic problem requires that he allocate his resources to A rather than to B; and so on.

From the perspective defined by the goal of correctly solving his economic problem, an individual may judge his actions as being either efficient or otherwise. From the point of view of his own chosen goals, considering the varying degrees of urgency that he has assigned to these goals, the individual may frown at a particular course of action as being at variance with his goal program. Such a course of action is "inefficient," "wasteful," and "irrational"; it fails to aim at the most important of the chosen goals.

The goal of "efficiency" is not really a separate goal in its own right. Efficiency is nothing else, in the present context, than the consistent pursuit of other goals. Consistency in the pursuit of goals calls for a refusal to apply resources to achieve one goal when this implies forsaking a still more highly cherished goal. Inefficiency is thus synonymous with inconsistency. An inefficient course of action is one that is inconsistent with a given program of goals. A course of action that is inefficient with respect to one set of goals may be highly efficient with respect to a different set. But the point is that, in making plans, individuals have in mind given sets of goals. With respect to *this* set of goals, they seek a consistent, efficient course of action.

SOCIETY AND THE ECONOMIC PROBLEM

Economists frequently speak of the economic problem facing society. What they usually have in mind is something closely similar to the economic problem faced by individuals. But the legitimacy of this interpretation of the term "economic problem" is by no means clear, and the limitations on its use in this sense must be understood. Discussions that deal with the economic problem facing society assume a group of human beings, on the one hand, having numerous different desires for consumer goods and services and, on the other hand, having command of a body of productive resources. The economic problem facing the society is, once again, that of securing *efficiency*. The problem consists in constructing an organized social system that will most efficiently utilize the limited resources of "society" for the satisfaction of the desires of "society" for consumer goods and services. Once again a successful solution of this problem calls for "consistency"—a pattern of activity and production that should faithfully reflect the respective weights assigned to each of the goals that it is desired to satisfy.[1]

The limitations surrounding this use of the term "economic problem" arise from the fact that society is made up of numerous individuals. Each individual can be viewed as independently selecting his goal program. And in a market economy especially, each individual adopts his own courses of action to achieve his goals. It is therefore unrealistic to speak of society as a single unit seeking to allocate resources in order to faithfully reflect "its" given hierarchy of goals. Society has no single mind where the goals of different individuals can be ranked on a single scale.

Nevertheless, there is a sense where one form of societal organization can be termed "more efficient" than another. For example, a market economy, as we shall see, is unquestionably more "efficient" than a system of self-sufficient individual "economies," because *each individual* shows by his voluntary participation in the market that he is better off under the former than the latter. Thus, each individual finds he can most efficiently solve his own economic problem by cooperating with other individuals through division of labor and the market. Any form of voluntary social cooperation emerges only because *each* participant seeks in this way to further his *own* goals. If he participates in a social system of any kind, he does so in the interests of his own efficiency; his participation is a method of solving his own economic problem.

We will be speaking of the efficiency or inefficiency of a social system in this sense. We are not invoking the notion of a society having *its* goals in any sense apart from the goals of the individuals making up the society. Efficiency for a social system means the efficiency with which it permits its individual members to achieve their several goals.

---

1. This statement of the nature of the economic problem facing a society is worthy of notice. Most nineteenth-century economists (and many laymen today) use the adjective "economic" to denote a relationship to *wealth* (more or less carefully defined). Most economists today, however, recognize that the term "economic problem" is fundamentally suited to denote the problem discussed in the text.

THE PROBLEM OF COORDINATION

However, when individuals seek to fulfill their purposes through some form of social cooperation, the efficiency of the social system in the above sense depends on the degree of *coordination* with which the separate activities of the participants are carried on. The cooperation of individuals requires that their actions fit into an overall pattern of organization. The fundamental point is that the source of the advantages of social cooperation over individual autarky exists in the possibilities that social cooperation opens up for *specialization and division of labor.* It is efficient, for example, to participate in a market economy (instead of being a self-sufficient Robinson Crusoe) because the value of one's specialized services to the market is higher than the value of all that one could produce by spreading one's efforts over numerous branches of production for one's own consumption.[2]

Now, the very factor *specialization,* which can make social cooperation "efficient" for each of the cooperating individuals, *itself* introduces problems upon whose successful solution the worthwhileness of specialization depends. Clearly, if everyone specialized in the same kind of production, specialization would be worse than useless. A social system will emerge only if the system promises individuals a way of cooperating with others *in an efficient way;* that is, only if the system *coordinates* the specialized activities of the participants.

In this chapter we discuss the market economy with respect to the way it coordinates the activities of its participants. We do not "judge" the degree of success that the market economy attains in this regard either as compared with other economic systems or as to its own "efficiency." We are concerned with finding out *how* the patterns of relationships existing in the market process succeed at all in organizing numberless, independently planned actions into a social system that efficiently serves the purposes of its participants.

The general problem of coordination can be reduced, for a market economy, into a number of fairly distinct special problems. First, we will outline these problems, and then proceed in subsequent sections to discuss how these problems are solved by the market.

1. The economy must somehow or other develop a system of "priorities" governing *what goods and services should be produced.* Resources are

---

2. The classic statement of the advantages to be derived from the division of labor is in the opening chapter of Adam Smith's *Wealth of Nations.* See also Mises, L. v., *Human Action,* Yale University Press, New Haven, Connecticut, 1949, pp. 157–164.

clearly insufficient to produce everything that the participants would like to enjoy. There must be some way to decide on the kinds and quantities of products to which resources should be allocated; this involves the notion of "priorities." If Mr. Smith wants a new coat, and Mrs. Jones wants a new dress, then there must be some method of *ranking* these two wants so as to guide producers in making their decisions as to what to produce. If one viewed society as having wants that, in principle, can be ranked on a *single* scale of absolute "importance," then this problem would be simply that of discovering this ranking. Such a view of things recognizes the possibility of declaring Mr. Smith's need for a coat to be somehow or other more or less "urgent" *from the standpoint of society* than Mrs. Jones's need for a dress. Efficiency in the operation of the economy requires that, in this view of things, the system find out *which* want is the more urgent and then direct producers to give it corresponding priority.

But even when it has become clear that no objective way exists of determining the relative importance of the wants of different individuals "from the point of view of society" in any such *absolute* sense (if any meaning at all can be attached to this term), the problem of ranking must and can be solved. For participation in a market economy to be attractive, individuals must be assured that *some* reasonably satisfactory—and definite—method will be used to assign priorities to the wants of all the different participants. From the point of view of coordination, participants must be assured that the decision of any individual entrepreneur to produce a given commodity is consistent with this priority system. The priority system used need not be able to lay claim to the achievement of ultimate justice or fairness. Participants must merely be convinced that the degrees of importance that the market attaches to different wants are such as to make the market system profitable from their own individual points of view.[3]

---

3. The notion of priority in satisfying the wishes of market participants should be interpreted very broadly. Under this heading should be included, for example, at least part of the function frequently assigned to an economic system of providing for *growth*. Insofar as growth involves a problem of resource allocation (for example insofar as it involves denying Mr. Smith's wants today in order that Mrs. Jones's grandchildren should enjoy a better life in the future), the market must determine the rate of growth of the economy on some basis of priorities. It is also true that the priority attached by consumers to present consumption over future consumption may be such that no growth at all (or even economic decline) may be the most "efficient" outcome.

2. A second problem of coordination relates to the way resources are combined to produce those goods or services to which priority in production has somehow been assigned. Once it has been decided that a certain good is to be produced, the next step is to decide on the *method of production to be used*. Very often there are a number of different methods of production that are technically capable of yielding a desired commodity. Drinking water can be brought from the mountains or extracted from the sea. The economic system requires a device that will guide the producer of the commodity to use the most efficient method of production—efficiency in production being measured with respect to the economy as a whole. The "correct" method of production means the correct combination of resources. The correct combination of resources used to produce a given commodity will leave as a remainder, out of the entire available stock of resources, that body of resources able to produce the greatest quantity of goods in their order of priority. In other words, production is carried on efficiently, from the viewpoint of society, when it interferes *least* with the rest of production.

Clearly, with innumerable producers making independent decisions as to production techniques, the economy must *coordinate* these decisions so as to ensure that each producer uses those resources least needed elsewhere in the economy. Just as products can be produced in different ways, so resources can be used to produce different products. It is in the interest of *each* market participant that each unit of each resource be directed toward the production of that product where it will be used most efficiently—in the sense stated above.

3. The essence of the market economy is specialization and division of labor in production; production, moreover, invariably involves the cooperation of the productive services of several different resources. For both these reasons it follows that, in a market economy, resources are generally used in processes of production which go to satisfy the wants of others than the owners of the resources themselves, and/or do not permit the productive contribution of any particular unit of a resource to be distinguished or identified. A truck driver transports food from one city to another. He himself may need very little of this food; and it is quite impossible to identify what portion of the utility of transportation is attributable to his services, what portion is attributable to the truck, to the highways, and so on. All this creates a problem of compensating each participant in the system for his productive contribution as a resource owner (or entrepreneur). If an individual is to participate in the economy, some definite

system must exist, which will ensure that he will receive a share of what is being produced.[4] An efficient system will provide sufficient reward to each participant to enable all participants to enjoy the benefits of the widest possible range of resource services.

HOW THE MARKET SOLVES THE PROBLEMS OF COORDINATION

In a market economy these problems of coordination find their solution in the market process. The key role is played by market *prices*. The reasonable success that a market economy is able to attain in the solution of the three coordination problems outlined in the previous section is the consequence of a market process that determines prices. Market prices guide individual decision makers toward decisions that tend to consider implicitly all the relevant conditions prevailing in the market.

Thus, the *single* process that determines the course of the various prices in a market continuously works toward the simultaneous solution of the three problems of coordination. These three, analytically distinct tasks are fulfilled as aspects of the *same* market process market prices emerge from. This will become apparent in the following paragraphs as we discuss the different aspects of the market solution.

1. In a market economy the task of production is carried out by entrepreneurs in search of profits. Where an entrepreneur has the choice of producing two products at equal cost, he will produce that which promises to sell for the highest price. Thus, *priorities* in a market economy are assigned to different goods by the process that determines their *prices*. Where equivalent combinations of resources can produce different products, it is the product that can command the highest market price that top priority is automatically assigned to.

Much of our study is concerned with the process by which the market price of products is determined. Generally, it is obvious even at this point, however, that those products for which consumers are prepared to undergo the greatest pecuniary sacrifice will tend (other things being equal) to command the highest prices; so thus, the market tends to consider these products as socially more "important." Resources will tend to be purchased by entrepreneurs for use in the production of the relatively higher-priced goods. Changes in the urgency with which

---

4. From a short-run viewpoint this coordinating problem is frequently seen as the problem of *distributing* the national product. Some of the early economists saw the principal task of economics as being the elucidation of the laws governing distribution.

consumers are anxious to obtain specific goods will tend to be reflected in changes in their prices and hence in the priority that the market attaches to their production. The more responsive the price system is to changes in consumer preferences, the more accurately will the decisions of producers be in conformity with the priority system based on pecuniary sacrifice.

This kind of priority system is frequently described as *consumer sovereignty*. It is the consumers' acts of purchase, translated into market forces, which determine market prices, and thus give directions to the producers as to what should be produced. Changes in consumer preferences, which are responsible for the price changes, compel producers to alter their production processes. Any non-market obstacles placed in the way of the pricing process thus necessarily interfere with the priority system that consumers have set up. It must always be borne in mind that such a priority system cannot necessarily lay claim to any kind of *ethical* excellence. All that can be claimed for the priority system is that it offers potential market participants more attractive alternatives than are available to them otherwise.

2. That production in a market economy is undertaken for profit also has definite consequences with respect to the second task of coordination. When a given product can be produced by different methods of production, it is most profitable to use the cheapest method of production. The entrepreneur will therefore tend to use this method of production. The cheapest method of production is that which requires the smallest expenditure for the resources used. Whether or not one production process is cheaper (and therefore more likely to be employed) than another depends not only on the quantities of resources required for the processes, but also on their *prices*. The market value of different resource combinations influences the decisions of producers to use more machinery or less, more skilled labor or less, a larger plant or a smaller, and so on.

Now, as with the prices of products, the analysis of the determination of the prices of resources must wait until later chapters in this book. But generally it is not difficult to see what factors are at work in the determination of resource prices, and to appreciate how these factors relate to the coordination problem of securing the use of "socially efficient" methods of production. Market prices are the basis of cost calculation by producers. The price of each resource tends toward the point where all supplies of the resource available at this price are bought by producers.[5] Producers tend to bid up resource prices in order to secure resources for the production of given products for as long as it is profitable to do so; thus, at the market price, the resource will be used by producers of those products in whose production the resource yields greatest profits. Producers bidding for the resource to produce a product in which the resource will be relatively *less* profitable will soon find it impossible to compete with the producers of more valuable products. In buying the cheapest resources (among all those resources that are for him technically equivalent), the producer will therefore tend to be buying those resources *least* valuable elsewhere in the economy—"valuable," that is, in the sense of being able to cater to consumer wants having higher (pecuniary sacrifice) priority.

It cannot be expected, to be sure, that at any one time the market process should have succeeded in securing *complete* coordination of decisions concerning methods of production. Inevitably, at any one time, certain processes of production will be carried on using resources some units of which could be used more valuably in other production processes. So long as the market is competitive, however, the existence of such opportunities for increased efficiency will *tend* to be discovered and exploited by profit-seeking entrepreneurs. The market process will constantly tend to rearrange and reshuffle the allocation of productive resources so as to conform more closely with the most recent changes in the patterns of available resources and consumer preferences.[6]

3. The price system a market economy has its setting in is responsible also for the solution of the third problem of coordination, that of determining the individual rewards to be received by each of the resource owners cooperating in the productive process. This function is fulfilled as a different aspect of the same pricing process that determines resource allocation and the organization of production. Resource owners selling the services of their resources in the market secure prices that are determined by the interaction of resource supply and entrepreneurial demand. Acting in their capacity of consumers, the resource owners will in turn use the money prices, which they receive in the resource markets (their

5. The sentence in the text needs to be qualified to some extent. It is possible that a resource is so plentiful or so low in productivity that even if the price falls to practically zero, it does not pay to employ the entire supply for production.

6. See more on this point in Ch. 13.

"incomes"), to buy goods in the product markets. Thus, the market value of the goods and services a consumer can buy with his income is determined by the value that the market places upon the services that, in his capacity of resource owner, he has furnished to the production process.

The real incomes received by consumers are therefore determined by the *prices* that emerge in the market for the services of the various resources. In general, the price of a resource depends on its productivity in the different branches of production. When a resource owner is otherwise indifferent to the use his resource will be applied to, he will sell its services to the highest bidder. The highest bidder will tend to be that entrepreneur to whose profit calculations the services of additional quantities of the resource add most. The market process therefore tends to ensure the apportioning of rewards among cooperating resource owners in a way that attracts resources to their most productive uses. At the same time each individual resource owner participating in the market process is able to enjoy the fruits of the production of the market to an extent depending on the usefulness to the market of the productive services that he is willing to supply on these terms. That portion of production that is not earned by resource owners is received by entrepreneurs as pure profit. We now consider briefly the factors that determine the size of profits, and especially the coordinating functions that profits fulfill.

THE COORDINATING FUNCTION OF PROFITS IN A MARKET ECONOMY

In the previous sections it was seen that the market process simultaneously solves the three fundamental problems of economic coordination through the price system. The emergence of a price structure reflects a priority system that guides resources to (what this priority system pronounces to be) their most productive uses. But the price system is not "automatic"; it functions only as the expression of human actions. In particular the price system is the expression of entrepreneurial decisions consciously planned and executed. Entrepreneurial decisions are made with the purpose of winning profits.

Profits are to be won whenever something can be sold for a price higher than the price it can be bought at (or higher than the sum of the prices of everything needed for its production). For an entrepreneur to win profits it is necessary, *first,* that such a price discrepancy exist; and *second,* that the entrepreneur know that it exists. Now, for a price discrepancy to exist, it is necessary that those willing to sell the commodity (or the factors necessary for its production) for the lower price and those willing to buy the commodity at the higher price be unaware of each other's attitudes. If these sellers and buyers knew each other's attitudes, these would soon be altered to eliminate the price discrepancy. The entrepreneur wins profits by becoming aware, earlier than others, of the hitherto unknown discrepancy (reflected in the price differential) between the attitudes of those willing to sell for less and of those willing to buy for more.

It is the characteristic of the real world to which the analysis of market theory may be applied that, at any one time, numerous instances occur of the kind of ignorance that makes it possible for price discrepancies and profits to emerge. Each market participant knows some of the market facts relevant to his own situation, but is ignorant of a great many more. Among the alternatives from which Market Participant A believes he has to choose, some particularly attractive alternative is usually missing (obtainable by dealing with Market Participant B) which might have been included if only A and B would have known of each other's situation and attitude. From the point of view of an imaginary, disinterested outsider knowing all these facts, both A and B are the losers due to their ignorance of some market facts. *From the point of view of the omniscient outsider,* the market *always* has room for a reshuffling of resources or goods according to the pattern that would take place if the market participants themselves were not in ignorance of the opportunities available to them.

It is here that we can see the essential character of the coordinating functions performed by the market process. The market process tends to present market participants with alternatives that approximate those opportunities they would choose if they possessed all the relevant information. The market process achieves this *without* making it necessary for market participants to learn all this detailed information. Instead, the market reveals any lack of coordination resulting from ignorance by market participants of potentially available opportunities through the emergence of price discrepancies. Ignorance of available opportunities then equates to ignorance of price discrepancies. Where this kind of ignorance persists, the opportunity exists for the first discoverers of the price discrepancy to step in and win profits. In doing this they wipe out the price discrepancy itself, and thus remove the lack of coordination that resulted from the limited market knowledge of market participants.

The quest for profits thus serves as a complete substitute for the search for conditions where ignorance exists on the part of market participants of the opportunities available to them. In the quest for profits the latter search has been replaced by a simple search for price discrepancies. Wherever discrepancies exist between prices paid for identical goods, or between prices paid for goods and those paid for everything required for their production, then the imaginary omniscient economist could point out possibilities for reallocation of goods or resources that would benefit all concerned. The market tends to act to achieve precisely this reallocation by offering prizes (profits) for the detection and removal of price discrepancies. It is thus the activity of the entrepreneur in his search for profits that serves as the driving force of the price system, enabling it to solve the problems of coordination outlined in the previous sections of this chapter.

SUMMARY

Chapter 3 examines the operation of a market system, with respect to the way it achieves the *goals* or functions that its participants may seek to fulfill through this means of social organization.

An "economic problem" consists for an individual in ensuring that the resources at his disposal be utilized in the most effective manner possible, from the point of view of his own cherished goals. With some reservations, it is possible to speak of an economic problem facing society in general, and of the "efficiency" with which a form of social organization fulfills the goals set for it.

For a system of social cooperation, efficiency requires the coordination of separate activities. Social cooperation opens up the way to the improved fulfillment of individual wants through division of labor; but division of labor is beneficial only where carried on in a coordinated fashion. Coordination involves (a) the development of a *priority system for the satisfaction of wants*, (b) some way of determining the *method of production* to be employed for each adopted project, and (c) a way of *assigning rewards* to the individuals cooperating jointly in productive activities.

The market simultaneously solves these coordinating problems through the *price* system. Prices determine the priority with which the various possible products will be produced on the basis of consumer demand working through the entrepreneurial search for profits. The same process guides entrepreneurs to the employment of definite methods of production (those which can achieve a given result at the lowest money cost). At the same time the pricing process assigns prices to the services of those cooperating in production. The driving force in the process is thus the entrepreneurial search for profits, leading to the production of products commanding the highest prices (for given production costs) and to the employment of the resources involving least cost (for a given productive purpose).

SUGGESTED READINGS

Knight, F. H., *The Economic Organization*, Kelley and Millman Inc., New York, 1951, pp. 3–30.

Mises, L. v., *Human Action*, Yale University Press, New Haven, Connecticut, 1949, pp. 694–697, 258–323.

In this and the succeeding chapters we discuss the theory of the demand side of the market. Our task will be to explain the way the alternatives presented to each consumer by the market determine the way he spends his income and the quantities of each good that he decides to purchase.

In the present chapter a framework is set forth within which individual consumer demand theory intuitively "fits." This is the notion of *marginal utility*. It must be stressed that utility theory provides no explanation in terms of any external observable criteria. It merely provides a logical means of mental orderliness in bringing coherence into a description of individual behavior. It provides a framework by which an internal consistency can be introduced into the explanation of consumer adjustment to changes in market data. The fact that this framework is intuitively and introspectively valid makes it extremely valuable in explaining the actions of market participants.

This chapter provides the conceptual apparatus that is then put to work in Chapter 5 in interpreting individual allocation of income. In Chapter 6 the analysis is extended to cover the demand for particular commodities as expressed by the market as a whole and as it reacts to given changes. The analysis will be built on the basis of understanding the individual demand behavior of which market demand is itself the resultant. In Chapter 7 we apply our analysis to a market process that might develop in an economy where only consumer goods are bought and sold.

THE SCALE OF VALUES

The fundamental premise the theory of demand (and, therefore, also market theory in its entirety) is built upon is that *men do not consider all their desires to be of equal importance*. Each of us wishes to enjoy the services of innumerable types of commodities, to achieve a variety of cherished goals. For the analysis of human action, it is of the first moment that we *rank* these inclinations and desires as either more or less urgent. Whenever we are forced *to choose* between the satisfaction of two inclinations, one of them takes precedence over the other.

That men are *able* to arrange their preferences in order of importance is inherent in the nature of man himself; that men are *forced* to make such a ranking is imposed by the brute fact of scarcity that places man constantly in the position of being unable to satisfy all his desires. It is this scarcity that thrusts on man the necessity to choose. And it is in the act of choice that man does, in fact, rank the available alternatives. The renounced alternatives, by their very renunciation, are declared less urgent than the alternative that is chosen.

At any given time, a man finds himself possessed of a multitude of desires. He would like to eat, drink, read, walk, or simply sleep. The foundation of the theory of demand is the recognition that all his desires, all the goals he deems worthy of achievement, may be considered as making up a *scale of values*, arranged in their order of importance. This ordered array is set up, for any number of man's desires, whenever he is forced to choose between them. When man eats, then he pronounces the goal of eating to be superior on the value scale *of this moment* to any of the other activities he might have engaged in. When, at another time, he goes on a hike, then it is this form of recreation that has been set aside as more urgently desired *at the moment* than other forms of activity.[1]

Acting man, at every moment of his consciousness, is forced to choose among a number of possible courses of action. It is of the essence of action that it aims at encompassing the fulfillment of as many of the actor's desires as is possible, *in the order of their urgency*. That is, a man always acts to ensure that no desire is satisfied at the expense of the satisfaction of some more important want. This, after all, is only a different way of expressing the fact that man is intent on successfully achieving his goals. "Achieving one's goals" means *renouncing* the achievement of a specific goal should it interfere with the achievement of a goal considered more important.

In the actuality of the everyday world, human beings are able to satisfy their wants only through directing their efforts toward appropriate *means* for such satisfaction. A man who wishes to eat may purchase food, cook food, or simply put on a hat and coat and go to a restaurant. His actions have been intermediary to the goal of eating. "Eating" is the *end* of his

---

1. It is unnecessary, and may in fact be misleading, to consider a scale of values as existing for a consumer, in any sense, *apart from his acts of choice*. All that is meant here is that when man is forced to choose, he is *at that moment* forced to arrange his values in order of importance. In particular, the notion of a given scale of values does *not* imply any *necessary permanence* for the rankings under consideration.

present endeavors; the *means* that he adopts for the attainment of his end can be an act of purchase, cooking, or walking to the restaurant. It is rare indeed that any act a man undertakes can be considered only an end in itself; in most cases actions are aimed at some goal that, upon examination, proves to be only intermediate to the attainment of some more "ultimate" purpose; and so on.

For our purposes it is not so much the distinction between ends and means that is of importance. Rather it is desired to emphasize that when men act to obtain the means necessary to fulfill their more ultimate goals, they are actuated by the same kind of calculation as when they aim at their goals directly. In particular, it is noted that the very considerations that constrain man to arrange his desires in order of their importance force him to make an identical arrangement among the means necessary to the fulfillment of these desires. In his attempts to obtain the means for the satisfaction of his wants, man directs his first efforts to the attainment of those means that minister to ends highest on the value scale. When forced, as in fact he constantly is forced, to choose between alternative bundles of "means," man places the means in their appropriate rankings within the value scale. He is careful not to follow any course of action that would secure him the means of satisfying any desire, where this would be at the expense of items higher on the value scale—that is, at the expense of wants (or means for the satisfaction of wants) considered more urgent.

It is this complete scale of values that man at once sets up and follows, whenever he is called upon to choose. Man's actions are invariably carried out under the constraint of some such value scale. Our analysis of demand theory is built on the logical consequences of the existence of such a scale—of the fact that man's desires and the means to the satisfaction of these desires are not of equal "significance." By "significance" we mean simply "importance," judged by the yardstick set up by a man's value scale. The terms "significance," "importance," "urgency," and the like are used throughout demand theory to allow the idea of value ranking to embrace *all* objects and courses of action that man considers as desirable or worthy of attainment. A man may be in a position where he must choose between quite heterogeneous objects or values. He may be forced to choose whether to rush over his breakfast or to miss his train; whether not to tell the truth or to lose his job; whether to increase his costs by granting a salary increase to an employee or to risk being labeled a "skinflint." No matter how unmatched the relevant alternatives may appear, the very fact that he is called upon to choose between them means that man must somehow rank them on the same scale. Thus, this scale must be far wider than one intended merely to rank values as more physically pleasurable or less, as more morally acceptable or less, as more esthetically appealing or less; it must, or more accurately, *does* rank objects and courses of action as simply more worthy of action or less. An item higher on the value scale, for action, is more "significant" than an item below it.

MARGINAL UTILITY

In the theory of demand, the term *utility* is to be understood as denoting simply "significance," in the sense set forth in the previous section. As such the utility concept is fundamental to the theory of demand and to the understanding of the determination of prices. In this and in the next chapters we use the utility concept to analyze the actions of the consumer and the way his actions are adjusted to changes in basic market data. Our discussion begins with an illustration of the notion of *marginal utility* as it is reflected in a simple exchange transaction between two men and then proceeds to use marginal utility as a tool in the subsequent analysis.

Imagine two men *A* and *B*. Each possesses a quantity of both fish and fruit. However, *A* would gladly give up some of his fish if this would secure him more fruit; *B* is ready to give up some of his fruit if this will increase his supply of fish. When *A* and *B* become aware of this situation, exchange ensues. We will suppose that *A* gives 3 lbs. of his fish to *B* and obtains 10 lbs. of *B*'s fruit in exchange. Let us restate this simple case using utility terminology, from *A*'s point of view.

Both fish and fruit have utility for *A*; *A* would prefer, other things being equal, to have more fish than less fish and more fruit than less fruit. However, the utility to *A* of the 10 lbs. of fruit that he obtains from *B* is greater than that of the 3 lbs. of fish that *A* yields in exchange. For *B*, of course, the case is the reverse. The utility to him of the 3 lbs. of fish that he obtains is greater than that of the 10 lbs. of fruit that he yields.

Now, it must be noticed, that when we compare for *A* the utilities of fruit and fish, we are *not* comparing the significance of fruit-in-general with that of fish-in-general. Such a comparison clearly has no meaning for a science of human action, since nobody is ever forced to choose between two such alternatives. All that is involved in the utility comparison is the utility of the quantity of fruit that *A* acquires with that of the quantity of fish that he yields. These are the relevant "fruit" and "fish" involved in the comparison. To emphasize this limitation, we describe the situation for A by saying that for him the *marginal utility* of fruit is higher than that of fish. We are able to assert that, on A's scale of values, the marginal utility of 10 lbs. of fruit is higher than that of 3 lbs. of fish. The significance to A of the prospective 10 lbs. of additional fruit is placed higher than the significance of the 3 lbs. of fish that are to be renounced.

When the transaction has been completed, A has successfully pursued a course of action that has substituted a more valuable package for one less valuable. He was not called upon to choose between fish and fruit. He had no need to compare fish-in-general with fruit-in-general, nor even to compare all his own fish with all his own or B's fruit. The only choice forced on A was to compare the significance of fish and fruit *at the margin*. At issue was the loss of *some* fish as compared with the gain of *some* fruit. What A was called upon to decide was whether the *difference* to him involved in the loss of the 3 lbs. of fish meant more or less to him than the difference involved in the gain of the 10 lbs. of fruit. The fact that A chose to exchange signifies that the marginal utility to him of 10 lbs. of fruit was greater than the marginal utility to him of the 3 lbs. of fish.

DIMINISHING MARGINAL UTILITY

We can now develop a principle of far-reaching significance in economics generally and in demand theory in particular. This principle is usually referred to as *diminishing marginal utility*. A clear understanding of this principle will provide the key to much of the subsequent discussion.

Imagine a man who has had to decide how much of a particular commodity to buy. Let us suppose that he was able to obtain as many units of the commodity as he pleases at a fixed price of $\$P$ per unit and that he has finally purchased N units. We say that his action demonstrates that he prefers N units of the commodity to the amount of $\$P \times N$, which he has to pay for them. He has chosen between the alternatives of either paying the sum $\$PN$ (and gaining N units) or going without the quantity N of the commodity.

This way of expressing the choice that faced the man, while correct as far as it goes, does not fully set forth the actual complexity of the decision he has made. Our buyer, who actually buys N units, could have bought, if he had desired, either more than N units or less than N units. The full range of alternatives open to him include:

Buying Possibilities	Cost
Buying none of the commodity	no money
Buying 1 unit	P
Buying 2 units	$2P$
. . .	. . .
Buying $N-1$ units	$(N-1)P$
Buying N units	NP
Buying $N+1$ units	$(N+1)P$
. . .	. . .

In comparing these successive alternatives one with another, the prospective buyer assesses the differences (marginal utility) that successive additional units of the commodity would make to him; and he weighs these differences against those involved in the prospective loss of successive additional sums of money. The principle of diminishing marginal utility focuses attention on the marginal utility attached to successive additional units of the commodity.

The acquisition of additional units of a commodity enables the buyer to satisfy a successively larger number of wants. The acquisition of the mth unit of a commodity by one who already possesses $m-1$ units means that he will now be able to satisfy a want that, if only $m-1$ units would be possessed, must have gone unsatisfied. It is clear, upon reflection, that this want whose satisfaction is made possible by the acquisition of the mth unit must rank higher on the man's scale of values than the want that depends for its satisfaction on the acquisition of the $(m+1)$th unit. For when a man acquires the mth unit, he will have to choose—out of all the wants that must go unsatisfied when only $m-1$ units are possessed—that particular want whose satisfaction the acquisition of this mth unit should, in fact, make possible. And, of course, it will be the most important of these wants that will be chosen. Furthermore, of the still remaining unsatisfied wants, it will be the next most important one that will be selected for satisfaction upon acquisition of the $(m+1)$th unit.

Similarly, looking at the same situation from the opposite direction, it is obvious that if the man who possesses $m-1$ units were to *lose* one of them, then he would see to it that the want that must now go unsatisfied will be the *least* important of all hitherto satisfied wants. Of the remaining yet satisfied wants, it must be the *next* least important that would be sacrificed, were yet another unit to be lost.

To restate the contents of the preceding paragraphs compactly, we can say that the

Marginal utility of the mth unit is lower than that of the (m − 1)th unit and higher than that of the (m + 1)th unit.

This conclusion is the principle of diminishing marginal utility.

The principle readily lends itself to illustration. Consider, for example, an air passenger packing his valise and allowed to take with him baggage of only limited weight. He surveys the articles he would like to take but which weigh, let us say, 5 lbs. in excess of the limit. Clearly, the 5 lbs. of his possessions that will be excluded will be those the passenger believes to be least urgently required for the trip, among all the 5-lb. groups of articles that can be removed. Suppose that a sudden change in regulations reduces the permitted weight by 5 lbs.; then yet another 5 lbs. of articles will have to be excluded. The latter will be possessions that, while more desired for the trip than those previously excluded, are yet not as indispensable as the articles still packed in the valise. The marginal utility of allowed baggage, in terms of 5-lb. units of impedimenta, increases as the baggage allowance dwindles and diminishes as the baggage allowance increases.

Some words of clarification are in order with respect to the meaning of "marginal." Let us imagine six physically similar shirts each bearing a different number. A man owns the shirts numbered 1, 2, 3, and 4. He contemplates the purchase of the shirt numbered 5 and then of the shirt numbered 6. His decision requires the comparison of three situations: (a) possession of shirts 1, 2, 3, and 4; (b) possession of shirts 1, 2, 3, 4, and 5; and (c) possession of shirts 1, 2, 3, 4, 5, and 6. As discussed, such comparison involves the marginal utility of "a fifth" and of "a sixth" shirt. If each shirt is priced at $5, then the decision whether or not to purchase the fifth shirt will hinge on whether a fifth shirt has greater utility than $5 or not. The marginal shirt in this case happens to be the shirt bearing number 5. And similarly for the sixth shirt.

The law of diminishing utility tells us that the marginal utility of the sixth shirt will be lower than that of the fifth. The acquisition of the fifth shirt, let us say, enables the man to fulfill a particular engagement without appearing in a soiled or frayed shirt. The sixth shirt will obviously make no difference at all to this engagement; it can affect only some other occasion, less important than this engagement.

It must be made clear that the fifth and sixth shirts, as well as each of the four already possessed, being different units of the same good, are perfect substitutes for one another. The shirt numbered 6 has lower utility than that numbered 5 only *because it is to be acquired later.* Once the man has bought the sixth shirt, it may well be that the shirt numbered 6 may actually be worn for the most important occasion. When we say that a sixth shirt has lower utility value than a fifth, what we actually mean then is that the utility of *any* one shirt, when six shirts are owned, is lower than that of any shirt in a five-shirt wardrobe. This is so because the utility of any shirt in a man's wardrobe means simply the difference its loss would make to him. A man owning shirts numbered 1 to 6, contemplating the loss of shirt number 3, is in exactly the same position as if he would be contemplating the loss of shirt number 6. Any use shirt number 3 would be put to, were shirt number 6 to be sacrificed, can be perfectly served by one of the other shirts, when it is shirt number 3 that is to be given up. The marginal utility of any one particular unit in a stock of shirts, or any other good, even the marginal utility of the unit devoted to a more important use than any of the other units, is exactly the same as the marginal utility of the unit devoted to the *least* important use—since it is this least important use that is at stake.

This rather obvious fact can be fruitfully borne in mind throughout economics whenever the adjective "marginal" appears.

THE MARGINAL UTILITIES OF RELATED GOODS

It is useful for many purposes to distinguish between goods that, for a given consumer, are unrelated and goods that are related. *Unrelated goods* are those whose marginal utility depends only on the quantity of it possessed, not on the quantity possessed of the others. *Related goods,* on the other hand, are any group of goods whose marginal utility depends, in some way, not only on the quantities of the good itself possessed, but also on the quantities possessed of the other goods in the group.

The relationship between related goods can be one of two kinds. Related goods can be either *complementary* to one another or *substitutes* for one another.

Goods that are complementary to one another are those the consumer in some way considers as cooperating together in the satisfaction of a particular want. Automobiles and gasoline, for example, are complementary goods. Pens, paper, and ink are complementary goods. Usually complementary goods may combine in different proportions to satisfy the particular want they are complementary to. Where they are useful only when combined in some fixed proportion, it is useful to consider them as constituting parts of one good. It is hardly more worthwhile to consider separately the items making up a pair of shoes than it would be to consider the utility of water as made up of the utility of hydrogen and oxygen. (Of course, where goods are complementary with respect to one use, but are independently useful elsewhere, it is convenient to keep them distinct.) Complementary goods are distinguished in that for each such good, its marginal utility to the consumer rises, other things being equal, as the quantities possessed of the goods complementary to it increases. The more paper that the owner of a pen acquires, the more significant a bottle of ink may appear to him.

Goods that are substitutes for one another are those the consumer considers capable, to some degree, of satisfying the same particular want. Potatoes and bread, for example, are to a degree capable of satisfying the same wants that are satisfied by the other. Airline transportation and railroad transportation are substitutes, to a degree, each for one another. It is to be noted that when two physically dissimilar commodities are *perfect* substitutes for one another—where, that is, there is no purpose served by a given quantity of the one that cannot be served equally well by a given quantity of the other—then, from an economic point of view, they are not "different" goods at all. If, for example, there were *no* purpose for which a blue pencil is used that is not perfectly served by a red pencil, and vice versa, then it would not be expedient to distinguish economically between red and blue pencils at all; they would be used interchangeably. If two nickels could perform all the uses required of a dime, and vice versa, then the two coins would make up an economically homogeneous kind of good. Within this economically homogeneous group there would be, it is true, physical differences—some members of the group being made up of two nickels, the other being each one dime. But this would be as irrelevant as, say, the different registration numbers on two identical automobiles where the difference in number is the only physical means of distinction between them.

Most substitute goods are, however, only imperfect substitutes for one another. A characteristic of goods that a consumer considers as substitutes for one another is that the marginal utility to him of any such good declines, other things being the same, as the quantity possessed of the substitute goods increases. The more rapidly the marginal utility declines in this manner, the more perfect is the substitute relationship between the goods. The special case, as we have seen, of perfect substitutes is one where the marginal utility of the one good declines, with increased possession of the other, exactly as rapidly as it would decline were the quantities possessed of this good itself to be increased in the same proportions.

MARGINAL UTILITY—SOME FURTHER REMARKS

It is worthwhile at this point to emphasize a number of points concerning the marginal utility concept as we have used it thus far. These points will serve to clarify the content of our utility analysis and, at the same time, point to the way our analysis is related to the very earliest attempts to use the tool of marginal utility.

The Paradox of Value

Modern utility theory emerged in the 1870s at the hands of Jevons, Menger, and Walras. One of the earliest uses of the theory was to sweep away a misunderstanding that had prevented the earlier classical economists from using the utility concept to explain prices.

The earlier writers found themselves unable to explain the prices of goods by reference to the use-value or utility of these goods. To be sure, the prices of many goods seem to reflect their relative degrees of usefulness to men; the classical economists would have welcomed such a theory. But they were troubled by the many goods whose prices seemed to defy any such explanation. Diamonds, for example, are clearly much less important for human life than water, yet the price of water is quite negligible compared with that of diamonds. This paradox had forced the classical economists to seek an entirely different method of explaining prices.

Marginal utility theory is able to dispose of the problem quite simply. The basis for the paradox was the premise that water is more significant for man than are diamonds. This premise is no doubt correct, but not in a way that can support the classical conclusions. Water, in the abstract, is no doubt more important than diamonds in the abstract. But for human action the greater importance of water over diamonds must be demonstrated through choice among alternatives. For an analysis of human action no other meaning can be attached to the term "more important." From this point of view the greater importance of water must mean that we assume if a man has to choose between water and diamonds, he will choose water. But for the statement of alternatives a man must choose among, it is clearly insufficient to specify only that these are water and diamonds. One must specify the terms and conditions on which he is to choose. And here the irrelevance of the "greater importance of water over diamonds" for understanding their relative prices becomes immediately clear.

Water is more important than diamonds only where a man must choose between renouncing *all* water or renouncing *all* diamonds. Faced with such a choice it is indeed likely that a man will place diamonds distinctly in second place. But this kind of choice is one that the market does *not* confront the consumer with and therefore cannot have bearing on the determination of market prices. In the market a man buying or refraining from buying water is choosing not merely whether to have water or not to have water, but whether to have some *additional* quantity of water or not; and similarly, of course, for diamonds. Thus, the law of diminishing marginal utility provides the key.

The marginal utility of water cannot be said to be either higher or lower than that of diamonds until there are first specified (a) the size of the marginal unit and (b) the margin at which marginal quantities of water and diamonds are being compared. The marginal utility of water is indeed *lower* than that of diamonds—when a small quantity of water is compared with a similar weight of diamonds and when the loss of this small quantity of water would still leave the consumer with ample water. These are, in fact, the conditions under which consumers choose whether to buy water or diamonds. The quantity of water usually available is ample; thus, the margin at which an additional quantity of water is valued is such as to make its marginal utility low, according to the law of diminishing marginal utility. On the other hand, diamonds are usually possessed in sufficiently small amounts to ensure that the typically sized marginal unit still possesses high marginal utility.

If conditions were otherwise, prices would indeed reflect the altered conditions. If, for example, a thirsty owner of diamonds were to bargain in a desert with the owner of a quantity of water, we would indeed expect to find the price of water far from negligible. Clearly, in these circumstances, the marginal utility of water must be immensely higher than under normal conditions. Here, indeed, water would show itself as "more important for man than diamonds."

The Subjective Character of Utility

The concept of utility as we have developed it thus far in this chapter, and as we shall use it to analyze the demand side of the market, is essentially a *subjective* concept. We must not consider utility as in anyway intrinsic to an object or service. A good is not to be thought of as bearing a tag inscribed with some degree of utility. We do not require any philosophical sophistication to distinguish sharply between the utility relevant to the analysis of human actions and such qualities as the mass, extension, and even color or beauty of an object. For the analysis of demand this distinction is of the greatest importance.

For the economist, what is relevant is merely that a consumer prefers some specific quantity of a good or service to some specific quantity of the same or another good or service. One alternative is considered to satisfy a want that is more urgent than that which could be satisfied by the rejected alternative. The relatively greater want-satisfying power of the first good or service is called its greater utility. Of course, "want-satisfying power" springs from some quality, real or imagined, associated with the use or enjoyment of the good or service. The utility of coal springs from its heating powers, that of a painting from its artistic merits; the utility of a shoeshine is associated with an appropriate glossiness, the utility of a textbook with the knowledge it confers. But all these are the specific qualities that characterize goods or services on the *basis* of which one good is preferred over another. Acting man considers these "objective" qualities of the goods among which he chooses; he weighs, with more or less expert knowledge, the relative objective merits of the goods and then arranges them on *one* scale—the scale of preference.

Man cannot "objectively" compare the glossiness of a newly shined pair of shoes with the thermal capacity of a quantity of fuel, but he must sometimes choose between them. When he chooses he is arranging them in order of "importance." There is a homogeneous common denominator that makes it possible to compare them: that of their relative positions on the utility scale. The one is more urgent, significant, and important than the other. The economist, concerned exclusively with the logic of choice, needs only to be indirectly conscious of the "objective" qualities of goods. It is not the intensity of these qualities, but the degree of subjectively felt significance with which the law of diminishing marginal utility is concerned, and from which demand analysis takes its start.

Several corollaries follow immediately from the establishment of the subjective character of utility. Most important is the implication that the utilities of the same good for two different people *cannot be compared*. This, it is noted, is saying considerably more than that it is possible for the same good to have *different* utilities to two different people. It is even saying more than that there is no conceivable *way of discovering* for which of two people a given good has more utility. The impossibility of interpersonal utility comparisons implies that *no meaning at all* can be attached to a statement comparing the utilities of the same (or different) goods to two people.

Utility refers to relative position on a value scale. A good of greater utility is higher on the scale and thereby preferred over a good of lower utility. There is no single value scale on which a specific "good-for-*A*" can take up a position relative to a "good-for-*B*"; there is no conceivable act of "choice" that should "prefer" a good for *A* rather than for *B*.

The impossibility of comparing the utility of a good for two people does not affect, of course, the fact that each of us frequently engages in comparisons concerning the relative "usefulness" of a good to different people. We say that a hungry man "needs" food more than one who has just dined. We try to give charity "where it will do most good"; we distribute gifts among our friends or children where we think they will be the most useful or pleasurable. All this is quite in order, but it does not involve any comparisons of that utility demand analysis depends upon. An outsider *C* is entitled to his opinion, however irrational, as to how a quantity of a good "ought" to be shared out between two other people, *A* and *B*. Frequently he does so by placing himself mentally in the positions of both these people simultaneously. But it is always his choice, always his assessment of relative "urgency," which operates in such decisions.

Another, and a related, implication of the subjective character of utility is that utility must be clearly distinguished from both ethical values and psychological pleasure-pain sensations. As far as ethics is concerned, the matter is straightforward. In studying demand, we are interested in the patterns of action that follow from given tastes, no matter what these tastes may be. Utility refers to the importance attached by man to possession of goods. What degrees of importance a man attaches to different goods is indeed a matter determined in part by his ethical values. But just as the economist analyzes the demand for coal not by reference to its technological thermal capacity but to the subjective significance that men attach to coal (of course chiefly on technical, objective grounds), quite similarly the economist analyzes the demand for goods (flowers or bullets, knowledge, or liquor) by starting out in a quite "positive" way, and without the need for any moral evaluation, from men's demonstrated preferences.

The distinction between the utility used in demand theory and pleasure-pain sensations should be equally clear cut. The distinction must be especially stressed because many of the earliest expositions of utility analysis did fail, in fact, to recognize such a distinction or were phrased as if they failed to do so. This failure was both unfortunate and unnecessary. The utility of a loaf of bread, insofar as demand theory is concerned, is not to be identified either with the hunger pangs suffered for lack of the bread or with the sensation of satiety experienced upon its consumption. These sensations may be "real" and important enough, but like ethical values, *underlie* the preferences that men reveal in their actions. A man's value scale and the utility to him of given commodities are doubtless dependent on the intensity of these sensations. But the economist must be satisfied to commence from the colorless fact of preference.

Utility as a Relative Concept

We conceive of utility as a purely relative notion. In saying that a good has utility to a man, we mean that it possesses importance, or significance, to him because of its power to remove uneasiness. As we have seen, "importance" and "significance" take on meaning only in the context of a comparison with other goods. Utility reveals itself only in acts of choice when two or more goods are being *compared*. Thus, it is quite meaningless to conceive of the utility of a loaf of bread, as it were, in a vacuum. All we can say is that a loaf of bread may have either more or less utility than a glass of beer, a news magazine, or twenty cents.

If utility could be identified with some "objective" property of a good, say its mass, calorific value, or even moral worth, then the concept would not depend on the relationship between one good and another. But the utility of demand analysis refers to none of these objective qualities and does, therefore, by its very definition, imply a comparison with other goods or services. Utility refers to position on a scale of values. Without other goods or services, there is no scale of values and hence no utility concept at all.

The relative character of utility means that men's preferences can be the subject of interpersonal comparisons. There is, as we have seen, no value scale upon which the relative positions of a loaf-of-bread-for-A and a loaf-of-bread-for-B can be observed. But it may be possible for an observer to discover whether a loaf of bread bears the same relationship to twenty cents on A's scale of values as it does on B's; and it may be possible to assert that a loaf of bread has greater utility to A than twenty cents, but that for B the situation is reversed. In fact, this kind of assertion is, as we shall discover, the foundation of market theory.

The Ordinal Character of Utility

Two conflicting approaches to utility theory are met in the literature. The older (but by no means extinct) approach was to treat the utility of a good for an individual as a magnitude to which, in principle, a cardinal number could be assigned. An apple has, let us say, 10 units of utility; a shirt, 50 units; and so on. Such an approach involves the postulation of a numerical scale of utility against which the utilities of goods might—again only in principle—be measured with precision.[2] The theoretical concept of numerical quantities of utility involves, again, the notion that a larger "quantity of utility" (one, that is, comprising a larger number of "units" of utility) is built up through the addition of smaller quantities of utility or of units of utility. A good with utility of 10 possesses *10 times* the utility of a good with unit utility; and so on. The cardinal utility approach would consider a man enlarging his stock of a good as, at the same time, increasing his store of utility afforded by possession of the good. The *total* store of utility afforded by the entire stock would be the sum of the successive increments of utility obtained as the stock successively expanded from the acquisition of the first unit up to the addition of the last acquired unit. The *rate* at which the addition of successive physical units of the good increases the total utility of a stock of the good is termed (in the cardinal terminology) the "marginal utility" of the good.[3]

The ideas, however, underlying the cardinal approach present considerable conceptual difficulty. Without attempting to enlarge on this difficulty, we can contrast this approach with the currently more accepted *ordinal* approach. This view denies the very notion of cardinal quantities of utility. The only numbers that can be assigned to utilities are ordinal

---

2. As can be imagined, cardinal utility theorists encountered serious difficulties in attempts to devise methods of measuring this utility. The earliest notions of cardinal utility arose out of the vain attempts to build an economic theory of consumer choice based on the psychological *content* of the feelings of satisfaction (associated with different acts of consumption) that account for a man's preference of one good over another. On the other hand, ordinal utility, as we have seen, is quite distinct from such psychological magnitudes.

3. The statement that a man acts so as to achieve his goals in order of their importance to him is translated directly, in cardinal-utility terminology, into the statement that he acts so as to *maximize* his total utility. In this context marginal utility is employed most conveniently as a mathematical tool simplifying the analytical task of finding the maximum position.

numbers. Utilities can be arranged *in order;* for example, first, second, and so on. They cannot however be assigned numerical magnitude. A shirt may be said to have greater utility than an apple; one may not say *how many times* the utility of the shirt is greater. A "unit" of utility has no meaning for the ordinal approach. When men value goods, they arrange them in order of value; they do not attach cardinal numbers to them.

The discussion we have presented in this chapter follows the ordinal approach to utility. For us, the utility of a good corresponds to a ranking on the scale of values; to speak of the utility of a good is to involve only the comparison of its significance with that of some other good. An important consequence of our adopting this ordinal viewpoint is that the term "marginal utility" is used in this book in a somewhat different sense from its use in a "cardinal" approach. This matter of terminology needs a brief explanation.

Total Utility and Marginal Utility

For a cardinal utility theorist, we have seen, the term "marginal utility" is used in contradistinction to "total utility." Total utility refers to the quantity of (cardinal) utility afforded by a stock of a commodity. Marginal utility refers to the *rate* at which total utility changes as the size of the stock of the commodity changes. An approximation to this rate of change of total utility is given by the amount of change in that utility resulting from a one-unit increase in the stock of the commodity. (Sometimes cardinal utility theorists loosely refer to this approximation as "marginal utility.")[4]

For ordinal utility theory, such a distinction between total and marginal utility is not called for. Since there is no cardinal quantity of utility that increases, there can be no such concept as a rate of change of such a quantity. For an ordinal theory, *marginal utility* means the significance attached to the addition to (or decrease of) the quantity possessed of a good by the marginal unit. It does not, it must be noticed, refer to *a change in the significance* of the stock of the good, but to the significance of a change in the size of the stock. But *total utility,* too, for the ordinal theorist means the significance attached to the acquisition or loss of a given stock of the commodity. Both the utility of a stock of a good and the marginal utility of a marginal unit being added (or subtracted) from the stock "are total utilities" (in that they do not refer to "rates of change"); but, and more

---

4. The total utility of a stock of a commodity is thus the sum of the marginal utilities of the units making up the stock, taken successively.

important, at the same time they are both "marginal utilities" in the sense that the utility of *any* quantity of a good, large or small, implies that this quantity is being considered "marginally"—that is, that somebody is contemplating the acquisition or loss of this quantity.

The "marginal unit," in fact, is never anything else than the unit *that happens to be under consideration.* It is the unit relevant to the act of choice confronting a man. The *size* of this unit depends only on the circumstances of the situation where a choice has become necessary. A man may be contemplating the purchase of several shirts. For certain sums of money, he can buy one, two, or several shirts. In choosing among the alternatives open to him, the man will be comparing the marginal utilities of the appropriate number of shirts—that is, *the smallest number of shirts separating one possible decision from another.* If any number of shirts can be bought, then a single shirt is the marginal unit; if shirts can be bought only in packages of three, then three shirts make up the marginal unit—and the decision whether or not to buy additional shirts will involve the difference that three more shirts will make to the purchaser's sense of well-being. Suppose a situation where a man is forced to choose between purchasing all of a supply of shirts or of obtaining none at all; then the entire supply would be the relevant "unit." The man must assess the difference that the entire supply would mean to him in considering the attractiveness of the price it can be had at. In such a situation the marginal unit is the entire supply, and the man is in a position where the "marginal utility of shirts" means nothing else than the significance to him of this entire shirt supply.

MARGINAL UTILITY AND THE CONDITIONS FOR EXCHANGE

The utility analysis discussed in this chapter provides a framework within which to understand the emergence of exchange between individuals. Interpersonal exchange is the essence of the market process, and market theory is devoted to the explanation of the way objects will be produced for exchange, the quantities that will be offered for exchange, and the rates at which different exchanges will take place. Here we analyze the basic conditions that exist when two individuals exchange goods. This analysis will be fundamental to much of the subsequent material in this book.

The conditions for exchange exist between two individuals *A, B,* whenever a specific quantity of a good possessed by *A* is ranked lower on his value scale than a specific quantity of a good possessed by *B,* while the ordering is the reverse on *B*'s value scale. That is, wherever the marginal utility of a quantity of one good possessed by *A* is lower for *A* than that of a quantity of another good possessed by *B*, while for *B* the marginal utility of the latter quantity is the lower, then each of the two gain by giving up what is less important to him in exchange for what is more important.

If these conditions are absent, no exchange can take place. It is not sufficient that *A* ranks *B*'s brand new automobile higher than his own ancient jalopy; if *B* concurs in *A*'s relative valuation, both vehicles will remain where they are. No exchange will take place freely unless each party believes that he will be better off having made the exchange. This fundamental and self-evident truth is the central theme of the market process and of its theory.

The implications of these conclusions are far reaching. Where two men each possess both of two goods, then, as we have seen, any difference in the rankings that specific quantities of the two goods occupy on the value scales of the two men will result in exchange if the two men are "in the same market" (that is, if they are each in contact with the other and aware of the other's relative ranking). This is so because it will benefit each man to give some of the good he values less for some of the good he values more. A state of rest, where both men, although in the same market, do not barter, can exist therefore only *when both men rank both goods in the same order* on their individual scales of value. But if this is so for two goods, it is so for *any* two goods. Thus, for two men to be in a state of rest with respect to each other, each must rank the marginal quantities of *all* the goods, which both possess, in exactly the same order as does the other.

Moreover, if this is the condition for absence of exchange between two men, it must be so also for *any* two men. Thus, for a market to be at rest, *each* participant in a market must rank each one of the goods he possesses in exactly the same order of significance, at the margin, as does every other participant in the market.

To put the same proposition in a different and more useful form, in any market a tendency will exist for each participant to barter in the marketplace so long as the relative marginal utilities to him of all the goods he possesses is in anyway different from those of any other participant with respect to those that he possesses. As each participant exchanges, the marginal utility of given quantities of the goods that he sacrifices rises (in accordance with the law of diminishing utility), while that of given quantities of the goods that he acquires correspondingly falls. The process of exchange thus raises those marginal utilities that had been relatively low (that is, of the goods that the owners for this reason wished to sell) and lowers those marginal utilities that had been relatively higher (that is, of the goods that the owner for this reason wished to buy). Hence, as the exchange process continues, the value scale of each member of the market tends toward consistency with that of every other member, with respect to the goods possessed by each member.

As men's tastes change, as for various reasons the quantities and kinds of the commodities and services each man possesses change, the relative marginal utilities of the goods he possesses alter for each participant in the market and thus, again and again, diverge from the rankings of other participants. There is thus constant recurrence of opportunities for each participant to exchange profitably.

The *rates* exchanges will take place at, of course, are closely bound up with the *degree* of divergence between the value scales of different participants. These are matters that will concern us in later chapters. Our discussion has been carried on in barter terms consistent with our assumption that exchange is carried on with the assistance of a medium of exchange that only facilitates, and in no way distorts, the expression by men of their relative valuations of real goods and services.

SUMMARY

Acting men, in choosing between available alternatives, arrange them in order of preference. The scale of values made up in this way indicates the relative *marginal utilities* of different specific quantities of different goods and services. Men act so as to replace a good of lower marginal utility by one of higher marginal utility.

The marginal utility of successively available additional units to a stock of a commodity steadily diminishes, other things being equal. This is the *law of diminishing marginal utility*.

Goods are either *related* or *unrelated*. Related goods may be either *complementary* to one another or *substitutes* (rivals) for one another. Complements are goods whose marginal utility rises, other things being the same, as the quantity possessed of the others increases. Substitutes are goods whose marginal utility falls, other things being the same, as the quantity of the others increases. Unrelated goods are those whose marginal utilities are unaffected by the quantities possessed of the other.

The marginal utility view is able to resolve the classical paradox concerning the relative values of diamonds and water. The utility concept is *subjective* and *relative* in character. The utility of a good refers to nothing inherent in the good itself and is meaningless unless it refers to a comparison with the utility of something else. Utility is an *ordinal* concept. No cardinal "units" of utility are implied in utility theory. "Marginal utility" is therefore to be interpreted not as the "rate of change of total utility," but as the (total) utility afforded by an increment of a good or service.

The utility theory provides the framework to understand exchange between market participants. Exchange will take place wherever the value scale rankings of two goods possessed by one man are different for him than the corresponding ranking for another man. In a market there is therefore a constant tendency for participants to exchange so that the value scale of each represents rankings identical with that of every other participant, for goods possessed by each of them.

SUGGESTED READINGS

Wicksteed, P. H., *The Common Sense of Political Economy*, Routledge and Kegan Paul Ltd., London, 1933, pp. 1–125.

Mises, L. v., *Human Action*, Yale University Press, New Haven, Connecticut, 1949, pp. 119–127.

Rothbard, M., "Toward a Reconstruction of Utility and Welfare Economics," in *On Freedom and Free Enterprise*, D. Van Nostrand Co., Inc., Princeton, New Jersey, 1956, pp. 232–243.

5   CONSUMER INCOME ALLOCATION

We have developed thus far the tool of marginal utility. We must now put this tool to use in analyzing the pattern of consumer behavior in spending his income in the marketplace on the goods and services he desires. Such an analysis (a) will enable us to understand the forces of *demand* as they are felt in the market, and (b) will help explain the ways demand may be expected to adjust to changes in relevant market facts. The analysis will thus give us perhaps the most important link in the chain of causation through which the market mechanism works.

MARGINAL UTILITY AND THE ALLOCATION OF INCOME

The consumer decides at any given time on what goods to buy, and in what quantities to buy them, on the basis of *three* sets of factors. *First,* the consumer consults his own scale of values, built upon his personal tastes, and the requirements of his own particular situation. *Second,* the consumer at any given time finds himself with a limited amount of money with which to buy (or, considering purchases over time, finds himself with limited money income per unit of time).[1] *Third,* the consumer faces a market where each good he is interested in is obtainable only at a definite price. The consumer finds, that is, that the expenditure of all his income on a particular good will provide him with a definite and limited quantity of the good; but, more important, that the expenditure of this amount might also provide a large number of alternative combinations of purchases, the contents of each combination being, with given expenditure, rigidly determined by the prices of the goods entering into

---

1. A consumer finds himself with given money income only *after* he has made his decisions concerning the quantity of his labor services, for example, that he will offer to the market at going wage rates. Taking a broader perspective, it should be clear that the terms on which a resource owner will make offers to sell resource services to the market depend on the direct satisfaction that he might himself derive, *as consumer,* by *not* selling them (for example, the utility to him of leisure), as compared with the consumer satisfaction that he can secure from their proceeds in the market. The analysis of consumer decisions can be extended to take explicit notice of all this. In such an analysis money income would not be one of the ultimate determinants of consumption expenditures; its place would be taken by the "income" the consumer is endowed with in his capacity of resource owner; that is, the flow of resource services he is naturally endowed with and free to sell in the market if he wishes. See p. 245.

the combination, and the proportion of expenditure allocated to each of the goods in the combination.

The essence of the problem facing the consumer thus consists in choosing one out of an immense number of alternative assortments of goods. A man may spend all his income per unit of time on good *A*, or all of it on good *B*, or good *C*, and so on. But he may spend all his income on some combination of the goods *A*, *B*, *C*. He must decide on which goods to include in his combination of purchases.[2] Confining our attention to the man's *consumption* expenditures, it is clear that with his own given value scale of the moment, he will act to secure, so far as is possible, as many of the goods and services he desires *in their order of importance to him*. In other words, he will act to make sure that *no one item* of the available goods, which he does *not* buy, is of greater significance to him (that is, is of higher utility) than any item, obtainable for the same expenditure, which he *does* buy. Let us ponder the implications of this proposition.

Our consumer, with, let us say, $100 to spend on consumption, may if he desires spend everything on shirts at, say, $4 per shirt. But if he spends $4 on a shirt, this is because he can find no article, available for $4, of greater utility. If he can buy a steak dinner for $4, and a steak dinner has greater utility than a shirt, he will buy the dinner, not the shirt. If he spends *all* his $100 on shirts, this can only mean that having even a twenty-fifth new shirt is more important than a single meal. Now several new shirts may have greater utility than eating, but the law of diminishing utility tells us that, relative to a first steak dinner, each additional shirt will have lower and lower utility. At some point, it is likely, the consumer will feel that another shirt has less utility than a first dinner, and expenditure will have somehow to be divided between dinners and shirts.

In fact, consumers usually buy a host of different kinds of goods: shirts, meals, haircuts, TV sets, college tuition, theatre tickets, and cigarettes. The important point to observe is that the movement from selecting one possible combination of goods to the selection of a differently proportioned combination involves shifting dollars between different goods *at the margin*. The one combination calls for fewer dollars spent on

---

2. He must further decide, of course, what portion of his income to allocate to *saving*. Although the analysis of this chapter can be applied to deal explicitly with this question, our discussion will apply most simply to the situation where the consumer does not wish to save anything. For further analysis of consumer decisions that have, like decisions to save, a bearing on the future, see below in the Appendix on multi-period planning, pp. 335–345.

the theatre, but more dollars spent on food; a little leaner budget for clothing, a little more liberality for books. Any selected combination of goods could be discarded in favor of some other combination simply by drawing back the margin of expenditures on one or more items and correspondingly advancing the margin of spending in other branches of consumption. The conditions for such a movement on the part of a consumer are simply that the marginal utility of the additional units in the new combination be greater than the discarded units in the old. The condition for consumer equilibrium (that is, the position where the consumer takes no action to improve his position) is that the marginal utility to be gained by adding any amount of money to any branch of consumption be offset by the marginal utility sacrificed by subtracting this sum of money from any of the already adopted branches of consumption.

The law of diminishing utility explains how consumers approach their equilibrium positions. Suppose a consumer has provisionally allocated his income so that he is spending "more than he needs" on food and "less than he needs" on clothing. Then he is in a position where several dollars taken from the food budget could be more advantageously put to use added to the clothing allocation. The marginal utility of several dollars' worth of clothing is greater than that of the same number of dollars' worth of food. The consumer's actions will remove this discrepancy. As he withdraws dollars from food, the marginal utility of a dollar's worth of food rises; as he adds dollars to clothing, the marginal utility of a dollar's worth of clothing falls. This narrows the gap between the marginal utilities of food and clothing, until it no longer pays to transfer expenditure from one to the other. By his actions the consumer has improved his position and thus at the same time reached a position where further improvement cannot be achieved.

THE POSITION OF CONSUMER'S EQUILIBRIUM

The degree of precision to which a consumer may be able to carry the allocation of his income will depend on the sizes of the marginal units of the goods available to him. If these goods are each divisible into very small physical units and can be purchased in any desired number of these small units, then income allocation can be made as precise as the consumer wishes; that is, as precise as the consumer feels worthwhile in view of the difficulty of choosing carefully between a number of closely similar alternatives. Disregarding the disutility of deliberation, it may be possible for the consumer to allocate his income so carefully that the further shift of even one penny of expenditure from any one good to any other must result in a gain from the new purchase that is more than offset by the sacrifice of the old.[3]

It is very possible, however, that the goods obtainable in the market are available only in units of considerable size. In such a situation, the consumer contemplating shifts in expenditure at the margins of different goods can consider only the possibility of reallocating sums of money that are of some size. The decision whether or not to purchase a second car may involve comparing the marginal utility of a car on the one hand, and several thousand dollars' worth of other commodities on the other hand. There can be no question here of shifting about pennies, dimes, or even dollars at the different margins of expenditure. Nevertheless, it can be said, here too, that the consumer will act to secure that assortment of goods so that no opportunity still remains to reduce the expenditure on any items, by any amount, in favor of other items, without the marginal utility of the additional purchases being lower than the marginal utility of the eliminated purchases.

At the position of equilibrium for a consumer, the following conditions hold with respect to any two kinds of goods available to him. Consider the higher priced of the two goods (that is, the one whose marginal unit is of such a size that it sells at the higher price). Consider the marginal utility of one unit (to be lost by *restricting* expenditure on this good by the price of one unit); denote this by a. (That is, a is an ordinal number denoting the relative position of this unit on the consumer's utility scale.) Consider the marginal utility of the unit to be gained by *expanding* expenditure on this good by the price of one unit; denote this by b. (Of course, b will denote a position lower than a.) Consider now the number of units of the lower-priced good that can be purchased for the price of a unit of the higher-priced good. Denote by c the (ordinal) marginal utility of *this*

---

3. Cardinal utility theorists translated this condition directly into "the equi-marginal principle." Denoting the cardinal marginal utility of a unit of commodity a by the symbol M_a (in utility units), and its price by the symbol P_a (in money units), it follows that the cardinal quantity of utility that can be bought with a unit of money is (approximately) M_a/P_a. The equi-marginal principle requires that, for utility maximization, income be distributed among any two commodities a and b in such a way that $M_a/P_a = M_b/P_b$ (approximately). In the absence of such an income distribution, a net gain in utility could be obtained by transferring expenditure from one commodity to the other. The discussion in the text presents the logic of the corresponding ordinal utility conditions; in addition, the discussion in the text makes allowance for marginal units of various sizes.

number of units (of the lower-priced good) to be lost should expenditure on this lower-priced good be *contracted* (in favor of a unit of the higher-priced good); denote by d the marginal utility of the same number of units of the lower-priced good to be *gained* at the expense of a unit of the higher-priced good. (Again, of course, d will denote a position lower than c.) At equilibrium, for *any* two goods, a will be higher on the ordinal utility scale than d (so that the consumer will not give up a unit of the higher-priced good in favor of a number of units of the lower-priced good), *and* c will rank higher on the ordinal scale than b (so that the consumer will not buy an *additional* unit of the higher-priced good at the expense of a number of units of the lower-priced good).[4]

A GEOMETRICAL ILLUSTRATION

The allocation of income by a consumer can be illustrated graphically. We consider, in the diagram (Figure 5-1), the allocation of expenditure between two goods X and Y (assuming the total expenditure on both goods to be fixed). Any point (such as P_1) in the diagram represents a "bundle" made up of a quantity of X, represented by the abscissa of the point (such as OS for the point P_1) and a quantity of Y, represented by the ordinate of the point (such as OR for the point P_1). With given expenditure allotted to be spent wholly on X and Y a consumer faced with given market prices for X and Y finds that he can acquire only a limited number of "bundles"; only a limited number of points in the X–Y field in the diagram are actually open to him.

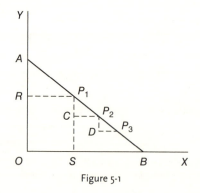

Figure 5-1

4. The consumer must of course compare the marginal utility a, not only with d, but also with the possibilities available for using the income (required to purchase a) to purchase, instead, a package made up of additional quantities of *several* alternative commodities.

It is fairly easy to describe a line (AB) drawn so that it passes through all points open to the consumer. The consumer, we suppose, can buy any amount of the good X at the price p_x per unit; and he can buy any amount of good Y at the price p_y per unit. Then if we denote the allotted amount to be spent on X and Y by M, it is clear that if all of M is spent on X, the number of units of X that can be bought is M/p_x. Similarly, if all of M be spent on Y, the number of units of Y that can be bought is M/p_y. Marking off the distance OB along the X-axis, where OB represents the quantity M/p_x; and marking off the distance OA along the Y-axis, so that OA represents the quantity M/p_y; it is clear that B and A are two of the points on the X–Y field that are open to the consumer. If he spends all on X, he can place himself at B; if he spends all on Y, he can place himself at A. If, however, he desires to purchase a bundle that contains not Y alone but some quantity of X together with the quantity OR of Y, then the quantity of X that will be included in the bundle must be determined. Instead of spending all of M (that is, $OA \times p_y$) on Y, the consumer wishes to spend only the amount $OR \times p_y$ on Y. This leaves him with $M - (OR \times p_y)$ to spend on X. Now $M = OA \times p_y$ so that the consumer has, to spend on X, the amount $(OA - OR)p_y$ or $AR \times p_y$. At a price, per unit of X, of p_x, this amount will therefore yield $AR \times p_y/p_x$ units of X. Denoting this quantity of X by the distance OS (= RP_1), we have discovered that the point P_1 is a point open to the consumer. It represents a bundle of OR of Y and OS of X.

It is easy and of some importance to show that the point P_1 must lie (on our assumption) on the straight line AB. The straight line AB has the downward slope OA/OB. But $OA = M/p_y$ and $OB = M/p_x$ so that $OA/OB = p_x/p_y$. Consider the line joining AP_1; it has the downward slope AR/RP_1. But $RP_1 = AR \times p_y/p_x$ (by definition) so that $AR/RP_1 = p_x/p_y$. The slope of AP_1 is thus the same as that of AB; P_1 (and thus in general *any* point representing a bundle of goods that can be purchased with the allotted expenditure) must lie along AB. AB joins all the "bundles" that are available to the consumer with his allotted expenditure; it is frequently called the *opportunity line*.

The consumer must thus select a point on AB representing the allocation of this expenditure most satisfactory to him. Suppose the consumer is at point P_1; then he will act to improve his position by moving along AB either toward A or B, until he reaches the point of consumer equilibrium. A movement, for example, from P_1 to P_2 implies that P_2 is an alternative that is preferred over P_1. The point P_2 represents a bundle that contains a little more of X (CP_2 of X) and a little less of Y (CP_1 of Y) than the bundle at P_1. If movement occurs from P_1 to P_2 this means that the consumer has compared the marginal utility of CP_2 of X with that of CP_1 of Y and considers the former to be higher than the latter. He considers the gain of CP_2 additional X more than sufficient to outweigh the sacrifice of CP_1 of Y. The market enables the consumer to translate his preferences into action. He is able to sell CP_1 of Y and buy CP_2 more of X; in the diagram he has moved from P_1 to P_2.

If P_2 is a point preferred over all other points on the opportunity line, the consumer acts to attain P_2, thereby rejecting all the other alternatives open to him (that is, refraining from selecting any other point on the line). At P_2 the consumer is at equilibrium. The diagram shows how this equilibrium position differs from other positions, say P_3 or P_1, on the line. The size of the increments of Y and X, respectively, P_1C and CP_2 between P_1 and P_2, or P_2D and DP_3 between P_2 and P_3, are, let us suppose, the smallest that can be exchanged for one another. At P_3 the consumer is not at equilibrium, because he prefers the additional quantity of Y, P_2D to the marginal quantity DP_3 of X. He will therefore shift $DP_3 \times p_x$ ($= P_2D \times p_y$) of expenditure from X to Y. Similarly, as we saw, at point P_1 the consumer shifted $P_1C \times p_y$ ($= CP_2 \times p_x$) of expenditure from Y to X. Only at P_2 will the consumer not act to alter his position, because, on the one hand, the marginal utility of P_2D of Y is higher than that of an additional DP_3 of X, while on the other hand the marginal utility of CP_2 of X is higher than that of P_1C of Y.

THE EFFECTS OF CHANGES

We have been describing the pattern of consumer action in the marketplace. We have seen that a given income enables the consumer to take advantage of goods available in the market so as to place himself in the most advantageous position that the relative prices of these goods permit. The consumer achieves this by adjusting the proportions of his income spent on different kinds of goods so that a transfer of money from the margin of spending on one good to that spent on another is not profitable.

The conditions for equilibrium thus involved (a) his own relative preferences and tastes, (b) his income, and (c) the prices of the different goods available. We now turn to examine the effect on consumer allocation of income brought about by changes in each of these three groups of factors.

1. *Change of Tastes*

Consumer equilibrium was determined in part by tastes, because it was the consumer's relative eagerness to obtain different goods that determined the marginal utilities of the goods at various margins of expenditures. If, after reaching equilibrium, the consumer's tastes change or his circumstances change, then it is likely that he will no longer be in equilibrium. A man who has achieved equilibrium in the summer may soon be impelled to action by the imminent threat of a severe winter.

A change of tastes means simply a reordering of the relative positions of items on the consumer's scale of values. One good, or a number of units of the good at the margin, will now occupy a higher position in the utility scale. Necessarily this means that some other good or goods, or units of them, now occupy relatively lower positions.

This will affect equilibrium by altering the marginal utilities of the several kinds of goods so that the marginal utilities of the units of some kinds of goods (which would have to be given up should expenditure upon them be curtailed) are now relatively lower, while the marginal utilities of additional units of the goods (to be gained should expenditure on *them* be expanded) are now relatively higher. It may well be wise to switch some expenditure from the former goods to the latter.

In the diagram (Figure 5-2) a consumer was initially in equilibrium at the point P_2. This means that a movement from P_2 to P_3 (which was possible since it is along the opportunity line AB) was not taken because the marginal utility of DP_2 of Y was higher to the consumer than that of DP_3 of X. Suppose however that the consumer's tastes change, shifting somewhat away from Y toward X. Then it may well be that the relation between the marginal utility of DP_3 of X to that of DP_2 of Y is reversed. If so, P_2 is no longer an equilibrium position, and the consumer acts to achieve the situation P_3.

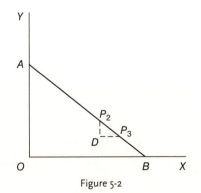

Figure 5-2

2. Change of Income

A consumer attains equilibrium with expenditure upon different goods and services. If the total amount available for spending, let us say, had been considerably larger, the consumer's equilibrium pattern of expenditure allocation would probably be rather different. How would the consumer's allocation of income be altered if his income were larger (everything else, tastes as well as prices, remaining unchanged)?

A larger total expenditure *must* mean, of course, that a larger quantity of *some* goods will be bought, but it is unlikely indeed that the increased expenditure will be spread proportionally among *all* the goods that the consumer buys. Some goods will be bought in much larger quantities, some goods will be bought in only slightly larger quantities, and some goods may be bought in exactly the same quantities as with lower total expenditure, while it is quite possible for the amount bought of some goods to be actually *lower* with the higher total expenditure. When the larger total expenditure now available makes it possible to acquire (superior quality) goods that are close substitutes for a good of lower quality that was bought with lower income, then it is likely that the amount bought of this "inferior good" will *decrease* as total expenditures increase.

In general, the proportion of increased available expenditure allocated to any one good will express a number of factors. Where the marginal utility of a good diminishes, with its increased consumption, relatively rapidly as compared with other goods so that the utility of the marginal dollar becomes higher when spent on other goods, a shift of income allocation toward other goods will occur. Again, as noted before, the effect of increased income on the consumption of a good will depend on the relationship between the marginal utility of this good, and the advancing margin of consumption of *other* goods, which is made possible by an increased income.

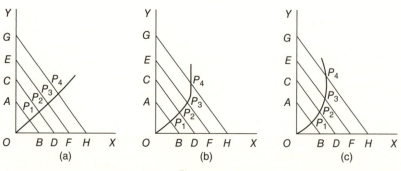

Figure 5-3

The possibilities thus outlined can be illustrated with the type of diagram used in the previous section. In the diagram [Figure 5-3(a)], the line AB is the opportunity line, and P_1, the consumer's equilibrium position, for a consumer with a given expenditure ($OA \times p_y = M_1$) that is to be spent wholly on the goods X, Y, these goods being available in unlimited amounts at given constant prices p_x, p_y, respectively. The line CD represents an opportunity line (with P_2 the equilibrium position) for the consumer where the available expenditure is no longer M_1 (= $OA \times p_y$) but some larger sum $M_2 = OC \times p_y$. The prices of X, Y have not been changed so that the line CD is parallel to AB (with its slope p_x/p_y). The new opportunity line clearly enables the consumer to purchase bundles containing larger quantities of both X and Y. The new equilibrium position P_2 is clearly more satisfactory than the position P_1 to which the consumer would be limited by the smaller budget allocation M_1. It is possible to draw any number of lines parallel to AB, such as EF, GH, and so on, each of which represents the opportunity lines for the consumer if his budget allocation of X and Y were progressively increased. And on each of these opportunity lines we may denote the corresponding bundle that the consumer would select (that is, the respective positions of consumer equilibrium) by the points P_3, P_4, and so on. Thus, the line joining these equilibrium points P_1, P_2, P_3, . . . denotes the different bundles that the consumer would select at different budget levels. This line is frequently called the *income-consumption line*.

The three diagrams describe the possible effects that a rise in available expenditure may have on the consumption of the good X. In Figure 5-3(a), the income-consumption line shows a continual increase in the quantity of X that would be bought with increasing total expenditure. Figure 5-3(b) describes a good whose consumption increases with increases in total expenditures, until a point is reached where further increases in "income" are channeled entirely into other goods, no further quantities of X being bought. Figure 5-3(c) describes the situation with respect to an "inferior" good whose consumption actually declines after "income" rises beyond a certain point.

Generalizing from the two-goods situation where we examined the effects upon consumption of different budget allocations for total expenditure on the two goods, we can easily understand the differences in income allocation at different income levels. It is impossible to say anything about the income-consumption line for any one particular good. The proportion allocated for given goods will probably alter with changes in income. Which goods will get a relatively larger share of lower incomes and which a larger share of higher incomes, will depend, once again, on the particular tastes of the consumer under consideration, on what he considers an "inferior" good, and on the availability and prices of other goods upon which he can spend the increases in income. These effects upon income allocation of changes in income have an important bearing, as we shall see, on the effects upon income allocation of *price changes* for particular goods.

3. Change of Prices

The most important kind of change theory attempts to grapple with is that of prices. Supposing that a consumer's preferences, tastes, and income are given; what can be said about the different ways he would allocate income with different prevailing sets of prices? And, in particular, can any definite statement be made concerning the relationship between consumption of a *particular* good and its price, other things being assumed to remain unchanged?

Now we have seen that relative prices play a key role in determining the allocation of income by a consumer in a given situation. The consumer acts to reach a position where a shift of expenditure from any one kind of good to any other would mean substituting a less preferred for a more preferred situation. The selection of such a position involves valuation of the *quantity* of each good that must be relinquished or gained, consequent on such a contemplated shift in any given amount of expenditure. These quantities in turn depend, for any given expenditure, upon the *prices* of each good.

A consumer who has planned the allocation of his budget in the light of a definite set of prices, but who later discovers that the actual prices are different from what he has previously believed, will find it necessary to make adjustments in his purchasing plans. He will find that it is no longer the case that a shift of expenditure at the margin from one good to another cannot improve his position. He will find, say, that whereas with the erroneously assumed prices, a dollar withdrawn from the planned meat allocation and added on for bread meant the sacrifice of a quantity of meat that has higher utility than that of the additional bread, under the new prices this may not be so at all. He will find, perhaps, that with the price of meat higher than was originally believed, the quantity of meat that is sacrificed in contracting the margin of expenditure upon it by a dollar is so reduced that its marginal utility is now lower than that of the additional quantity of bread this dollar can buy. He will buy less meat and more bread.

In order to analyze the effects of price changes upon a consumer's allocation of income, we can perform a mental experiment. We can imagine a given set of prices for the available goods, and we can imagine a consumer spending his income on these goods according to his tastes and preferences. His allocation, as we have seen, would be such that the shift of any amount of expenditure from any one good to any other would mean replacing one quantity having higher marginal utility, with another quantity having lower marginal utility. Now we imagine sudden drastic changes in the prices of many goods, while the consumer's money income and his tastes are assumed not to have changed. The prices of some goods have risen, some more than others; the prices of some goods have fallen, some more than others; the prices of other goods, perhaps, have not changed at all.

We can now classify the possible consequences of this change in prices in *three* possible ways. *First,* it is possible that since prices have altered so drastically, the consumer finds that the *purchasing power of his income has increased* in the sense that he finds it possible to spend his income on exactly the same goods, in the same quantities, as before, and yet have some income left over unspent.[5] *Second,* it is possible that the change in prices has been such as to *reduce the purchasing power of the consumer's income* in the sense that he finds it impossible to purchase, even if he would wish to do so, the same bundle of goods previously bought. And *third,* it is just possible that price increases and decreases so offset one another that the consumer's income is *exactly sufficient* to buy the bundle of goods previously bought.

Let us take up this last case. Although the consumer's income and tastes are assumed to be unchanged, it is clear that the previous bundle, although still within his reach, is no longer necessarily the most preferred among the alternatives open to him. The alterations in the relative prices

5. This is only one of the possible senses intended to be conveyed by the phrase "an increase in purchasing power." Where a sum of money may be spent on a number of different goods that undergo various independent price changes, it is not possible to assert unambiguously whether the sum of money can purchase more or less than before, unless it is specified how the sum is to be allocated among the various goods. Any index of purchasing power must correspond to some such (arbitrary) specification. The Laspeyres method of price-index construction is based on the interpretation of "increases in purchasing power" employed in the text.

of goods make it *possible* for the consumer to translate his income into bundles made up of quantities and proportions of goods different from those making up the bundles among which he chose previously. The new bundles may well include one or several that are preferable to the alternatives previously available and even preferable to the bundle previously selected. In fact this is likely to be the case.

As we have seen, the consequence of the change in prices is to alter the relative marginal utilities of those quantities of different goods that it is contemplated to add or subtract at the respective margins by shifting expenditure among goods. A "dollar's worth" of the goods that have risen in price will now tend to have lower marginal utilities, since a dollar now buys only a reduced quantity, while, on the other hand, a "dollar's worth" of the goods whose price has fallen will correspondingly tend to have higher marginal utilities. This will express itself in the actions of the consumer by his shifting expenditure away from the former goods toward goods either of the latter group or of those whose prices have not changed, while, in addition, he will tend to shift expenditure at the margin away from goods whose prices have not changed toward those that have fallen in price. The proportions in which expenditure will shift away from the different goods whose prices had risen will depend on the rapidity with which the respective marginal utilities rise as the margin of consumption is drawn back. As expenditure is shifted away from any one good, the marginal utility of a "dollar's worth" of that good rises (while at the same time the marginal utility of a dollar's worth of the other goods whose margin of consumption is being advanced, falls), until the consumer no longer wishes to transfer expenditure. The goods whose marginal utility rises most rapidly with decreasing consumption will be those from which the least expenditure will be shifted. On the other hand, among those goods toward which expenditure is being shifted, the consumer will shift expenditure least toward the goods whose marginal utility *falls* most rapidly with an advancing margin of consumption.

The net result of this readjustment would thus be a tendency for the consumer to increase the purchase of goods whose prices have fallen and curtail the purchases of goods whose prices have risen, in accordance with the sets of factors discussed above. However, there are additional complications that have to be borne in mind in connection with the purchase of *related goods*. As seen earlier, the marginal utility of a good falls, other things remaining the same, with increased possession of substitute goods; and, on the other hand, rises, other things remaining the same, with increased possession of goods complementary to it. It has already been noted that an increase in income, by bringing within reach goods of a superior quality and so reducing the marginal utility of inferior goods for which the superior product is a substitute, may actually bring about the curtailment of purchases of the inferior good. In the case of price changes, similar effects may occur. A fall in the price of a given good, leading to a shift of expenditure toward it, may so increase the marginal utility of a second good complementary to it that expenditure on the second may be increased although its price has not fallen or even risen. Similarly, it may happen that consequent on a changing pattern of prices, the expenditure on a certain good may rise (thereby reducing the marginal utility of a second good for which the first is a substitute) to a degree sufficient to cause a shift of expenditure away from the second, even though its price may actually have fallen.

Where the prices of the various goods have changed, *increasing* the purchasing power of the consumer's income, in the sense that this is more than sufficient to purchase the previously purchased bundle of goods, these complications assume added importance. Where price changes of this kind have occurred, the consumer will desire to alter the makeup of his purchases, not only because relative prices have changed (altering the utility of a dollar's worth of expenditure at the margins of the various goods as discussed in the previous paragraphs). He will wish to do so for an important additional reason. The purchase of the original bundle would, at the new prices, leave unspent income to be spent in the present period. This additional expenditure would be distributed by the consumer, among the various goods, *as if an increase in his income had occurred.* In such a situation the effect of the changed prices upon income allocation is as if compounded of *two* distinct kinds of change. *First,* the alteration in prices includes the pure change in relative prices dealt with in the preceding paragraphs; *second,* it includes the equivalent of an increase in income, and we must expect the same kind of effects on income allocation that we discovered to occur in that situation.

In the same way, where the change in prices *diminishes* the purchasing power of a man's income so that he can no longer buy the previously purchased bundle of goods, we must expect the consumer to act in a way reflecting *two* kinds of change. *First,* his actions will reflect the change in the utility of a dollar's expenditure at the margin for each good that has been caused by the change in relative prices. *Second,* his actions will reflect a reduction in his income and a consequent necessity to draw back the margin of expenditure on the various goods, consistent with the normal analysis of such an income change.

Price Change for a Single Good

The special case of a price change of a single good will enable us to grasp more clearly the argument of the previous section and will at the same time focus attention directly on the factors underlying the usual analysis of the market demand for an individual commodity.

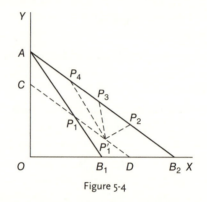

Figure 5-4

For this purpose we return to the two-commodity world employed in the earlier diagrams of this chapter. AB_1 is the opportunity line of a consumer with income M_1 faced with prices p_{x_1} and p_{y_1} for X and Y, respectively; P_1 denotes the position of consumer equilibrium. A change in the price of X now occurs, *lowering* it to p_{x_2}; the price of Y has not changed. The change in market data has altered the opportunity line from AB_1 to AB_2 in the following manner. Since the price of Y and the consumer's income have not changed from p_{y_1} and M_1, respectively, A is still a point on the opportunity line, since expenditure of M_1 entirely on Y would still yield OA $(= M_1/p_{y_1})$ of Y. However, since the price of X has fallen from p_{x_1} to p_{x_2}, the amount of X that could be bought by spending all of M_1 on X will have increased from OB_1 $(= M_1/p_{x_1})$ to OB_2 $(= M_1/p_{x_2})$. The slope of the opportunity line has fallen from p_{x_1}/p_{y_1} to p_{x_2}/p_{y_1}.

The altered price of X has thus brought within the consumer's reach a whole new series of alternatives to choose from (many of them containing more of both X and Y than was included in the bundle at P_1). Let us analyze three different possible positions of consumer equilibrium on the new opportunity line; namely, the points P_2, P_3, and P_4. Points P_2 and P_3 imply that as a result of the fall in the price of X, the consumer will tend to buy a larger quantity of X (since P_2 and P_3 are to the right of P_1); while P_4 implies a curtailment of the quantity purchased of X as a result of its fall in price.

To assist in this analysis we draw, through the point P_1, the line CD, parallel to the new opportunity line AB_2. This line represents the opportunities available *at the new set of prices* (p_{y_1}/p_{x_2}), for the consumer whose *income is just sufficient at these prices, to purchase the bundle* P_1. The three lines AB_1, AB_2, and CD express the situation of the consumer in the face of the fall in the price of X. AB_1 sets forth the alternatives open to him, with income M_1, at the old prices; AB_2 sets forth the alternatives open to him, when, with his income and the price of Y unchanged, the price of X falls. Clearly, this situation means that his income M_1 has risen in purchasing power, in the sense that, if he were to buy the bundle P_1, some unspent income would still be left. This is shown in the diagram by P_1 being below the new opportunity line AB_2. The line CD sets forth the alternatives open to the consumer if he was in some way prevented from enjoying this rise in the purchasing power of his income. That is to say we put the consumer in a position where, acting in a market with the new prices, he is permitted to spend only that amount of money now needed to buy the previously purchased bundle P_1. The relation CD to AB_1, shows the new alternatives opened to the consumer by *a pure change in relative prices,* without any alteration in the purchasing power of his income (in the above defined sense).[6] The relation of AB_2 to CD shows the new alternatives opened by the consumer by a pure rise in income (from $OC \times p_{y_1}$ to $OA \times p_{y_1}$ [$= M_1$], with the price of X and Y unchanged at p_{x_2} and p_{y_1}, respectively). The relation of AB_2 to AB_1, then, shows in *combination* the new alternatives opened to the consumer who has experienced a change in relative prices as well as a rise in the purchasing power of his income.

Considering the opportunity line CD (and comparing it with AB_1), it is clear that the consumer would tend to select a bundle on CD that lies to the right of P_1. Since the price of X has fallen relative to that of Y, the

6. Corresponding to other possible senses of the term "purchasing power of income," other CD lines may be drawn. For each such possible construction, a "substitution effect" will result (and therefore also an "income effect") somewhat different from that described in the text. For a survey of the possibilities in this regard, see Machlup, F., "Professor Hicks' 'Revision of Demand Theory,'" *American Economic Review,* March, 1957, p. 125.

consumer will find that a dollar's worth of X at the margin has increased in quantity, while that of Y has decreased. This will tend, as we have seen, to make the marginal utility of a dollar's worth of X higher than that of Y (at P_1), leading the consumer to shift some of his expenditure from Y to X. It is clear, then, that insofar as the fall in the price of X has merely changed the relative prices of X and Y (that is, abstracting from the rise in the purchasing power of the consumer's income), the consumer will tend to substitute X for Y, as compared with his previous purchase of P_1. This shift toward X, from P_1 to (say) P'_1, is known as the *substitution effect*.

Because the change in the price of X, besides altering the *relative* prices of X and Y, has actually *increased the purchasing power* of the consumer's income, we should look to the concept of the income-consumption line discussed earlier in this chapter. The income-consumption line, we saw, passes through the different positions of consumer equilibrium that would be taken up as his income increased, while prices of goods remained unchanged. The problem in our own case is to understand the way a consumer with opportunity line CD, and equilibrium position P'_1, will allocate his income when his opportunity line rises to AB_2. This involves the shape of the income-consumption line passing through P'_1. As we saw, the slope of such a line may be either positive or negative.

In the diagram the dotted line $P'_1 P_2$ shows a positively inclined income-consumption line. This line depicts a situation for a consumer who, having chosen the bundle P'_1 out of the series of alternatives open to him shown by CD, would buy more of X if his income were increased. For such a consumer, a change in opportunity line from AB_1 to AB_2 will result in a change in equilibrium position from P_1 to P_2. The fall in the price of X will move the consumer to *increase* the quantity of X that he buys; *first*, as a result of the substitution effect (from P_1 to P'_1), and *second*, as a result of the *income effect* from P'_1 to P_2. The effect of a fall in the price of X represents the combined effects of a pure change in relative price (which by itself would move the consumer to buy bundle P'_1); and, in addition, of a rise in the consumer's purchasing power (which at the *new prices* would move the consumer to replace bundle P'_1 by P_2). For the positively inclined income-consumption line $P'_1 P_2$, the income effect, like the substitution effect, shows that the fall in the price of X results in an increased demand for X by the consumer.

Where, on the other hand, the income-consumption line passing through P'_1 has a *negative* slope, the results of a fall in the price of X are somewhat less definite. Such a slope represents the actions of a consumer to whom X is an "inferior" good; thus, a rise in his income moves him to replace it by additional purchases of Y. The fall in the price of X, besides altering the purely relative prices of X and Y in the favor of X, has also increased the consumer's real income. The change in relative prices, as before, will yield a positive substitution effect; the consumer would (abstracting from the change in purchasing power) move from P_1 to the right, to P'_1. But the income effect in this case is negative. The increase in real income will tend to *reduce* the quantity of X that the consumer will purchase. *Two* possibilities exist; either the negative income effect is, or is not, greater than the substitution effect. The *first* possibility is shown in the diagram by the dotted line P'_1P_4; its slope is so steeply negative that P_4 is to the left of P_1. This depicts the extremely rare case where a fall in the price of a good actually *decreases* the quantity that a consumer will purchase. (Such goods are called "Giffen-goods.") The *second* possibility, where the negative income effect is not greater than the positive substitution effect, is shown by the line P'_1P_3. Although, in this case, the fall in the price of X results in an increase in the quantity purchased, as shown by P_3 being to the right of P_1; nevertheless, the increase is not as great as it would have been if the price fall had not involved a rise in the consumer's real income.

THE INDIVIDUAL DEMAND CURVE

The analysis of the allocation by the consumer of his consumption expenditure, which has occupied much of this chapter thus far, provides us with the background necessary for the understanding of the consumer's *demand curve* for specific goods. This traditional tool of price theory relies heavily upon the analysis of the effect of price changes upon income allocation discussed in preceding pages.

The demand curve is the graphic representation of a very important conceptual tool. The analysis of consumer income allocation has taught us that the manner in which a consumer will divide his expenditure between various available goods depends on a host of factors: the kinds of goods available, the preferences of the consumer himself, the size of his income, and the prices the various goods can be bought for. Focusing attention on any *one* commodity, and inquiring into the quantity of it that a consumer will tend to buy, we face a highly complex problem because of the many factors that have a share in determining this quantity. The economic theorist attempts to introduce a measure of conceptual order into this problem by concentrating on what is, from his point of view, the key factor—namely, the price of the good itself. He asks himself, what effect a given change in its price will have upon the quantity of a commodity demanded by a consumer, assuming the other determining factors to be given and, for the purposes of this mental experiment, unchanging. By abstracting in this way from the effects of other factors, the economist is able to extract a simple relationship between its market price and the quantity of a good that a consumer will buy. The demand curve depicts this relationship graphically.

In the diagram (Figure 5-5), the horizontal axis, as in the previous diagrams, represents the *quantity* of the good X that a consumer may buy. The vertical axis, unlike those in the earlier diagrams, represents here the *price* of X. A point in the price-quantity field associates a given quantity with a given price for the good. The point R, for example, associates the quantity OQ of X with a price of OP dollars per unit for X. For a consumer the point R is a relevant point if, at the price of $OP per unit of X, he actually buys the quantity OQ (during a given period of time). The curve DD′ joins all those points that are relevant for the consumer. The abscissa of the curve, for any given price ordinate, indicates the quantity that the consumer will take at the price.[7] The curve abstracts from all the many other kinds of change that might alter the quantity taken by a consumer, and concentrates on the consumer's response to price changes, other things being left unchanged.

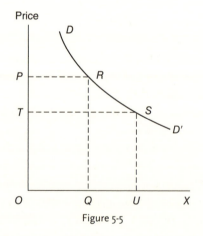

Figure 5-5

7. The individual demand curve may be looked at from another, no less important angle. A point on the demand curve represents the *highest* price per unit that the consumer will be prepared to pay (if forced to do so) for a given *quantity* of the commodity.

Although the demand curve, both as a diagrammatic aid and as a conceptual tool, depends on "other things remaining equal," it cannot of course exist in a vacuum. The demand curve associates with each price of a good the quantity that a consumer will buy under a *given* set of conditions with respect to those "other things." A demand curve is drawn for a consumer with a definite income, facing a definite subjective value scale of his own. A change in any of these other things will cause the entire demand curve to change: the set of quantities of a good that a consumer will buy at different prices, under one set of these "other" conditions, being quite different from those relevant to different conditions. A rise in income, for example, may shift a demand curve to the right (or, for an inferior good, to the left) and, besides changing its *position,* will probably also change its *shape.*

The demand curve of the individual consumer for a single commodity is thus just one piece in the complex jigsaw puzzle that is made up by the understanding of the different ways the consumer would allocate his income in response to different sets of conditions. Its usefulness in analysis, we will discover, is not so much in explaining the actions of the consumer himself; these are best understood by attacking the problem of income allocation on marginal utility lines. The demand curve becomes of value in helping explain the forces that, in the market, are being exerted by individuals *upon* the price of particular goods. And for this reason it becomes fruitful to concentrate attention on the (admittedly partial) relationship existing between price and quantity alone.

The *shape* of the demand curve of the individual is of considerable theoretical importance. This is especially so when we consider, in the next chapter, the shape of *market* demand curves derived from the individual curves. The question we are faced with is whether any *generalizations* can be made concerning the relationship between the quantity a consumer will buy of a good and its price, which should be valid under all possible assumptions regarding relevant "other things." Can we say, for example, that a lower price for a good will invariably be accompanied by a larger purchase of it on the part of a consumer—no matter what the particular good may be, no matter what the income of the consumer may be (that is assumed to be constant), and no matter what the (constant) prices of other goods are assumed to be? Or can we at least make some such generalization that should be valid under a limited but specified range of conditions?

Our marginal utility analysis of consumer income allocation enables us to provide answers to these questions. We saw that a fall (rise) in the price of one good, other things being equal, affects a consumer's action in *two* ways. *First,* it alters the relative prices of goods in favor (at the expense) of this good so that the marginal utility of an additional dollar's worth of this good is now higher (lower) than that of a dollar's worth of other goods, at the margin. This moves the consumer to replace expenditure at the margin on other goods by additional expenditure on a good that has become cheaper, and vice versa for a good that has become more expensive. This substitution effect will tend to make a *negatively sloping* demand curve, showing that a consumer will buy more of a good as its price falls. This effect is perfectly general. The *second* way a fall (rise) in the price of a good affects the consumer's actions (and thus the shape of his demand curve) results, as we have seen, from the fact that a change in *one* price alone, which leaves all other things "the same," is *by that very token* the change in price that at the same time changes the real income of the consumer. A fall (rise) in one price can only leave the consumer with more (less) than sufficient money income than is required, at the new price, to buy the old bundle of purchases. This income effect, of course, is likely to be extremely small in the case of a moderate price change for a commodity that occupies a relatively minor place in the budget. Moreover, the income effect of a fall in price of a good that is not "inferior" tends, we have seen, to *increase* the quantity purchased. The negative slope of the demand curve that we found to be associated with the substitution effect is thus *reinforced* by the income effect.

Even for inferior goods the negative income effect may still leave the demand curve sloping downward to the right. Since this effect may in the real world be expected to be very small, where it exists it is likely that a fall in price of even an inferior good will increase the quantity that a consumer will buy. The theoretical possibility does exist, of course, that a fall in price of a good may have so strong a negative income effect as to make a demand curve with a positive slope, representing the case where a man will buy more of a good when its price is higher. This constitutes the so-called "Giffen-paradox."

SOME REMARKS ON EXPECTATIONS

The analysis of this chapter has been almost purely formal in character, and this has enabled us to group together under "tastes and preferences," a host of factors that have a bearing on the way a consumer will allocate his income, and on the shape of his demand curve for a particular commodity or service. Several further remarks are necessary in this regard, in order to prevent possible misunderstanding of the scope of the tools of demand analysis, due to the simplicity of the framework that we have been using.

Demand analysis is concerned with the way the consumer acts in spending his income. Our analysis has been *static* in the sense that we have assumed a *given* scale of values and worked out the consequences for consumer behavior of changes in income and prices in the light of the given scale of preferences. We discussed the consequences upon consumer actions of a formal *change* in his relative preferences, from one value scale to a different one. This procedure, valid in itself, must not lead us to believe that we have not taken into account the fact that acting human beings are *forward* looking; that they act on the basis of *expectations, anticipations, and uncertainty;* and, of course that, in consequence, they frequently make "mistakes." In the course of time, human beings "learn by their mistakes" and constantly revise their assessment of future requirements and their interpretations of current market events. All this must certainly be kept in mind and lies very close indeed to the core of the possibility of a science of human action.

For the purposes of demand analysis, these aspects of action are understood as reflected in the tastes and preferences of the moment under consideration; they are implicit in the marginal utilities associated by consumers with given quantities of specified goods and services. The marginal utility of an air conditioner depends, for a consumer at the start of summer, on his guess of the heat expected in the coming months. The demand curve for air conditioners for this consumer will reflect all his guesses in this respect. It will reflect, perhaps, his guess as to the degree of discomfort to be expected in the various rooms of his home; it will reflect, perhaps, his guess how an air conditioner in one room will help to lessen or increase the discomfort in adjoining rooms.[8] No matter what uncertainties enter into his choice, his scale of values will still reflect the law of diminishing utility—utility, of course, itself reflecting the expectations and estimates of the consumer. The psychology of choice in the face of risk and uncertainty would certainly help in making concrete statements about the actual choices made. For the formal analysis of "static" demand this is unnecessary.

8. See the Appendix on multi-period planning for an outline of the way current market decisions depend upon expectations concerning future market conditions.

These considerations must be kept in mind when the tools of demand analysis are applied to the real (dynamic) world. A rise in price for a particular commodity, for example, may bring about a revision by a consumer of his estimates of future prices, and therefore of the significance of additional current purchases of the good. This must be interpreted as a shift in consumer "tastes." It would be inadvisable to apply a demand curve that has reference to one set of expectations, to a different set. The recognition of the limitations of the demand curve is of importance in exploiting its appropriate usefulness and in pointing to the directions where more refined analysis is called for.

SUMMARY

Marginal utility analysis enables us to explain the way a consumer will allocate his income. He will act to share expenditure between different commodities and services so that (having regard to the disutility of careful deliberation) no further opportunity exists to shift any amount of money from the margin of expenditure on one good to that of another, without sacrificing a quantity with higher marginal utility for one of lower marginal utility. A consumer will act, "exchanging" marginal quantities of one good for another, so tending toward such an "equilibrium" position.

The content of the "bundle" purchased at this position depends on (a) the consumer's tastes and preferences, (b) his income, and (c) the market prices of the various goods. Alteration in any of these sets of data will lead the consumer to alter the allocation of his income toward a position in equilibrium with respect to the new sets of data.

The analysis focuses particular attention on the effects of *price* changes. In general, a fall in the price of a (non-inferior) commodity, other things being equal, results (a) in a tendency for the consumer to purchase more of the good, as a consequence of the *substitution effect* of the change in purely relative prices; and (b) in a tendency for more of the good to be bought as a consequence of the *income effect* of the rise in the consumer's purchasing power (brought about by the fall in the one price). For inferior goods, the substitution effect is not different, but this may be partly offset (or in exceptional cases be more than completely offset) by the negative character of the income effect.

The *demand curve* for any good of an individual consumer presents the relationship between the possible prices of the good and the quantities of it that he will buy. It assumes *given* conditions with respect to tastes (including expectations), income, and prices of other goods. Insofar as a change in price can *itself* affect these other conditions, the demand curve cannot be used without further refinement.

SUGGESTED READINGS

Böhm-Bawerk, E. v., *Capital and Interest*, Vol. 2, *Positive Theory of Capital*, Libertarian Press, South Holland, Illinois, 1959, Bk. 3, Part A.

Marshall, A., *Principles of Economics*, The Macmillan Co., London, 1936, Bk. 3, Chs. 1, 2, 3.

Knight, F. H., *Risk, Uncertainty and Profit*, Reprint, University of London, London, 1957, Ch. 3.

Hicks, J. R., *Value and Capital*, Oxford University Press, New York, 1946, Part I.

Machlup, F., "Professor Hicks' 'Revision of Demand Theory,'" *American Economic Review*, March, 1957.

6 MARKET DEMAND

In this chapter we will carry forward the analysis of consumer demand from the individual to the market. Each individual, we found, attempts to allocate his consumption expenditures among various available goods according to fairly well-defined principles. There will therefore be in the market, at any one time, a demand for particular goods and services made up of demands of individuals as determined by their allocation of expenditures. Analysis of market demand carries us a significant step nearer a complete understanding of the way prices for particular goods emerge, and of why prices for particular goods change relatively to the prices of other goods in the way they do. At the same time market demand analysis is solidly founded on the theory of individual demand explored in the preceding chapters. It serves, therefore, as one of the most important links relating *market* phenomena back to the actions of the *individual* participant in the market process.

MARKET DEMAND

In a market, at any one time, a set of prices prevails for the various goods and services available. In addition, consumers have limited sums of money available for current expenditure. Each consumer acts to allocate his current expenditure so as to improve his position as far as possible. The data of the market, at the same time, describe the opportunities open to each consumer and outline the limitations of these opportunities. Each consumer consults his own tastes and preferences in deciding which opportunities he should grasp. For him, his available expenditure and the prices of the marketplace determine his actions according to his own scale of values.

Looking at the market as a whole, therefore, we see a mass of individuals each attempting to secure definite quantities of different goods and services according to the market data of the moment and their own individual scales of value. The result is that for each particular commodity or service, the market as a whole is bidding definite sums of money for definite quantities of the good. The determinants of the particular bids made by the market as a whole for particular goods are of course the very same as those that guide individuals in their demand for goods, since it is the aggregate of these actions that constitutes market demand.

As we shall discover in later chapters, the bids made by the market as a whole play a decisive role in the determination of subsequent market events. It is the peculiarity of market prices that they emerge as a result of actions taken at the beckoning of other prices. Analysis of market demand therefore is directed to help us in understanding its influence on the emergence of subsequent prices. Considerable assistance in this regard is afforded by the analysis of the market demand for *particular commodities* taken independently, and it is therefore with this aspect of the subject that this chapter principally deals.

The quantity of any one commodity for which the market as a whole bids depends, then, on the tastes of the individuals for this and other commodities, on the incomes of the individuals, and on the prices of this and other commodities that the individuals believe are the relevant market prices they are free to bid at. In analyzing the quantities of the specific good that the market will seek to buy during a given period of time, we once again focus attention on *price* as a key determinant. We assume that consumers' individual incomes are given, that prices of other goods are given, and that each individual is endowed with a given scale of values— and we ask how much (per unit of time) the market would seek to buy of the commodity under consideration at various different prices. This question can be answered by our analysis of the individual demand for the particular commodity. At a given price for the commodity, each individual would seek to buy a particular quantity of it. Summing these quantities for all individuals gives the quantity that the market as a whole would seek to buy at this price. Repeating this operation for a series of possible prices yields the *market demand schedule*—the list of quantities of the good that the market will seek to buy at the series of prices. If the individual demand schedules for participants in the market indicate that *each* such participant would seek to purchase a larger quantity of the commodity at lower than at higher prices, then the market schedule will express this in the very same way. The market demand schedule is only the aggregate expression of a series of alternative potential actions of individuals.[1]

1. There may of course be goods for which a relevant market demand schedule exists but for which no individual demand schedules are relevant. Stock examples are goods that are typically consumed in common by a large number of people, such as major-league baseball, concerts, and so on. For such goods it is hardly useful to talk of individual consumer demand schedules; the prospective consumers must somehow band together to buy them—whence the market demand schedule. In a market economy entrepreneurial activity frequently serves prospective consumers of such goods by undertaking the task of organizing production and then selling "tickets of admission." In any event, the price that the market as a whole is prepared to pay for a given quantity

As we have seen, the analysis of demand for a particular commodity at different possible prices, but with nothing else permitted to change, means the analysis of individual behavior when subject to (a) pure changes in relative prices, together with (b) changes in the purchasing power of income. While the effects of the latter changes, we saw, do not always run the same way, the effects of pure changes in relative price are, in fact, invariably to increase the quantity of a commodity that individuals seek to buy as the price falls. The demand of the market as a whole will therefore faithfully reflect these tendencies.

THE MARKET DEMAND CURVE

The graphic representation of the market demand schedule yields the *market demand curve*. The curve represents the "lateral summation" of all the individual demand curves for the commodity under consideration. Any point on the market demand curve shows by its abscissa the quantity that the market will seek to buy (during a given period of time) at the price represented by the ordinate of the point. The length of this abscissa is found by adding together the abscissae of those points on all the individual demand curves with the same price ordinates as the point on the market demand curve. Suppose, for example, that Figures 6-1(a), (b), (c) represent the individual demand curves of a number of market participants for a commodity. Then points P_a, P_b, P_c indicate that at a given price OA for the commodity, these participants will seek to buy quantities OB_a, OB_b, OB_c, respectively. The quantity that will be sought for the market as a whole at price OA is indicated in Figure 6-2 by the point P_q. This quantity OQ is made up by adding together OB_a, OB_b, OB_c, and so on for all the market participants. Thus, the market curve DD_q can be thought of as obtained by "adding together sideways" the individual demand curves DD_a, DD_b, DD_c, and so on. (It will be noticed that the quantity axis for the market demand curve represents a far greater order of magnitude than the corresponding axes in the individual curves.) It is clear that the shape of the market demand curve DD_q depends completely on the shapes of the individual curves DD_a, DD_b, DD_c, and so on. The reaction of the market as a whole to a particular change in price is made up entirely of the individual reactions.

---

of such goods is made up of the shares of the total cost various individuals are prepared to pay for the privilege of admission.

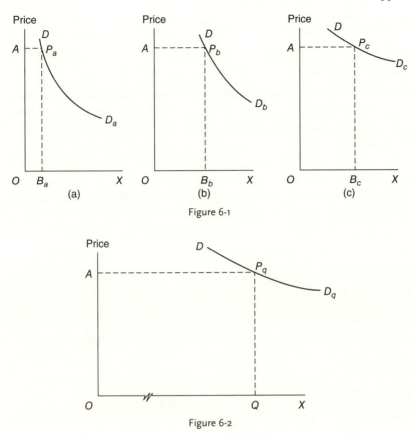

Figure 6-1

Figure 6-2

The market demand curve is a graphic device for presenting compactly a series of postulated relationships. It can, of course, only tell us
what we have already put into it, but it is nevertheless a highly useful
aid in organizing our thinking about both the determination and effects
of price changes. *Two* kinds of questions can be answered, at least in
principle, by the organization of our information into the framework of
the demand curve. *First,* the curve lists the quantities that the market as
a whole will bid for at *different given prices.* Here price is the independent
variable, with quantity the variable that is made to depend on the prevailing price. (From this point of view, the demand curve would ordinarily
be expected to have its axes transposed, with quantity measured along
the vertical axis. The prevailing practice, however, is the one sanctioned
by long economic usage and is thus well-entrenched.) *Second,* the curve
lists the prices that given quantities of the commodity can bring if placed

on the market.[2] Here it is price that we seek to make dependent on the quantity.

It should be emphasized that the demand curve relates quantity to price in the two ways mentioned, corresponding to two different ways the term "price" is used in analysis. When we ask what quantity the market will demand at a given price, we are speaking about a *hypothetical* or *provisional* price. As we shall see, the fact that a given quantity will be asked may in fact be the reason why the provisional price may rise or fall, or why the hypothetical price cannot in fact become actual. On the other hand, when we ask what price a given supply will bring on the market, we are asking about the price that will in fact be realized in the market under the postulated circumstances.

The use of the demand curve must never mislead us into treating "price" and "quantity" as being somehow mechanically related, apart from the actions of individual market participants. Any statement making quantity bought depend on price asked, or making price determined depend on quantity offered, must be interpreted as summing up the purposeful actions of individual human beings in response to definite alternatives being offered to them or in response to a change in the terms of the available alternatives.

DEMAND ELASTICITY

The mental tool that is represented by the demand curve attacks the problem, we have seen, by focusing attention on the influence exerted by *price* upon the quantities that will be bought by individuals and by the market as a whole. This involves the process of mentally "freezing" all the other factors that have any bearing on the quantity purchased and allowing the price to vary. Using marginal utility analysis, we were able to make the generalization that (with the possible exception of certain "inferior" goods) a fall in price, other things remaining unchanged, is associated with a greater quantity of goods desired to be purchased. In graphic terms, this meant that the demand curve slopes downward to the

2. This second view of the market demand curve corresponds to the alternative view of the individual demand curve to which reference was made on p. 86, n. 7. A point on the market demand curve thus denotes the highest uniform price a given quantity of the commodity can be sold at in the market without any remainder being left unsold. In Ch. 7 we will see that this implies that when the quantity has been sold at this price, all consumers who have *failed* to buy (even the most eager among them) are not prepared to pay any higher price for additional units.

right. It is useful to further classify demand curves, within the sweep of this generalization, on the basis of their *elasticities*.

The concept of elasticity, as applied to demand, refers to the degree of sensitivity to the influence exerted by price that individuals show with respect to the quantity of a good they seek to buy. A lower price, we found, generally means a larger quantity being purchased. But "larger quantity" can mean "slightly larger quantity," or "much larger quantity," depending on the responsiveness of the individuals or group of individuals to price changes. Demand curves can be ranked in this way as either more elastic or less elastic. One demand curve is more elastic than a second if a given change in price exerts a more powerful influence on quantity purchased in the first than in the second situation. In the diagram, a decrease in price from p to p' means an increase in quantity purchased from q to q_a for the demand situation shown by the curve DD_a, but an increase only from q to q_b for the demand situation shown by DD_b. DD_a is more elastic than DD_b. The concept of elasticity refers both to demand curves of individuals and of markets. The demand curve of one individual for sugar may be more or less elastic than his own demand curve for meat; it may be more or less elastic than his neighbor's demand for sugar.

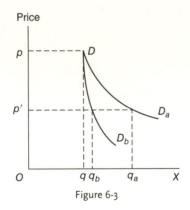

Figure 6-3

MEASURES OF ELASTICITY

In order to rank different demand situations in order of their elasticities, the elasticity concept must be defined with more precision than we have thus far attempted. Specifically, we must spell out what is meant by the statement that a given change in price "exerts a more powerful influence on quantity purchased" in one situation than in another. The diagram used in the previous section suggests that one curve is more elastic than another if its slope is less steep than that of the other. In this case we found a given fall in price resulted in a larger quantity being bought where the curve fell less steeply.

This, however, is unambiguously true only in the special case of that diagram where both curves referred to the same quantity axes, and the initial position was common to both curves. In general, slope is a misleading indicator of relative elasticity. Where the elasticities of demand for two commodities are being compared, there is no obvious equivalence in their units of quantity that should make it possible to compare the effects of given price changes. A drop in price of say $10, increases the demand for suits by 2 per year and increases the demand for steel by 5 tons. How does one compare 5 tons with 2 suits? Moreover, the slope of any demand curve depends entirely on the scale used for both quantity and price.

The standard measure of elasticity makes the concept independent of the size of the units the quantities or the prices happen to be expressed in. Elasticity is measured by the *proportional* change in quantity purchased, that is associated with a given *proportional* change in price. If a 10% drop in the price of one good is accompanied by a 50% increase in quantity demanded, while a similar drop in the price of a second good brings about only a 5% increase, then the first demand situation is more elastic over the specified price range than the second.

More specifically, absolute measures of elasticity are assigned to demand situations in the following way. A fall in price, which results in an increase in the quantity purchased, may or may not increase the money value of the purchases. On the one hand, a bigger quantity is being purchased; but on the other hand, a lower price per unit is being charged. Where the fall in price causes the quantity of purchases to increase in an amount more than sufficient to offset the lower price per unit so that total money value of the volume of sales *increases,* then the demand is said to be *elastic* or to have an elasticity of more than one. Where a price fall increases quantity demanded just sufficiently to offset the lower price per unit so that the money value of total sales is unchanged, then the demand is said to be of *unitary elasticity* or to have an elasticity of one. Where a price fall causes quantity demanded to increase so little as to be insufficient to maintain the original value of the volume of sales in the face of the lower price per unit, then the demand curve is said to be *inelastic* or to have an elasticity of less than one. The extreme cases are those of perfectly elastic demand and perfectly inelastic demand.

In Figure 6-4(a), D_e is a perfectly elastic demand curve. No matter whether the supply is q_1 or q_2, the same price can be obtained. Total money value of sales can be increased to any desired amount without lowering prices even slightly; the volume of sales can be increased without limit, even without lower prices per unit.

In Figure 6-4(b), D_i is a perfectly inelastic demand curve. It reflects a situation where there is no response to a price change. Lowering the price here simply diminishes the value of total sales by reducing the revenue per unit without in any way increasing the number of units sold.

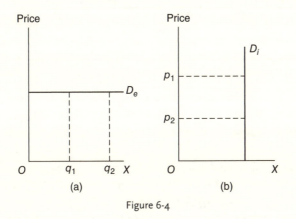

Figure 6-4

It should be clear from this discussion that, in general, it is meaningless to speak about the elasticity of "a demand curve." Elasticity, as a concept that is measurable, at least in principle, relates to a response to a *given price change*. In speaking of the elasticity of a demand curve, one must specify the *particular range* of prices over which the response of quantity taken to price changes is being measured.[3] This can be illustrated by means of Figure 6-5.

3. The term "elasticity of demand" is frequently reserved for the elasticity concept as measured over an infinitesimally small portion of the demand curve. Where p, q respectively represent the price and quantity at a point on the demand curve, and Δp, Δq represent infinitesimally small changes in price or in quantity, the elasticity of demand at that point is calculated as $\Delta q/q \div \Delta p/p$. (It will be observed that for a downward-sloping demand curve this formula will result in a negative number, since Δq and Δp are of opposite sign to one another.) Where the range over which demand elasticity is to be measured is of finite size, the point elasticity formula will yield various values depending on the particular values of p, q inserted in the formula. A number of "arc elasticity" formulas have been devised to yield unique elasticity values for such cases. (For further discussion of this point see e.g. Weintraub, S., *Price Theory*, Pitman Publishing Corp., New York, 1949, pp. 46–48.)

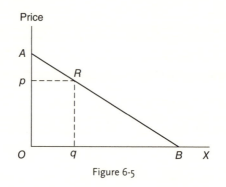

Figure 6-5

In the diagram *AB* is a straight line representing a demand curve. With any point *R* on the demand curve, is associated the amount of sales revenue it yields. This sales revenue is, of course, the product (*pq*) of (a) the price per unit (*p*), and (b) the number of units sold at that price (*q*). The elasticity of the demand curve in the region of any such point *R* depends, we have seen, on whether the value of *pq* rises with a fall in price (elastic demand) or falls (inelastic). With a straight line demand curve such as *AB*, starting at *A* and going down to *B*, the value of *p* × *q* rises from zero, reaches a maximum, and declines once again, at *B* to zero. It is clearly impossible to call the demand either elastic or inelastic. At high prices demand is elastic (lowering the prices increases total revenue); in the neighborhood of the price at which revenue is a maximum, elasticity is approximately unitary (because a fairly small price change in that neighborhood leaves total revenue about the same); while at the lower prices (where a further fall in price would reduce total revenue) demand is distinctly inelastic.

Elasticity measures apply, of course, both to individual and market demand. In all cases an inelastic demand over a given price range means that individuals are only slightly responsive to the price changes. Only a significant price fall is sufficient to attract any increase in the quantity that market participants will buy; only a significant price rise is sufficient to force a cutback in quantity purchased. In marginal utility terms, an individual whose demand for a good is inelastic ranks a unit of the good on his value scale *very much higher* than those units of other goods that are lower on the scale; and, on the other hand, he ranks the unit of this good *very much lower* than those units of other goods that are higher on the scale. Evidence of this is the fact that a moderate change in price is unable to alter the relative position on the value scale, with respect to fixed quantities of other goods, occupied by a "dollar's worth" of this good—even though the size of a "dollar's worth" is now larger or smaller than before the price change.

On the other hand, an individual whose demand for a good is elastic ranks a unit of this good with respect to given sized units of other goods in such a way that even a small change in relative price makes it attractive for him to shift expenditure at the margin between this good and the other alternatives available. In the market as a whole the elasticities of demand curves manifest themselves, as we have seen, in the change in the amount of total sales revenue which is expected to follow a fall or rise in price.

MARKET DEMAND AS SEEN BY THE INDIVIDUAL ENTREPRENEUR

Thus far we have discussed market demand as a whole. We have seen that this concept focuses on the quantities the market will ask at different market prices. These quantities, we found, reflect the quantities that the individual market participants separately ask at these prices. We must now put ourselves in the position of the individual firm producing goods for sale and ask how market demand appears from this position. The perspective on market demand, which we have already gained, together with that on market demand as seen by the firm, which we now consider, will enable us at a subsequent stage to understand how the interlocking chains of decisions of buyers and producers determine market prices and the output of both individual firms and entire industries.

To the individual entrepreneur operating a firm in an industry, the relevance of market demand does not hinge directly on the relation between market price and the quantity that the market as a whole will seek to buy. For him market demand is relevant only as it relates to the quantities that the market will buy of *his* product, and to the prices that *he* may charge, other factors remaining unchanged. He is interested, in other words, in the different alternatives the market as a whole might present to *him* as a result of alterations by *him* in the alternatives that he presents to the market.

It is clear that the alternatives the market as a whole presents to any one entrepreneur, in response to a given price posted by him, depend on a number of factors besides the shape of the market demand curve, or its elasticity in the neighborhood of this price. The quantities of a commodity that the market will seek to buy altogether at a given *market* price depend, we have seen, on a number of factors, including the prices and availability of other goods. The quantities of a good the market seeks to buy from any one entrepreneur, at a given price charged by him, will depend, in addition to all the factors that we found operative upon market demand—upon the prices and availability *elsewhere* of the *same* good. This plays an important role in explaining the different ways prices and output are determined in monopolized and competitive markets.

If we place ourselves in the position of a firm that *monopolizes* the particular commodity, then the relevant demand curve is *identical with the demand curve of the market as a whole*. In such a situation the *only* alternatives (with respect, it must be emphasized, to purchase of the monopolized product) available to market participants are those offered by the monopolist. The only competition he faces is that of other goods and services; thus, the quantities of *this* good that the market will seek to buy from the monopolist are identical, for each price, with the quantities that the market as a whole would seek to buy altogether, at the same *market prices*, from a market of competing producers.

The elasticity of the demand curve facing a monopolist, over any price range, is thus the same as that of the market demand curve. The decisions of the monopolist concerning what price to ask will therefore hinge, partly, on his estimation of the elasticity of demand of the market, since it is this factor that reflects the alternative amounts of revenue the market permits him to choose from.

The situation is quite different when viewed by an entrepreneur whose product is made available to the market by other producers as well. The *competitive* entrepreneur realizes that there is a going market price at which the market can buy elsewhere. If he himself asks a higher price than that asked elsewhere in the market, it is plain that everybody will go elsewhere when the same good is available more cheaply. On the other hand, it is equally plain to the competitive entrepreneur that even a moderate reduction of his price below that asked elsewhere in the market will attract a large number of buyers to him. In other words, if he offers the market alternatives less favorable to consumers than those offered by his competitors, the quantity of his products the market will ask for will be very slight; if he offers alternatives more attractive to the consumers than those offered elsewhere, the quantity asked of his product will be very large. The elasticity of the demand of the market for *his* output is thus very high—much higher than that of the market demand curve as a whole. The individual entrepreneur in a competitive market knows that the consumers will be highly responsive to any price change on *his* part.

Whether or not the elasticity of demand faced by a competitive firm will be *infinitely* high (that is, whether the demand curve facing it will be a horizontal straight line) depends largely on the degree of similarity between the products offered by the competing firms. If these products are *exactly the same in all respects,* from the point of view of consumers, then indeed any one entrepreneur will find that a very small reduction in price (from slightly above the market price to slightly below the market price) will increase his sales revenue from zero to very large amounts indeed.

If the similarity between the products, as seen by the consumers, is not quite perfect, however, then the elasticity of demand faced by any one competing firm, while probably very high, will be something less than infinite. Thus, a slight reduction by one corner drugstore on the retail prices charged for a branded commodity, say toothpaste, will not attract *all* the customers for toothpaste away from other drugstores that have not made the price cut. This is because "toothpaste available at one drugstore" may not be *perfectly* similar to "toothpaste available at another drugstore," from the consumers' point of view. The *physical* identity of the branded merchandise is not necessarily the relevant criterion here; to some consumers one drugstore may be a few steps further away than another, one drugstore may be more pleasant to do business in than another, and so on. Where there is some (real or imagined) physical difference between two closely similar products, such as two different kinds of toothpaste, or an identical toothpaste marketed under two different brand names, then of course we can similarly expect the demand curve facing any one seller to be highly, but still less than infinitely, elastic.

These considerations need to be borne in mind when we come to analyze the market forces determining prices in various types of markets.

DEMAND AND REVENUE

Our discussion of the demand curve and its elasticity faced by the firm suffices to make clear the relationship between demand and revenue. The entrepreneur is interested in knowing all the alternatives open to him. Among the key alternatives concerning which he desires information are the various amounts of sales revenue that may be expected to be forthcoming under specific circumstances of price and output. Here the demand curve facing the firm plays the decisive role.

Let us suppose that a firm believes itself to be confronted with a demand curve DD_1. This means that he can sell a particular quantity, OB, of the good at a price OA per unit. There are a number of revenue concepts implicit in this price-quantity relationship, and the entrepreneur may be interested in each of them for particular purposes. The most obvious revenue concept is that of *total revenue*. If he is able to sell the quantity *OB* at a price of $*OA* per unit, then he receives the quantity *OB* × *OA* dollars in total sales revenue. This figure is clearly important to the entrepreneur, because by subtracting the total costs of its production from the total revenue of a given quantity of output, he can immediately calculate the profit associated with a given level of output. In graphic terms, the total revenue for any output *OB* is represented by the area of the rectangle *OBRA* (that is, quantity, *OB*, multiplied by price, *OA*).

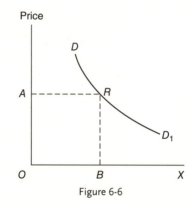

Figure 6-6

A second and related concept is that of *average revenue* per unit of output. Since the total revenue from the sale of the quantity *OB* is *OB* × *OA*, it follows that the revenue *per unit* is $\dfrac{OB \times OA}{OB}$; that is, $*OA* per unit. *OA* was the price *each* unit of the quantity *OB* can be sold at and is thus, of course, the average revenue for this number of units received by the entrepreneur. It is noted that as the quantity of output increases (in the situation shown in Figure 6-6), the revenue obtained per unit of output *declines*. Larger quantities of output can only be sold by the firm at progressively lower prices since the demand curve facing it slopes downward to the right. It can be seen, in fact, that the curve of demand facing the firm is identical with a curve relating the firm's average revenue from output to the size of the output. Any point on the demand curve facing the firm, showing the quantity that the market will buy of the firm's products at a given price, shows at the same time the price per unit this quantity of output can be sold at—which, from the point of view of the firm's books, means the revenue, per unit of output, obtained from this level of output. The coincidence of the demand curve facing a firm, with the firm's curve of average revenue for output, holds true, in this way, regardless of the slope of the demand curve. If a firm is in a highly competitive market so that the elasticity of the demand it faces is very high, then it will find that it is able to expand output with hardly any drop in the revenue obtained per unit. The average revenue curve in this case, like the demand curve, is very nearly a horizontal straight line.

Another related concept is *marginal revenue*. Marginal revenue is the amount of revenue at stake in any decision whether or not to produce a given marginal unit. Suppose a firm could obtain $1,000 total revenue by producing and selling 100 units of a commodity, and an increase of output by 1 unit would raise total revenue to $1,005; the marginal revenue of a 101st unit would be $5. The addition to output and sales of a 101st unit means an additional $5 in total revenue. Any decision as to expansion or contraction of output by any given number of units must hinge partly on the difference to total revenue made by the number of units under consideration.[4]

It is worthwhile to notice some straightforward arithmetical relationships between total, average, and marginal revenue.[5] (1) The average revenue of any output, as we have seen, is simply the total revenue obtained from that output divided by the number of units of the output. (2) The marginal revenue of any marginal unit, we saw, is the *difference* between the total revenue of output including this unit and the total revenue of output excluding this unit. The marginal revenue of the 101st unit is thus the difference between the total revenue from 101 units and the revenue from 100 units. (3) It follows directly that the total revenue of, say, 101 units is equal to the sum of the marginal revenues of the 1st, 2nd, 3rd, . . . and 101st units (since the marginal revenue of each unit of output is the amount added on the total revenue by the decision to step up output to

4. The reader will observe the parallel between the notion of marginal utility (dealt with in the preceding chapter) and that of marginal revenue treated here. Both notions (like other marginal concepts we will be dealing with) focus attention on the *difference* that a proposed additional unit of something (such as "quantity sold") makes in some calculation (such as an estimate of revenue) made by an interested individual. An important respect in which marginal revenue differs from (ordinal) marginal utility is that the former notion (unlike the later) refers to a cardinal number (a specific sum of money).

5. Analogous relationships exist between the total, average, and marginal values for all cardinal magnitudes (such as cost, output, and so on).

include this unit).[6] (4) If revenue per unit of output (average revenue) were the same for all levels of output, this must mean that the marginal revenue of any one unit is the same as that of any other unit, *and* that the value of this marginal revenue is the same as the average revenue. If a firm can sell any amount it pleases at a constant price, then this price is by definition both average revenue and marginal revenue. Thus, where a firm faces a perfectly elastic (horizontal) demand curve, this curve, beside being coincident with the average revenue curve, coincides also with the marginal revenue curve. (5) Where average revenue falls with increasing output, then marginal revenue must be less than average revenue. If the additional revenue obtained by adding a marginal unit to a given level of output were more than the revenue per unit of this level of output, then the revenue per unit of the expanded level of output would be increased. If marginal revenue were the same as the previous revenue per unit, then the revenue per unit would not change with the expanded output. Falling average revenue thus signifies a marginal revenue less than the average. It is possible for average revenue to fall so low that marginal revenue is negative. Such a situation exists when increased output can be sold only at so low a price that total revenue *declines* with the expanded output.

The marginal revenue of any particular unit of output thus clearly depends on the slope of the demand curve facing the firm at this level of output—that is on the *elasticity* of the demand curve in the neighborhood of this output.[7] For a demand curve of less than perfect elasticity, increased output requires a lower price. Whether this increase in output raises total revenue, lowers it, or leaves it unchanged, depends, we found, on demand elasticity over the relevant range. With elastic demand, total revenue increased; with inelastic demand, total revenue declined; with unitary elasticity, total revenue remained unchanged. Therefore, with a downward-sloping demand curve, we can generalize by saying that (a) *positive* marginal revenue (that is, rising total revenue) is associated with *elastic* demand, (b) *negative* marginal revenue (that is, falling total revenue)

6. Graphically, therefore, the area below the marginal revenue curve up to a given sales quantity may represent the total revenue for that quantity.

7. Mathematically the relationship between price (p), marginal revenue (MR), and elasticity of demand (ε) is represented by the formula $MR = p + p/\varepsilon$. For a downward-sloping demand curve (for which the value of ε is negative), marginal revenue, therefore, will be *less* than price by a quantity p/ε (disregarding the sign of ε). The more elastic the demand curve, the nearer the marginal revenue curve will lie to the demand curve.

is associated with *inelastic* demand, and (c) *zero* marginal revenue (that is, total revenue unchanged with increased output) is associated with demand of *unitary* elasticity.[8]

DEMAND AND THE PRICES OF OTHER GOODS

Throughout the discussions of individual and market demand, it has been emphasized that the quantity of any one commodity that will be asked for in the market at any given price depends in large part on the prices and availability of other goods and services. The number of air reservations to Florida beach resorts at a given price depends in part on the price of train tickets over the same distance, on the availability and price tag of alternative resorts, and may even depend partly on the prices of quite different kinds of goods. Each consumer, we found, allocates his income among an immense variety of goods according to their relative marginal utilities. The amount of income he will seek to spend on any one good depends not only on the marginal utility of a "dollar's worth" of this good, but also on the marginal utility of a dollar's worth of all other goods. This dependency on the prices of other goods is aggregated in the market so the quantity of any one commodity that the market as a whole seeks to buy at a given price depends heavily on the particular pattern of prices prevailing for other goods. The concept of *cross elasticity* is of some importance in this connection.

Cross elasticity gauges the degree of sensitivity of demand for *one* product to price changes in a *different* product. Supposing there is a 50% rise in the price of college tuition; what can be said about the quantity of college textbooks that will be bought at a given price? Very likely there will be a decline. On the other hand, what is likely to happen to the demand for the services of employment agencies that specialize in jobs for high-school graduates? Clearly an increase is to be expected. The cross-elasticity concept ranks the various possible degrees of relationship between prices of goods and demand for other goods.

Cross elasticity may thus be either positive or negative. *Positive cross elasticity* exists between two goods when a change in the price of one, other things remaining unchanged, causes the quantity bought of the other to

8. From the formula in the preceding footnote, it follows immediately that at a point where elasticity is unitary, marginal revenue is zero. A special case is where total revenue is unchanged for all points on the demand curve. For such a "constant outlay curve," marginal revenue is zero, and elasticity unitary, for all points on the curve.

move in the *same* direction. This is likely to be the case when most of the consumers consider the two goods as substitutes for one another. A rise in the price of the one good would thus stimulate a switch to the other good. *Negative cross elasticity,* on the other hand, exists between two goods when a change in the price of one, other things remaining unchanged, causes the quantity purchased of the other good to change in the *opposite* direction. This is likely to exist where the two goods are regarded by the bulk of consumers as *complementary* to one another. A rise in the price of one good tends to raise the price of the group of complementary goods that are used to satisfy some desire. This tends to reduce the quantity purchased of the group as a whole and therefore also of each good in the group.

If the consumers relate the goods strongly to each other (that is, if they are very close substitutes, or if they are almost invariably used together in consumption), then the cross elasticities also will be of a high (positive or negative) degree. (A *measure* of cross elasticity relates the percentage change in the quantity bought of one commodity to a given percentage change in the price of the other.) If the relation between the goods is weak, then the cross elasticity between them will be very low. A price fall in one good will cause only a slight shift of expenditure away from *any one* other good (although the total shift may be considerable).

DEMAND AS A MARKET FORCE

It must be emphasized that consumer demand constitutes a vibrant, *active* market force, with a powerful positive impact on resource alloca-tion, prices, and other market phenomena. We must not allow the formal presentation of demand analysis to create an image of market demand as being merely passive, responding to changes in market prices but without itself exerting any active influence on the market. Nothing could misstate more grossly the true operation of demand in the marketplace. While a more complete understanding of the operation of demand forces in the market must wait until we discuss the determination of market prices, our discussion of demand cannot close without making clear the positive nature of this market force.

Consumers are human beings acting purposefully to improve their positions. At any one time they find themselves able to choose among a number of alternatives. As acting men they are intent on making sure that no more desirable alternative exists other than those that they see before them. To this end consumers are constantly experimenting with new goods, new brands, and different stores. In selecting from among the available alternatives those they deem most attractive, consumers are at the same time rejecting the remaining alternatives. In making these selections and rejections, consumers are making known to the market the choices the *producers* have to choose from. Consumers in the market-place are not only aware of the choices available at *current* prices but are aware that by offering producers more attractive prices, they may themselves be able to secure even more desirable buying possibilities.

Moreover, the true power exerted by demand forces can only be appreciated by mentally relaxing the *ceteris paribus* assumptions underlying the demand curve of a given instant. In the ever-changing complex of real world conditions, consumers continually revise their relative valuations of available alternatives. Producers are subjected to a steady flow of information that apprises them of the most recently expressed preferences of the market and helps them gauge possible future preferences. As a consequence of changing demand patterns, it happens continually that the bids made today by consumers, on the basis of yesterday's prevailing prices, prevent all the desired choices from being successfully completed. It becomes continually apparent to consumers, that is, that they must revise their opinions of the actual choices they are free to make selections and rejections among. When we have studied the complex of factors that affect the decisions of producers, we will be in a position to understand the constant agitation by which the market seeks to adjust the mutually offered alternatives of producers and consumers to the ever-changing conditions on both sides of the market.

It must be stressed once again that market demand does not present itself as a single homogeneous force. It is not simply a matter of a *single* "market" bid being placed for a quantity of a commodity being sold at a given price. The aggregation of individual demand schedules into a market schedule, and its expression by the market demand curve must not mislead one into forgetting that market demand for a given good is the force felt by the bids of individual buyers. Some of the buyers of the good are more "eager" than others; that is, some buyers will be more active in offering producers more attractive alternatives or will be more likely to accept an alternative that other buyers reject. This must be kept in mind when interpreting a market curve. For each buyer individually, too, it must not be forgotten that his "eagerness" to buy a particular commodity is not homogeneous. The very law of diminishing marginal utility, which as we found is responsible for the characteristic downward slope of the individual demand curve, makes implicit in such a curve the fact that buyers display less "eagerness" for successive *single units* of the commodity. The determination of price, we shall discover, depends quite fundamentally on this "discrete" character of demand, on the fact that bargains are made not with consumers as a whole but with *individual* buyers contemplating the wisdom of acquiring *additional* units of a commodity.

Finally, we must draw attention once again to the way consumers *adjust* to changes in the availability of goods and the consequences of this propensity for the demand of particular commodities. Suppose a sudden stoppage occurs in the availability of a particular commodity or service; for example, a cessation of commuter service occasioned by a strike. Consumers of this particular service now find themselves barred from a previously available alternative. This will have an immediate consequence upon the demand for both related and unrelated goods. Income allocated to commuter service most likely will be allocated to services that are *substitutes* for commuter service. Taxicab service and car-rental services will now be patronized by consumers on a larger scale, even at the previous prices. (Of course, this will tend to exert a pressure on these prices to rise; but there will be more of this in later chapters.) On the other hand, goods and services in someway *complementary* to commuter service will experience a decline in the quantity purchased at given prices. Newsstand literature that is particularly suited for commuter reading, perhaps, will suffer such a decline. Even the demand for entirely unrelated goods may alter somewhat as a reshuffling of income initiates a tendency toward a quite different pattern of consumer equilibrium.

These short-run effects can be expected to give way, if the strike persists so long as to force the complete closing down of the line, let us say, to a permanent readjustment of consumer demand, other things remaining the same. The human race has shown remarkable ingenuity at discovering "substitute" goods and services, especially when allowed a long period of adjustment. In our example we can expect the closing down of a commuter line to increase the "long-run" demand by the erstwhile commuter communities for automobiles, to decrease the demand for new residences in these communities, to increase the demand for new residences in other communities, and so on.

This type of ability to adjust has important implications for demand analysis. The point is sometimes expressed by saying that in the long run the demand for a particular commodity is likely to be considerably more elastic than in the short run. This means that given price changes can be expected to cause more drastic shifts of demand away from the goods that have become relatively more expensive, toward those that have become relatively cheaper, as a longer period of adjustment is contemplated. As human beings acting to improve their positions, consumers adjust to a worsening of the available alternatives by seeking new ones. The discovery and effective utilization of new methods to satisfy wants takes time.

SUMMARY

The *market demand schedule* lists the different quantities of a given commodity that will be asked for by the market as a whole at given prices. It is made up of the sums of the individual purchases that would be made by market participants at the different prices. The graphic representation of this market demand schedule is the *market demand curve*.

The shape of the market demand curve depends on the individual curves and is thus characteristically downward sloping. The proportion in which the quantity purchased increases with a given percentage fall in price measures the *elasticity* of demand over the given price range. If a fall in price is associated with so great an increase in quantity bought that total revenue increases, we call the demand *elastic;* if total revenue remains unchanged, the elasticity is *unitary;* if total revenue declines, the demand is *inelastic.* A perfectly inelastic demand situation is associated with a demand curve that is vertical over the relevant range; a perfectly elastic situation is associated with a horizontal demand curve.

From the point of view of the individual firm, the demand for his product depends also on the prices charged by the firm's competitors. If there is very little difference, in the opinion of consumers, between the products of the firm and those available elsewhere, demand will be highly elastic with respect to the prices charged by the firm. If the firm monopolizes the production of his product, the elasticity of demand is the same as that of the entire market for this good.

Associated with a demand curve are several revenue concepts: (a) the *total revenue* of a given output, (b) the *average revenue* or revenue per unit of output, and (c) the *marginal revenue* of any contemplated change in output level. These three concepts are related arithmetically and change, with changing level of output, in a way that depends on the elasticity of the demand curve.

The relationship between consumer demand for any two goods is expressed in the concept of *cross elasticity* of demand. This concept relates to the degree in which the quantity demanded of one good changes as a result of a given percentage change in the price of another good. Cross elasticity may be either *positive* (between goods that consumers regard as substitutes for one another) or *negative* (between goods regarded as *complementary* to one another).

Demand is an *active market force* that constantly forces producers to revise their estimates of the alternatives they can choose from. Market demand expresses itself in bids for *particular* quantities of commodities by *particular* individual buyers. Demand by consumers, where thwarted from the attainment of particular objectives, adjusts by an increased demand for substitute goods as part of a general reallocation of individual consumer income. This adjustment takes time to become fully worked out, so that the elasticity of demand for particular commodities tends frequently to be higher as a longer period of adjustment is considered.

SUGGESTED READINGS

Marshall, A., *Principles of Economics,* 8th ed., The Macmillan Co., London, 1936,
    Bk. 3, Ch. 4.
Stigler, G. J., *The Theory of Price,* rev. ed., The Macmillan Co., New York, 1952, Ch. 3.
Stackelberg, H. v., *The Theory of the Market Economy,* Oxford University Press,
    New York, 1952, pp. 164–171.

7 MARKET PROCESS IN A PURE EXCHANGE ECONOMY

Until now we have been concerned with the way consumers make decisions when faced with the necessity of choosing between alternatives given by the market. We assumed consumers were faced with an array of products that could be bought at given prices. We investigated the principles by which the consumer allocated his income among the array of purchase possibilities, focusing attention in particular on the kinds of changes in the data that could alter the consumer's allocation pattern.

This analysis, based as it was on the assumption of opportunities determined externally, did not deal with the really essential elements of the market process. We have been assuming that the facts governing the relevant decision were presented in some definite but unexplained way by the external world, as market data. Just as an individual is forced to adjust himself passively to the physical laws governing his surroundings, so we also assumed him to face the prices of the goods that he wished to buy as being determined completely by impersonal and external forces. But the market process is itself continually modifying, disrupting, and adjusting the market phenomena that govern the decisions of the market participants. Our real task is to understand *this* process.

A market process is the result of the *interaction* between the decisions made by all the participants in a market. In a market system where products are produced and sold to consumers by entrepreneurs who have produced by combining resources purchased from resources owners, the market process results from the impingement upon each other of the plans made by consumers, entrepreneurs, and resource owners. Each of the participants in the market, at any one time, makes his decisions on the basis of what he believes to be given market data. Out of the mutual interplay of these numerous decisions, and of their influence upon subsequent decisions, the market process of price and production determination emerges.

In the previous chapters we investigated the elements of the market process that must be explained by consumer theory. In Chapters 8 and 9 we will investigate those elements that must be explained by the theory of production. These elements are based on the assumption of data given by the market that the individual consumer or producer must passively adjust himself to. In Chapters 10 and 11 we take up the full analysis of the complex market process emerging from the compounding in the marketplace of all these separate elements. The analysis in the preceding chapters, and in Chapters 8 and 9, is introduced not primarily for its own intrinsic importance but as an indispensable help to the understanding of the complex strands of cause and effect making up the market process.

The present chapter is introduced at this point as a step toward the understanding of the market process in its full complexity. In this chapter we show how *a market process could emerge in a market made up of consumers only.* We imagine an economy where *no production is possible;* all commodities are obtained costlessly by natural endowment. Exchange could and probably would take place in such a society. The actions of individuals in such an exchange economy would be governed by the principles analyzed in the preceding chapters. Market phenomena would be derived purely from the interaction of the decisions of the consumer participants. Although this kind of market is unlikely to correspond to any real society, its thorough analysis will prove extremely valuable for the analysis of the more complex market processes involving production activities. There are chains of logic that apply with equal validity to any kind of market. They can be perceived with especial clarity in a simple market such as we consider in this chapter. We will be drawing heavily upon this chapter when we come to consider markets, in Chapters 10 and 11, involving production as well as simply exchange and consumption.

THE NATURE OF COMPETITION

Any investigation of the process that determines prices and production programs must take careful account of the *competitive element* inherent in market activity. In the final analysis, the market process relies most heavily upon this element. We may view the market process as the mechanism that determines the opportunities that market participants find most advantageous to offer other participants and that in this way also determines the particular opportunities that will be embraced in the market. A market process may be defined as *competitive* when the opportunities that market participants feel constrained to offer to the market are only those opportunities

> *that they believe to be more attractive (or at least no less attractive) to the market than comparable opportunities being offered by others.*

Each market participant is forced to act with the realization that the opportunities he would *like* to offer to the market (that is, those that, if accepted, would yield him the greatest advantage) will be rejected by the market (that is, they will yield no advantage at all) if they are considered less attractive than those made available by his competitors.

In general, then, the competitive market process tends to ensure that each participant will offer to the market those opportunities that, if embraced, will prove most advantageous to himself—not out of *all* possible opportunities that he could offer, but out of those opportunities he is able to offer that he believes at least not less attractive to the market than those of others. This is a very general proposition that applies to both buyers and sellers and is sufficient to narrowly delimit the range within which exchange opportunities emerge and are embraced in the marketplace. Our task in this chapter is to reduce this general proposition to more specific statements that can be applied to particular conditions.

A SIMPLE CASE OF PRICE COMPETITION

The simplest possible case where we may observe and analyze the competitive process at work is that of the market for a single homogeneous commodity, which cannot be produced by human action, but which is each day obtained costlessly from nature by a large number of market participants. The careful analysis of what can be expected to take place in this simplest of cases will prove of great value in the analysis of the more complicated cases to be taken up later.

Participating (at least potentially) in the market for our commodity are all those individuals who, on the one hand, might be induced to buy quantities of it if the price is low enough, and those who, on the other hand, possess some units of the commodity and might be induced to sell quantities of it if the price is high enough. Since we avert our eyes from everything except the one commodity, competition can only take the form of offering more attractive opportunities in terms of higher prices offered or lower prices asked. The factor that determines the quantity of the commodity a potential buyer might wish to buy at each of a series of different prices (graphically expressed by his demand curve) is the marginal utility to him of additional units of the commodity. Similarly, since production of further units of the commodity is assumed to be impossible, the factor that determines the quantity of the commodity its owner would be willing to sell at given prices is the marginal utility to him of the units of the commodity under consideration. (This can easily be seen by observing that what an owner of the commodity does not sell, he is keeping for himself. Clearly the quantity of the commodity he wishes to keep for himself depends on the marginal utility of the relevant units of commodity as compared with what can be obtained by selling them.) Our discussion in earlier chapters of the significance of the law of diminishing utility will lead us generally to expect that at higher prices, all market participants will wish to hold less of the commodity. The higher the price of the commodity, the less attractive it generally becomes to hold a unit of it instead of what its value in money could buy of other commodities. Fewer non-owners (and owners) of the commodity will be willing to buy quantities of it, while more owners of the commodity will be willing to sell it. On the other hand, the lower the price of the commodity, the more attractive it generally becomes to hold a unit of it instead of its value in other commodities. More non-owners of the commodity will be willing to buy, while fewer owners will be willing to sell (more of them, in fact, joining the non-owners in being prepared to add to their holdings). If we assume an appropriate discrepancy between the marginal utility of the product for some holders of it and that for others in the market, we have a situation where conditions for mutually profitable exchange exist. The problem is to explain the terms exchange will take place upon.

The competitive process of price determination in a market such as this can be grasped most easily by first imagining a quite impossible situation—where each market participant is fully aware of the quantities that the rest of the market would wish to buy and sell at each possible price. This "perfect knowledge" implies that each buyer and seller knows both what sellers would be prepared to sell at each possible price (if it could be obtained), and also what can be sold at each of these prices. In other words each buyer and seller knows the limiting price *above* which a given quantity of the commodity cannot be *sold,* as determined by the willingness to buy of the most eager buyers; each participant also knows, for any given quantity of the commodity, the limiting price *below* which it cannot be *bought,* as determined by the willingness to sell of the most eager sellers.

In this situation it is easy to describe the outcome. The knowledge possessed by the buyers and sellers will ensure that the prices asked for by sellers will be similar to those offered by buyers, and will be within a narrow range—the limits of this range being easy to define. Our assumption of perfect knowledge on the part of each buyer and seller means that he knows the best offers available to him, as well as the best offers available to others and against which he must compete. Each potential buyer knows (a) the lowest price it is *not* necessary to bid above in order to induce each given seller to sell given quantities, and (b) the highest price it *is* necessary to bid above in order to ensure (if it proves desirable to do so) that given quantities of the commodity are not bought by less eager buyers than himself. Similarly, each potential seller knows (a) the highest price it is not necessary to go below in order to induce each buyer to buy given quantities, and (b) the lowest price it is necessary to offer to sell below in order to ensure (if it proves desirable to do so) that given quantities of product are not sold by less eager sellers than himself.

It follows that the range of possible prices that may emerge in our market must necessarily include only

those prices at which the quantity of the commodity that buyers would be willing to buy (at these prices) is no greater and no less than the quantity that sellers would be willing to sell (at these prices).

No exchange could take place at higher prices; buyers would not offer such higher prices (nor, in fact, would sellers waste their time in asking these prices).[1] No buyer would offer such higher prices because he knows that the lower price is quite sufficiently high to induce the more eager sellers to supply all that buyers would ask at that lower price. (No seller would waste time in asking such higher prices because he knows that buyers can find an adequate number of sellers sufficiently eager to supply all the units of product that would be asked for at the lower price.) On the other hand, no exchange could take place at prices *below* the range specified above: no sellers would accept lower prices. He would not do so because he knows that the higher price is quite sufficiently low to attract all the buyers necessary to buy what the sellers would offer at that higher price.

With perfect knowledge assumed, this definite outcome will emerge immediately without haggling, or exploratory, "mistaken" acts of exchange at "wrong" prices. Perfect knowledge would ensure that each participant resign himself immediately to what he correctly believes to be the best opportunity he can obtain. He *knows* that he cannot obtain a superior opportunity because he knows that everybody else has the same perfect knowledge that he does, thus even those who might otherwise be prepared

---

1. A special case of great importance is where at any price greater than zero, the quantity of the commodity that would be offered for sale exceeds the quantity that would be bought. For such a good, it is clear, no finite positive price can be maintained; it becomes a free good whose ownership does not yield command over other commodities through exchange.

to provide superior opportunities know perfectly well it is unnecessary for them to do so. (No seller, as we saw, would waste his time asking prices higher than the above specified range.) Moreover (and this will be of the utmost importance when we extend the analysis of our simple case to more complex ones), there is an *additional* reason why a seller (for example) would not waste his time asking the higher prices. And this is quite apart from the fact that he knows he would find no buyer equipped, as he must assume each buyer to be, with perfect knowledge, ready to buy at the higher prices. This additional reason is that the seller knows that were any buyers to offer (inexplicably, and in error) a price higher than he really need pay, he (the seller) could hardly expect to get the sale. He would realize that such a buyer would be inundated with offers of numerous competing sellers eager to sell at a price higher than they can get elsewhere. It would be clear to any seller that this kind of error on the part of a buyer would be immediately self-correcting.

The price resulting from this reasoning process has several interesting properties that become apparent as one follows the logic of its determination. The price is so *low,* on the one hand, that almost all those who buy at the price would have been willing (if this had been necessary) to pay higher prices to secure what they are buying. On the other hand, the price is so *high* that almost all those who sell at the price would have been willing (if this had been necessary) to sell for lower prices. The reason why all the buyers do *not* have to pay higher prices is that the *marginal* buyers would *not* be willing to accept the last units bought, at any higher price. Competition among sellers therefore ensures that *no* buyer pays more than the marginal buyer. The other buyers thus gain what is often termed a *buyer's surplus,* representing a sheer gain arising through their purchases. Similarly, the reason why all the sellers do *not* have to sell for lower prices is that the *marginal* sellers would *not* be willing to sell the last units sold, at any lower price. Competition among buyers forces up the prices received by *all* sellers to the price acceptable to the marginal seller. The other sellers gain, in this way, a *seller's surplus.* The two-sided competition of many sellers and many buyers forces price within the range specified above—on the one hand, no higher than necessary to attract *all* the sellers needed to sell what buyers would be willing to buy at the price, and on the other hand, no lower than necessary to attract all the buyers needed to buy what sellers would be willing to sell at the price.

The logic of the discussion may be presented also in a somewhat different manner. Imagine two lists, one for sellers and one for buyers, in which market participants are ranked in order of their eagerness to sell or to buy the commodity. In the sellers' list the first line is assigned to the participant prepared to sell a *single* unit to the market at a price lower than that offered by anyone else; the second line is assigned to the seller prepared to sell a *second* unit to the market at a price lower than anything offered by everybody else (except the occupant of the first line). Of course both lines may be occupied by the same person. And so on, each successive line raising the price successive units can be induced to be offered to the market at. In the buyers' list, similarly, the first line is assigned to the buyer prepared to pay the highest price for a single unit of the commodity; the second line is assigned to the buyer (who may be the same person as the first buyer) prepared to pay a price for a *second* unit that is higher than anything that would be offered anywhere else in the market (besides, of course, the price that would be paid by the occupant of the first line). A comparison of the sellers' and buyers' lists would reveal that the most eager buyers (those high on the list) are prepared to pay much more for specified quantities of the commodity than would be demanded by the most eager sellers (those correspondingly high on the sellers' list). As one moved down both lists this gap would gradually narrow since the prices on successive lines on the sellers' list are rising, while those on the successive lines on the buyer's list are falling. When the line is reached where the seller's offer is *higher* than the corresponding buyer's bid, the unit has been reached where its seller cannot expect to find a buyer for it. Any buyer sufficiently eager to pay the high price the seller asks for it can find more eager sellers prepared to sell for less. Conversely this unit is also the unit for which a prospective buyer cannot find a seller. Any seller sufficiently eager to sell for the low price the buyer offers for it can find more eager buyers prepared to buy for more. The preceding unit, on the other hand (that relating to the preceding line in the list), can be sold since the buyer cannot find anyone prepared to sell for less, nor can the seller find anyone prepared to buy for more. The four prices represented by the offers and bids of the buyers and sellers ranked on these two lines of the lists delimit the price range within which equilibrium market price will be confined. The upper limit to the range is the *lower* of the following two prices (out of the four): the price corresponding to the buyer's bid on the higher of the two lines, and the price corresponding to the seller's offer on the lower of the two lines. (A price higher than the lowest of these two would *either* exclude a buyer necessary to take the last unit offered for sale at this price, *or* it would attract a seller of one unit more than can be sold at the price.) The lower limit to the range is the *higher* of the remaining two prices. (A price lower than this lower limit would *either* attract a buyer of one more unit than will be offered for sale at the price, *or* it would exclude the seller of the last unit necessary to supply all the buyers willing to buy at the price.) These buyer-seller pairs involved in defining the upper and lower limits to the price range are known in the literature as the "marginal pairs."[2]

The logic of this kind of price determination throws immediate light on the consequences of certain possible *changes* in the basic data. It is clear, for example, that a change in tastes, which raises the marginal utility of the product under consideration for the market participants, must have the immediate effect of a rise in price (with no other changes in the data). An increase in the marginal utility of the good means that for any given quantity of the commodity, buyers will be prepared, if they have to, to offer higher prices. Similarly, sellers will be willing to sell given quantities of the commodity only at higher prices. The resulting price will therefore be higher than before the change. A sudden increase in the quantity of the commodity that is in existence, on the other hand, will cause a fall in price. The marginal utility of a unit of the commodity will now be lower than before for holders of it. This follows from the law of diminishing utility, since holders are on the average holding larger stocks of the commodity. The consequence is a fall in price according to the above outlined logic of competitive price determination with perfect knowledge.

SIMPLE PRICE COMPETITION WITHOUT PERFECT KNOWLEDGE

Our analysis of the competitive determination of price in a market for a single unproducible commodity must now be extended to cover also the case where knowledge is less than perfect. Certainly we have to expect that in a real world, buyers and sellers will to some degree be ignorant of the prices that they must offer or ask in order to outstrip competitors and to attract advantageous exchange opportunities. It follows that some exchanges will probably take place, at least in the beginning, at prices significantly higher or lower than the price range defined in the previous section.

2. See Böhm-Bawerk, E. v., *Capital and Interest,* Vol. 2 (translated by G. D. Huncke), Libertarian Press, South Holland, Illinois, 1959, pp. 224–225. In the appendix to this chapter, a translation into diagrams of the logic of the competitive price will be found, together with further discussion of competitive price determination.

The important link between the case analyzed in the previous section and the more realistic case we are now dealing with is that the price range immediately realized in the preceding case must be recognized as being also the *equilibrium* price range for the present situation. It will be recalled from earlier chapters that a state of equilibrium is a state that would be maintained unchanged so long as the basic data (of the situation being analyzed) do not themselves change.[3] By describing the price range defined in the preceding section as being also the condition for equilibrium in the present imperfect-knowledge case, we mean, then, that if by chance sellers were to ask and buyers were to offer only prices lying within this range, no upward or downward revisions of price would ensue for subsequent exchanges so long as the basic data of the case continued unaltered. This is clearly the case, since prices in this range would clear the markets; all bids made at this price would be accepted, since offers to sell precisely the same quantity at this price are being made at the same time. No buyer making a bid, and no seller making an offer, needs to make revisions.

But this piece of information does not by itself tell us very much about the prices that will actually be determined in the kind of market we are attempting to grapple with. Without the perfect knowledge that we were assuming in the preceding section, we can expect, as we have seen, the equilibrium conditions to be established at the outset only by purest chance. And if the prices and conditions that prevail at the outset are not those of equilibrium, we are faced afresh with the problem of describing the competitive process of market price determination.

We will assume that trading is carried on during trading "days." (A trading "day" is a period of time so short that a course of action planned for one "day" cannot or will not be revised during the day "itself.") We will further assume that market participants do not have any reason to consider any prices except those that will prevail "today"; in other words we eliminate possible complications arising out of speculative behavior. Nobody in our market is holding back from buying (selling) "today" merely in the hope of lower (higher) prices tomorrow or later on.[4] Market participants, whatever the degree of their knowledge of market conditions, can be expected, then, to use their knowledge in the following obvious way.

3. See especially in Ch. 2, pp. 23–25.

4. For an outline of some of the complications introduced by the possibilities for speculation, see pp. 339–340 in the Appendix on multi-period planning.

Each potential buyer will bid prices for specific quantities of the commodity only up to the point determined, *first*, by the marginal utility to him of the commodity, and *second*, by the lowest price that he *believes* sufficiently high to induce sellers to sell, as well as sufficiently high to outbid his less eager competitors—in other words the lowest price he can buy at in the market today. Similarly, each potential seller will offer quantities of the product for sale at prices whose lower limit will be set, *first*, by the marginal significance of the commodity to himself, and *second*, by the highest price that he believes sufficiently low to induce buyers to buy, as well as sufficiently low to eliminate any less eager sellers who may be in competition with him—in other words the highest price he believes he can obtain in the market today.[5]

The absence of perfect knowledge implies that some (probably most) of the resultant bids and offers, on a given trading day, will be made in error. Buyers will bid prices either higher than necessary to obtain what they want or lower (and below what they might have been prepared to offer if they had been better informed) than necessary to obtain what they want. Similarly, sellers will offer to sell either for prices lower than necessary or higher (and above what the sellers themselves, if better informed, might have been willing to accept) than necessary to sell their commodities. It will be observed that the mistakes that can be made are of *two* possible kinds. *First*, bids and offers may be mistaken because

> *they unwittingly pass up superior opportunities (the particular market participants are ignorant of) in favor of the inferior opportunities*

(buyers offer to pay higher prices than they "really" need to; sellers offer to sell for prices lower than those they can "really" secure elsewhere). *Second*, bids and offers may be mistaken because

> *they deliberately pass up desirable opportunities in the erroneous belief that still more attractive opportunities can be secured*

---

5. Since we are assuming only imperfect knowledge, it is likely that participants are aware that some of their expectations are likely to be mistaken. In our analysis, however, we will continue to assume that each participant is able to crystallize all his guesses and doubts into a *single*-valued expectation he acts upon as if with certainty. The reader will recognize this as a simplification; it is the task of a theory of uncertainty to replace this simplification by a more sophisticated analysis of human action. For one such theory see Shackle, G. L. S., *Expectation in Economics*, Cambridge University Press, London, 1949.

(for example, buyers refuse to offer prices high enough to obtain what they want, even though if better informed they would have done so, because they believe the lower prices that they are bidding can buy the product somewhere in the market).

Two distinct possible reactions may emerge in the market consequent upon, and corresponding to, these two kinds of "mistaken" bids and offers. The *first* kind of error probably means that in some parts of the market, on a given day, prices are higher than in others. Imperfect knowledge has brought about an imperfect market which we may define loosely as one where prices are not immediately uniform. This discrepancy between prices will set into motion arbitrage operations on subsequent "days" as soon as the discrepancy is discovered. That is, as soon as knowledge increases just sufficiently for somebody to discover the consequences of the previously imperfect knowledge, a part of these consequences will tend to be eliminated. Men will buy where the price is low in order to sell where it is high, and in so doing they will bring about a tendency toward a uniform price.

The *second* kind of error means that some prospective buyers and sellers are disappointed—they find their bids to buy rejected as too low or their offers to sell rejected as too high. We are entitled to assume that insofar as knowledge of market conditions for a given day is concerned, our prospective buyers and sellers are capable of learning from experience gained on previous days (although throughout our analysis we are holding all the *data* of the situation—especially the buying and selling attitudes and expectations of the participants—constant from each trading day to the next). Buyers who yesterday found themselves disappointed in their bids to buy (because they bid too low) will revise upward their estimates of the prices necessary today to obtain the product; prospective sellers who found themselves disappointed yesterday because they asked prices that were too high will realize that they must lower them today if they are to meet the competition of other sellers. In other words, the disappointment associated with a seller's discovery during a trading day that "the price" of the product is lower than he had believed simply means that on the following day he will start with a lower and more nearly correct estimate of the price that will clear the market. And similarly for buyers who discover that they had a falsely optimistic estimate of market price.

The two kinds of reaction outlined in the preceding paragraphs make up the agitation that characterizes a competitive market groping toward the equilibrium position. It is clear that so long as prices are outside the equilibrium range (which we found to be realized immediately in the case where perfect knowledge is assumed), the market must seethe with changing patterns of exchange activity. Prospective buyers and sellers change their bids and offers, price discrepancies are discovered, exploited (and in this way destroyed)—all this alters the opportunity patterns being embraced in the market. The *direction* of these changes is toward the position described by conditions of equilibrium. Supposing, to recapitulate, that *all* prices asked and bid are initially *above* the equilibrium range; it is clear there would be some unaccepted offers to sell. The disappointment of those making these offers will teach them (even when some exchanges have taken place at these higher prices) that the higher prices are above the highest price that is low enough to sell the quantities of the products that they would be willing to sell. Their subsequent bids, competing with each other, will be lower—in the direction of equilibrium. On the other hand, with *all* prices asked and bids falling initially *below* the equilibrium range, the disappointment of unsatisfied prospective buyers in competition with each other would raise the bid prices toward the equilibrium price range. To consider the remaining possibility, if some bids are above and some below the equilibrium range, and some selling offers are also above and some below the range, then if not all the selling offers above the range are accepted, nor all the bids below the range accepted, the same adjustments will occur. But even if the bids below the range are exactly matched by the offers to sell below the range, and the bids and offers at above the range prices also match perfectly, the price discrepancies would invite arbitrage activity. The commodity would be bought where its price is below the range, and sold where its price is above the range. And this would go on until the below the range prices rise, and the above the range prices fall, to a single price. This single price can only lie in the equilibrium range. Any other price would generate the disappointments and adjustments outlined above.

Besides explaining the way the competitive market process determines prices, our analysis indicates also the way the market determines the *quantities* of the commodity that will be sold. In equilibrium of course, the quantity sold is no greater and no smaller than that which both buyers would be prepared to buy and sellers prepared to sell at the going price. During the time equilibrium has not yet been attained, so that prices are either all above, all below, or partly above and partly below the equilibrium price range, we must generally expect a *smaller* quantity to be sold than in equilibrium. This occurs because at prices higher than the equilibrium price range, buyers will buy only a smaller quantity; while at prices below the equilibrium price range, sellers will sell only a smaller quantity.

Our analysis, simple as it is, can be used to explain a host of matters. It is easy to see, for example, how it could be used to explain a persistent rise in the price of a commodity, or a persistent rise in the quantity of a commodity sold. In these and similar cases, the analytical framework enables the observer of the real world to look for those factors that his theory suggests may play a key role in the explanation he is seeking. Our analysis is also the foundation for the exploration of more complex situations, one of which we must now consider.

THE MARKET FOR SEVERAL NON-PRODUCIBLE GOODS:
THE PROBLEM

Still avoiding the complexities associated with existence of costs of production, by assuming all commodities sold in our market to be non-producible, we must now extend our analysis to the case where market activity is possible in a number of *different* commodities. We may formulate the problem by first setting forth our assumptions. There are a large number of potential participants in the market. Each potential participant is endowed at the start of each day with an initial package containing quantities of a number of different commodities. This package we may call his daily "income." The package may be of different size and composition for each market participant, and in his package a participant may find some of the included commodities present in greater quantities than others. All we need assume is that each day each participant is endowed (by nature, since we exclude production) with the same package as yesterday; no commodity is saved from yesterday. Each day, regardless of yesterday's experiences, participants arrive on the market with the same tastes as they possessed on the previous day. Thus, for any one participant at the start of each day, the marginal utilities of the various commodities on the market are exactly the same as they were at the start of the previous day. Additional units of all available commodities are ranked on his value scale in exactly the same order as at the start of the previous day.

Endowed with different initial daily incomes and tastes, different market participants can be expected to arrive at the market each having a *different* scale of values with respect to the various commodities. These differences in relative significance attached by different people to marginal quantities of the various commodities mean that opportunities may exist for each of the various market participants to improve his position by exchanging with other participants. Market activity will ensue. Goods will be bartered until nobody is aware of further opportunities for mutually profitable exchange. During the course of such a trading day, specific quantities of the various commodities will have changed hands, and each of the transactions will have been effected on particular terms.

Our problem is to discover what market forces are operative in determining (a) the quantities of the various commodities exchanged during any one day, and (b) the terms these exchanges are made on. We must discover further whether the market transactions of any one day can be expected of *themselves* to bring about changes in the market transactions of the following day. In other words, can we expect market participants to *revise* their willingness to buy or to sell commodities at yesterday's rates of exchange, purely as a result of yesterday's market experiences (that is, *without* any changes in the basic data, incomes, tastes, and so on)? If our analysis does lead us to expect such changes, we must further inquire into the pattern that these changes will describe over time, whether these changes may finally come to a halt, and, if so, into the conditions that would be thus indefinitely maintained.

This description of the problem posed by the multi-commodity market makes us immediately aware of a complication that was not present in the case of the analysis of the single-commodity market. Our analysis of the market for the single commodity was based on the notion of the existence of a definite upper limit to the price that a potential buyer would be prepared to pay for a commodity if market conditions forced him to do so. Such an upper limit, of course, can be considered definite only on the assumption of definitely known opportunities alternative to the purchase of the commodity. So long as we were, as in the previous sections, confining our attention to the single commodity, such an assumption was appropriate. We were able to assume a specific pattern of prices governing the availability of other goods, and, holding these other conditions unchanged, we were able to proceed with our analysis.

In our present problem we are unable to proceed in this way. We are now explicitly broadening the scope of our analysis to embrace an entire group of commodities. We wish to investigate the process by which the prices and quantities exchanged of *all* the commodities are determined. The upper limits to the bids that a prospective buyer might be prepared to make for a given quantity of one commodity cannot be thought of without considering the market situation—itself an object of our inquiry—with respect to all the other commodities. Our analysis of the multi-commodity market must clearly take full account of this complication.

THE EQUILIBRIUM SITUATION FOR
THE MULTI-COMMODITY MARKET

As in the single-commodity case considered in the preceding sections, it proves pedagogically convenient to approach our task by attacking it indirectly. Our principal aim is to explain the way the market transactions of any one day force potential buyers and sellers to *revise* their market plans, and, in so doing, to bring about *alterations* in the market transactions for the following day. We wish to discover how the mutual impact of numerous, possibly inconsistent, market plans, forges out new patterns of exchange based on the disappointments encountered or opportunities discovered in the course of exchange. We will, however, approach this task by first explaining the relationships that would perforce have to exist among the transactions in a multi-commodity market, if these transactions be required *not* to lead to any plan revisions by market participants on subsequent days. A firm understanding of the state of affairs, which would lead *nobody* to make any alterations in his market activities, will clarify the kinds of change that *will* occur under any other conditions.

At the start of each trading day, it will be recalled, we assume numerous exchange opportunities to exist among the market participants. For the transactions of any one trading day to be consistent with equilibrium (so that they may be repeated without alteration on subsequent days), it is necessary that they exhaust *all* possibilities of mutually profitable exchange. So long, for example, as the price pattern ruling on a particular trading day does not set in motion exchange between two market participants, who might cheerfully have exchanged at some other set of prices, it is obvious that sooner or later the situation will demand and achieve its own correction.

If the equilibrium pattern of market transactions must be such as to exhaust all possible opportunities for exchange, then these transactions must clearly bring about a very special *reshuffling of the pattern of commodity ownership*. At the beginning of each day the commodities bestowed by nature on the economy are distributed among individuals in one way. At the close of the day's market transactions, if these are to be consistent with equilibrium, the pattern of ownership of commodities should leave no two individuals in a position with respect to one another that could present the conditions for mutually profitable exchange. The analysis of earlier chapters enables us to characterize such a pattern of commodity ownership with clarity. At the close of a day's market transactions in an equilibrium market, the various commodities will be owned by market participants in such a way that, with respect to marginal units of these commodities, *the value scales of all participants shall be identical.*[6]

When the ownership of commodities has been redistributed in this way, through exchange, no further transfer of commodities between any two commodity owners could possibly be proposed that would leave *both* parties better off with the transfer than without it. This is obvious. Let us suppose that one of the parties prefers the additional quantity of the commodity that it is proposed he acquire over that he is to give up. Then, since all participants have already attained identical scales of value, it follows that the other party to the commodity transfer values the two quantities of goods in exactly the same way. And this means that he prefers the quantity of the commodity that it is proposed that he *give up* over that it is proposed he acquire. No exchange opportunity can exist.

What the particular ownership pattern in a given situation must be, if it is to fulfill the condition of identical value ranking by all market participants, will depend on two sets of factors. On the one hand, it will depend on the different tastes of the various market participants (since these will govern their respective value scales); and on the other hand, it will depend on the initial quantities of the various commodities each participant is endowed with at the start of the trading day (since no ownership pattern can emerge that should leave anyone worse off than at the start of the day). *If* one could discover the way a market participant, owning a particular array of the various commodities, would rank additional units of these various commodities on his value scale; *and if* this could be discovered also in turn for each of the possible cases in which the array of commodities he owns might be somehow different; *and if* corresponding sets of discoveries could be made in turn for each of the various market participants—then, taking into account the initial commodity endowments, we would have the data to determine the pattern of commodity ownership that would prevail at the close of trading in an equilibrium market.[7]

6. This identity, at the close of equilibrium trading, between the value rankings of different market participants holds only with respect to the marginal units of (a) those goods that each of the participants holds a stock of at the close of the day and (b) those goods that can be bought and sold. With respect to a good that some participants possess no stock of at the close of the day, all that can be said is that it ranks relatively higher on the value scales of those who do hold some of it than on the scales of those who do not.

7. Whether or not the initial commodity endowments and the value scales of the various participants do, in fact, permit the existence of such an ownership pattern

We may assume that these data are sufficient to determine uniquely the required *pattern of ownership* at the close of trading in the equilibrium market—namely, that pattern that yields identical scales of value with respect to additional quantities of goods. The next step is to discover what determines the *transactions* in the equilibrium market; that is, those transactions that will *lead* to the above described final pattern of commodity ownership.

It will be recalled that a trading "day" is defined as being so short that no plan changes can be made *during* a single day. Bids and offers made at the start of a day are to be maintained unchanged throughout the day. It follows that in looking for the transactions of an equilibrium market, we are looking for a *single* set of prices for the various commodities that will permit market participants voluntarily to continue the reshuffling of commodity ownership through exchange, until the ownership pattern outlined in the previous paragraphs is reached. In the equilibrium market there will be a single price for each commodity (clearly, *two* prices for the same commodity must result in arbitrage activity on subsequent days, altering either or both of the two prices). And with the required unique set of prices for the various commodities expected to govern the market throughout the day, in equilibrium, market participants will be induced to buy and sell the various commodities in precisely those quantities that will result in the final pattern of commodity ownership outlined above. In other words, with these prices ruling, *each* market participant will convert during the day his initial commodity endowment into a particular commodity bundle more desirable to him than any other one available at the market prices. The distribution of commodity bundles at the end of the equilibrium trading day will be such that no opportunities for exchange exist between any two participants; thus, no one is led to revise his market plan for the following day.[8]

Now, the preceding paragraphs describe the conditions that would have to be fulfilled before we could pronounce a multi-commodity market to

---

(and of only one such pattern), is a question, not of price theory proper, but rather of mathematics. (In mathematical economics the proof that such a pattern does exist is known as an "existence theorem." We will assume that such a unique pattern does exist and that complete knowledge of market data enables this pattern to be completely specified.)

8. Here, too, we will assume that such a set of prices is mathematically feasible and can be derived from a complete knowledge of market data.

be in equilibrium. In the subsequent sections we will be concerned with our principal problem—what goes in a multi-commodity market where these conditions have *not* been fulfilled. At this point, the most fruitful approach to this task will be to show that, exactly as was the case with the single-commodity market, the equilibrium conditions *would* be immediately fulfilled if all participants possessed, and knew each other to possess, perfect knowledge of all relevant market data.

Our analysis of the single-commodity market (with perfect knowledge) proceeded from the following self-evident propositions. No prospective buyer would be prepared to pay more for a commodity than its price elsewhere in the market; nor would he waste time by offering to buy at a lower price than that at which others are prepared to buy elsewhere in the market. No seller would be prepared to sell the commodity for less than it could bring elsewhere in the market; nor would he waste time trying to sell it for more than the price it can be obtained for elsewhere in the market. We may translate the logic of these propositions into corresponding statements having reference to the multi-commodity market with perfect knowledge.

Consider any participant in such a market, contemplating the conversion of his initial commodity endowment into a preferred bundle by exchange in the market. He must sell some items and buy others; he must calculate the price offers and bids he should make. It is clear that the *ratio* between the price that he bids for one good and the price he offers to sell a second good for

> must not be different than the ratio of the prices these two goods can be bought and sold at elsewhere in the market.

This is readily seen. Suppose the two goods in question to be A and B respectively, and suppose the market price of A to be k times the market price of B. Then our market participant, knowing this, will under no circumstances make bids and offers to buy A and sell B (or, vice versa, to sell A and buy B) that would yield a ratio between the price of A to the price of B, either greater or smaller than k. He would not offer to buy A at *more* than k times the price he is offering to sell B for. Such a course of action would mean that he would give up *more* of B, in order to buy a given quantity of A, than he would have to give up elsewhere in the market; by the same token, he would be providing the market with quantities of B at a *lower* cost (in terms of A necessary to be sacrificed in exchange) than is called for elsewhere. On the other hand, our market participant would not offer to buy A at *less* than k times the price he offers to sell B for. To do so would mean to ask a price for *B* that would be *greater* (measured in terms of quantity of *A* required to be given up in exchange for a unit of *B*) than is being asked elsewhere; by the same token, such a course of action would mean an offer to buy *A* at a price that would be *lower* (measured in terms of quantity of *B* offered in exchange for a unit of *A*) than sellers of *A* can obtain elsewhere in the market.

It follows from these propositions that for *each* pair of commodities, each of the perfectly informed market participants will seek in turn to make price bids and offers bearing ratios that should coincide with that reached by the other participants. Extending this to all the commodities, it follows that each market participant will seek, and is aware that each of his fellow participants is likewise seeking, a unique set of relative prices for all the commodities that should be common to all participants. With each participant equipped with the same complete information concerning individual tastes and initial commodity endowments, it is not difficult to see which particular pattern of relative prices will immediately emerge from their calculations. It can only be the particular set of relative prices that we found to satisfy the conditions for an equilibrium market.[9]

No participant would make the error of entering the market in the belief that some *other* set of relative prices, according to which he should adjust his own buying and selling plans, would prevail. With perfect knowledge, such a possibility (which would of course mean the violation of the conditions for equilibrium) is precluded. With perfect knowledge, a participant would know (and would know that everybody knows) that any other set of relative prices would *not* bring the market, during the day, into that pattern of commodity ownership that we found characteristic of the close of a day in the equilibrium market. Such a set of relative prices must then lead to the failure by some of the market participants to exploit among themselves a number of mutually profitable exchange opportunities. Such a set of relative prices cannot be assumed to be allowed to prevail, then, insofar as these interested participants can be counted upon to take advantage of all opportunities for mutually gainful exchange. Knowing this, each participant would correctly calculate what the set of market prices will be. The conditions for an equilibrium market would be immediately satisfied.

9. The reader will observe that in this, as well as in parallel succeeding discussions, our assumption of perfect knowledge includes also the assumption of the ability to make instantaneous calculations of required information from the data.

THE MULTI-COMMODITY MARKET
WITHOUT PERFECT KNOWLEDGE

Our awareness of the relationships that would exist in a multi-commodity market in equilibrium, and our understanding of how these relationships would be immediately realized in a world of perfect knowledge, must now be used in extending our analysis further. We must now examine the multi-commodity market where knowledge is *not* perfect and which *cannot* therefore be expected to fulfill equilibrium conditions. Once again we assume that each day there is some initial endowment of a bundle of commodities for each market participant; that these endowments may differ among participants but are the same for any one participant from day to day; and that while participants may differ among each other in their tastes, any one participant arrives in the market each day with the same tastes as yesterday, regardless of yesterday's market or other activities.

The imperfection of knowledge means that the typical participant will know of the tastes and initial commodity endowments of only a small number of his fellow participants, and he will have only fragmentary—and possibly incorrect—knowledge of these. Were all these market participants to come into contact with each other for the first time without any experience whatsoever of earlier price relationships, the first exchange transactions would probably be made, on a very small scale, within fairly close groups of persons aware more or less completely of one another's situations. Any buying or selling plans on a wider scale could be made only on the basis of guesses regarding market conditions that very likely would be proved mistaken. Even when the scope of exchange is broadened to embrace the entire market, we must expect the individual buying and selling plans of different participants to be made on information gathered, for each of them, from the experience of only small segments of the market. These plans will prove themselves mutually inconsistent; knowledge of their inadequacy will be gained by the plan makers through the discovery of superior opportunities lost because of adherence to such a plan, or through the direct disappointment of goals sought to be achieved by the plans. It will be instructive to work through in detail the simple logic of such a sequence of (a) plans made and executed on the basis of mistaken knowledge; (b) the discovery of the unplanned sacrifice of desirable opportunities, or the non-attainment of planned objectives, due to this limited knowledge; and (c) the revision of plans for future trading, in the light of the information gained from these market experiences.

Let us consider two market participants *a* and *b*. We will assume *a* to start his day with a given, nature-endowed bundle of commodities, including the commodities A and B, in such a proportion that he would gladly give up a number of units (let us say any number up to *m*) of B in order to *gain* a single additional unit of A. On the other hand, *b* starts his day with an endowment such that *his* tastes would lead him to *give up* a unit of A in order to acquire a number of units of B (let us say any number *l* or higher, with *l* < *m*).

Both *a* and *b* enter the market with estimates of the ratio between the price of A and the price of B that will rule in the market during the day. On the one hand, *a* expects the price of A to be *k* times the price of B; that is, he expects to be able to acquire commodity A by selling commodity B at the rate of *k* units of B for each unit of A acquired. On the other hand, *b* expects the price of A to be *n* times the price of B (with *k* < *l* < *m* < *n*). Thus, he expects to be able to acquire *n* units of commodity B in the market for each unit of A that he sells in the market.

It is not difficult to understand the plans that *a* will formulate and follow on the basis of his estimate. He believes it possible to acquire a single unit of A for the sacrifice of *k* units of B. He does not think it necessary to sacrifice any *more* than *k* units of B per unit of A; on the other hand, he does not hope to be able to acquire a unit of A for the sacrifice of *less* than *k* units of B. He will refuse, therefore, to enter into any transactions that will yield *less* than one unit of A for the sacrifice of *k* units of B. And, again, he will not waste his time in seeking to obtain *more* than one unit of A for *k* units of B. Or, to repeat the sense of the previous sentences in different words, *a* will refuse any transactions calling for the sacrifice of *more* than *k* units of B per unit of A; and he will not waste time seeking to obtain A at the sacrifice, per unit of A, of *less* than *k* units of B. (Of course, were *a* to find that a unit of A could not only not be obtained for *k* units of B, but could not even be obtained for anything less than the sacrifice of more than *m* units of B, he would refuse to sell B to get A, not only because he believes that better opportunities are available but also because trade on such terms would, on our assumptions above, make him subjectively *worse* off than at the start of the day.)[10]

Similarly, *b* will refuse to enter into any transactions to sell A and buy B, which will yield him *less* than *n* units of B per unit of A, because he is

---

10. In fact if the ratio of the price of A to that of B is *very* large, *a* will actually *sell* some units of A in order to acquire B.

sure that he can obtain better terms elsewhere in the market. (Moreover, any transactions that yield, per unit of A, not only less than n units of B, but even less than l units of B, will be rejected for the additional reason that trade on such terms would leave b actually worse off than at the start of the day.)[11] Again, b will not waste time seeking to acquire *more* than n units of B in exchange for the sale of one unit of A. To repeat these obvious propositions in different words, b will refuse transactions calling for the sacrifice of *more* than one unit of A per n units of B; and he will waste no time seeking to acquire n units of B in exchange for *less* than one unit of A.

It is clear that a and b *could* both gain through mutual exchange, with a selling B and buying A, and b selling A and buying B, at any ratio of the price of A to the price of B lying between l and m. So long as a can obtain a unit of A for less than m units of B, and so long as b can obtain at least l units of B for one unit of A, each can gain from trade. Since l < m, there is clearly a range of price ratios that can create mutually profitable barter. But it is equally clear that with their differing estimates of market conditions, a and b will not come to terms with one another, since each believes he can do better elsewhere. On the one hand, a will not give more than k units of B for one unit of A; on the other hand, b will not accept less than n units of B for one unit of A. Since k < n, no trade between a and b can result. But let us consider the possible relations that these estimates on the part of a and b may bear to the actualities of the market. A number of cases may be considered in turn.

1. It is possible that both a and b might not be disappointed at all. It is possible that a might find people willing to buy B from him and sell A to him at prices yielding one unit of A for every k units of B. Similarly, it is possible that B might be able to sell one unit of A and buy n units of B. But together these possibilities simply mean that two prices exist in a single market either for A, or for B, or for both. This can continue only for as long as there is ignorance, among a and those with whom he deals, of what is going on among b and those with whom *he* deals (and vice versa). As soon as the price differentials are discovered, some market participants will find that it is profitable to buy A in the area where a deals, and sell it in the area where b deals; and to buy B in the area where b deals, and sell it in the area where a deals. In this way the price differentials will

---

11. And for *very* low ratios of the price of A to that of B, b will even *sell* some units of B in order to acquire A.

tend to disappear, and in the course of time both a and b will revise their estimates of the price ratio between A and B, closer and closer together.

2. Another possibility is that the prices of A and B in the market are such that one unit of A can be had in exchange for a particular number of units of B that is greater than k but smaller than n. (In this and the succeeding cases we ignore the possibility of more than one set of prices for the various commodities in the same market, such as was considered in the preceding paragraph.) It is clear that a will buy no A on these terms, since he believes he can get A elsewhere in the market with a smaller sacrifice of B. (And if the market prices are such that one unit of A requires the sale of more than m units of B, then a would be actually worse off by such a trade.) But at the end of the day a will find himself disappointed in his hopes; he will not have bought any A with the proceeds from the sale of B. He will have discovered that he has passed up profitable opportunities (to get A by sacrificing B at ratios calling for more than k of B) in the vain hope of obtaining A for the sacrifice of only k of B per unit of A. (Of course the lost opportunities would have been profitable for a, on our assumptions, only if the $A:B$ ratio, while less than $1:k$, was not less than $1:m$.) In making his plans for the succeeding trading days, a will revise downward his estimate of the relative price of B and revise upward his estimate of the relative price of A.

As far as concerns b, the situation is rather similar. He will not sell A in order to buy B, at the going rate of one of A to less than n of B, because he thinks he can get n full units of B for the sacrifice of one unit of A, elsewhere in the market. At the end of the day, he too is disappointed. He will have discovered that he has passed up desirable opportunities (of getting something less than n units of B for the sacrifice of a unit of A) in the vain hope of obtaining a more advantageous deal. (Of course, the lost opportunities would have been desirable, on our assumptions, only if the $A:B$ ratios, while greater than $1:n$, are no greater than $1:l$.) In making his plans for the succeeding trading days, b will revise upward his estimate of the relative price of B and revise downward his estimate of the relative price of A.

3. A third possibility is that in the market, the price of A is *less* than k times the price of B; thus, a unit of A is equivalent in the market to less than k units of B.

(a) Let us consider b's reaction first. It should be clear that b will react in exactly the same way we saw that he would react when the price of A was more than k times (but less than n times) the price of B. He would refuse to trade at market prices. He would do this (on our assumptions) for *two* reasons. *First*, *b* would argue that if he wished to buy *B* by selling *A*, he could do so much more advantageously (on his estimation of market conditions) elsewhere in the market (where he expects to secure as much as *n* units of *B* per unit of *A* sold.) *Second*, since we assumed that under no circumstances would *b* buy *B* by selling *A* should the relative price of *B* rise to the rate of less than *l* units of *B* per unit of *A* sold, *b* will consider himself only to lose subjectively, that is, to be worse off by trading *A* for *B* at market rates. (In fact *b*, after his discovery of the market rates of exchange, might be tempted in the future to *sell B* and buy *A*.) At the close of the day, *b* will have discovered how grossly he had underestimated the relative price of *B*; and in making his plans for the future, he will revise upward his estimate of the relative price of *B* and revise downward his estimate of the relative price of *A*.

It is worthwhile to consider briefly, for this case, the impact of these changes in *b*'s plans upon the market. Suppose that the initial market prices of *A* and *B* were at variance with the fundamental data of the market in such a degree that with the given ratio between the market price of *A* and that of *B*, too many people planned to convert *A* into *B* as against those planning to convert *B* into *A* (in other words that the relative price of *B* was too low and that of *A* too high). In this case *b*'s original estimate of the relative price of *B* was even lower than that "erroneously" ruling in the market. Since the market as a whole "erred" in pricing *B* relatively too low and *A* relatively too high, some of those who planned to sell *A* and buy *B* must necessarily be disappointed. We have already seen that since *b*'s estimate of the relative *market* valuation of *B* was even lower, his plans, too, were of course bound to be disappointed. (As it happens, *b*'s misjudgment of the relative market valuation of *A* and *B* may even have helped to make the misjudgment by the *market* more serious in its consequences. This can be seen by observing that if *b* had known that in the market one unit of *A* could be had for so little of *B*, he might have *sold B* to buy *A*, thereby helping to make less serious the general movement to convert *A* into *B*.) In any event, as *b*'s disappointment, along with that of others, tends to raise estimates of the relative price of *B* and lower estimates of the relative price of *A*, the market prices of subsequent trading days tend to lower the number of units of *B* obtainable through the sale of a unit of *A*. (This is so since we are observing that the terms transactions are effected upon depend directly upon the estimates of prospective market prices held by market participants.) This adjustment in the relative prices of A and B will tend to eliminate the discrepancy between the quantity of A, which people wish to convert into B, and the quantity of A, into which people wish to convert B.

On the other hand, suppose that the market prices of A and B on the initial trading day were at variance with the fundamental conditions of the market, but, this time, in the opposite direction. Suppose, that is, that the going prices induced too many people to plan to convert B into A, as compared with those planning to convert A into B (in other words that the price of B was relatively too high and that of A relatively too low). In this case b's original mistaken estimate of the relative prices of A and B in the markets tends, if anything, to make less acute the immediate consequences of the "erroneously" high relative valuation placed upon B by the market. At the ruling relative market prices, it is true, too many people are attempting to sell B and buy A, as compared with those who can be induced at these prices to sell A and buy B. Inevitably, some of the former will find their plans disappointed. But if b had correctly estimated the relative prices of A and B on the market, he too might (as we have seen) have attempted to sell B and buy A. (Of course b's *own* misjudgment of market prices led him to make plans to sell A and buy B on terms that again could only be disappointed.) In any event the disappointment of those who find that they are not able to sell B in order to buy A at going market prices will result in lower estimates of the relative price of B and higher estimates of the relative price of A. Similarly, b's estimates of relative market prices will be revised (in the reverse direction) toward the new relative market prices.

(b) Let us now turn to consider a's reaction to a market where one unit of A is equivalent in value to less than k units of B (that is, less than a has expected and planned for). Since a enters the market expecting (and willing) to have to sacrifice k units of B in order to be in a position to buy one unit of A, he will waste no time seeking more advantageous terms. He might not, in fact, discover the unexpectedly favorable terms on which he can convert B into A until the close of the day. At the close of the day he will certainly revise his estimate of tomorrow's relative market price of A downward, and that of B upward.

Let us suppose that the relative market price of A is too high, and that of B too low, so that too many people are induced to convert A into B, as compared with those wishing to convert B into A. Then if a's error in the estimation of prices kept him back from converting B into A, this would tend to accelerate somewhat the market tendency lowering the relative price of A and raising that of B. At the original prices, some of those wishing to sell A and buy B are disappointed. If a remained in ignorance of the opportunities that all these people are prepared to afford him, more of them will have been disappointed than need have been the case.

On the other hand, if the relative market price of A is too low, and that of B too high, so that too many people are led to attempt to convert B into A, a's ignorance of what is available in the market would not make any real difference to subsequent market movements. If a had known of the opportunities available in the market for the conversion of B into A and was not to be disappointed in them, someone else instead would have been disappointed. In any event the market would proceed to price A relatively higher, and B relatively lower, than before.[12]

MONOPOLY IN A PURE EXCHANGE MARKET

Thus far we have been proceeding on the assumption that any prospective buyer of a commodity is able, in seeking out the best possible terms, to choose from among a number of holders of the commodity. On this assumption, any prospective seller of the commodity, deliberating upon the price he should ask for the commodity, knows, as we have seen, that he will only be wasting his time if he demands a price any higher than the lowest price asked by his competitors. The possibility of one seller charging a higher price for a commodity than another seller can arise only from ignorance on the part of one or other of the sellers or the knowledge on the part of the first seller that some prospective buyers are ignorant of the opportunities made available by the second seller. Under these circumstances the market process ensures that the prices charged by the different sellers will move toward each other until the equilibrium price range is achieved. In other words the competitive market process tends to ensure that no seller charge a price for a commodity higher than that which the most eager among the sellers is prepared to accept in order to sell an additional unit of it. This state of affairs assumes, of course, that although the initial commodity endowments of the different market participants are not alike, nevertheless each commodity is present in significant amounts in the endowments of a considerable number of participants.

A special case arises when a particular commodity is present each day in the initial endowment of only one of the participants. This participant may of course be unwilling to sell any units of this rare commodity.

---

12. Similar analysis may be employed to work out the consequences, for the plans of a and b respectively, of a market where the price of A is more than n times the price of B.

He may rank each unit of it, which he possesses, higher on his subjective value scale than any additional quantity of any other commodity. But it is possible that he might be glad to give up some of this rare commodity in exchange for appropriate quantities of some other commodities (and this is of course more likely to be the case when his endowment of the rare commodity is large, and his endowment of other commodities meager). In this situation the participant thus favored is in a position to act as a *monopolist* with respect to the commodity he has sole possession of.[13]

A monopolist is in the unique position of being able to demand a price for the monopolized commodity without paying regard to prices charged for the commodity by other sellers, since no such other sellers exist. Although he knows, like the sellers of any other commodity, that for each quantity of his commodity there is a price it cannot be sold above, for him this upper limit is not set by the actions of other sellers of this commodity. This upper limit is determined by the subjective valuation of this commodity of its prospective buyers as compared with other commodities. It is misleading, as we shall see, to say that the monopolist is exempt from competition, but he certainly does not have to meet the competition of other sellers of *his* commodity.

The competition that the monopolist does have to meet is from the actions of sellers of other commodities. When the monopolist asks a particular price for his commodity, any buyer of a unit of it, with a given set of market prices for the other commodities, must sacrifice definite quantities of one or more of these other commodities in order to be able to buy the unit of the monopolized commodity. The lower the prices obtained by the sellers of other commodities, the larger must be the quantities of these other commodities that must be sacrificed in order to buy a unit of the monopolized commodity. Similarly, with given prices of the other commodities, any increase in the price per unit demanded by the monopolist again calls for larger sacrifices of other commodities in order to acquire a unit of the monopolized commodity.

Thus, the monopolist who is attempting to convert his initial commodity endowment into the most desirable commodity bundle possible through exchange is faced with a special problem. Like every other participant in the market, he must make estimates of the prices that will rule in the market for all the other commodities. But whereas other participants

---

13. The reader may imagine a group of islanders who have divided up their island into equal holdings, in one of which oil is discovered.

must make an estimate of the market price of every commodity that they sell (one reason for this being that these prices will set the upper limit to those that they themselves can demand), a monopolist is not obliged nor is he able to estimate a market price for the monopolized commodity. He must himself set the price. He knows that too high a price will lead many prospective buyers to exchange their own commodities for commodities other than the monopolized one (where they are able to secure better terms). On the other hand, it is not difficult to perceive a lower limit to the price that the monopolist might conceivably be willing to sell any given quantity of his commodity at. This lower limit is set for a monopolist as for anyone else by the point at which the subjective sacrifice involved in the sale of the given quantity of the commodity ranks higher on the seller's value scale than the additional quantities of other commodities whose purchase would be made possible by the sale.

No matter what price he charges, the monopolist knows that he can sell only a smaller quantity than it would be possible to sell at a lower price. This, by itself, might mean that he would be refusing to sell some units of the monopolized commodity, even though he actually values the quantities of other commodities obtainable in exchange for those units more highly than those units themselves. On the other hand, by keeping the price higher and thus admittedly reducing the quantity of the monopolized commodity sold, the monopolist *may* be able to obtain *more* in exchange for the units of his commodity, which he is able to sell at the high price, than he could obtain by selling a larger quantity at the lower price. Of course, the competition provided by the sellers of other commodities may be so effective that the monopolist's most advantageous course of action must be to charge a very low price indeed. In such a case any increase in the price would reduce the number of units sold so drastically that the increase in price for those remaining units that can be sold is insufficient to make up the lost revenue. The elasticity of demand for the monopolized commodity is of relevance in this regard. The strength of the competition of other commodities is reflected in the elasticity of demand of the monopolized commodity at all points on the demand curve. If the demand curve for the commodity is inelastic at any particular price-quantity point, it will be better for the monopolist to charge a higher price rather than that corresponding to the point. With demand inelastic at a certain point, total revenue is greater with the smaller quantity sold at the higher price. The particular price that the monopolist will attempt to select will permit a quantity to be sold that yields more revenue than any other price-quantity combination. At this stage elasticity of demand will be unitary.[14]

One particular feature of the monopoly situation is especially worthy of note. The monopolist's power to force buyers to pay higher prices is a result of his ability to restrict the quantity of the commodity that he puts on sale. It is this feature that distinguishes the monopoly price from the competitive price. When a seller of a commodity is competing with other sellers of the same commodity, he is not in a position to deliberately raise the price by holding some of the commodity off the market. Were such a competing seller to hold back some of his commodity, his customers would certainly not be prepared to pay higher prices in order to secure their share of the reduced supply. They would simply buy elsewhere. But when a monopolist holds back part of a supply of his commodity (even though he might be able to sell all of it at a low price, and even though the supply thus held back is perhaps of no use at all to him personally), he may be in a position to drive up the price.[15] Those most eager to obtain the commodity now find that in order to bid it away from other less eager

14. The optimum price decision for the monopolist can be illustrated by a diagram. Let AR be the market demand curve for the monopolized good. This line will therefore be the monopolist's average revenue line, and the MR line will show his marginal revenue. At the point P, marginal revenue is zero (and the point elasticity of demand unitary). At this point the monopolist will be maximizing his revenue. Since he has no costs (and we are ignoring his own demand for the good), this point is therefore the best for him.

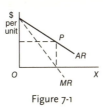

Figure 7-1

15. An interesting special case is where the monopolized good is present so plentifully in the monopolist's endowment that it would, under competitive conditions, have been a free good. If the plentiful endowment had been distributed among the endowments of many participants, none of them could have gained command over other goods through exchange, by virtue of ownership of this plentifully endowed commodity. Under competition there is so much of the commodity that even the lowest positive price would bring forth a supply of it on the market in excess of the aggregate quantity that participants wish to buy. The monopolist, by restricting the quantity that he offers to the market, may be able to turn the free good into one that commands a positive price.

competing buyers, they must offer prices these other buyers are unable or unwilling to match. The degree to which a monopolist may be able to force up the price in this way, depends, as we have seen, on the degree of competition provided by other commodities, reflected in the elasticity of demand for the monopolized commodity.

So long as the number of monopolized commodities is not large, as compared with the total number of commodities on the market, the existence of monopoly elements in an exchange market does not seriously upset the analysis of this chapter. Monopoly elements will distort somewhat both the pattern of prices of the various commodities and the quantities of them exchanged in the market, but the logic of price determination is not fundamentally altered. The *results* are different, but the market process operates in an essentially unaltered manner. When we consider the case of a monopolist-producer, we will return once again to an analysis of the effects upon the efficiency of the entire market system that are introduced by monopoly elements.

THE AGITATION OF THE MARKET

The analysis of this chapter places us in a position to understand the seething agitation of changing prices that can be expected in any large pure exchange market, even in the absence of any changes in initial commodity endowments or changes in tastes.

Each participant in the market will be constantly scanning the latest prices of the various commodities in making his market plans for the day. Market participants will be constantly revising their estimates of the prices they must expect to pay when buying the various commodities, and the prices they can expect to obtain by selling them, in the light of their experiences, and disappointments, in yesterday's market. In earlier sections of this chapter we examined the kind of logic entailed in making decisions concerning two commodities. In a market with many goods, the same logic will be constantly applied to every possible pair of commodities and every possible pair of groups of commodities.

The prices ruling on any one day will reflect the estimates for that day, on the part of the market participants, of the entire set of relative market prices. With these estimates in mind, each participant will seek to transform his initial commodity endowment into the most desirable bundle of commodities he can obtain by buying and selling in the market. His plans will be made according to the logic of consumer choice discussed in earlier chapters. He will go out into the market with a plan calling for the purchase of definite quantities of specified commodities, and the sale of quantities of other commodities, all at the expected prices. These plans of the various market participants, made on the basis of imperfect and fragmentary knowledge, are almost certain to fail to mesh completely. There will inevitably be disappointed plans, as well as the realization that inferior opportunities have been seized at the expense of superior opportunities that have remained unknown.

These disappointments and discoveries will lead to a new set of estimates for the following day and a new set of buying and selling plans. This kind of agitation will proceed for as long as the set of prices expected to rule in the market is in any way different from those that fulfill the conditions for the equilibrium market. Whenever the prices are such that the relative values of any two commodities, A and B, induces too many people to convert A into B, as compared with those wishing to convert B into A, conditions exist that will bring about a readjustment in prices in the direction of reducing previous "disappointments."

In this process of market agitation the market participants with the keenest judgment of market conditions will be the most successful. Even though in this chapter we are not allowing any commodities to be produced, and are not permitting any activity to be based on speculation, there is still a range within which the entrepreneur can exercise his peculiar function. Whenever one man has superior knowledge of what is going on in the various sections of the market, he is in a position to buy and sell more advantageously than others. He will be able to buy the goods he wishes to buy where prices are lowest, and sell those he wishes to sell where prices are highest. When his superior knowledge suggests that the *same* good is available at different prices in the same market, he will engage in arbitrage to take advantage of the price differential. In this way some participants will buy goods in the market only to resell them immediately at a profit. By this kind of activity the superior knowledge of the entrepreneur is placed at the disposal of all the participants in a market. More and more people discover that he is willing to pay higher-than-usual prices in those market areas where the price of a good is low; more and more others discover that he is willing to sell for lower-than-usual prices in those market areas where the price of a good is high. The competition of all the market participants, each seeking the best opportunities available in the market, places pressure upon each of them to secure the most accurate market information and, in turn, to supply the market with the most attractive opportunities possible.

Only in the absence of market equilibrium, and in the state of incomplete knowledge on the part of market participants, does market agitation and entrepreneurial activity emerge. Market equilibrium, and the set of conditions necessary for the existence of equilibrium prices, represent a mental construction whose most useful purpose is to help understand the nature of the market activity that is characteristic of the *absence* of equilibrium. Sometimes expressions are used by economists suggesting that the market situation satisfying the conditions for equilibrium marked out by a given set of data is achieved, more or less automatically and immediately, by the mere existence of these data. Such a notion would overlook the process whereby equilibrium could conceivably be reached. It would bestow upon the state of equilibrium an emphasis that hardly fits into the analysis of any imaginable real world where the basic data of the market, tastes and initial commodity endowments, are themselves subject to drastic changes over time.

This becomes immediately apparent when one does, in fact, attempt to apply the analysis of this chapter to a world of change. Thus far we have been employing "static" assumptions. We have been assuming that each day each participant is endowed with the same initial commodity bundle as yesterday; that each day each participant, regardless of past experiences, has the same tastes as yesterday. The only difference between one market day and the following one was that plans made for trading during the latter day are based on estimates of prices learned through the market experience of the previous day. Agitation in the market was caused by rapid changes in plans made by the various participants as market experience steadily spread more information and repeatedly indicated fresh opportunities for profitable trade. When one superimposes upon this already complicated picture a particular pattern of unforeseen changes in initial commodity-endowments and in individual tastes, things become far more complex.

With changes in incomes and tastes, market agitation proceeds from *two* analytically distinct sets of causes. First of all, as in our previous analysis, participants each day will revise their trading plans under the impact of the disappointments and other market experiences of the previous trading day. In addition, participants will be revising their plans simply because they face a new set of conditions. They find themselves with a scale of values, with respect to additional quantities of the various commodities, different from yesterday, because they no longer have the same tastes and attitudes as yesterday, and because they find themselves in possession of initial stocks of the various commodities different from yesterday. Any market changes that might have brought trade closer to the equilibrium pattern, from the standpoint of yesterday's income and tastes, is continually disrupted by the emergence today of a totally different structure of income and tastes. Long before equilibrium conditions appropriate to the data of any one day have been attained, the market is faced with data calling for a totally different set of equilibrium conditions.

In addition, once we admit changes in tastes and income into our analysis, we must include the possibility that market participants, in planning their buying and selling for the day, make guesses concerning the changes, in the incomes and tastes of other people, that might have taken place. In other words participants might not rely on the knowledge gained during the market experience of the previous day. In this way a new source of imperfection in market knowledge is opened up; namely, that due to inability to correctly gauge changes in tastes and incomes. On the other hand, a new range for entrepreneurial activity is opened at the same time. Those with a keener sense of the tastes and attitudes of others, and those with swifter access to relevant information, are in a position to foresee more accurately the set of market prices that will emerge on a particular day and will be able to profit by exploiting their superior knowledge.

All this suggests that in any real world where static assumptions are useful only as preliminary tools, the market will be characterized by continual agitation, a constant seething and absence of placidity. By focusing our attention on the data relevant for a particular day, we can understand the changes likely to be generated in the market purely by *these* data, and then we can proceed to examine the likely consequences upon individual market plans generated by the impact of a particular change in tastes or incomes. In this kind of analysis, the static analysis making up this chapter has its most fruitful applications.[16]

SUMMARY

Chapter 7 examines the market process as it would proceed in an economy where no production is possible. The process is based on the interplay of

---

16. In the Appendix dealing with multi-period planning, the reader will find (see pp. 335 ff) an outline of how the market process would work in a pure exchange economy when each of the participants is free to make decisions to transfer consumption from one period of time to later periods.

numerous individual *consumer* decisions (each consumer being naturally endowed with some bundle of commodities). The analysis of the market process in such a pure exchange economy will facilitate the analysis in later chapters of more complex and realistic models.

In the market each individual finds it necessary to *compete* with others. He is forced either as buyer or seller to offer opportunities to the market that are no less attractive than those made by others.

The competitive process can be most easily analyzed by reference to the market for a *single* commodity; by imagining what would occur *if knowledge were perfect,* it is possible to state immediately the conditions for equilibrium in such a market. The detailed analysis of why these conditions and no others can be consistent with equilibrium represents the basis for all further market analysis.

When the perfect-knowledge assumption is abandoned, further analysis shows how initial buying and selling decisions that fail to dovetail give rise to "disappointments" and thus lead to revised decisions that are gradually adjusted toward the equilibrium pattern.

Still further analysis extends the range of inquiry to the market process involving *numerous* consumer goods. This case is considerably more complicated than the preceding one. Nevertheless, once again the state of affairs that would result from universally perfect knowledge is shown to be the equilibrium situation for the multi-commodity market. Detailed analysis shows how the absence of perfect knowledge brings about "mistaken" decisions, and how the disappointments suffered as a consequence convey the information required for revisions of these decisions in the "right" direction.

By imagining cases where one or more of the commodities appear in the endowments of only *one* market participant, it is possible to analyze how the market process operates in the presence of *monopoly.* The analysis of the decisions of a monopolist in a world without production serves as an introduction to the more complicated monopoly cases to be considered later.

The analysis of a pure exchange economy clarifies why a market may be expected to be in constant agitation as a consequence of the acquisition of new knowledge. Moreover it becomes clear, in particular, how such agitation is set in motion by the activities of *entrepreneurs* who become aware, more swiftly than others, of the most advantageous opportunities available.

SUGGESTED READINGS

Böhm-Bawerk, E. v., *Capital and Interest*, Vol. 2, *Positive Theory of Capital*, Libertarian Press, South Holland, Illinois, 1959, Bk. 3, Part B, Chs. 2, 3.

Wicksteed, P. H., *Common Sense of Political Economy*, Routledge and Kegan Paul Ltd., London, 1933, pp. 493–526.

Wicksell, K., *Lectures on Political Economy*, Routledge and Kegan Paul Ltd., London, 1951, Vol. 1, Part 1.

APPENDIX

In this appendix a diagrammatic exposition is presented of the factors that determine the equilibrium price of a single non-producible commodity in a competitive market. This exposition will at the same time clarify the statement that price is determined by supply and demand.

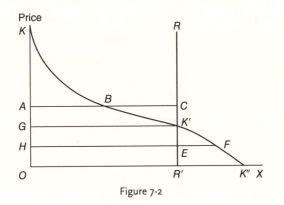

Figure 7-2

In Figure 7-2, the horizontal axis measures quantities of the commodity, while prices (whether bid or asked) are measured along the vertical axis. Since we deal with a non-producible commodity, a certain fixed quantity of it is owned (during each period of time) by market participants as a whole. (This quantity of the commodity, we assume, is endowed by nature to holders of it, during each period.) It is from this stock that any purchases must be made in a given period. The size of this stock of the commodity is represented in the diagram by the distance OR'. RR' is a vertical line erected on R'. The line $KK'K''$ is drawn so that the abscissa of any point on the line represents the quantity of the commodity that the *holders* of the commodity would like, in aggregate, to own, when the market price of the commodity is represented by the ordinate of the point. Thus, when the price of the commodity is OA, holders of it wish to keep for their own use, in aggregate, only the quantity AB. Since AB is less than AC (= OR'), which is the aggregate quantity that holders actually do own, it follows that at price *AB,* holders of the commodity seek to sell the quantity *BC* out of their holdings. At a lower price, *OG,* holders of the commodity do not wish (in aggregate) to sell any amount at all; they wish to keep their entire endowments for their own use. Should the price be lower yet, holders would attempt (vainly, of course) to *increase* their holdings by buying more. Thus at price *OH,* the owners of the commodity would be seeking to buy the additional aggregate quantity *EF* (*besides* the quantities of the commodity that *non*-holders might seek to buy). It is clear, then, that the segment *K'K"* (of the *KK'K"*) line represents (with *K'* being on the price axis) the (aggregate) demand curve for the commodity of the group of market participants who are naturally endowed with holdings of the commodity. (Similarly, it is clear, the horizontal distances between the *KK'* segment, and *RK',* represent the quantities of the commodity that will be supplied to the market, at various prices greater than *OG.*)

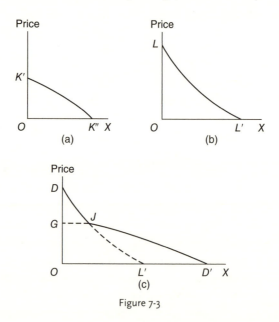

Figure 7-3

In Figure 7-3(a), the *K'K"* segment is drawn separately (with *K'* on the price axis). In Figure 7-3(b), the line *LL'* represents the demand curve for the commodity of all market participants who are *not* naturally endowed with quantities of it. Figure 7-3(c), shows the line *DD'* obtained by lateral summation of the *K'K"*, *LL'* lines. Any point on the line shows the aggregate quantity that will be purchased at a given price by the entire market.

It is clear that for prices higher than *OG*, the *DD′* line is identical with the *LL′* line (since we have seen that no holders of the commodity would wish to buy at prices higher than *OG*).

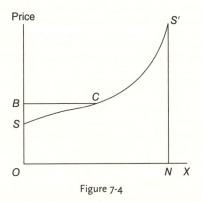

Figure 7-4

In Figure 7-4, the *SS′* line is the market supply curve for the commodity. This shows, for each possible price, the aggregate quantity that would be offered for sale by the initial commodity holders. It is clear that for any price (such as *OB*), the abscissa of the corresponding point on the supply curve (such as *C*) is identical with the horizontal distance between the *KK′* and *K′R* lines in Figure 7-2 (such as *BC*). (In fact it is obvious that the supply curve is derived from Figure 7-2 simply by reversing the *KK′* segment about the axis *K′R*. Keeping *K′* in its initial position in Figure 7-2, and transposing the *KK′* line until it lies symmetrically to the right of the *K′R* line, yields the line *SS′*. Thus, *OS* = *OG* = *R′K′*; *OR′* = *ON*; and *NS′* = *OK*.)

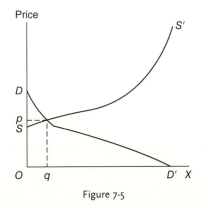

Figure 7-5

In Figure 7-5, the *DD′* line [from Figure 7-3(c)] has been superimposed upon the *SS′* line (of Figure 7-4). This is the typical supply-demand diagram. It demonstrates that the equilibrium market price will be p and that the quantity of commodity sold will be q, yielded by the intersection of the curves. A higher price would mean that sellers would be induced to offer a quantity greater than that which buyers wish to buy at the price; a lower price would mean that buyers would seek to buy a quantity greater than that which sellers are prepared to sell at the price.

It is unnecessary, in the case of the non-producible commodity that we are considering, to isolate the market supply curve (as was done in Figures 7-4 and 7-5). Since the SS' line was derived, as we have seen, directly from Figure 7-2, it is clear that market "supply" is nothing else but an indirect reflection of the strength (or weakness) of the *demand* for the commodity by its initial holders (as seen in the line $KK'K''$ in Figure 7-2). This can be seen very clearly by considering Figure 7-6. In this figure the line TT' is obtained by the lateral summation of the line $KK'K''$ (from Figure 7-2), and the line LL' [from Figure 7-3(b)]. This line is *not* the market demand curve. This line represents, for each price, the aggregate quantity of the commodity that the market would like to *own* at that price. (This quantity thus includes some quantities of the commodity that the initial holders of it do, in fact, already own.) By erecting the ordinate $R'P$ on R' (where OR', as in Figure 7-2, represents the entire endowment of the commodity), it can be shown that equilibrium market price must be $R'P$. At any price below $R'P$, the market as a whole would be seeking to acquire or to retain an aggregate amount greater than is in existence. Competition would drive prices higher. On the other hand, at any price greater than $R'P$, the market would seek to hold in aggregate a quantity falling short of the natural endowment. The competition of unwilling commodity holders would drive the price down.

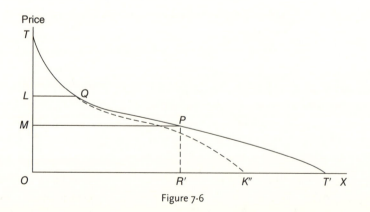

Figure 7-6

It can be shown easily that the result obtained in Figure 7-6 is identical with that obtained by isolating supply from demand, as in Figure 7-5. The abscissa of a point on the TT' line is the sum of the abscissas of the corresponding points on the $KK'K''$ line and the LL' line. The first of these latter two abscissas is equal to the distance OR' minus the horizontal distance between the point and the RR' line (for prices above OG). For the price at which the abscissa of the point on the TT' line is equal to OR' (as at P in Figure 7-6), therefore, it follows that the abscissa of the corresponding point on the LL' line equals the horizontal distance between the KK' line and the RK' line. But this latter distance is equal to the abscissa of the corresponding point on the SS' line (for all prices above OG); while the former distance is equal to the abscissa of the corresponding point on the DD' line (for prices above OG). Thus, the price the TT' line intersects the $R'P$ line at (in Figure 7-6) is the same price the DD' and SS' lines intersect at (in Figure 7-5). (The proof is formally valid also for prices below OG, but at such prices no exchange at all would ensue, since no quantities at all of the commodity would be supplied by holders of it at such prices.)

Figure 7-6 (as compared with Figure 7-5) emphasizes the supremacy of demand considerations in the determination of the price of a nonproducible good. Price is determined by the strength of the demand for the commodity; the demand of those who already hold some of it, and the demand of those who hold none of it. On the other hand, the diagrams leading up to Figure 7-5 demonstrate also the *quantity* of the commodity that will be bought at the market price, depending on the initial distribution of holdings. Figure 7-6 emphasizes, then, that the initial distribution of holdings, while it affects the equilibrium quantity sold, can in no way affect the equilibrium market price (with a given demand situation).[17]

The line TT' can be considered as ranking the degrees of eagerness with which *all* market participants desire to hold successive single units of the commodity. (In this ranking, therefore, are merged both the "sellers' list" and the "buyers' list" referred to in the text of this chapter.) When the unit is reached that exhausts the entire endowment of the commodity, market price is represented directly by the eagerness to hold this unit of the market participant involved (that is, the market participant who is more eager to own this unit—in terms of his readiness to pay higher

---

17. For further discussion of this point, and of other matters discussed in this appendix, see Wicksteed, P., *Common Sense of Political Economy*, Routledge and Kegan Paul Ltd., London, Bk. 2, Ch. 4.

prices for it or to forgo the opportunity to sell it for higher prices—than is anyone else). All the *more* eager owners (or would-be owners) enjoy a consumer's surplus to the extent that they need sacrifice, for a unit of the commodity, only the amount that the marginal consumer of the commodity is prepared to sacrifice (instead of the higher sums that they themselves would be prepared to sacrifice, if this were necessary).

Finally we may notice the special case where the $KK'K''$ line (of Figure 7-2) is a vertical line at the origin (and thus coinciding with the price axis). This case corresponds to the situation where those holding the commodity initially have *no* desire to own any of it, no matter how low the price. The SS' line corresponding to such a situation is, of course, also a vertical straight line erected at a distance OR' from the price-axis (since the quantity supplied at a given price is the horizontal distance from the $KK'K''$ line at that price to the RR' line, and this distance is now the same for all prices, the distance OR'). Demand in this case is dependent entirely on the demand of the non-holders. Supply is completely inelastic. With a given aggregate commodity endowment, market price will depend entirely on the strength of the demand of non-holders; supply will be completely passive in this respect. The standard example of this kind of situation is that of a market for perishable fish caught by fishermen. Ignoring the demand of the fishermen for fish as food for their own families, it is clear that the entire catch will be thrown on the market for whatever it can bring. With given demand strength, price will depend on the quantity endowed (that is, the size of the catch); with a given sized catch, price will depend solely on the strength of demand for fish on the part of the public. This situation is illustrated in Figure 7-7. Here SS' is a vertical line; market price will depend only on (a) the shape and position of the DD' line, and (b) on the distance OS.

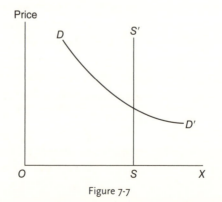

Figure 7-7

8 PRODUCTION THEORY

Thus far, our analysis of individual economic activity and of the interaction in the market of the economic activity of numerous individuals has been confined to a world where no production was considered possible. The market process we were able to analyze was a process where all participants participated directly as consumers. Our principal purpose in this book, however, is to analyze a market process where the wants of participants in their role of consumers may be met not only through exchange but also by acts of *production* from resources. In the pure exchange economy of the preceding chapter, a participant could improve his position (from that he finds himself placed in by natural endowment at the start of each day) only through acts of exchange. In the full market process, which we wish to investigate, a participant may improve his position not only by direct exchange of endowed consumer good for endowed consumer good but also by acts of production and of exchanges of resources and products for the resources and products of others.

In this and the following chapter we take up the analysis of the activity of the individual participant in his role of *producer*. In Chapters 10 and 11 we will examine the market process forged out of the interactions of numerous individuals acting in their capacities of resource owner, producer, and consumer. The economic analysis of production affects the analysis of the market process, of course, through the supply side. In this chapter and the next we inquire into the way the quantity of product that will be offered to the market at a given product price depends upon the pattern of production costs. In this chapter we lay the groundwork by setting up the problem of production in its proper *economic* framework, indicating the kinds of alternatives a would-be producer is free to choose among, and showing especially how this range of alternatives is circumscribed by what we will discover to be the *Laws of Variable Proportions*. In Chapter 9 we will proceed to show how the principles of production theory, developed in the present chapter, can be applied to the analysis of production costs and upon the way these costs affect supply.

THE ECONOMIC ASPECT OF PRODUCTION

The economist examines production from a very special point of view. From a purely physical perspective, of course, production is simply the process where quantities of raw materials and labor are transformed into quantities of product, the quantities being rigidly determined by the laws of physical science. For the technologist the interest lies wholly in these physical laws, describing the various results that can be expected to follow on different patterns of resource combination.

The economist's perspective on production, however, is a quite different one. Production is a process not of physical nature but of human action. In seeking to improve their positions, men find it worthwhile to act as producers as well as consumers. As consumers they act to spend their incomes on the goods and services they consider most important. In exactly the same way they may seek to improve their positions by *producing* goods and services—either those they consider most important for themselves or those that can be sold to command the goods they consider most important. The very same categories, such as purpose, means, ends, and cost, which make possible the analysis of consumer demand, reappear unchanged in connection with the actions of men engaged in production. And the economist analyzes production with *these* categories making up the focus of his attention, rather than the physical laws within whose framework productive activity is carried on.

The essence of the economist's outlook is thus that he sees the producer as a man *making choices among alternatives* of a certain order of complexity. By considering the range of possible alternatives, the economist is able to analyze the way these choices are made and the way action will change in response to changes in the range of alternatives that choice is made from.

PRODUCTION BY THE ISOLATED INDIVIDUAL

Production would take place of course, even in the absence of a market. Robinson Crusoe and his production plans are accorded frequent attention in economic treatises. An isolated individual finds himself with a severely limited stock of goods ready for immediate consumption. These may not be sufficient to satisfy even his immediate subsistence needs and fall very short of satisfying all his "wants." On the other hand, he finds himself in command of productive resources of certain kinds and in certain quantities. He himself is capable of supplying labor power—for a more or less definite number of hours per day and possibly capable of being applied in a number of directions requiring special skills and aptitudes. He has possibly at his disposal raw materials of various kinds, as well as perhaps a number of tools, or, at any rate, natural objects capable of being used, with or without alteration, as rough implements. He finds himself, finally, subject to rigid physical laws that determine quite precisely the outcomes of different ways resources are combined. These are the data.

With these data at his disposal, the isolated individual recognizes that he is faced with choice among rather definite alternative situations. It is a physical law that a plot of land, a quantity of seed, a number of implements, and a good deal of labor can yield a crop of grain. This *fact* is translated by man as constituting *an opportunity;* the discovery of this fact means the recognition of one alternative open to him, if he sees fit to adopt it. The individual, however, will be aware that the data afford other opportunities as well. He may see himself capable of building a house, planting a vegetable garden, or catching fish or game. Finally, he is certainly aware of the opportunity, through leisure, to avoid expending labor altogether, and thus to leave untapped also the other resources—except insofar as they can be used for direct enjoyment such as sunning oneself on the plot of land. Of course, *ignorance* on the part of the individual may blind him to a number of possible opportunities that the data of his situation actually make feasible. He may not know his own skills, he may not know the full capabilities of the soil, raw materials, and implements at his disposal. He may be ignorant of the techniques by which his resources can be most successfully exploited. But the opportunities he is ignorant of simply do not enter into the range of alternatives he recognizes his power to choose from, and in no way affect his actions (except, of course, insofar as he may *believe* there are opportunities he is ignorant of and for whose discovery he is prepared to forgo other already known alternatives).

Even the *known* alternative courses of action the individual "producer" is able to choose from, it must be further noticed, are by no means *certain* in their outcomes. The physical laws the farmer knows and on the basis of which he plants his crops, tell him also that unfavorable weather can drastically alter the results of his activities. And the farmer can know little of weather conditions months in the future. To some extent, in fact, *every* course of activity open to him leaves some range of uncertainty concerning the outcome.

Thus, when the isolated individual has finally ploughed his field; sown, grown, and reaped a crop of wheat; the productive process constitutes in retrospect an example of human action capable of analysis from the economic point of view. In producing his crop of wheat the farmer has made and carried out a chain of *decisions*. (a) He decided to put his resources to productive use rather than leave them unused, or used only for leisure purposes. (b) He decided to grow wheat rather than produce another type of product, and to grow wheat rather than any other crop. (c) He decided on the method of production that he used, what tools to use, what kind of ploughing and planting methods to employ, how to irrigate, and so on. (d) He decided on the *size* of crop to raise; that is, he decided on the quantity of his total supply of resources to apply to this one branch of production.

These decisions meant choice among alternatives. They meant the rejection of other alternatives in favor of those adopted. In order to obtain his wheat the farmer sacrificed possible leisure; he sacrificed those other goods whose production would have been possible with the resources actually devoted to wheat; he rejected alternative methods of raising wheat, alternatively proportioned combinations of the resources, and alternatively proportioned allocation of the resources between wheat and other uses. To the isolated individual *these rejected and sacrificed alternatives* are his *costs of production*. The production of wheat cost him leisure; it cost him a possible tobacco crop, corn crop, a house, or anything that could have been produced with any other disposition of the resources that the farmer devoted to wheat.

The decision to incur these costs, of course, was simply the decision to produce wheat rather than any of these other goods with any other methods. Its basis was the *preference* of the producer for what he could obtain from his resources when devoted to wheat (in the way they *were* devoted), over what he believed he could obtain from these resources on any other disposition. This preference, of course, was completely subjective; it expressed his taste for wheat as compared with other goods and other crops; it expressed his relative degree of confidence in his success as a wheat grower in the face of the inevitable uncertainties, as compared with his assessment of the uncertainties in the other kinds and methods of production; and throughout, this preference expressed his subjective beliefs as to the objective efficacy of the different ways of using resources, these beliefs being based perhaps on supposed scientific knowledge, religious convictions, or reliance on magic. One of the main differences between such "preference" for the production of wheat (with a specific method of production), on the one hand, and "preference" as it appears in direct consumer behavior, on the other hand, lies merely in the complexity of the operating influences expressed in the former. While it is true that production yields a product that is *measurable* and thus differs radically from the utility that is involved in the analysis of demand, nevertheless these subjective factors, especially when an obtainable product is considered *ex ante,* go far to maintain the essential homogeneity of human action in both consumption and production.

Whether or not the costs conceived in this sense of forgone alternatives were justified in retrospect depends on a number of factors. Looking back at this use of his resources, the producer may *regret* his decisions. He may have discovered that the alternatives he chose among were not quite as he had imagined them to be. Perhaps the soil was less fertile than imagined; perhaps he discovered himself to dislike agricultural labor more than he had thought; perhaps events proved him overoptimistic to the uncertain factors in farming, and perhaps overpessimistic to the uncertainties in other kinds of production; perhaps experience showed him mistaken in the supposed scientific or other knowledge on whose basis he assessed the outcomes of different productive efforts. And, of course, during the wheat production, the farmer's tastes may have changed so that he no longer prefers wheat over, say, vegetables. Under these circumstances, the producer's product proves to be worth less than it cost to produce—he has incurred a "loss." In other words, the producer thinks he made the "wrong" decisions; one or more of the rejected alternatives has proved preferable to the one adopted.

But, of course, it may well be that the producer is highly satisfied with his course of actions. Events may have proven his choice among alternatives an eminently wise one. The costs in this case are considered well expended—the producer has "profited" by his actions. All this means is that the wheat produced is still preferred over the goods that might have been produced with the same resources.

Looked at in this way, it is not difficult to understand how production decisions depend on the data of the situation and to envisage the alterations in the production pattern of the individual that would be the consequence of changes in these data. The same isolated individual might engage in a different kind of production if the available alternatives were different, or if his subjective tastes or his way of gauging future uncertainties were different. If the available resources were different in kind, relative quantities, or quality, the individual would find the opportunities he could choose among rather different. The discovery of a new tract of fertile land, the discovery of new techniques—even the discovery, through bitter experience, of the mistakes made in the past use of the *same* resources— will alter the range of alternatives and may well bring about different production patterns.

The analysis of the productive activity of the isolated individual could be carried much further. But our principal interest is in the theory of production as it is carried on in the market economy. The case of Crusoe production was merely an introduction to the more complex kind of production decisions performed under the guiding pressure of market forces. And we shall find that the more detailed analysis of production for the market covers the activities of the autarkic producer as well.

PRODUCTION IN SOCIETY

It is possible to imagine a society where all production would be carried on without a market. Such would be a society of self-sufficient farmers each growing his own food, making his own clothes, and providing for all his other wants to the best of his own unaided ability. Resources would be neither bought nor sold; each autarkic producer would use only his own resources. Products would be neither bought nor sold; each household would enjoy only the fruits of its own productive efforts. For the purposes of economic analysis, such a society would be simply a congregation of isolated islanders.

Our analysis of demand has already shown that a society without exchange is extremely unlikely. The discrepancies between the scales of value of the different householders are likely to generate situations where exchange of consumer goods between numerous pairs of householders are mutually profitable. Where the individuals are engaged in production, the scope for such profitable exchanges becomes greatly widened. This occurs because the resources at the command of different individuals are likely to be different. In the first place, this will generate exchange of *resources* to some extent; and in the second place (especially where pronounced differences in resources cannot be diminished through direct exchange—for example, special labor skills), this will generate a continual recurrence of situations where the *products* of different individuals, each produced with resources relatively unavailable to the other producers, can be profitably exchanged against one another.

This fosters the further development of the phenomenon of *division of labor*—a social process that takes advantage of the intransferable special resources at the disposal of individual members of society and forges out of them the social organization of production through exchanges in the marketplace. It is unnecessary to expand here on the advantages of division of labor.[1] It is sufficient to notice that the process of division of labor feeds on itself, continually making possible further gains for individuals

---

1. The classic statement of the advantages of division of labor is Smith, Adam, *The Wealth of Nations*, Bk. 1, Ch. 1; see also Mises, L. v., *Human Action*, Yale University Press, New Haven, Connecticut, 1949, pp. 157–164.

by progressively wider and more intricate division of labor. The economic history of modern society consists chiefly in such a progressive widening of the range of specialization and exchange.

Production in a society based on division of labor, specialization, and exchange is carried on with almost complete responsiveness to the pressure of market forces. Individuals produce primarily for sale on the market; they produce largely with resources bought in the market. The production decisions are thus made on the basis of alternatives and *opportunities rigidly determined by market prices,* in addition to the framework of purely physical laws production is carried on within. This chapter is principally concerned with production as it is carried on within the market economy, to which we now turn.

PRODUCTION IN THE MARKET ECONOMY

Production decisions in a market economy are made by *entrepreneurs.* Entrepreneurs take the initiative in undertaking productive activity in conjunction with the market, buying and combining the productive resources to obtain the product, and selling the product on the market. The essential element in the entrepreneurial role is, for the economist, that the entrepreneur undertakes ventures whose outcome is uncertain. This speculative element is present, to be sure, in *all* human action, since action being necessarily involved in the flow of time is always directed at some moment in the future—and hence is always undertaken in the face of uncertainty. Nevertheless, in economic analysis we distinguish, in every act of buying or selling, between this "entrepreneurial" element on the one hand, and the act of buying or selling seen as if it could be carried on with uncertainty absent. In production within the framework of a market society, the decisions to produce are *essentially* entrepreneurial. All the resources required for the emergence of the product can be bought in the market; the entrepreneur in actually buying them—and thus allowing the product to emerge—has made his decisions to pay prices for the resources completely on the basis of his appraisal of the future value of the product to him in the market. In this sense decisions to produce are purely speculative: they involve the present purchase of resources (that is, the purchase of the "product" in the form necessary to physically produce it) in the hope of being able to resell them (that is, to sell the "resources" in the form of the finished product) at a higher price in the future.

The direct motive for production in the market economy is thus the profit motive in its simplest sense. Under the impulse of this motive the entrepreneur makes his choices among the alternatives the market offers to him. The *range* of these alternatives depends on the extent of the market and on the degree of specialization already attained. In a highly developed market economy an entrepreneur must choose from innumerable possibilities; he can choose to produce any of innumerable kinds of goods and services—the necessary resources can be obtained somewhere at a price; and he can choose to produce any one particular good by any one of the possibly numerous methods technologically conceivable for the purpose.

Very few of these alternatives, however, promise to be profitable. An entrepreneur might produce air in a laboratory—but this product would fetch nothing in the market. He might produce shoes by hiring labor to make them by hand and be able to sell them for a price—but would probably be unable to recoup his costs. To win profits the entrepreneur must seek to produce a good, the resources for whose production can be bought for a sum less than the sum likely to be obtainable from the product's sale. The entrepreneur scans the available alternatives in order to seek those offering the *greatest* difference between these two sums.

Specifically, the entrepreneur must decide (a) *what good* to produce; (b) *what quantity*, per unit of time, to produce of this product; and (c) *what method* of production to employ. Included in these basic decisions, of course, are decisions where to buy resources, where to sell the product, what quality of resources to use, and so on. The market presents the possibilities; quantities of given resources can be bought for given prices and quantities of given product can be expected to be sold for given prices. Technical facts determine the quantities of product obtainable from given resource combinations. The entrepreneur, at any given moment, seeks the one opportunity he believes to be most profitable.

Once an entrepreneur has embarked upon a productive venture, he frequently finds that his choices as to production in later periods of time are to a considerable extent decisively influenced by his past activities. A man who has been a shoe producer for some years may have gained so thorough a knowledge of this line that continuation in it seems for this reason alone the most profitable available productive enterprise. A man may have in the past purchased equipment for the production of a certain commodity, and the continued availability to him of this equipment makes the production of this commodity the most profitable available undertaking in subsequent periods. This frequently tends to make individual entrepreneurs identify themselves with the production of definite commodities or services. Thus, the decision an entrepreneur must make as to *what* to produce frequently does not have to be explicitly made at all; it is only at fairly wide intervals that this question demands even casual attention.

This is the reason why a good deal of the analysis of production in the market economy centers around the *theory of the firm*. The firm is an entrepreneurial unit committed to some degree to the production of a specific output. The theory of the firm involves principally its decisions as to the level of its output and the particular resource combination to employ. It must never be forgotten, however, that entrepreneurs are as completely under the discipline of the market with respect to the product that they produce as with all aspects of their productive activities. Entrepreneurs constantly experiment with new products, diversify their output, close down plants, and switch to other products under the pressure of market prices. The decision of a firm to continue with an established line of products means that this line promises greater profits than other lines of product. It is of the essence of the market process that the pattern of production changes in response to changes in the basic data, namely, the resources available to the economy and the wishes of the consumer. Both kinds of change will exert a decisive influence on the type of product that an entrepreneur will be producing at different periods of time.

FACTORS OF PRODUCTION

In order to produce products the entrepreneur must buy resources. Resources sufficient for the production of a given product are known as the *factors of production*. A factor of production (also termed an *input*) may be a commodity, such as a raw material; or a service, such as a type of skilled or unskilled labor; or a piece of information, such as the knowledge of a technical formula. It is obvious that there are innumerable such factors, different kinds of raw materials, different kinds of tools and equipment, different kinds of labor services, and so on. At one time economists considered it expedient to group factors into three broad classes: *land, labor,* and *capital*. Capital was the produced "factor," the class of resources that had been produced, in turn, through the combination of other resources. Land and labor were the "original" factors, "labor" including all services provided directly by human beings and "land" covering all other nature-given objects and services that could be used for production.

This classification was adopted on the belief that different economic laws governed the returns earned in the market by each of these classes. This belief is no longer held by modern economists so that this classification, while it provides a grouping useful enough for a number of purposes, is no longer considered as expressing a distinction of any fundamental *economic* significance. The laws governing the prices of productive factors are common to them all.

Nevertheless, it is economically significant to distinguish some important characteristics attached to some groups of factors that play a role in the determination of the actions of producers, with respect to both these and other factors. Such characteristics, for example, are the *substitutability* and *complementarity* of factors. We have already met these categories in the theory of demand. The fact that a productive process, unlike an act of consumer choice, yields a *measurable* result makes it possible to formulate the categories, in the case of productive factors, in a somewhat different way. A given quantity of factor *A* is a *substitute* for a given quantity of a factor *B* when, in a process of production that utilizes factor *B,* the outcome expected of the process is unchanged with the replacement of the given quantity of factor *B* by the given quantity of factor *A*. If the conditions under which the quantities of the two factors could be obtained were completely similar, then an entrepreneur would have no reason to prefer the one quantity of factor over the other. It may be immaterial, for example, to the owner of a factory whether its walls are painted grey or green. Grey and green paint are to this extent substitutes.

Perfect substitutability would mean that under *all* circumstances a given quantity of factor *B* is a substitute for a given quantity of factor *A*. No matter what the purpose is, no matter how much of factor *A* or factor *B* is already being used, a replacement of the quantity of the one factor by that of the other leaves the expected outcome unchanged. It is noticed that if two goods or services were discovered to be perfect substitutes for one another in production in this way, then we would consider them, from the economic point of view, as constituting a *single* factor of production. Economic goods, whether those of lowest order (consumer goods) or of higher order (factors of production) are considered as units of the same good not on the basis of physical homogeneity but on the basis of *economic* homogeneity. Units of a physically homogeneous group are considered the "same good" because there is no reason to prefer one unit over any other. If there is no reason to prefer, for any purpose, a unit of one good over a fixed number of units of a physically different good, then, economically speaking, a unit of the first good, and the fixed number of units of the second good, are both units of the same good, even though there may be physical differences between them.

The concept of substitutability thus provides the basis for distinguishing between factors. *A single factor consists of all goods or services that are perfect substitutes for one another.* A factor A is not the same as a different factor B, if the two are not perfect substitutes for one another. Thus, while for some purposes grey and green paint are substitutes for one another, nevertheless they are two distinct factors of production since there are numerous purposes for which only the one or the other will do. Substitution between different factors, we will discover, plays an important role in the decisions made by the entrepreneur.

Complementarity in the case of factors of production is very similar to complementarity in the case of consumer goods. Factor B is complementary to factor A if a given increase in the employment of A (other things remaining unchanged) yields an increment of output that is greater when a larger quantity of factor B cooperates in the process than when a smaller quantity of B is in use. Production invariably requires the cooperation of a number of factors. Raw material without labor can yield no product. Labor without materials and equipment yields no product. Even a singer requires a hall or a stage to produce his product. One factor by itself cannot produce. It requires the cooperation of complementary factors of production. A given factor for the production of a certain product may require the cooperation of a complementary factor which has no close substitutes. In order to produce a typed letter a secretary can do nothing without a typewriter. Or merely the cooperation is required of any one of a group of factors that are to some extent substitutes for each other. In either case, as we will see, the quantity of a factor an entrepreneur will buy depends in part on the price and availability of the factors complementary to it. The typical situation with a productive process is that a group of complementary factors is required between which, however, a degree of substitutability exists. This will be discussed later in this chapter.

Another category relating to factors that must be discussed is *specificity*. A resource is a factor *specific* to the production of a certain product when there is no other product it can be a factor for. The resource is either employed in the production of one particular product, or it must remain unemployed. A spare part designed to fit a machine of a particular make might be mentioned as a possible example of a specific factor; it is likely to be useless for any other purpose. It is extremely difficult, however, to give a good example of a completely specific factor. Specificity must be considered as the limiting case in a spectrum that ranks factors according to their *versatility*. A factor that is non-specific is to some degree versatile—it is useful for more than one productive purpose. Although it is difficult to locate examples of perfectly specific factors, it is not at all a difficult task to find factors with extremely low versatility. Such factors are considered as *specialized* for the production of one or more products. From the point of view of the entrepreneur, it is far more productive in these productive processes than in any others. An intricate machine may be "specialized" because its use as scrap is far less productive than the use it was designed for.

The specific or specialized character of a factor plays an important part in decisions concerning the disposition of resources in production. In the case of the isolated individual as a producer, use of a factor in a production process for which it is specific involves no opportunity cost. The product that he obtains by the use of the factor in its particular use is not offset by the loss of any product that he could have obtained by employing it in any other way. He will tend to use this factor rather than its substitutes, wherever these substitutes have alternative uses. In a market economy the entrepreneur of a firm in an industry where a factor is specific, however, cannot expect to obtain the factor without cost. Although the factor will not be sought by any other industry, nevertheless, other firms in the same industry will be competing for it thus forcing up its price. The factor specific to a certain *industry* will hardly be specific to a particular *firm* within the industry. From the point of view of the owner of the resource, however, the price he receives for its allocation to any one firm in the industry is greater than the minimum necessary to persuade him to allow it to be used in the industry. This is so since he can obtain nothing by selling it to a firm in any other industry. It follows that anything causing the income to the owner of a specific factor to fall (for example, a special tax on the income from this resource) will have no effect (at any rate in the short run) on production.

Entrepreneurial decision making concerning the purchase of factors will be influenced considerably by the institutional circumstances defining the length of time the commitment is to be made for. A man buying a machine makes a decision relevant not only to the immediate production period but to periods in the future as well. On the other hand, when a firm rents a machine (on a short-term lease), the decision to purchase the machine's services may be reviewed at fairly frequent intervals. Labor services are usually bought on a short-term basis, but if labor could be bought only through long-term contracts (or if one could buy labor only through buying a slave) then here too the decision would have overriding influence on future production periods. When making a long-term factor purchase of this kind, the entrepreneur, besides engaging in current production, is *investing* resources for the sake of *future* production and profits. While it is true that *some* element of investment is present in all productive activities, nevertheless, in a first analysis of production theory the complications introduced by these investment components are often conveniently ignored. There is considerable justification for initially abstracting from the existence of time differences between the purchase of factors of production and the sale of the product. For most of the remainder of this chapter we will consider production from the point of view of this simplification. We must of course not allow this simplification to obscure the essentially speculative character of production. But it will enable us to abstract provisionally from the complications introduced by the once-for-all purchase of factors that will yield productive services over a period of time. These are principally (a) the complication that current decision making is powerfully influenced by past decisions on such purchases, and (b) the complications introduced into an entrepreneur's decision making for current production, by the fact that a part of the price he pays for factors needed for such current production may only be recouped by the production yielded by these factors in future periods of time.[2]

PRODUCTION FUNCTIONS AND ISOQUANTS

Much of what has been discussed thus far in this chapter can be summarized and formalized with the aid of the concept of the *production function*. In mathematics a function is the expression of the precise relationship existing between a number of variables, where the value of one of the variables depends on the value of the others. The production function formalizes the relationship between the quantity of output yielded by a productive process, and the quantities of the various inputs used in that process. Thus a single typed letter is produced by combining some minutes of secretarial services, a sheet of paper, the use of a typewriter for some minutes, and so on. Algebraically a production function may be written $x = f(a_1, a_2, a_3, \ldots, a_n)$. The equation reports that the quantity x, of the product X, that is produced, depends on the quantities $a_1, a_2, a_3, \ldots,$ a_n (of the inputs $A_1, A_2, A_3, \ldots, A_n$, respectively) employed in the productive process. The factors, for which the quantities are not zero, are the complementary factors for the production of X. If the quantity of any of

---

2. In the Appendix on multi-period planning (see pp. 340 ff) some explicit attention is paid to the *time-consuming* aspect of all production.

the a's in the production function has a constant value, for a given value of x, in all possible methods of production, then the factor concerned has no substitutes. As a rule, however, it will be the case that for a given quantity x, the a quantities are variables, denoting a degree of substitutability between the A's.

For the analysis of production it is frequently convenient to visualize the available alternatives with the aid of graphical methods. In this regard the production function is of particular use. The limitations of three-dimensional space make it necessary to limit the exposition to a production function involving only two variable productive factors, but the insights thus obtained can be intuitively extended to more complex processes.

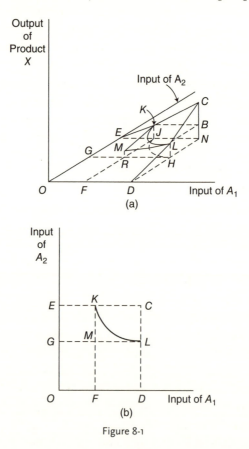

Figure 8-1

In the diagram [Figure 8-1(a)] the two horizontal axes refer respectively to the quantities used (per unit of time) of two factors, A_1, A_2, and the vertical axis refers to the quantity of output of the product X that is produced by the factors (during the given time period). A point in the space (such as the point C) relates a quantity of the factor A_1 (such as the quantity OD) and a quantity of the factor A_2 (such as the quantity OE), with a quantity (CN) of the product X. If the relationship associated with such a point is technically feasible, then the point is said to be on the *production surface*. The production surface (of which $ODCE$ in the diagram is an arbitrarily cut portion) represents the outputs possible with all conceivable combinations of the two factors.[3] The line KL is drawn on the production surface so that all points on the line are the same vertical distance from the horizontal plane passing through the origin. The line KL thus indicates all the different ways of combining factors A_1, A_2, that will produce a given quantity of output. Thus, for example, in the diagram the output LH can be produced either by using the quantity OD of A_1 together with the quantity OG of A_2, or by using the quantity OF of A_1 together with OE of A_2, or by using any of the other combinations corresponding to points on the line KL.

The situation set forth in Figure 8-1(a) can be conveniently further analyzed by means of a number of separate two-dimensional diagrams. Thus Figure 8-1(b) shows a projection of the production surface onto the horizontal plane passing through the origin—a "map" of the surface. The line KL appears here as a "contour line" on the production surface, representing points of equal "altitude." Such a line is termed an *isoquant*. For any production surface there will be any number of such isoquants, one for each possible output level. The coordinates of any point on this line represent for the entrepreneur one of the alternative "packages" of inputs that he may be able to buy in order to produce a given output.

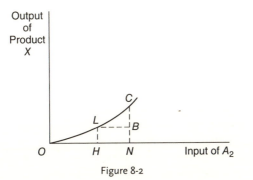

Figure 8-2

3. The notion of a *surface* presupposes continuity in the production function. This implies divisibility of the inputs and outputs. Production theory, while simplified by such assumptions, does not depend on them for the validity of its general theorems.

In Figure 8-2 the diagram shows a vertical section of the production surface parallel to the XA_2 plane through the point C (or better, it can be considered as the projection of this section onto the XA_2 plane so that O is at the origin). The curve thus represents the quantities of product that can be obtained by employing alternative quantities of one factor, A_2, in combination with a fixed quantity (OD) of the other factor, A_1. Thus (always keeping this quantity of A_1 unchanged), the employment of OH of factor A_2 yields HL of output, and the employment of the quantity ON yields NC. The increment of factor A_2, in the quantity HN, thus yields an additional output of BC (other things, especially the quantity of factor A_1, remaining unchanged). The quantity BC is termed the *marginal increment of product* corresponding to the input increment HN.[4] This quantity, as we shall see, has considerable significance for entrepreneurial decision making. An entrepreneur is always faced with the alternative of purchasing an *additional quantity of a particular factor.* To assess the attractiveness of any such alternative, it is first necessary for the entrepreneur to judge what difference *this* increment of factor will make to output. This difference is the marginal increment of product generated by the additional quantity of factor.

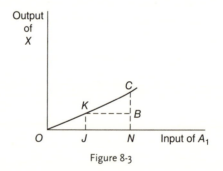

Figure 8-3

4. For continuous total product curves (such as in Figure 8-2), the *slope* of the curve at any point (such as at C) measures the *rate* output increases at with increasing input (of A_2) when the input level is shown, by the abscissa of the point (such as the quantity ON). In the literature this rate of output increase is known as the *marginal product* of A_2 (when it is employed in volume ON). The notion of a marginal increment of product corresponding to specific increments of input, used in the text, does not require the postulation of perfectly divisible inputs or outputs. The marginal increment of product has the dimensions of products; marginal product has the dimensions of product per unit of input. For small input increments, marginal increment of product is thus approximately equal to marginal product times the increment in input.

In Figure 8-3 an analogous diagram is drawn to show the alternative outputs that can be produced with different quantities of input of the factor A_1, the quantity of factor A_2, this time, being held unchanged at OE. The curve OC is thus the projection, onto the XA_1 plane, of the vertical section through the production surface at C parallel to this plane. The quantity BC is the marginal increment of output associated with the input increment JN of factor A_1.

At any point on the production surface, the relationships between the marginal increments of output corresponding to the various variable factors spell out the alternatives open to the entrepreneur. As we shall see the first question asked by an entrepreneur concerning a given process of production is whether it is the cheapest method of producing the given quantity of output. This is the question of whether the process, corresponding to a point on the production surface, is cheaper than any other point on the same isoquant. This question resolves itself into two components. The one component asks which other physical combinations of factors are able to yield the same output; the second component concerns the money costs of these different input combinations. Leaving aside the latter problem at this stage, it is clear that the first part of the question asks about the various additional quantities of, say, factor A_1 required to keep the level of output unchanged when various quantities of the other factor, A_2, are withdrawn from the productive process.

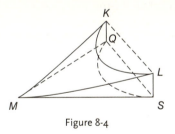

Figure 8-4

The relationships can be visualized with the aid of Figure 8-4. Here MKL is an (enlarged) portion of the production surface bounded by (a) the solid line KL, a small portion of an isoquant line; (b) KM, the line of intersection of the production surface through K by a vertical plane perpendicular to one of the factor axes, say, A_1 (so that the line MQ is horizontal, and is indicating increasing input of A_2, toward Q); and (c) LM, the line of intersection of the production surface through L by a vertical plane perpendicular to the other factor axis (so that the line MS is horizontal, perpendicular to MQ, and is indicating increasing input of A_1 toward S). The curved line QS is the projection of the isoquant segment KL onto the horizontal plane through M. To an entrepreneur weighing a productive process corresponding to the point K, the answer to the question considered in the previous paragraph, insofar as it concerns the possibility of point L, is that in order to offset a loss of the quantity MQ of input of factor A_2, it is necessary to expand the input of A_1 by the increment MS. An entrepreneur producing the quantity of output shown by the point K can maintain the same level of output by withdrawing MQ of factor A_2 and adding MS of factor A_1. The relation between MQ and MS thus measures the *rate at which factors can be substituted for one another at the margin*. From the diagram it is clear that the required relationship between the increments of factor MQ and MS is defined by the condition that each is associated with the same marginal increment of product (in our case shown as being the quantity KQ, equal to LS). If one unit of factor A_1 has a higher marginal increment of product (at the relevant margin) than one unit of factor A_2, then the increment of A_2 required to offset the withdrawal of a unit of A_1 will of course have to be larger than one unit.

THE SHAPE OF THE ISOQUANT AND THE SUBSTITUTABILITY OF FACTORS

Thus, the shape of the isoquants is the graphical expression of the degree of substitutability between the two factors used in production. The slope of a straight line drawn connecting two points on an isoquant measures the degree of substitutability over this range. Thus, if in Figure 8-4 the straight line KL had been drawn, its slope with respect to the A_2 axis (like the slope of the straight line QS) would be MS/MQ, showing the quantity of the one factor required to offset a withdrawal of a given quantity of the other. The steeper the slope of KL, the greater would be MS in relation to MQ, showing that A_1 would be less good a substitute for A_2 at the margin. For a continuous isoquant line, with the points drawn closer and closer together, the slope of the line joining them becomes very nearly the slope of the isoquant itself at a point. This slope measures the *marginal rate of substitution* of factor A_1 for the factor A_2; that is, the increment of factor A_1 necessary to keep output level unchanged when a small reduction is made in the employment of factor A_2.[5]

---

5. For a continuous isoquant line, this marginal rate of substitution of A_1 for A_2 is then mathematically equal to the ratio of the marginal product of A_2 to that of A_1.

The importance of the slope of the isoquants in this regard can be spotlighted by contemplating two extreme theoretical situations, one where no substitution at all is possible between the factors, the second where the factors are perfect substitutes for one another (so that there is no economic justification for distinguishing between them).

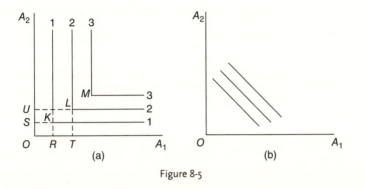

Figure 8-5

In Figure 8-5(a) isoquants are drawn that require the cooperation of two factors A_1, A_2, *in a fixed proportion*. Thus the point K, for example, yields a level of output 1, using OR of A_1 and OS of A_2. The point L, corresponding to a level of output twice that of K, requires OT (which is twice OR) of A_1, and OU (which is twice OS) of A_2. An increase in the quantity of factor A_1 used, without the required proportional rise in factor A_2 used, yields no additional output whatsoever. This is indicated by the shape of the isoquant family. At K, for example, increases in either A_1, or A_2, separately, yield no increase in output so that the isoquant is perfectly horizontal to the right of K (showing that an increase in A_1, by itself, does not lift output at all) and is on the other hand perfectly vertical above K (showing that an increase in A_2, by itself, does not raise output at all). A higher output is achieved only when *both* factors are raised proportionately. An example of such a process might be the bottling of a beverage that can be sold only in a given-size bottle. Each additional unit of output requires the employment of one additional bottle, plus one additional unit of the beverage. Use of two or more empty bottles does not yield any product; neither does the use of additional beverage—in *any* amount—without bottles.

Such a case is one where there is no substitutability between factors. This is expressed in the L-shaped pattern of the isoquant family. The marginal rate of substitution of A_1 for A_2 in the vertical portion of the isoquants is zero, since the slope of the isoquant with respect to the A_2 axis is zero. No additional units at all of A_1 are needed to offset the withdrawal of units of A_2 (because the quantity of A_2 available, compared with that of A_1, had been greater than that required by the fixed proportion). On the other hand, in the horizontal portion of the isoquants, the marginal rate of substitution of A_1 for A_2 is infinitely large (as is the slope of the isoquant with respect to the A_2 axis), showing that no matter how much additional A_1 might be used, it would be insufficient to offset the loss of even a small quantity of A_2. The level of output depends, not on the quantity of either input by itself, but on the number of "units" each of which is compounded of a fixed quantity of the one factor together with a fixed quantity of the other factor. An entrepreneur, in making his decisions as to the quantities of input that he should purchase, will in fact treat units of the two inputs as component parts of a single unit of a composite factor—in the same way as he would treat the two blades of a pair of scissors.

The diagram in Figure 8-5(b), on the other hand, depicts the diametrically opposed situation where the factors used in production are perfect substitutes. Here the isoquants are downward-sloping parallel straight lines throughout their extensions, showing that the *same* additional quantity of any one of the factors can always be used instead of a given quantity of the other factor. The marginal rate of substitution of one factor for the other is thus constant at all points on the diagram and is neither zero nor infinite.

However, the two cases shown in Figure 8-5(a) and in Figure 8-5(b) are extreme, limiting cases. In the real world the proportions between inputs seldom are technologically completely fixed. Usually there is room for some alteration in input proportions without altogether wasting any input. On the other hand, we have already seen that if two factors were perfect substitutes in production, then they would be classed together as units of an economically homogeneous group of goods. Typical isoquants, therefore, will be neither parallel to the factor axis nor straight lines throughout their length. They will express the fact that inputs are *partial substitutes* for one another; that within limits, a withdrawal of one input can be offset by additional use of the other input, but that such substitution becomes more and more impractical. The marginal rate of substitution of one factor for the other becomes greater and greater as the substitution is carried forward. Greater and greater quantities of a factor are needed to replace given withdrawn quantities of the other factor as the replacement goes on. The typical situation is thus one where the proportion in which the factors will be used, while not fixed absolutely by technological considerations, is yet by no means a matter of complete indifference.[6]

These possibilities are sometimes described with the assistance of the concept of the *elasticity of substitution*. The elasticity of substitution between two factors measures the degree to which it is possible to substitute one of the factors for the other, without bringing about more than a given increase in the marginal rate of substitution of the first factor for the second.[7] A high elasticity of substitution characterizes two factors substitution can take place freely between, without causing more than a moderate worsening of the rate further substitution can be made at. In the special case of perfect substitutes, the elasticity of substitution is infinite. No matter how far substitution has been carried, it is always possible to carry it still further at the same rate of substitution. There is in such a case no "optimal" proportion, deviation from which makes further substitution more and more disadvantageous.

A low elasticity of substitution, on the other hand, characterizes two factors from which best results can be obtained only by combining them in rather definite proportions. A significant deviation from these proportions brings about a very sharp drop in efficiency, so that the more the one factor has been substituted for the other (thereby departing from the best proportions), the more disadvantageous are the terms on which still further units of the first factor can be substituted for the second. In the special case of factors, the proportions between which are technologically fixed with complete rigidity, the elasticity of substitution is zero at the point of fixed proportions. When the quantity used of one of the factors, relative to the quantity used of the second factor, is slightly less than is

---

6. These considerations governing the substitutability of *factors* have their counterparts (in the theory of consumer demand) with respect to substitutability between *commodities* in consumption. We saw in earlier chapters that as a consumer gives up quantities of one good in order to acquire additional units of a second, he tends to be willing to continue such exchange only on increasingly attractive terms.

7. Mathematically the elasticity of substitution between two factors A_1 and A_2 is defined as $d\left(\dfrac{A_1}{A_2}\right) / d\left(MRS_{A_1 A_2}\right) \times MRS_{A_1 A_2} / \dfrac{A_1}{A_2}$, where $MRS_{A_1 A_2}$ is the marginal rate of substitution of A_1 for A_2. The $d\left(\dfrac{A_1}{A_2}\right)$ term denotes the change in the use of A_1 as compared to that of A_2. The $d\left(MRS_{A_1 A_2}\right)$ term denotes the change in the marginal rate of substitution. The remaining terms are introduced to make the result independent of the size of units used.

required by the fixed proportion, then its marginal rate of substitution for the second is, we have seen, zero. As soon as the quantity of the first factor has been raised to meet the required proportion, its marginal rate of substitution for the second has risen to infinity (no amount of it can offset the slightest reduction in the amount used of the second factor). Such an abrupt rise in the marginal rate of substitution, brought about by only the slightest alteration in the relative employments of the factors, constitutes zero elasticity of substitution.

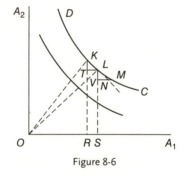

Figure 8-6

The typical processes of production lie somewhere in between these two extremes. The isoquant family will show a pattern that is exemplified, at least for a portion of the production surface, in Figure 8-6. In the diagram the isoquants are drawn convex to the origin. An entrepreneur who has been operating at point K can maintain the same level of output by withdrawing the quantity KT of input A_2 and increasing by quantity TL the input of factor A_1. By moving from the production situation at K to that at L, the entrepreneur increases the proportion in which input A_1 is employed relatively to A_2, from the proportion RO/KR to SO/LS. This is shown graphically by the reduction in slope from that of the line OK to that of the line OL. The convexity of the isoquant means that a further withdrawal of LV (drawn to be equal to KT) from the quantity employed of factor A_2 will require, for the maintenance of the output level, an additional quantity VM of A_1 that is *greater* than TL (which had been previously required). The extension of a straight line joining KL to N (that is, continued substitution on the same terms) would bring it into the neighborhood of lower isoquants. The convexity of the isoquant means that substitution of either factor for the other, if carried on at a constant rate of substitution, would bring about progressively lower output yields.

The elasticity of substitution at any point on one of these "typical" isoquants depends on the convexity of the curves. If the isoquants are only slightly convex (or, at any rate, in that portion of an isoquant where the curvature is slight), the marginal rate of substitution (shown by the slope of the isoquant) changes only slowly so that the elasticity of substitution over the relevant range is high. This is the case for the central portion of the isoquants. Thus, in the region of KL in the diagram, a given percentage change in the ratio of A_1/A_2 used does not alter the slope of the isoquant as considerably, for example, as it does in the neighborhood of MC. The elasticity of substitution is thus quite high in the central portion of an isoquant (corresponding to efficiently proportioned combinations of factors) but drops rapidly at the outer portions of the isoquants where a small amount of substitution brings about a rather sharp deterioration in the terms on which further substitution can take place. Thus, at the point C, the isoquant is parallel to the A_1 axis. This means that the marginal rate of substitution of A_1 for A_2 has reached an infinite level: no amount of additional A_1 can maintain output should the input of A_2 be cut slightly. From a point slightly to the left of C, to the point C, this marginal rate of substitution has jumped from a finite (high) level to a level greater than any assignable value—this corresponds to an elasticity of substitution very close indeed to zero.

It is now quite easy to perceive the relation between what we have called the "typical" isoquant, and the two special cases between which it is intermediate. The case of rigid, technically fixed proportions is one where the central portion of the typical isoquant has become shrunk to a single point. It is as if points C and D coincided; the range where some substitution is possible (and where the elasticity of substitution is not zero) has become narrowed to the vanishing point. On the other hand, the case of perfectly substitutable factors is one where the central portion of the typical isoquant extends throughout the production surface. The range of high (in fact, infinite) elasticity of substitution is not bounded by any limits whatsoever.

CHANGES IN FACTOR PROPORTIONS, AND CHANGES IN THE SCALE OF FACTOR EMPLOYMENT

The insights gained in the preceding section should make it easy to distinguish between the effects of *two* quite different kinds of changes that can be made in the input of productive factors. The *first* kind of change is alteration in the *proportions* in which the various factors are combined. The *second* kind of change is alteration in the *scale* in which inputs combined in a given proportion are applied. Here too the isoquant map provides useful graphic aid in showing the two kinds of input changes.

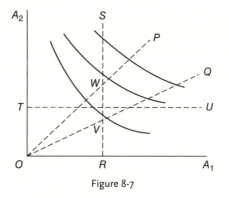

Figure 8-7

In Figure 8-7 a number of dotted straight lines are superimposed upon an isoquant map. OP and OQ are straight lines meeting the origin, differing from one another in their slopes; SR is parallel to the A_2 axis, and TU is parallel to the A_1 axis. Any two points on a straight line passing through the origin (such as W, P on the line OP) represent two combinations of the factors A_1 and A_2, in both of which the factors are combined *in the same proportions*. The difference between inputs at the two points is one purely of *scale*. Just as an architect may construct a scale model of a building (retaining the *relative* proportions of all lengths while reducing all *absolute* lengths by a constant scale factor), so too the point W, for example, is a "model" of the input situation at the point P (retaining relative proportions but with absolute measurements of factor input multiplied by the scale factor, in this case OW/OP). An increase in the scale of input, of course, may take place with *any* given proportions of factor combination; that is, along *any* straight line passing through the origin.

Points on *different* straight lines passing through the origin correspond to combinations of factors between which there is a difference in the *proportions* of the factors employed. Thus, for example, the point W differs from the point V, and the point Q in that W is characterized by a ratio of the quantity employed of A_2 to that of A_1, which is equal to the fraction WR/OR (the tangent of the angle WOR), while both V and Q have a ratio of A_2 to A_1 equal to VR/OR (the tangent of the angle VOR).

RETURNS TO SCALE

The problem of defining the consequences upon output of a change in the scale of input is the source of the concept of *returns to scale*. If a given percentage change in the scale of inputs brings about the same percentage change in output, then the production process is said to yield *constant returns to scale.* If one hour's employment of a typist's services, together with the use of given typing facilities, can produce 10 typed pages, and the employment of two typists, each similarly equipped, yields 20 pages in the same time, then constant returns have prevailed. On the isoquant map this would be expressed by the condition that intercepts (marked off along a straight line passing through the origin) between pairs of iso-quants have lengths proportional to the differences between the output levels represented by the respective isoquants. Equal increments of output should mark off equal distances along any straight line passing through the origin.

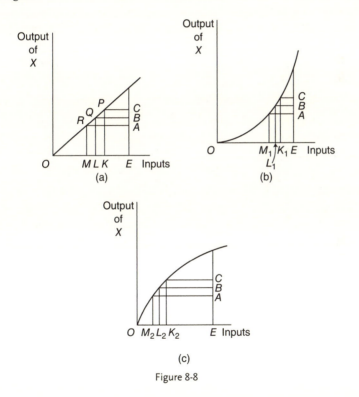

Figure 8-8

If a vertical section were made of a production surface characterized by constant returns to scale, along any horizontal straight line passing through the origin, we would obtain a situation shown in Figure 8-8(a). Output is measured along the vertical axis; AB, BC represent equal incre-ments of output. The section of the production surface shows a *straight line* so that the contour lines corresponding to output levels A, B, C, appear as the points R, Q, P, with $RQ = QP$. On an isoquant map this is translated

as generating equal distances ($ML = LK$) between isoquants corresponding to output levels separated by equal output increments ($AB = BC$).

If a productive process were to be characterized by *increasing returns to
scale*, the section of the production surface would be *convex* from below
[as in Figure 8-8(b)] so that equal output increments would correspond
to unequal distances between contour lines; the higher the output level,
the shorter will be the distance between isoquants corresponding to a
given output increment. Thus L_1K_1 (corresponding to output increment
BC) is *shorter* than M_1L_1 (corresponding to output increment AB, which is
equal to BC). If there were decreasing returns to scale, the situation would
be reversed, as in Figure 8-8(c), with L_2K_2 (which corresponds to output
increment BC) *longer* than M_2L_2 (which corresponds to the equal increment AB at a lower level of output).

While intuitively it might seem almost obvious that constant returns
to scale must prevail universally, with a doubling of *all* factors in a given
combination yielding a doubled output, and so on, it is impossible to make
any a priori generalizations to this effect. In the real world, moreover, it
is extremely difficult to discover cases where an increase has occurred in
all factors. Usually it is discovered that some important ingredient in a
productive process (for example, managerial skill) has stayed unchanged
during an increase in all other inputs. Where this has been the case, the
changes in output cannot be attributed to a pure change in scale. Along
with the change in scale, in such cases there has occurred also a shift in
the *proportions* in which the factors, whose input was increased, are combined with the factor whose input was not increased.

THE LAWS OF VARIABLE PROPORTIONS: THE PROBLEM

We have already noticed some of the consequences of an alteration in
factor proportions. We saw that as the proportion used of one factor
increased (relative to a second factor), substitution of the first for the
second becomes more and more difficult, if a given output level was to
be maintained. Our focus of attention, in that situation, was a change in
factor proportions *under the condition that the level of output be unchanged.*
But the problem of changed factor proportions is of importance in several
other aspects. One such problem, for example, is the effect upon output of
changes in factor proportions, *under the condition that total cost of production be unchanged.* This will be taken up in a later section of this chapter.

At this point we are interested in yet another aspect of the problem of
effects of variations in factor proportions. We are concerned with the effect

exerted by an increase in the ratio of the quantity in which one factor is employed, relative to the quantity in which a second factor is employed upon (1) *the output per unit* (a) of the factor being used relatively more freely, (b) of the factor being used relatively more sparingly; and (2) the *incremental effect* upon output brought about by additional input (a) of the factor being used relatively more freely, and (b) of the factor being used relatively more sparingly. Our examination of these matters will be confined to the simplest case, that of a process of production yielding constant returns to scale. It is clear that as the ratio of employment of one factor to that of a second is increased from very low values to very high ones, there is an initial stage where the first is spread very sparsely, so to speak, over the second factor, and a final stage where the second factor is spread very sparsely over the first. This symmetry between the initial and the final stages will be reflected in the above measurements of the efficiency of the two factors. The behavior, during the initial stage, of the output per unit of the factor that is being used sparingly in this stage will be mirrored, during the final stage, in the behavior of the output per unit of the other factor. And the same will be the case with the incremental effects on output of additional inputs of the two factors in these two stages.

Inquiries have been made by economists throughout the history of the science into the effects upon both the per-unit efficiency and the marginal effectiveness of factors between which the input proportions are undergoing variations. These investigations have tended to focus attention on one particular way that an alteration in input proportions can be achieved, the attention paid to this case arising in part from its supposed relevance to real-world situations. The case most frequently considered involved *successive increments in the input of one factor to a fixed quantity of another factor.* In the history of economic thought this case has been dealt with under the name "the law of diminishing returns"; in the real world the case was exemplified whenever an alteration occurs in the quantity of labor and capital applied to the cultivation of a given acreage of land.

While we too will investigate the effects on production efficiency of variations in input proportions, by references to this case, it must be stressed that the importance of the case lies purely in the change in input proportions that it exemplifies. The fixed quantity of the one factor is not to be thought of as one of those "other things" that are so often held unchanged in economics. It is, on the contrary, the means through which factor proportions can be altered under particular circumstances. For this reason it is probably better to use the newer term *laws of variable proportions* in place of "law of diminishing returns." What these laws describe, once again, can be visualized with the aid of an isoquant map drawn to express the results determined by these laws. In the diagram (Figure 8-9), the isoquants (on a production surface characterized by constant returns to scale) are drawn convex to the origin (that is, with what we found to be their typical shape, due to the imperfect substitutability of the factors). However, the isoquant lines have now been extended to the point where they slope upward in their outer regions.

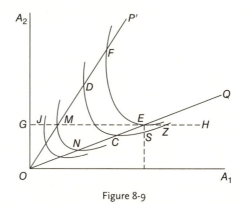

Figure 8-9

This pattern of isoquant map corresponds to a particular set of technical conditions that, according to the laws of variable proportions, are typical of production processes. A portion of an isoquant that slopes upward is to be interpreted as the situation where a *withdrawal* of one of the factors from the productive process, keeping the input of the other factor constant (for example, a movement from the point Z in the diagram to the point E), actually *increases* the level of output (shown in the diagram by the fact E is on a higher isoquant than Z). A positively sloping isoquant thus corresponds to the case where the marginal increment of product associated with an increase in the input of one of the factors is negative. The lines OP, OQ, separate the upward sloping portions of the isoquants from the other regions. Thus, between the lines OP and OQ, all isoquants are negatively sloped. The lines OP, OQ, are called *ridge lines* and pass, by their definition, through all those points where isoquants are *vertical* (such as points M, D, F), and through all the points where isoquants are *horizontal* (such as points N, C, E).

THE LAWS OF VARIABLE PROPORTIONS

The behavior of output according to the laws of variable proportions can be examined by considering in the diagram (Figure 8-9) the line GH

drawn parallel to the A_1 axis. Points on this line correspond to combinations of the input of a fixed quantity (OG) of factor A_2, together with the input of different quantities of factor A_1. As we move to the right along the line GH, we are considering the effects of combining greater and greater quantities of A_1 with the fixed quantity of A_2.[8] In so doing, of course, we are *decreasing the ratio* of the quantity of A_2 employed relative to the quantity of A_1 employed. (Thus if straight lines were drawn joining the origin to points M and E, we would find that the slope of a straight line OE would be less than that of a straight line OM.)

Now as we move from G toward M (where the line GH is intersected by the ridge line OP), we cross higher and higher isoquant lines; total output is steadily increasing. But so long as the point M has not been reached, the isoquants slope upward since we are outside the ridge line. This means that at any point between G and M, output could be *greater* if there were *less* of the fixed factor A_2. In this range there is *too much* of the fixed factor in relation to the variable factor. While the marginal increment of output corresponding to increases in the input of the variable input is positive (for all points in this range), that corresponding to increases in the fixed input is *negative*. (That is, for any point between G and M the output is higher than it would have been if the quantity of the fixed input had been greater.)

As we move further to the right, from the point M to the point E, we are in the region between the two ridge lines. Within this range, movement to the right still brings us to higher isoquant lines; successive increments of the variable factor bring about progressively higher levels of output. Also, in this region, the isoquants slope downward. Marginal increments of output corresponding to increases in *either* factor would be positive. At any point between M and E, output is lower than it would have been if the quantity of either input would have been greater.

As we move still further to the right, we reach the region outside the second ridge line OQ. In this range, every increase in the input of the variable factor *decreases* output (shown by the intersection of GH with lower

---

8. When we talk of "a movement to the right" along a line, we do not, of course, mean a *temporal* succession of cases (each one of which is more to the right than the ones actually earlier *in time*). Different points on an isoquant map refer to *alternative* situations possible at *one* moment in time. A "movement to the right" means, then, that we proceed to *consider* successively the situations more to the right as alternatives to those more to the left, which we *consider* first.

isoquants). Output is higher than it would be if the input of the variable factors (A_1) were greater, but lower than it would be if the quantity of the fixed input (A_2) had been greater. There is too much here of the variable factor A_1 in relation to the quantity of fixed factor A_2 available. The fixed factor is being overworked.

From these considerations it is possible to develop a rather complete description of the effect that different input proportions will have upon both the per-unit and the incremental effectiveness of the factors. We must remember that for the case of constant returns to scale, which we are considering, points on an isoquant map that lie on the same straight line through the origin correspond to situations where the per-unit output of any one of the factors is the same for both points, and where the marginal effectiveness of any one of the factors is the same for both points.[9] This means that these measures of factor effectiveness depend only on the ratio of input proportions, not on scale. Thus in Figure 8-10, the diagram (which selects certain features of Figure 8-9 for emphasis) shows (besides the line GH) the line WZ drawn parallel to the A_2 axis, so that the situation at V' on GH is the same (with respect to the per-unit and marginal effectiveness of the factors) as at the point V on WZ; the situation at B on GH is the same as at B' on WZ; and so on.

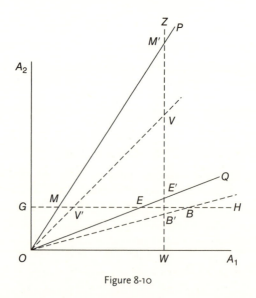

Figure 8-10

9. For proofs of these mathematical propositions, see Allen, R. G. D., *Mathematical Analysis for Economists*, The Macmillan Co., London, 1938, pp. 317–322.

Now as we moved to the right along GH, total output rose steadily until point E (on the ridge line OQ) and then declined. Since the quantity of A_2 did not change during this movement, it follows that the output attributable to one unit of A_2 rose steadily until E and then declined. This is an important result. We have seen that movement to the right along GH is equivalent (insofar as the effectiveness of units of the factors is concerned) to a movement downward along WZ. We are thus able to state that a movement downward along WZ increases the output per unit of A_2 until point E', after which the output per unit of A_2 falls. (With constant returns to scale the ridge lines are straight lines through the origin; thus, E, E' are both points on the ridge line.) Said another way, a movement upward along WZ first increases the per-unit output attributable to A_2 and then decreases it. This is an even more important result. It tells us that *with one factor constant* (here A_1, held fixed at an input of OW), *successive increments of a second factor bring about first a steady increase and then a steady decrease in the per-unit output attributable to this second (variable) factor.* Similarly, the output per unit of A_1 steadily increases with movement upward along WZ until M' (on the ridge line OP), after which it declines (since A_1 is constant along WZ, and total output rises till M' and then falls). Hence for movement to the right along GH the output per unit of A_1 rises until M and then declines steadily thereafter.

We can restate the results of the previous paragraph in the following terms. As the ratio of the employment of one factor to that of a second is steadily increased from very low values to very high values, the following changes appear in the output per unit of each of the factors.

1. *At first, for each of the factors being used, the per-unit output increases.* This is seen for the factor used relatively freely in this stage, from the behavior of the output per unit of A_2, during the movement to the right along GH from G to M. The same is seen for the factor used relatively sparingly in this stage, from the behavior of the output per unit of A_1, during the movement to the right along GH from G to M.

2. *A range follows during which the output per unit of the factor whose relative employment is being decreased rises steadily* (this is seen from the behavior of the output of A_2 during the movement to the right along GH, from M to E); *while the output per unit of the factor whose relative employment is being increased falls steadily* (this is seen from the behavior of the output of A_1 during the movement to the right along GH, from M to E).

3. *Then there is a final stage where, for each of the factors, the per-unit output decreases* (this is seen for both factors—the one being used sparingly in this stage, A_2; and the one being used relatively freely in this stage, A_1—by the behavior of the per-unit output of each in a movement to the right along GH, to the right of E).

We are also in a position to set forth the consequences of altered input proportions upon the effectiveness *at the margin* of units of the factors. We have seen that a movement to the right along GH (that is, the addition of successive increments of input A_1 to a fixed input of A_2) brought about a rise in the output per unit of A_1 until the ridge line at M, after which it fell. In other words, so long as the input of A_1 (for the given quantity of A_2) is less than indicated by the point M, each additional unit of A_1 brought about such an addition to total output that the output per unit of A_1 was raised. This means that in this range the marginal effectiveness of A_1 was greater than the average effectiveness of A_1. Moreover, in the range along GH moving from M to E, the effect of adding a unit of A_1 brought about so small an addition to output that the output per unit of A_1 was lowered. This means that in this range the marginal effectiveness of A_1 was lower than the average effectiveness of A_1. Finally, moving along GH to the right of E, we found that each additional unit of A_1 actually reduced total output; the marginal effectiveness of A_1 in this range is therefore negative.

Similarly, for a movement upward along WZ it can be seen that until the ridge line at E', the marginal effectiveness of A_2 (added to a fixed input of A_1) is greater than the average effectiveness of A_2; that above E' the marginal effectiveness is lower than the average effectiveness, and that above M' the marginal effectiveness is actually negative. Translating the movement up WZ into the equivalent but reversed movement *to the right* along GH, we see that until the point M, the marginal effectiveness of A_2 is negative; that between M and E the marginal effectiveness of A_2 is positive but below the average effectiveness of A_2, while to the right of E the marginal effectiveness is greater than the average effectiveness of A_2.

We can restate the results of the preceding paragraphs as follows. As the ratio of the employment of one factor to that of a second is steadily increased from very low values to very high values, the following changes occur in the effectiveness at the margin of additional units of input of each of the factors.

1. *At first the factor that is being used relatively freely in this stage is negatively effective at the margin*—this is seen in the negative marginal effectiveness

of A_2 in the movement along GH to the right until M; *while the factor being used relatively sparingly in this stage is positively effective at the margin* (and has a marginal effectiveness greater than its average effectiveness in this stage)—this is seen in the marginal effectiveness of A_1 in the movement to the right along GH to M.

2. *A range follows where the factor whose relative employment is being decreased is positively and increasingly effective at the margin* (although not as effective as the factor as a whole is, per unit, in this range)—this is seen in the effectiveness at the margin of A_2 along GH from M to E; *while the factor whose relative employment is being increased has an effectiveness at the margin that is positive but steadily declining* (so that it is below the overall per-unit effectiveness of the factor in this range)—this is seen in the effectiveness at the margin of A_1 along GH from M to E.

3. *There is a final stage where the factor whose relative employment has been decreased has an effectiveness at the margin that has risen higher than the overall per-unit effectiveness of the factor in this range, while the factor whose relative employment has been increased is negatively effective at the margin.*

The laws of variable proportions can now be expressed compactly in the form of a table.

Ratio of A_1/A_2	Effectiveness of Factor (A_1) Being Used in Greater and Greater Proportion.		Effectiveness of Factor (A_2) Being Used in Smaller and Smaller Proportion.	
	Average effectiveness	Effectiveness at the margin	Average effectiveness	Effectiveness at the margin
Stage 1 Very low A_1/A_2 ratio	Increasing	Greater than average	Increasing	Negative
Stage 2 Intermediate A_1/A_2 ratio	Falling	Falling (but positive) and less than the average	Increasing	Positive, increasing, but less than the average effectiveness
Stage 3 Very high A_1/A_2 ratio	Falling	Negative	Falling	Greater than the average

The interest these laws have held for economists over the past century and a half, we have noticed, has been largely confined to the special case where successive increments of a variable factor (such as labor) are added to a given quantity of a "fixed" factor (such as land). The traditional "law of diminishing returns" was formulated for this case, either (a) in terms of the average product of the variable input (that is, its product per unit) or (b) in terms of the marginal increment of product brought about by unit additions to the variable input.[10] The central point in either formulation was that *eventually* the average product and the marginal increment of product would both *diminish*. One or two points may be noticed concerning these formulations. First of all, they do not assert that these variables will *always* be decreasing. In fact, it will be seen from our analysis that if there is any point (on a production surface characterized by constant returns to scale) where the addition of a unit of one factor by itself will diminish total output, then there is a range where the average product of that factor is increasing. Marginal increment of product also may be increasing initially, but the point where it begins to decline will be *before* the point where average product begins to decline. (This has sometimes caused unnecessary confusion as to the point where "diminishing returns set in," due to confusion between the two formulations of the law.)

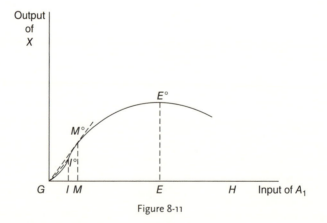

Figure 8-11

10. For the proof that these two formulations are *not* mathematically equivalent (as economists have sometimes believed), see Menger, K., "The Laws of Returns, A Study in Meta-Economics," *Economic Activity Analysis* (edited by Morgenstern, O.), John Wiley and Sons, Inc., New York, 1954.

Most of these considerations can be seen in Figure 8-11, which is a vertical section of the production surface along the line GH. The curve shown is thus the curve of total output corresponding to increasing input of A_1 (with a fixed input of A_2). The curve that has been drawn is continuous; thus, we can observe the way average output changes for very small changes in input, and also the way *marginal output* changes continuously.[11] The average output of any quantity of input A_1 is shown by the slope of the straight line joining the origin to the total output curve at the relevant point. Thus for input GI of A_1, that output is $II°$, and average output is therefore $II°/GI$, which measures the slope of the angle $I°GI$. Marginal output at any level of input of A_1 is shown by the slope of the total output curve itself at the relevant point, since this is the limit of the rate per unit of input at which the curve rises for very small increments of input.

It will be seen that until $I°$, the output curve rises more and more steeply (corresponding to rising marginal product of A_1) and thereafter rises less steeply (corresponding to falling, but positive, marginal product).[12] At the point $E°$, when total output is at a maximum, the slope is zero (horizontal), corresponding to zero marginal product for A_1; thereafter the slope is downward, corresponding to negative marginal product. It will be seen further that straight lines drawn joining the origin to successive points on the output curve have steeper and steeper slopes until the point $M°$ (where the slope of the line $GM°$ is also the slope of the output curve itself, $GM°$ being tangent to the output curve at this point); after $M°$ the lines have lower and lower slopes. This corresponds to rising average product of A_1 until the point M and steadily declining average product thereafter.

It will be readily seen that M, E, correspond to the two points in the isoquant map where the line GH was intersected by the two ridge lines. The *first* stage, described in the laws of variable proportions, thus corresponds to the portion of the curve from G to $M°$. In this region the average output of A_1 is increasing, and its marginal output is positive and greater than the average output (as seen by comparing the slope of the output curve at any point in this region, with the slope of the line joining this point to the origin). In the diagram, since this portion of the output curve was drawn

---

11. See in this chapter p. 167, n. 3.

12. Concerning whether the output curve passes through the origin (or begins to rise only to the right of the origin), see Knight, F. H., *Risk, Uncertainty and Profit*, University of London (reprint), London, 1957, p. 101, n.

concave from above, the marginal output also was increasing during a portion of the range. The *second* stage described in the laws of variable proportions corresponds to the portion of the output curve between $M°$ and $E°$. In this region the average and the marginal outputs are both decreasing (but positive). The *third* stage corresponds to the region to the right of $E°$; average output continues to fall and marginal output is negative. The points $M°$, and $E°$, have the special significance that for point $M°$ average output of A_1 is at a maximum, while at point $E°$ total output is at a maximum (with marginal output of A_1 zero).

Taking the more general approach, with the focus upon the *ratio* between the inputs of the two factors rather than on the absolute input of A_1, we can easily see the application of the *symmetry* noticed earlier. The situation in the first stage with respect to average and marginal output of A_1, with the quantity of A_1 increasing, is completely mirrored in the third section, with respect to average and marginal outputs of A_2 considered for a steadily *decreasing* input of A_1. In particular it is true that with constant returns to scale, wherever the ratio of the input of *either* of the factors to that of the other is so low that the average output of the first factor rises with its increased input, then the situation is such that the *other* factor is being so used that its marginal product is negative; output could be increased by discarding some of this other factor. Moreover, at $M°$, where the average product of A_1 is at a maximum, the marginal output of A_2 is zero (that is, the total output yielded with any fixed quantity of A_1 is maximized when A_2 is employed in the proportion denoted by the point M in Figure 8-11); and the converse of this proposition is true at the point $E°$.

ECONOMIC IMPLICATIONS OF THE
LAWS OF VARIABLE PROPORTIONS

The laws of variable proportions describe the pattern of technical conditions that make up the background of the alternatives the producer-entrepreneur is able to choose from. In the marketplace, the precise determination of these alternatives depends on the prices that quantities of the factors can be bought at in the market.

Several generalizations can be made immediately. No entrepreneur will under any circumstances employ a unit of a factor whose employment causes output to decline. Thus, the laws of variable proportions tell us immediately that there are opportunities open to the entrepreneur that he will unquestionably reject. The entrepreneur will not employ factors in a proportion that fits into either stage one or stage three of possible input proportions. In either of these regions greater output could be obtained simply by discontinuing the use of some of the factors. Thus, the very important result is established that the only portion of the production surface ever seriously under consideration is between the ridge lines. This means that any group of factors employed in production will be in such a proportion that (a) the per-unit output of each factor would be lower with increased input, and (b) the marginal increment of product of any factor would be lower with increased input.[13] (Increasing average or marginal products can occur only where one of the factors has negative marginal product; that is, in the regions outside the ridge lines.)

The goal of the entrepreneur is to produce his output at the lowest possible cost. Of all the available alternative ways of producing a given output, there will be one, or several, that require a smaller total outlay than the others. Or, to put the matter the other way around, of all the possible levels of output that it is possible to attain with a given cost outlay, one or several will be higher than the others. The entrepreneur will seek to combine inputs in that proportion that will squeeze the most output out of the cost outlay.

If either of the factors is a free good, it is very simple to determine the optimum factor proportion. Additional units of this factor can be obtained, for any given cost outlay, without forgoing the employment of any of the other factor that it might be desirable to employ. The entrepreneur, thus, must simply buy as much of the priced factor as the given cost outlay permits and then combine with it as much of the free factor as will maximize output. That is, he must choose the proportion of the factors at which the marginal output of the free good is zero (which is then also the point where the average output attributable to the priced factor is at a maximum). This point, of course, is at the boundary of the middle stage (within which all entrepreneurs will, as we have seen, necessarily operate) where the free good is employed relatively more freely.

THE LEAST-COST COMBINATION

Where, as is the usual case, both factors can be had only at a price, the problem of determining the *least-cost combination* of factors for a given

---

13. One conceivable exception to these generalizations may result from a producer's knowledge that the market price of his inputs and outputs depends very sensitively upon his own production decisions. For the remainder of this chapter we ignore this possibility.

output is very similar to the problem that the consumer faces in allocating his income among several goods. In both cases the goal will be to ensure that expenditure is distributed in such a way that were any sum of money to be withdrawn at the margin from one good in favor of another, the economizing individual would rank the sacrificed commodities higher on his value scale than the additional commodities. In the case of the consumer, the comparison involved the marginal utilities of the relevant commodities. For the producer the comparison can be made more objectively in terms of the output given up, and the additional output gained. Thus the least-cost factor combination, which the entrepreneur will consciously seek to achieve, will be attained when the marginal increment of product corresponding to the last "dollar's" worth of expenditure upon any one factor is greater than the marginal increment of product corresponding to a prospective additional expenditure of a dollar upon any other factor. If this situation does not prevail, there is room to gain output, on balance, by withdrawing money spent at the margin on one factor and expanding by this amount the sum spent on other factors. This transfer will go on with the consequence that the marginal increment of output corresponding to the factor from which expenditure is being withdrawn will steadily rise (because according to the law of variable proportions the relevant stage is always that where the marginal output falls with greater inputs), while that of the factors whose use is being expanded will fall, until the least-cost combination is attained.

It is easy to see that with small-sized marginal units of factor (with which the difference between the marginal increments of output corresponding to two successively acquired units of factor can be ignored), this least-cost combination condition can be stated as follows. The marginal increments of product corresponding to units of any two factors must be in the same proportion to one another as are their prices (MIP_{A_1}/MIP_{A_2} = price of A_1/price of A_2). A given sum of money (S) being spent at the margin on A_2 (buying the quantity S/P_{A_2}, with P_{A_2} the price of A_2) makes a difference to output responsible for $S \times MIP_{A_2}/P_{A_2}$ output (approximately); whereas the same amount of money spent on additional units of A_1 could buy S/P_{A_1} units, which could add (approximately) $S \times MIP_{A_1}/P_{A_1}$ in additional output. But if, say, $MIP_{A_1}/MIP_{A_2} > P_{A_1}/P_{A_2}$ then $MIP_{A_1}/P_{A_1} > MIP_{A_2}/P_{A_2}$ so that the transfer of expenditure at the margin from A_2 to A_1 would be worthwhile. Thus, only equality between the two fractions describes the situation where the least-cost combination has been attained.

GRAPHIC ILLUSTRATION OF THE LEAST-COST COMBINATION

The isoquant map provides, once again, a useful means for visualizing the particular choice of input proportions that an entrepreneur will make under given cost conditions. It is necessary to introduce once more a graphic device that we have already met in the theory of consumer income allocation—the constant expenditure curve. It will be recalled that if any two goods, A_1 and A_2, can be obtained in any amount at constant prices per unit (P_{A_1} and P_{A_2} respectively), then a line (BC in Figure 8-12) can be drawn tracing out all the different packages of the two goods that a given sum of money (say, S) can buy. For such a line, $OB = S/P_{A_2}$, and $OC = S/P_{A_1}$, so that the slope BC with respect to the A_1 axis is equal to P_{A_1}/P_{A_2}. In the case of production, such a line passes through all the different factor combinations that can be bought for a given cost outlay and is given the name *isocost line*.

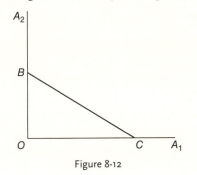

Figure 8-12

When the isocost line is superimposed on an isoquant map, the points where the isocost line is intersected by successive isoquants rank the different factor combinations in order of their productive efficiency. The particular choice of input proportions the entrepreneur seeks to achieve corresponds to the point on an isocost line where it meets the *highest* of these attainable isoquant levels.

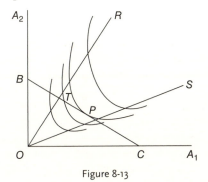

Figure 8-13

In Figure 8-13 the isocost line BC (corresponding to a ratio of $P_{A_1}/P_{A_2} =$ OB/OC) is superimposed upon an isoquant map. It is evident that the point P on the isocost corresponds to the particular factor combination that yields highest output. It is at this point that the isocost is just tangent to an isoquant. An any other point (for example, at T) the isocost can only cut an isoquant; thus, there is a higher level of output that can be obtained by giving up some of one input (for example, A_2) and employing instead additional units of the other (A_1). At P, a transfer in either direction would be disadvantageous because it could result only in lower output. Any level of output higher than at P is simply out of reach with this outlay.

It will be observed that at the point of tangency, the slope of the isoquant line is the same as that of the isocost; thus, this point fulfills the (approximate) condition that the additional quantity of any one factor necessary to offset the withdrawal from production of one unit of the other factor be equal to the ratio of the price per unit of the second factor to the price per unit of the first. This, of course, is simply the same condition developed in the previous section, that the ratio between the marginal increments of product corresponding to units of the two factors be equal to the ratio of their prices.[14]

This graphic derivation of the least-cost condition provides an interesting illustration of several of the principles developed in earlier sections of this chapter. Thus the significance of the fact that the factors are not perfect substitutes for one another is clearly brought out. If factors were perfect substitutes so that the isoquants were straight lines, then, if the slope of these isoquants were different from that of the isocost, there would be no point of tangency at all. Substitution of one factor for another

---

14. It may be observed at this point that much of the isoquant geometry developed in this chapter has, in the literature, a counterpart in consumer theory. In the literature the formal and diagrammatic analogy between consumer theory and production theory has been carried forward very extensively. Corresponding to the isoquant map in production theory, economists discuss the *indifference curve* map in the theory of the consumer. An indifference curve is a line drawn through all those different possible combinations of two commodities between which a consumer feels indifferent. The approach to consumer theory adopted in Chs. 4 and 5 made it unnecessary to resort to the use of indifference curves (concerning which there are some rather serious theoretical problems). The detailed discussion of isoquant maps in the present chapter, however, may be applied to consumer theory without significant alteration if it is desired to employ the indifference curve technique.

would continue until only the one factor would be used. If the slope of the isocost was that of the isoquants, then the isocost would coincide with an isoquant throughout its length; thus, no particular proportion between the two factors can be pronounced the most economic. (This, in fact, would be the case where, as we saw, the two factors make up one homogeneous group. The equality in isocost and isoquant slopes simply means that different prices are not being charged for economically identical units of factors.)

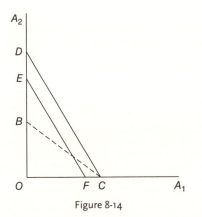

Figure 8-14

Movement along an isoquant corresponds to an alteration of input proportions. The fact that one such proportion is better than the others is the corollary of the fact that the factors are not perfect substitutes for each other. A change in the slope of the isocost (corresponding to a relative cheapening of one of the factors, compared with the other) will alter the point of tangency, either making a higher output possible for the same outlay or bringing down the possible level of output. In any event such a change will alter the optimum proportions of input in favor of the factor that has become relatively cheaper.[15]

15. By an extension of the analysis of the least-cost combination, an insight can be obtained into the notion of the *demand curve for a factor of production*. Such a curve, for any one producer, reflects the different quantities of the factor that he asks to buy at respectively different prices (all other things remaining unchanged). The lower the price of a factor, the larger will be the quantity that a producer will generally wish to buy. Our analysis explains part of the reason for this: the lower the price of a factor, the more it pays to substitute it in place of other factors. The lower the price of a factor,

With a given relation between factor prices, it is possible to draw a series of isocost lines, as *BC, DE, FG* . . . (in Figure 8-15). The respective points of tangency on these lines correspond to the different factor combinations that are optimum for successively higher levels of cost outlay. Each such point makes the most of the relevant cost outlay; the entrepreneur has to select that level of outlay, which, taken in conjunction with the price he can expect to get for his output, maximizes profits. The path joining these points of tangency is appropriately named the *expansion path*.

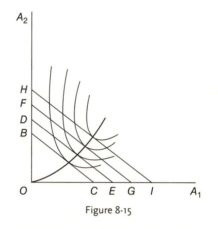

Figure 8-15

We can refer graphically, finally, to the special case where one of the factors is a free good, costing nothing to obtain. In this case, the isocost line will be a straight line parallel to the axis of the free input. It will show that a fixed quantity of the non-free input can be employed, with no limit on the free input. The point of tangency with the isoquants will be where the isoquants are vertical or horizontal; that is, on the ridge line. At this point, as much of the free input is being used as can be employed without diminishing possible output.

----

the greater becomes the marginal product derived from the last dollar spent on it. Consequently the producer must (even if he were not to expand his output as the result of the lower costs) switch expenditure at the margin from other resources to the now cheaper resource, in order to achieve the (new) least-cost combination. (See also Ch. 9, pp. 215–216, n. 10.)

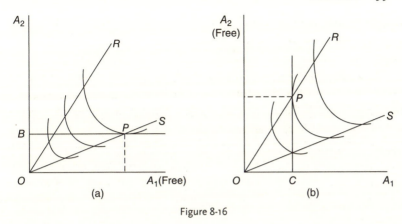

Figure 8-16

SUMMARY

Chapter 8 commences the analysis of the activity of the individual market participant in the role of *producer.* This analysis serves as the foundation for the examination of the *supply* side of the market. The economist sees the producer as making *choices among alternatives* of a special kind. These alternatives involve the various productive uses that the resources available to him might be put to. The rejected productive uses constitute the economic costs of production of any adopted process of production involving scarce resources. In society the efficiency of production is advanced through specialization and division of labor. The producer's alternatives are rigidly controlled by the market *prices* of the resources he must purchase for a given production process.

Production is carried on with factors of production. A unit of factor may possibly be related to a second unit of factor in a *substitute* relationship, or possibly in a *complementary* relationship. A unit of factor may be *specific* to the production of a certain product; it may be *specialized* for this particular production; or, on the other hand, it may be *versatile* in production.

Analysis of production decisions is formalized by the use of several mathematical and graphical concepts. Production possibilities are expressed in the *production function,* expressed graphically as the production *surface.* Contour lines on this surface are *isoquants.* The slope of the isoquants measure the substitutability between the cooperating factors. Extreme cases are those where either no substitution at all is possible (technically rigid proportions being required), or where the one factor may be substituted completely for the second. Typical production processes permit substitution between the complementary factors to a limited degree.

The isoquant geometry points up clearly the distinction between alterations in the *proportions* in which factors are combined, and alterations in the *scale* in which factors (combined in a given proportion) are applied. Alterations in scale yield alterations in output that may be characterized by *increasing returns to scale, decreasing returns to scale,* or *constant returns to scale.* Alterations in factor proportions yield alterations in output that are governed by the *laws of variable proportions.* Detailed analysis of the various possible cases throws light on the alternative possible ways of expressing these laws.

The economic implications of the laws of variable proportions include the delimitation of the best input combination a producer will employ under given technical and market conditions. The attainment of this "least-cost combination" may be analyzed both logically and graphically.

SUGGESTED READINGS

Knight, F. H., *Risk, Uncertainty and Profit,* University of London (reprint), London, 1957, Ch. 4.

Carlson, S., *A Study on the Pure Theory of Production,* Kelley and Millman Inc., New York, 1956.

Stonier, A. W., and W. C. Hague, *A Textbook of Economic Theory,* Longmans Green, London, 1953, Ch. 10.

9   COSTS AND SUPPLY

An understanding of the operation of the full market process must include, we have seen, the understanding of the forces acting to supply the market with the various produced goods and services. These forces determine the arrays of alternatives offered to prospective consumers. But we have seen that these forces are themselves conditioned by the circumstances under which entrepreneurs are able to engage in production. In particular the entrepreneur operates in a situation where his choice of product, his choice of production method, and his choice of volume of production must be made on the basis of the market facts relating to the prices of both products and factors. In order to produce any particular quantity of a particular product in a particular way, the entrepreneur must pay definite costs of production. The quantity of any one product that an entrepreneur will contribute to the market supply, thus, will depend partly on the costs incurred for this output. The quantity that the market as a whole will supply of any one product will in turn depend partly on the costs of production that must be incurred individually by entrepreneurs for the various possible levels of output.

In this chapter we carry further the analysis of the forces of supply. Leaning heavily on the principles of production discussed in the previous chapter, we examine especially the way costs of production of firms in a particular industry are likely to change with output. The chapter carries through the analysis to include the way the entrepreneur reacts to these alternative production opportunities and the way is thus cleared to the understanding of the forces of supply as they finally impinge on the market.

The focus of attention in this chapter is thus rather different from that of the previous chapter. There we studied production, examining the way output depended on the particular input combination employed. Here we adopt a point of view corollary to that of the previous chapter: here we are principally concerned with the way the costs of the firm depend on the level of output. Unless otherwise specified, it may be assumed throughout the chapter that for each output level, the least-cost combination problem has been solved. We turn first to a review of the ultimate meaning of *cost* and its place in production theory.

COSTS AND RENTS

The cost concept is bound up inseparably with the concept of human action. Action consists in choosing between alternatives. The adoption of any one specific alternative implicitly involves the rejection of other alternatives; in particular it involves the rejection of the "second-best" alternative—namely, that alternative that *would have been* adopted had the alternative that *was* actually adopted been unavailable. It is *this* rejected alternative that the economizing individual recognizes as the *cost* of the adopted alternative simply because *both* opportunities cannot be simultaneously adopted. A man may have to choose between the chance of opening a certain kind of store on the one hand, and retaining the friendship of a man engaged in the same line of business, on the other hand. If he adopts the former alternative, then he recognizes that his business has cost him his neighbor's friendship. Should he value the friendship more highly, then the cultivation and preservation of this friendship has cost him a possible lucrative business opening. Cost is made up of the conscious sacrifice of an available opportunity. This is the most general conception of the cost category.

For the isolated individual, the act of *production* involves a *particular* aspect of cost. The employment of a unit of a non-specific resource for the production of one particular product necessarily withholds it from making any contribution to the production of other products. A decision to make any particular use of a resource thus involves the sacrifice of other potential uses. This sacrifice constitutes the *cost of production* of a produced good. Every product is produced at the cost of some other product. This is the idea of *opportunity cost*.

Where production takes place within the framework of a market economy, the conception of cost of production is not quite so simple. While it is true that a firm owning a fleet of taxicabs *might* conceivably use the services of the cab drivers whom it employs to drive transcontinental freight trucks, this opportunity may not be an alternative normally taken into serious consideration. With effective division of labor, we have seen that an entrepreneur finds himself able—and called upon—to decide on the *kind* of product he is to produce only at relatively infrequent intervals. A taxicab firm does not ordinarily weigh the relative usefulness of its employees as cab or truck drivers. When it sends men into the streets with its cabs, the firm has immediately rejected, not the opportunity to send them into the highways with trucks, but the opportunity to refrain from hiring the men altogether. The rejected opportunity is normally thus the chance to save money costs paid to its cab drivers—including, of course, the chance to use the money saved to improve the quality of other inputs—perhaps to buy new cabs more frequently, perhaps to install a radio-dispatch system. In a market economy the individual entrepreneur considers as his costs of production the sums of money he is required to pay for factors in the market. A product is produced with the sacrifice of these sums of money. The alternative that is rejected is the opportunity to avoid both the act of production and the expenditure of money that it entails.

But the concept of opportunity cost, which we found in the case of the isolated individual producer, plays an important role in costs of production as they emerge in a market economy as well. There is an important sense in which the cost of production of any product is in fact the sacrificed opportunity of producing either some other product or the same product elsewhere. While it is true that the notion of cost pertains essentially to the alternatives forgone *by an individual* in his act of choice, a secondary connotation also is attached to it. The term "cost" is applied somewhat loosely to the *effects* of a given act of choice even where these are felt by an outsider. The decision of a man not to open up a particular business, in order to preserve a friendship with a potential competitor, may be said to have "cost" the consumers the advantages that would have ensued from their competition. In the same way, while the employment of drivers in one branch of industry costs the individual employers only definite sums of money, this employment, in a very real sense, "costs" other branches of industry the opportunity to use the services of these drivers. And, similarly, one can say that the employment of drivers by a particular employer "costs" other employers in the *same* industry the services of these drivers.

From this opportunity cost point of view, the "cost" of a particular decision may take on a number of quite different dimensions, depending on the point in the economic system upon which the effects of the decision are being assessed. From the point of view of taxicab firms, the employment of a driver by taxicab fleet *A* has the effect of withdrawing a potential driver from each of fleets *B, C,* and so on. From the point of view of consumers, however, such an employment has hardly any effect at all on cab service; but it *has* an effect on consumers insofar as other branches of industry are concerned. The cab driver's employment costs the consumer virtually nothing in terms of cab service, but it does cost them the use of the drivers in other kinds of service.

These considerations are not merely a questionably ingenious way of stretching the meaning of the word "cost." They point, in fact, to significant relationships in the operation of the market system. The key to the matter is that the sums of money that the individual producer considers as *his* costs of production tend to depend in a sensitive fashion upon these other opportunity costs of production. For a cab driver to be employed by any one employer, it is necessary that he be paid a wage (which are money costs of production from the employer's point of view) at least high enough to keep him from selling his services either to employers in other industries or to other employers in the taxicab industry itself. The employment of a driver at one point in the economy means the withdrawal of his potential services from other points in the economy. The *values* of these potential services to employers at these respective points are the measures of the relevant "costs" of the employment. At the same time these values set the amounts of money that these other employers will be willing to bid for these services. The wage actually paid must be at least high enough to outbid these amounts. Thus, an entrepreneur's money costs of production reflect in part also the value of the opportunity costs of production as felt by other employers and other industries.

The sums of money paid by the entrepreneur for a factor of production (and thus entering into his costs of production) can thus be analyzed into a number of distinct amounts. First, one part of the sum paid to a factor by a producer of a given product was necessary to attract and keep the factor in the industry producing this product. This amount would have to have been paid by any employer producing this product to prevent the factor from being successfully bid for by entrepreneurs producing other products. The size of this amount thus depends on the value placed by the entrepreneurs in these other industries, on the usefulness of the factor to them in their production activities. This element in the money costs of production paid out by the eventual employer of the factor thus measures that cost to consumers—often loosely termed the "social cost" of production—which takes the form of the lost products that might have been produced by entrepreneurs in other industries (the measurement being made by the appraisals of these entrepreneurs). This element is frequently termed the *transfer cost* of the factor, the amount that must be paid to the factor to keep it from being used by another industry. Any amount of money paid to a factor over and above its transfer cost cannot be considered as "costs," *from the point of view of the consumers choosing between products.* The assignment of a factor to the production of a particular product has not implied any loss of other possible products to consumers that can be valued above the transfer costs of the factor. From *this* point of view, sums of money paid for a factor above transfer costs are termed economic *rent* to the factor owner. The importance of the recognition of this second element, in the sums of money paid for factor services, lies in the realization that any payment of rent in this sense involves no exercise of influence upon the allocation of factors between *industries*.

Although from the point of view of consumers only transfer costs are true costs, insofar as the choice of product is concerned, there may be valid points of view from which the cost element in the payments to factors is considerably larger. What is rent from one point of view may well be true cost from another point of view. The amount of money that a particular employer must pay to ensure that the services of a factor are not snapped up by a rival producer of the same product is a true cost, in the sense that this sum is the decisive factor in the allocation of productive factors *between producers of the same product*. And even from the point of view of the consumer this kind of allocation is not a matter of indifference, since different producers may have different degrees of ability in efficiency of production. What is a rent, viewing the industry as a single unit, may be a cost, when the industry is viewed as consisting of producers of different entrepreneurial skills. An oilfield being exploited by a particular oil company commands a price a small part of which is necessary to withstand the competition of farmers for the land, the rest being necessary to outstrip the competition of other oil companies. This second portion of the price is rent from the viewpoint of the oil industry as a whole, but cost from the viewpoint of any one oil company.[1]

OPPORTUNITY COSTS AND SUPPLY THEORY

When it is realized that in a market economy as well, the costs that a producer's accountant reports to him are to be seen as reflecting opportunity costs in a real sense, then the dependency of the supply of particular products upon costs of production becomes visible in its proper context. It is apparent, for example, that the reason why all the resources of an economy are not channeled into the production of a single product is that the costs are too high, in *two* senses that are ultimately equivalent to one another. *First*, after a point the price that must be paid for the necessary factors would become very high indeed, far higher than could be justified by the value of the product produced. *Second*, the channeling of all resources into a single product means the complete cessation of the

1. See pp. 248–249, n. 12.

supply of any other goods; this sacrifice is too great. Both interpretations are ultimately equivalent in that the intolerable magnitude of the sacrifice of all other products manifests itself in the high prices that will be offered in the market for the other products, and hence for the resources required for their production.

These considerations point up a general tendency operating upon the supply of any one product.

The per-unit costs of production of any particular product tend in general to rise as the margin of output of this product is advanced.

Economic analysis of the conditions of supply of particular commodities hinges ultimately upon the degree to which this tendency is actually fulfilled as against the degree to which this tendency is thwarted by special circumstances. As more and more of a particular commodity is produced during a given period of time, fewer and fewer other commodities can be produced. By the principle of diminishing marginal utility, this means that the advancement, by successive units, of the margin of output of a particular product would involve the simultaneous *reduction* in importance of each additional unit of *this* product, and *increase* in importance of the units at the respective margins of output of *other* products. But this can only mean that the expansion of any one kind of production tends to entail, for each additional unit to be produced, the rejection of alternatives that are more and more difficult to ignore; a tendency toward increasing costs prevails. For the isolated individual, as for the market, the tendency toward increasing costs determines the margin of production for each good. The market process strives, as do the actions of the isolated individual, for a production pattern that strikes a balance between goods so that the opportunity costs of the production of each good be minimized. The output margin for each good tends to be at the point where an additional unit of it (whose utility *falls* with increased output) would no longer justify the opportunity cost of its production (which rises with increased output).

Ultimately, this is a general tendency that can hardly be escaped. The competitive market process may in fact be viewed as enforcing that organization of production that is enjoined by this principle of increasing cost. Nevertheless, this process is complicated by the different ways the tendency toward increasing cost actually makes itself felt in the cost data facing the individual entrepreneur. It is vastly complicated further by the possibility of ranges of production where there is no apparent tendency toward increasing costs. Most of this chapter is concerned with these complications. Our task will be to understand the selection by the entrepreneur (who produces *one* commodity) of that quantity of output that he will seek to supply to the market, out of the alternative output levels available to him. As was the case in the analysis of consumer demand, understanding the way the *individual producer* makes his output decisions will clarify the nature of the forces acting upon the *market supply* of particular products.

PROSPECTIVE AND RETROSPECTIVE COSTS

The insights afforded by viewing production costs as sacrificed opportunities are of particular value in distinguishing sharply between the costs of production concerning which the accountant informs the entrepreneur *after* a process of production has been completed on the one hand, and those costs of production that are, on the other hand, involved in the entrepreneur's decision making *before* embarking on a production process. We are directly concerned only with the latter in the analysis of supply (although, of course, the entrepreneur's anticipations of future costs are built on his experiences in previously completed production ventures).

An entrepreneur has produced a quantity of goods and wishes to determine in retrospect the total costs of his production. His financial records provide information concerning a large number of outlays that had to be incurred in order for the production to take place. First of all, far in advance of the actual production, the entrepreneur built or bought some kind of manufacturing plant. The books record both the sum paid for the plant and the interest the entrepreneur has had to pay (and which he may still be paying) on the capital raised to make the initial investment in the factory. These sums were incurred, it is true, in order to engage in production over a long period of time; they were not paid *solely* in order to produce the particular batch of goods whose costs of production the entrepreneur is now examining. Nevertheless, if these sums had not been paid, these particular goods could not have been produced. The entrepreneur is immediately conscious, in retrospect, of the difficulty in stating precisely what portion of these initially incurred sums of money are to be included in the costs of production of any particular batch of produced goods.

In addition, the entrepreneur's records mention sums paid, both in the past and during the period the goods were being manufactured, for maintenance and repairs to the plant and equipment. These sums also were incurred *not only* to produce one particular batch of goods. All these sums were more or less *necessary* in order that the particular batch of goods be produced, but the *amounts* thus paid seem to have little relation to the size of this batch of products. These sums, too, do not vary in any simple manner, in relation to the size of the batch of products whose costs of production are under examination.

But the entrepreneur's accounts may show further sums that do relate very precisely to this batch of goods. It may be possible to calculate, for example, the amount of money paid for the raw material used up in the production of these goods; it is possible to calculate the amount of money paid for the labor directly employed in their manufacture. These sums depend very plainly on the size of the batch of products under consideration. If a smaller batch had been produced, less raw material would have been bought and less labor would have been hired. It is quite possible, however, that some expenses, incurred for raw materials, labor, power, and other factors used up entirely in the production of this batch of goods, were undertaken in advance and would have required payment regardless of the quantity of goods produced. It is possible, for example, that some of the labor employed in the production is engaged under a contract providing for an annual salary, or that certain raw materials were already bought (or agreements for their purchase completed) well before the actual production decisions were made.

This wide variety of circumstances surrounding the expenses incurred in connection with the production of the goods may not altogether frustrate the entrepreneur who is trying to discover ex post facto what total figure to assign to the payments made for all the factors of production employed.[2] But this variety does point clearly to the fact that the costs of production involved in the *decisions* to produce may be quite different from the costs of production used to calculate the profit or loss relating

2. It will be remembered throughout the chapter that costs of production must, from the opportunity cost viewpoint, include not only the actual money expenditures that the producer makes to buy resources, but also those values of his own resources that he employs in production. The latter values are known as *implicit costs* and must be included in any *economic* tally of costs of production *both* prospectively and retrospectively. A producer who devotes his own labor to production is obviously sacrificing what he could earn in the market by his labor. (The accountant will, in this respect especially, frequently furnish records or estimates of "costs" that are different from those relevant to economic theory.) It should be observed that from the theoretical point of view, which sees production carried on by "pure" entrepreneurs who own no resources, *all* costs will be explicit. Implicit costs arise only in a real world where different market functions are performed in combination by a single market participant.

to a completed venture. The key point is that a *process of production takes time;*[3] thus, there are typically a number of opportunities to make production decisions, to revise them, to carry them forward, or to abandon them. At each such opportunity the entrepreneur makes his decision, based partly on the anticipated costs of production of the process. *For each such decision the relevant costs of production are different.*

When a process of production is being contemplated from the very beginning, the entrepreneur must try to anticipate *all* the expenses that the process will necessitate. These "full costs" are identical, in the entrepreneur's mind, with the costs that he expects to use at the end of the process in calculating the final profit or loss of the entire venture. But as the plan of production is put into operation, the entrepreneur again and again is called upon to decide whether the process should be continued as planned, continued with changes, or simply be abandoned. In making these decisions, the entrepreneur must still consider the costs of production necessary for a continuation of production. He must, as in all entrepreneurial decision making, balance expected revenue against expected costs. But in making this calculation,

> he pays no attention whatsoever to the expenses of production that he has already paid out (or that he has irrevocably committed himself to pay).

What has been paid has been paid. To be sure the entrepreneur will be conscious that his past actions and commitments have determined, in part, the circumstances under which future activity must be carried on. (He will be aware, for example, that a past commitment to pay annual interest sums on capital sunk into a plant will limit his future cash position.) But in comparing anticipated costs with anticipated revenues, the entrepreneur *pays no heed to those amounts that do not depend on his present decisions.* These past amounts may have been wisely or unwisely incurred, but there is nothing that can be done to alter the past. The aim must be to exploit *now* the favorable position the entrepreneur may find himself in (as a result of the past decisions that now appear to have been wise ones); or to make the best of a poor situation he may find himself in (as a result of past decisions that now appear to have been unwise ones). In *either* event, the way to achieve this aim is to make that decision, with respect to the continuation of the production process, that promises the widest

---

3. For further analysis of the *time-consuming* aspect of all production, see pp. 340 ff in the Appendix on multi-period planning.

margin between the revenue anticipated on the one hand, and the costs of production *yet* to be incurred through continuation of production, on the other hand.

When the statement is made that the quantity supplied to the market by the individual entrepreneur depends on his costs of production, the proposition may thus refer to many different situations in *each* of which it is valid, *mutatis mutandis*. It is true that the quantity supplied by an entrepreneur depends on his decisions as to the size of factory to build; and it is equally true that the quantity supplied depends on entrepreneurial decisions as to how heavily to utilize a given plant once it has been built; on the decisions as to how many machines to install; and, again, on subsequent decisions as to how fully to employ the available machines once they have been installed; and so on. For each of these decisions the relevant "costs of production" are different; yet there is clearly a sense where supply depends on *each* of these different conceptions of costs of production. The crucial point is obviously the *time* factor. There are forces acting upon supply which make themselves felt both frequently and rapidly; there are other forces, no less powerful, which influence supply less frequently and less rapidly.

In the economic literature it is sometimes convenient to group together the *short-run* influences upon supply, as distinct from the *long-run* forces. The latter are conceived as being felt only over those periods of time long enough to warrant reconsideration of the size of the firm's fixed plant. The "short-run" forces are felt whenever there is room for decisions as to the level of output to be achieved with a given plant. While this dichotomy is of considerable convenience (as will be seen in later chapters), it must not be regarded as more than a simplification. The truth is that a decision that an entrepreneur is called upon to make may vary, in respect to the permanence of its impact on production, through a wide spectrum. A sudden change in market conditions may influence the entrepreneur to step up production sharply. The immediately felt consequences, possibly, will be overtime employment of the labor force and intensive utilization of existing machinery. Should the change in conditions persist, the entrepreneur might initiate more frequent replacement of machines, recruitment of a larger permanent work-force, and so on. Finally, the entrepreneur might be called upon to decide whether or not to expand the size of the factory, whether or not to build an additional factory, and so on. Supply depends, in a different sense, upon each of these kinds of decisions. Each such decision is based on the *relevant* costs of production. In each case the entrepreneur is aware that the total relevant costs of production will vary with the size of the output concerning which the decision is to be made. Costs that do not vary in total amount with production are simply not relevant costs of production. They are sums that have already been incurred in past production decisions and therefore do not depend on, and cannot influence decisions concerning, the level of output now to be undertaken.[4]

CAPITAL GOODS AND COST THEORY

The foregoing discussion indicates the role played by *capital goods* in a theory of costs and supply. We have seen that the forces influencing the supply of a particular product are as numerous, and as different in their impact, as are the opportunities available to the entrepreneur to alter the progress of production. The main reason for the differences between the impacts of these various forces lies fundamentally in the *specificity* of the capital goods introduced at various stages of the process of production.

The concept of specificity in a factor of production refers, we have already seen, to the limitation of the usefulness of the factor to a narrow range of purposes. A specific factor is either used for these definite purposes, or it can be of no use at all. Factors of production, we saw in the previous chapter, are more specific or less specific, depending on their degree of versatility in production.

Any produced factor of production capable of yielding productive services over a period of time is a durable *capital good*.[5] Capital goods emerge as a result of past production of goods that were not consumed. Men

---

4. The distinction between long-run and short-run forces is responsible for the corresponding distinction, current in economic literature, between *fixed* costs and *variable* costs. Fixed costs are unchanging for the duration of the short run; variable costs are those that do change with changes in output even in the short run. From the long-run viewpoint there are no fixed costs; all are variable. The discussion in the text will have made it clear (a) that from the short-run point of view, expenditures that do not fall under the heading of variable costs are best considered, not as "fixed," but as not being costs at all; (b) that there may be a number of degrees of "fixity" in costs corresponding to the numerous junctures at which a producer may be forced to make decisions (and at which the expenditures previously irrevocably incurred are no longer weighed as cost factors in arriving at decisions).

5. For additional remarks on the nature of capital goods and their role in production and in market theory, see in the Appendix on multi-period planning, pp. 340–344.

produced, sacrificed labor and the services of other factors, in order to obtain goods that should yield their services in later production. Where the capital good is a durable one, the past production and utilization of productive services were undertaken in order to obtain a *stream* of such productive services in the future.

Now it is in the nature of things that capital goods are (at least to some degree) specific. When labor and raw materials have been combined to produce *any* material object, this object is more suitable for some purposes than for others. The labor applied in its manufacture *might* have been used to produce something else; but it happened to be used up in the production of *this* object. While it is sometimes said that capital goods represent "saved-up" labor (along with other productive services), the capital good cannot serve, in general, as a store of the versatility of the invested labor. A man may be able to dig holes in the ground with his bare hands. Instead he uses them to fashion a spade. The production of this capital good enables him to "save" his original labor for later use. When he uses his spade later to dig holes, he reaps (with more or less "profit") the fruits of his originally invested labor. But the spade, which serves as the "store" of labor, has stored it in a form that is *specific;* the original labor services (which *might* have been used to chop down trees) can be exploited, in their stored-up form, only to dig holes.

This necessarily specific character of capital goods is responsible for the heterogeneous nature of the cost forces acting upon supply. If capital goods were completely versatile, then the fact that past decisions have been made would in no way interfere with the necessity to weigh the *full* costs of production in making later decisions. Complete versatility in capital goods (conceived broadly as the capacity of a good to serve equally valuably in *any* productive process—and thus including complete mobility and ease of transferability between firms and industries) would mean that expenses paid out as a result of past decisions are completely retrievable. A new decision to continue a particular process of production will thus have taken into account the fact that this course of action means abandoning for the time being the possibility of recovering *all* the sums already sunk into the productive venture. Each decision made during the production process would then be made by comparing expected revenues with expected total costs—the latter including all sums, those already spent as well as those expected to be paid. The level of output will be determined on the basis of the *same* cost at each state of decision making (assuming no change in the market data concerning costs). Changes in the market prices of finished products would set up forces influencing supply that would not depend for their impact upon the time available for the impact to be felt. Forces able to exert a certain long-range impact would not exert any different pressure on supply than that exerted by forces felt within a very short time.

Capital goods, however, are not completely versatile. Once a decision has been made to invest in a certain machine, it is a commonplace that the sum invested can be recovered only at considerable loss, should the original production plans be abandoned later on. The machine will hardly be able to be used in other productive processes; and its value as scrap will be far less than the price paid for it. Moreover, even where the machine can be of use to similar firms, or to firms in other industries, the cost of transfer is likely to be such as to make full recovery of its purchase price impossible. Later decisions concerning the use to be made of the machines will therefore disregard a large part of the sums originally paid for the machines. The determination of supply in periods short enough to warrant no purchase of new machines will therefore be governed by cost considerations different from those influencing supply when longer periods (during which the costs of machines *may* be a pivotal factor) are under consideration.

The more durable the capital goods involved, the longer will be the time periods during which it may be possible, and wise, to ignore the cost of the capital goods. The more durable the capital goods, the longer it will be possible to use their services in production, without having to worry about their costs—since these services have been paid for already anyway.

A typical situation the entrepreneur finds himself in is where a factory, more or less well-equipped with certain machinery, has been already constructed. The existence of such a complex of durable, immobile, and specific factors exercises a profound influence on the relative attractiveness of the various alternatives available to the entrepreneur. The entrepreneur may be aware of new techniques of production that would enable a modern factory equipped with up-to-date machines to produce a larger output at a fraction of his present cost. He may be deterred from embracing this possibility because the wonderful new factory requires the outlay of money—*new* money, while the old factory, inefficient as it is, is available for use at almost no cost at all. The opportunity costs at *this* stage of producing a given output with the more "efficient" plant are *greater* than with the less "efficient" plant. Both from the point of view of the entrepreneur himself and from that of the consumers, the relevant opportunity costs indicate using up the old plant while it is still worthwhile. Only when the gap between the technical efficiencies of the new and the old plants has become so wide as to outweigh the cost disadvantage involved in the initial construction of the new plant (as compared with the old) will it be economically advantageous to scrap the old factory. Such a gap *may* occur while the "old" factory is still quite new; revolutions in technology *may* render recently constructed plants completely obsolete. But, more likely, it is necessary for the old plants to depreciate physically to a greater or lesser extent before it pays to build a newer and more efficient plant. In the interim period, during which repeated entrepreneurial deliberations pronounce the old factory the most advantageous, output levels will depend on the *additional* costs incurred by producing with the existing plant.

These additional costs required to cover the raw materials, labor, and other productive services used directly in the manufacture of the product will be found to vary, per unit of output, with the level of output itself. The existence of a fixed plant, which for the time being is not to be changed, exerts in itself a powerful influence on the relation between output level and per-unit production costs. This relationship must now be explored.

FACTOR DIVISIBILITY AND SHORT-RUN PER-UNIT COSTS

Production is carried on, we have seen, with the aid of capital goods. The more advanced the organization of production in an economy, the more durable will be the capital goods used in production, and the greater will be the proportion in which capital goods are combined with other complementary factors of production. The existence in a plant of any given complex of capital goods has *two* distinct implications for costs of production that the entrepreneur must consider in his daily production decisions. *First,* as discussed in the previous sections, the relevant costs in daily decisions will not include sums incurred in the past for the acquisition of the capital goods, insofar as these involve no current opportunity cost. *Second,* and it is this influence that is discussed in this section, a given complex of capital goods is itself the source of a definite pattern that the entrepreneur will find to characterize the way his relevant costs of production depend on the volume of output. This pattern in the costs of production is an inevitable consequence of the limited *divisibility* of capital goods; the pattern itself is an implication of the laws of variable proportions.

An entrepreneur has at his disposal a fully equipped plant. A decision to alter output will have the short-run effect, not of a plant being closed down (or another erected), but of a *different* quantity of variable factors being used complementarily with the *given* plant.

Any decision to alter production would thus have the immediate effect of altering the proportions in which the fixed plant and the variable productive factors are combined.

If capital goods and other factors were highly divisible, then a change in the volume of output would not necessarily entail an alteration in the input proportions of the different factors. For each level of output the optimum combination of factors would be employed. A 10% increase in the volume of output would call for alteration in the quantity employed of *each* of the factors wherever—and only wherever—this would meet the requirements for the new optimally proportioned input mix. With complete divisibility, there would be no obstacle preventing the exact desired adjustment in the employment of any factor. Thus, no efficiency in production would be gained, nor would any efficiency be lost, by an alteration in output volume, insofar as efficiency depends on input proportions.

But, of course, capital goods are only imperfectly divisible. An entrepreneur who owns one sewing machine can hardly increase or decrease his employment of sewing machines by 10%. An airline can alter the size of its fleet of planes only by adding or discarding planes in whole numbers. Therefore, an entrepreneur who slightly decreases the volume of his output must do so typically by combining a smaller quantity of variable inputs with an unchanged quantity of fixed capital equipment. Only if the cutback in production is considerable will the input of these capital goods be decreased. The more elaborate the capital goods involved, the greater the cutback (or the boost) in production will have to be before any alteration in the input of this factor is feasible.

The consequence of capital-goods-indivisibility is thus that different volumes of output are inevitably associated with differently proportioned input combinations. Thus, the laws of variable proportions clearly become relevant. Differently proportioned input combinations are in turn associated with different efficiencies in production. A change from one level of production to another means a change in the output that can be obtained from a given quantity of inputs. Put the other way around, this means that different volumes of output will be obtained at the cost of respectively different quantities of input per unit of output. Costs of production must change, per unit of output, with changing output itself, simply as a consequence of the laws of variable proportions.

We have already seen how the cost forces acting upon the supply of a product may exert their influence over different time periods. Some forces will be felt more swiftly, others will be felt only gradually, throughout longer periods of time. The main reason for this heterogeneity in cost forces stems, we have seen, from the existence of more or less fixed blocks of specific capital goods that are introduced at various stages in the process of production. Factor indivisibility, in which we are now directly interested, plays an obvious part in emphasizing this heterogeneity. The costs of erecting the firm's plant are "fixed," for considerable lengths of time, because it is only infrequently that it becomes feasible to change the entire plant. But if plant size were capable of being altered by small percentages, such alterations would seem profitable at far more frequent intervals. The fact that items such as heavy machinery and plant are *not* capable of such nicely adjusted alterations in size makes their costs relatively fixed over considerable periods. If plant size were easily variable, then even a rapid change in output volume might bring about some change in the size of plant.[6]

With the imperfect divisibility of capital goods, a fairly well-defined pattern of per-unit costs of production emerges. An entrepreneur finds himself with given fixed capital equipment, plant, and machinery. If the forces of demand were to move him to produce smaller and smaller output volumes, the immediate consequences would be that the variable inputs would be combined with the fixed inputs in smaller and smaller proportions. These proportions might be so low that the marginal increment of product corresponding to a small hypothetical increase in the fixed input might possibly be negative for low levels of output; in such a situation any increase in the variable inputs must raise the output per unit of variable inputs. The proportion of variable to fixed inputs would be less than optimal: the fixed plant would be greatly underutilized. If, on the other hand, the entrepreneur were moved by market demand to produce

6. Even if plants were perfectly versatile but able to be built only in a limited number of sizes, this indivisibility would mean that plant alteration is feasible only at fairly wide intervals. On the other hand, even if plants could be built in *any* desired size but were completely specific to one kind of production (or were, at any rate, completely immobile and thus unable to be transferred to other branches of production), plant alteration, once again, would be feasible only at long intervals. In the real world, then, *both* specificity and indivisibility combine to make expenditures for plant a cost only from the long-run view, and to bring about the typical pattern of variable costs discussed in the text.

larger and larger volumes of output, the situation would be reversed. Variable inputs would be combined with fixed inputs in greater and greater proportions. For one particular volume of output, the input proportions would be optimal. For greater outputs the fixed plant might be used more intensively than would be optimal; the average efficiency of the variable inputs would be falling. Although variable inputs would *never* be added by the entrepreneur in such volume as to make the corresponding marginal increments of product *negative,* nevertheless, the proportion of variable to fixed inputs may be so high as to render the marginal increment of product very low.

Translated into cost terms, our analysis thus yields fairly straightforward conclusions insofar as *short-run entrepreneurial decisions* are concerned. We recall that in day-to-day decision making, the fixed inputs entail no costs. The entrepreneur is called upon to make pecuniary sacrifices in order to obtain product, only through his purchases of variable factor services. The average efficiency in production of *these* services has been seen first to rise and then to fall as output is increased from very low to very high levels. Thus, the sacrifice of factor services, per unit of *output,* which the entrepreneur is called to make, would tend to fall, reach a minimum, and then rise for outputs raised higher and higher from very low levels. We may assume for the time being that the *prices* of factor services, which the entrepreneur is required to pay, do not depend on volume of output. It is then clear that the per-unit costs of production relevant to short-range entrepreneurial decisions will be high for low outputs, fall to a minimum for higher outputs, and then rise to higher levels once again as output is increased to the point where the fixed plant is being overutilized, so that decreasing average returns to the variable inputs prevail.

SHORT-RUN COSTS AND THEIR EFFECT ON SUPPLY

We have discovered that per-unit costs of production follow a characteristic pattern when the volume of production is changed within the framework of a given plant. This pattern suggests the way a producer with a given plan will make short-run output decisions, and the way these decisions will change with changes in the market conditions for his product. As we have seen, once a producer has constructed a plant, changes in market conditions only in fairly exceptional cases will bring him immediately to seek a different scale of plant. For the most part changes in market conditions will merely bring about revisions in the decisions concerning how heavily to utilize the given plant (that is, what quantities of variable inputs should be combined with the plant). These revisions will be made in the light of the short-run per-unit cost pattern that we have discovered.

Generally, a producer will seek to produce that volume of output (during a given period) that will yield the highest surplus of aggregate revenue over aggregate (relevant) costs of production. In contemplating any proposed volume of output (per period), an entrepreneur will always ask himself whether he could not do better by producing an output volume slightly larger, or slightly smaller, than that proposed. An output slightly *larger* than a proposed level would involve an increase in aggregate (relevant) costs of production; on the other hand, the increase would bring an increase in aggregate revenue. If the *marginal revenue* involved in this way (by the contemplated expansion of output beyond the level originally proposed) exceeds the *marginal cost* involved (the latter, of course, referring to the increment in *short-run* costs that are relevant with a given plant), then clearly the larger output is to be preferred over that originally proposed. Similarly, in contemplating a *contraction* of output below a proposed level, the producer will compare the *reduction* that this will allow in aggregate short-run production costs, with the associated reduction in aggregate revenue from product sales. Should the former exceed the latter, then the smaller output is to be preferred over that originally proposed.

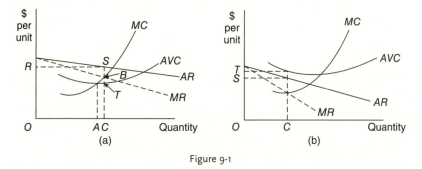

Figure 9-1

Diagrammatically, therefore, a producer will seek to produce that output (during each period) at which his marginal revenue curve intersects his marginal cost curve from above. In the diagram [Figure 9-1(a)] *AVC* is the curve of per-unit costs patterned according to the analysis of the preceding section. It shows that when the plant is combined with only a small quantity of variable inputs, the costs (of these variable inputs) per unit of output are high. These costs are shown to fall with increased utilization of the plant until (at the output *OA*) variable inputs are combined with the plant in optimum proportions, so that when the plant is combined with still greater quantities of variable inputs, the average efficiency of the latter fall and result in rising per-unit costs of production. MC is a curve showing the increments to aggregate variable costs corresponding to each successive unit of output.[7] This curve lies below the AVC line for outputs less that OA, and above the AVC line for larger outputs. For the output OA (at which per-unit costs are at a minimum), marginal cost is the same as per-unit cost.[8] An average revenue curve (AR) and a marginal revenue curve (MR) are also drawn in the diagram. The AR line expresses the producer's expectations respecting the prices at which he can expect to sell (during each period) the various possible output volumes under consideration.[9] (In drawing this AR line, we make, therefore, the some-what questionable assumption that the entrepreneur does in fact possess definite expectations on these points.) The MR line, then, expresses a set of implications of the AR line as drawn: it sets down, for each successive unit of output, the increment to aggregate revenue associated with its pro-duction and sale. (For any outputs q_n, q_{n+1}, which the producer expects to be able to sell at prices per unit, p_n, p_{n+1}, respectively, the marginal revenue associated with the $(n + 1)$th unit of output, is therefore $(q_{n+1} \cdot p_{n+1}) - q_n p_n$.)

With the cost and revenue curves shown, the producer will seek to produce an output volume OC. This he will be able to sell at a price CS. Any output greater than OC would be less than optimal from his point of view, since for each unit of output beyond OC the increment in costs exceeds the increment in revenue. Similarly, any contraction of output below OC would involve a sacrifice of revenue in excess of the diminution of aggregate costs of production. With output OC the firm is doing the best it can.[10]

7. The cost curves are drawn continuous. In a real world we might find, of course, that discontinuous curves would be a more faithful representation.

8. See pp. 105–106.

9. On the shape of the demand curve facing an entrepreneur, see pp. 101–103.

10. A word may be added here concerning the quantities of the various factors of production that the producer will be employing in order to produce the optimal output OC. These factors, of course, will be employed so as to make up the "least-cost combi-nation" (discussed at the end of Ch. 8). An alteration in the price of a factor of produc-tion will thus affect the quantity a producer will employ (as reflected in his demand curve for it) in *two* distinct ways. *First,* as we have already seen in Ch. 8 (n. 15), an altera-tion in the price of one factor will induce the producer to substitute a factor that has become relatively less expensive in place of one that has become relatively expensive (even if no alteration were to occur also in the scale of production). *Second,* an alteration

It is clear, then, that short-run output decisions will depend upon the expected demand for the producer's product, since upon this will depend his average revenue curve, and, in turn, his marginal revenue curve. Should expected demand be so weak that the producer can discover no volume of output where average revenue is greater than the relevant average cost of the variable inputs, he will produce no output. Thus in the diagram [Figure 9-1(b)] were he to produce even the quantity OC (where $MR = MC$), while doing better than at any other positive output, he would still be paying out *variable* costs for each unit of output that exceeds the corresponding revenue by the amount ST. (In addition, from the long-run point of view, he would be failing to earn anything toward the recovery of the costs sunk, in the past, in the fixed plant.) The producer, in this case, finds himself saddled with a plant that it does not pay to use at all, since nothing that it can be used to produce can be sold for enough to cover even the additional inputs that would now be required.

Should demand conditions be such that the output, for which marginal revenue just balances marginal cost, can be sold at a price per unit greater than the per-unit cost of variable inputs, then it will pay the producer to produce this volume of output. As we have seen, this volume of output (OC in the diagram) is to be preferred over any other positive output level (since $MC = MR$); and since for this output $AR > AVC$, the producer is better off with this output than with no output. Even if the excess of aggregate revenue over aggregate cost of variable inputs (that is, the amount $ST \times OC$ in Figure 9-2) is insufficient to cover the current quota of costs sunk in the fixed plant (so that from the longer-run point of view the decision to build the plant is seen to have been a mistaken one that has caused losses), nevertheless, the producer (who now cannot retrieve the past and can only do the best he can with the plant) can improve his position through producing OC. By so producing he earns enough revenue on each unit produced to cover all costs of variable inputs, and, in addition, to leave over the amount ST per unit of output (or the aggregate amount $ST \times OC$) toward the recovery of the sunk costs. From the short-run point of view this amount ($ST \times OC$) is "profit": the decision to produce can

---

in the price of a factor will change the level of output at which the marginal cost curve (duly modified to reflect the new least-cost combinations marked out by the new factor prices) intersects the marginal revenue curve. At all possible prices of a factor, however, it remains true that a producer will purchase that quantity of it such that the last dollar spent upon it yields a marginal product worth just more than a dollar.

improve the entrepreneur's position by this whole amount. (Should this amount of $ST \times OC$ exceed the entire sum sunk in the fixed plant, then, of course, the operation will be pronounced a profitable one from the longer-run point of view as well.)

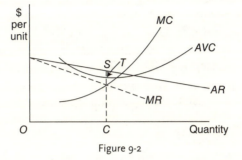

Figure 9-2

In general, it will be observed that the entrepreneur will in the short run be prepared to use his plant more intensively as the average and marginal revenue lines are higher on the diagram. Since marginal costs rise with increased output (after an initially falling phase), it follows that when, with a given cost picture, the intersection of the marginal revenue and marginal cost curves occurs at higher values of marginal revenue (due to an upward shift of both AR and MR), this intersection corresponds to a greater output volume. The more urgently his product is desired by consumers, the more willing a producer will be to employ his fixed plant more intensively.

In the special case where an entrepreneur feels that he faces a perfectly elastic demand situation (so that he believes himself able to sell any quantity he pleases at a given price), the average and marginal revenue curves coincide as a horizontal line (at the level of the given price). In this case the quantity of output that it will pay to produce can be seen simply as given by the intersection of the price line with the marginal cost curve. When different possible profitable prices are considered (still assuming perfectly elastic demand), the *marginal cost curve itself* now appears as the *supply curve* of the firm. For each possible profitable price, the quantity that it will pay the firm to produce is expressed, for this case, by the corresponding abscissa of the marginal cost curve.

Our understanding of the way the short-run output decisions of the individual producer depend on the intensity of the demand for his product suggests, in addition, the likely immediate consequences for industry supply of the product, of a change in the intensity of overall market demand for it. As the general demand for a particular product grows more intense, it is likely that each of the entrepreneurs (possessing plants designed for this product) will discover that the demand and marginal revenue curves for their respective individual outputs have shifted upward. Each producer will discover that additional units of input promise to add greater revenue increments than previously. Each will seek to expand output in the short run so that for the group of producers as a whole, the change in demand tends to bring about an immediate output expansion with existing plants. The process whereby the market achieves this kind of short-run adjustment of supply to changes in demand conditions will be more fully discussed in the succeeding chapters.

LONG-RUN COSTS AND SUPPLY

When an individual entrepreneur considers the wisdom of entering a particular industry, his basic decisions will not be governed by the pattern of short-run costs. From the long-run point of view an entrepreneur must decide whether or not an output level exists for this product that (when produced as efficiently as he knows that this output can be produced, and sold for as high a price as he knows that this output can be sold) promises net proceeds greater than he knows to be obtainable elsewhere. In estimating how cheaply various possible levels of output can be produced, the entrepreneur is in the long run free to consider production in various different sizes of plants. Of course, in taking the long-run view of production, he will have to include (in the costs of production of any proposed level of output) the cost of erecting the most appropriately sized plant, as well as the cost of the variable inputs that will subsequently be required. An entrepreneur who *has* already been producing in the industry must also constantly review his position from the long-run point of view. He must constantly ask whether some alternative plan of production (of the same product), possibly with a different size of plant, could not yield him higher net proceeds (even after considering the foremost advantage of his existing production set up, namely, the fact that he already has his given plant and does not have now to incur costs for it, as he would have to do with alternative production plans). And as his existing plant reaches the end of its life, the entrepreneur must certainly make his decisions with predominantly long-run considerations in mind.

In making these long-run decisions, therefore, entrepreneurs will examine the various proposed levels of output with so-called "long-run" costs in mind. The relevant cost of producing any proposed output volume, during each period of time, will now be the sum required for production when the scale of plant, together with all the inputs, can be selected with complete freedom out of *all* possible sizes and combinations (subject only to the constraint that the resulting cost sum be then the lowest known possible amount).[11] In contemplating any proposed volume of output, during each period of time, an entrepreneur taking a long-run view will ask whether a better position might not be secured by producing an output slightly larger, or slightly smaller, than that proposed. In comparing the proposed output with one slightly larger, he will compare the relevant marginal cost with marginal revenue. The marginal cost relevant for the long-run view is the difference between the aggregate costs of production (of the two volumes of output under consideration) when *each* of the respective aggregate costs is that which would result from the use of the plant size selected as best for *the particular volume of output under consideration.*[12]

11. In a real world where entrepreneurs hold expectations concerning the future only with considerable *uncertainty,* even this constraint will not necessarily be operative. The producer may well deliberately construct a plant, even though this plant will result in higher costs of production for the expected output volume than need be incurred with a differently constructed plant. He may make this decision simply because the first plant, while more expensive than the second, has the advantage of being more *adaptable* to possible deviations from the expected conditions. Concerning this see Stigler, G., "Production and Distribution in the Short Run," *Journal of Political Economy,* June, 1939.

12. Long-run cost curves are drawn to reflect these considerations. An assertion that the line *LAC* in the diagram is a long-run average cost curve amounts to the following statement. For the level of output expressed by the abscissa of any point on the line, its ordinate corresponds to the lowest per-unit costs of production possible for the output when (a) the producer is free to select any size of plant for each output level, and (b) the costs of production include *all* expenditures (which an entrepreneur who starts out without owning *any* resources must incur in order to produce the output).

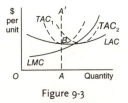

Figure 9-3

Although, once the entrepreneur has built his plant only "variable" costs need be considered in subsequent decision making, this is of course not the case for long-run

The pattern that long-run costs will follow as the entrepreneur considers a wide range of successively larger volumes of output will depend on the technological conditions governing the particular kind of production. Since there is freedom to vary the proportions of all factors used, there would seem (if we assume long-run divisibility of all factors) to be no room for the laws of variable proportions to operate. Divisibility of factors would permit the production of any proposed output with the least-cost combination of factors. With all factors divisible, this identical *proportion* of inputs, if desired, can be reproduced for the production of any other scale of output. It follows that (if we retain our temporary assumption of constant factor prices) any change in the per-unit cost of production, resulting from a change in output, must be attributed to the change in *scale* of production, not to any change in factor proportions. During a portion of the preceding chapter the analysis proceeded on the assumption of constant returns to scale. On this assumption the per-unit long-run costs of production would remain unchanged regardless of the scale of output (so long as factor prices do not change). Any proposed volume of output could then be produced, in the long-run view, at as low a per-unit cost as any other volume of output. Long-run marginal cost would be unchanged for all proposed output changes and would be the same as

---

purposes. Prospective costs, from the long-run view, are the sum of (a) the "fixed" cost of erecting the desired plant and (b) the variable costs appropriate to the selected size of plant. *With respect to a given proposed size of plant,* prospective costs per unit of output, from the long-run view, are thus obtained by dividing the sum of these two cost figures (for each output level possible with the plant) by the corresponding output quantity. (The cost curve thus derived is thus higher than the corresponding short-run [variable] average cost curve for this plant size, at each output level, by the quota of "fixed" cost assigned to a unit of output for that output level.) In the diagram the line TAC_1 is such a curve (for one size plant); TAC_2 is another. If one were to imagine such curves to be drawn for each possible size of plant, it is clear that the curve that cuts the vertical line AA' at the lowest point corresponds to the size of plant most suited to the production of the output OA; and similarly for all levels of output. AB thus emerges as the long-run cost per unit for an output volume OA; and the line of long-run average costs LAC is seen to be the "envelope" of all the TAC curves relevant respectively to all the various proposed levels of output.

The long-run marginal cost curve is drawn bearing the usual geometrical relationship to the corresponding average curve. At any given level of output, long-run marginal cost is equal to the short-run marginal cost for that level of output when the optimum-sized plant for the output is being used.

long-run per-unit cost. Any increase in intensity of market demand for the product of the industry could result in a larger aggregate supply, without any increase being necessary in the product price.[13]

Where, however, the required factors of production are only imperfectly divisible, it will not in general be possible to expand output by simply increasing the input of each factor in the same proportion. If there is a particular volume of output for which inputs, by chance, can be combined in an optimum proportion, a relatively small increase or decrease in output will result, with some inputs indivisible, in a less than optimally proportioned input combination. When an indivisible input is underutilized, expansion of output will lower per-unit costs. When output has expanded sufficiently so that optimal proportions are attained, further employment of additional units of the divisible factors without a corresponding increase in the input of the indivisible factors (due to this indivisibility) must raise per-unit costs. Thus, even where production might otherwise yield constant returns to scale, factor indivisibilities may cause rising or falling long-run costs.[14] In fact, it is possible (and sometimes convenient) to view *all* departures from constant returns to scale as being in principle the consequences of "indivisibilities."

13. The long-run average (and marginal) cost curve would thus be a horizontal straight line passing through the minimum points of all the *TAC* curves. (Of course, once a given sized plant has been built, the [short-run] marginal costs will nevertheless be rising.)

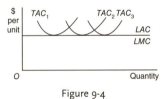

Figure 9-4

14. Many economists (for diverse reasons) have believed that the accompanying diagram illustrates the typical pattern of long-run costs.

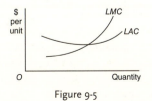

Figure 9-5

Whatever the pattern of long-run costs, which the technological conditions of the industry determine, an entrepreneur will formulate his long-run plans by comparing marginal cost with marginal revenue for each possible output. If there is no output at which the long-run average costs are fully balanced by expected average revenue, the entrepreneur will not enter the industry. Where the demand for his product is sufficiently strong for a range of outputs to be possible for which average cost is not greater than average revenue, the entrepreneur will choose to produce that output for which long-run marginal cost is just balanced by long-run marginal revenue. When he produces this output volume with the size of plant that minimizes its costs of production, he is doing the very best that he can.[15] Any other output, no matter how efficiently produced, must yield either a smaller surplus of aggregate revenue over aggregate costs, or even a deficit.

For the special case where an entrepreneur believes the demand for his product to be perfectly elastic (so that he can sell any volume of output without lowering the price), he will attempt, if it pays at all to be in the industry, to expand output (that is, to build larger and larger plants) so long as long-run average costs decline (that is, so long as there are increasing returns to scale). The size of plant that he should erect will be limited only by eventually rising long-run costs (when he will seek to build a size of plant for which his long-run marginal costs just balance his product price).

FACTOR PRICES AND SUPPLY

Cost curves and supply have been analyzed in the preceding sections on the assumption that the prices of productive factors do not change regardless of the level of output. So long as this assumption was retained, the

---

15. It needs to be stressed that long-run cost considerations do *not* require that the producer erect a plant of such a size that he use it subsequently at its most efficient level of utilization. In other words the *LAC* curve does *not* necessarily pass through the minimum points of the *TAC* curves. All that is necessary is that, for whatever output level it is decided to produce, a plant of necessary size be erected that minimizes its costs of production. This may well mean that this plant will then be used at less (or more) than *its* optimum level of utilization. This does not matter; the output that would be yielded by such "optimum" utilization of the plant could be produced more cheaply, it is likely, by underutilizing or overutilizing a different size of plant. Anyway, the aim is not to use plants at their most efficient levels of use, but to produce a given output with *its* most efficient combination of inputs.

only changes in the per-unit costs of production that were possible, as output increased, were those resulting from the *technological* conditions governing production. Thus, in the short run, per-unit costs changed as a result of the laws of variable proportions, while in the long run, costs depended on returns to scale. It was possible, we found, to make statements concerning supply (especially for the short run) based solely on these considerations. But we have already seen that the costs (and therefore the supply) of each product are governed by a paramount additional *economic* consideration. We know that when the output of any one product is expanded, a withdrawal is required of more and more units of factors away from potential employment in other branches of production. By the principle of diminishing marginal utility, therefore, the steady advancement of the margin of output of any one product involves the simultaneous *reduction* in importance of each additional unit of *this* product, and *increase* in importance of the units at the respective margins of output of *other* products.

This tendency must eventually express itself through the price mechanism. (In the succeeding chapters we will examine more closely *how* the market process would tend to make prices reflect such a tendency.) Eventually, entrepreneurs in the expanding industry would find on the one hand that their product has a lower price, and on the other hand that the various inputs can be bid away from other industries only at higher prices. As a result of the latter tendency, it is clear, producers will find that the per-unit costs of producing their product will tend to rise. Producers will attempt to escape some of the consequences of higher factor prices by altering the proportions of the various inputs, substituting factors whose prices have not risen (or which have risen less) in place of the factors whose prices have risen most. But the rising factor costs will ultimately raise the costs of production, and this will exert an appreciable effect on supply. The output for which an entrepreneur finds that marginal revenue is balanced by marginal cost will be a smaller one, as a result of rising factor costs. With a given intensity of demand for his product, the entrepreneur will therefore be prepared to supply only a smaller volume of output to the market.

If the entrepreneur is a relatively important buyer of a particular resource, he may find that the price of this input rises directly (and significantly) as a result of his own expansion of output and consequent increased purchases of the input. In such a case his own cost curves will directly incorporate the rising factor prices. Where the individual entrepreneur is a relatively unimportant purchaser of a particular input, its price will not rise appreciably as a result of his output expansion alone. But where a larger number of entrepreneurs are simultaneously expanding output (as a result, let us say, of an increase in demand), their competition will eventually force up the price of the required inputs.[16] In this case an individual entrepreneur will incorporate the consequences of rising factor prices in his long-run cost estimates only if he is able to forecast correctly the general expansion of his industry (and thus the higher prices). Entrepreneurial decisions made subsequent to a rise in factor prices, of course, will take them fully into account; thus, as the aggregate quantity supplied of the product increases, the resulting rise in factor prices will very definitely act as a drag upon further increases in supply.

It is not difficult to understand the various factors that determine the extent of the price rise of a particular resource consequent to expansion of production in a particular industry. The more important the industry (relative to all the industries employing this resource), the more sensitive the resource price will be to the expansion of the industry. Again, on the other hand, the more elastic the *overall* supply of this resource, the smaller will be the rise in its price necessary to expand output in one industry (since a small rise in price will call into production a greater aggregate supply of the resource, making it unnecessary to withdraw a great deal of the resource from other industries). The more easily a given resource can be replaced by other inputs (both in the expanding industry and in the others), the less rapidly will the industry expansion bring about a rise in the resource price. A small rise in its price will lead to its substitution by other inputs. Another consideration indirectly relevant to a rise in input prices, consequent on expansion of an industry, will be the demand conditions for the other products employing the inputs. The more sensitively the quantity demanded of the other products shrinks as a result of a rise in their prices (consequent on increases in factor prices and thus

16. Where a producer's cost curves rise in consequence of an expansion not of his own output, but of the output of his entire industry, the industry is said to be subject to *external diseconomies*. Rising costs come to the producer due to reasons "external" to his own operations. In theoretical literature attention is also paid to the industry that enjoys *external economies*. Here the costs of the individual producer *falls* as a consequence of expansion of the output of the industry as a whole. External economies are usually identified with such effects of expansion as more wide-spread knowledge, the possible cheapening of factors used, the increased possibilities of economies due to specialization, and so on.

also in the production costs of these other products), the less sharply will factor prices rise further as a result of the further growth of the expanding industry.

An analysis of all these determining factors is merely a way of assessing the actual opportunity cost of withdrawing productive resources from one use for more extensive employment in a different use. The pricing process conveys all the relevant information on this score through the extent that input prices rise. The entrepreneur in the expanding industry considers this information in assessing his own cost of production for different possible levels of output. His decision of the quantity of output to supply the market will then reflect his desire (motivated by the search for profit) to serve the market most faithfully in the light of (a) the intensity of demand for his product, and (b) the loss to the market of other potential products involved in the production of each successive unit of his own product.

SUMMARY

In Chapter 9 the analysis of the forces of supply is continued. Relying on the principles of production developed in the preceding chapter, the present chapter examines the way costs of production depend upon the level of output, and thus how producers make their output decisions.

The economist views cost from the *opportunity cost* point of view. (Any portion of a price paid for the use of a factor that does not reflect the foregone product that the factor could have rendered elsewhere is not a cost but *rent*.) From the opportunity cost point of view, the market governs the supply of any one product by balancing its value against that of the other products sacrificed through its production. This control is expressed through the impact of the producer's costs of production. The costs relevant to any particular production decision are those alternatives that, available immediately *before* the decision, were rejected by that decision. Since in the course of the production of a product it may be necessary to make successively a number of decisions, it is clear that the "cost of production" of the product cannot be unambiguously described unless a particular decision is identified as the focus of attention.

This relativity of costs springs partly from the *specificity* of the capital goods used in production. Because the costs incurred for capital goods at an early stage in production planning cannot subsequently be retrieved through switching them to other uses, it follows that these sunk costs are not costs at all from the point of view of subsequent production decisions.

The limited *divisibility* of capital goods is responsible for the typical way short-run costs depend upon the level of output. Output changes involve, as a consequence of the laws of returns, therefore, changes in factor efficiency, and thus in the per-unit cost of output. The resulting pattern of short-run costs makes it possible to understand the way a producer will make short-run adjustments in output as a consequence of changes in the data facing him.

In making decisions for the long run, on the other hand, producers must consider *all* prospective costs in a production process. In planning the size of plant, a producer must consider the way prospective changes in long-run output affect these overall costs. Involved in such alterations is the question of *returns to scale,* rather than the effect of changes in factor proportions.

A more complete analysis of a producer's decisions must consider, in addition, the possibility and the consequences of alterations in *factor prices.* The impact of such alterations will depend on the size of the producer with respect to the relevant factor market. The extent of the changes to be expected in factor prices as a result of the expansion of a given industry depends on the alternative uses of the factor and the conditions surrounding the elasticity of the factor's supply.

SUGGESTED READINGS

Viner, J., "Cost Curves and Supply Curves," *Zeitschrift für Nationalökonomie* (1931), reprinted in *Readings in Price Theory,* American Economic Association.

Chamberlin, E. H., *The Theory of Monopolistic Competition,* 7th ed., Harvard University Press, Cambridge, Massachusetts, 1956, Appendix B.

Mises, L. v., *Human Action,* Yale University Press, New Haven, Connecticut, 1949, pp. 336–347, 499–510.

10 PARTIAL MARKET PROCESSES—
THE DETERMINATION OF PRODUCT
PRICES AND FACTOR PRICES

We return now to consider the market process. In Chapter 7 we considered the kind of market process that would emerge in the absence of production. We assumed a society naturally endowed with a daily income of consumption goods of various kinds, and we then followed through the logic governing the emergence of exchange and prices. For that analysis the only prior theory that was required was the theory of consumer demand. On the basis of the theory of the demand of the individual consumer, we were able to work out the results of the interaction of the activities of numerous individuals for whom there are no production opportunities. However, in a society where men are able to further their purposes, not only by consuming what they find easily available, but also by using their resources to produce other goods, the market process becomes much more complex. (We have already obtained a bird's-eye view of this process in Chapters 2 and 3.) This process is based on the actions of individual human beings not only as consumers, but also as producers and as resource owners. The preceding two chapters have been devoted to the theory of production and costs, clarifying the behavior of the individual producer. In this chapter and the next we follow through the market process in a productive society, taking fuller account of productive activities and the market phenomena they give rise to. To a considerable extent we will be able to rely on the analysis of the simplified market process contained in Chapter 7.

In Chapter 7 each market participant was endowed daily with an initial bundle of consumer goods. In our present problem each market participant is endowed in addition with a bundle of productive resources. The market presents possibilities for each participant, through exchange, production, and possibly further exchange, to transform his initial endowment into one that is more desirable from his point of view. The interaction of all participants in the market generates, as we saw in Chapters 2 and 3, sub-markets where various resources are bought and sold, and also a great deal of entrepreneurial activity linking the various sub-markets together through production decisions.

The market process determines (a) the prices and quantities of each of the resources sold, (b) the quantities of each of the resources used in each branch of production, and (c) the quantities and prices of each of the products produced and sold. (We are aware, of course, that any number of intermediate products may be produced and sold, as well as consumption goods.) This market process consists in the concatenation of decisions on the part of market participants, decisions to buy and sell resources, decisions to use resources to produce products, and decisions to buy and sell products. As such, and as we have already seen, the process is a single one—*all* the decisions are to some degree dependent upon all other decisions, and in turn influence further decisions. Any separate analysis of part of the whole market process is justified only provisionally in the expectation that such analysis will throw light on the process in its entirety. We proceed, therefore, in the present chapter, to consider first the market process as it directly affects the output and prices of only a single *product*. We will then consider how the market process directly affects the employment and prices of only a single productive *factor*. The extension of these preliminary inquiries will then enable us in the next chapter to view and to analyze the market process as an indivisible unity.

THE MARKET FOR A SINGLE PRODUCT

In analyzing the market for a single product, we are adopting a "partial" approach. The only variables into whose value we inquire are those directly pertaining to the product itself, namely, its price, the method of production and the quantities of different resources used in its production, and the quantities produced by different firms. All other market phenomena are assumed, insofar as they might affect our own product market, to be "given" and (at least for most of our inquiry) unchanging. We ignore, for example, any effects upon other prices that might be brought about by the process of adjustment in the market for our own product and that might, in return, exert secondary repercussions upon our own market.

Thus, our problem is to explain the course of the market forces affecting the price, output, and organization of production of our one product.

We assume prospective consumers to be faced with known and stable prices that each of the other available products can be bought at. We assume entrepreneurs to be faced with known and stable prices that each of the available productive factors can be bought at, as well as with definite, technologically determined, possible methods of production. We assume that a large number of entrepreneurs have access to the factors of production. Consumers possess, in addition, definite tastes and incomes. We proceed to spell out the conditions for complete equilibrium in this product market.

LONG-RUN EQUILIBRIUM

Complete (or "long-run") equilibrium conditions require that a certain number of firms produce the product, each firm producing a certain quantity, and each firm producing with a certain method of production; that entrepreneurs sell and consumers buy the product in certain quantities and for certain prices—all these quantities and prices being such that no participant or prospective participant in the market should ever find any reason to alter his actions for the future. As for a definition of the equilibrium price of the product, we may to a large extent draw upon the analysis of Chapter 7.[1] In equilibrium there can be only a single price for the product ruling in the market (otherwise entrepreneurs would eventually discover the discrepancy in prices, and buy the product where its price is low, and sell it where its price is high, until the discrepancy should disappear). This price must be such that the quantity of the product that consumers wish to buy at this price is exactly the same as the quantity of product that entrepreneurs plan to produce in expectation of this price. Any other price would mean that, sooner or later, somebody (producer or prospective consumer) will find that his plans cannot be executed in the market. Of course, he would have ample reason to alter his future actions; the market would no longer be in equilibrium.

There are several further relationships implied by these conditions for the equilibrium price. If the price is to be such that nobody should see reason to alter his actions for the future, it must inspire, of course, no entrepreneur in the industry (nor any prospective entrepreneur) to make any alteration in output volume. This means that equilibrium conditions require that the relationship between the volume of output, the price of the product, and the given prices of the various resources make it disadvantageous for any entrepreneur to expand production (or to make plans for eventual expansion of production); but that this relationship also makes it disadvantageous to cut back production (or to make plans to cut back production eventually).

This means, first of all, that each entrepreneur must be producing an output volume for which the aggregate opportunity cost of production is

1. See pp. 115–125.

no greater in the long run than the total revenue obtainable from the sale of the products; and also that no producer who is *not* at present producing the product can see any prospect of producing any quantity of the product that should yield a revenue greater than the (opportunity) costs of its production. If these conditions are not satisfied, changes in output will occur sooner or later. If any producers are incurring losses (that is, if their long-run opportunity costs of production—the revenue they could acquire eventually if they transferred their resources to some other branch of production—exceed the revenue that they currently receive from their output), they will sooner or later alter their actions. This might not happen immediately, since many resources may not be transferable, and may thus involve no immediate opportunity costs (and thus involve no short-run losses) in their present use. But sooner or later entrepreneurs will retire from an industry that yields overall opportunities inferior to those available in other branches of production. On the other hand, if any outsider to the industry can perceive prospects of an output that should yield a revenue in excess of what he could earn elsewhere with the same resources, he will sooner or later attempt to enter the industry. Neither of these eventualities is consistent with equilibrium in the product market.

The above required equilibrium relationship means, in addition, that each entrepreneur will be producing an output volume and facing a demand curve for his product so that the following conditions are satisfied: (a) the marginal unit produced has added to total revenue an amount exceeding the corresponding increase in relevant total opportunity costs, and (b) the next unit that the entrepreneur just *fails* to produce would have added an increment to cost exceeding or equaling what it would add to revenue. This, we saw in the previous chapter, represents the optimum volume of output, relevant—*mutatis mutandis*—for both short- and long-run decisions. (If potential producers are so numerous that an increase in output by one of them leaves the price of the product, and hence marginal revenue, virtually unchanged, it is clear that such an optimum output is possible only where the relevant marginal costs increase with increases in output. If marginal costs do not increase with expansion of output, then, if a certain level of output is selected as satisfactory, still larger outputs will be still more satisfactory with declining marginal costs, or at least no less satisfactory with constant marginal costs. Neither of these possibilities is consistent with equilibrium, since there is no good reason why any entrepreneur should continue producing a given output volume instead of expanding to produce a larger one.)

To sum up, a market for a product will be in complete (long-run) equilibrium when the following mutually consistent sets of decisions are being made. (1) Each entrepreneur is producing (in response to the market price) an output whose (long-run and short-run) marginal costs bear the above described relationship to revenues. (2) Each consumer is desirous of buying, at the same market price, a quantity such that the aggregate thus demanded is exactly what producers are, in aggregate, producing. (3) For each producer the market price is no less than the average long-run costs of production for his volume of output. (4) No entrepreneur who is not presently producing can find any possibility of employing resources in this industry more lucratively than in other industries. These equilibrium conditions define the scale of plant for each producer, the levels of plant utilization, the output consumed by each consumer, and the market price.

Assuming a unique pattern of decisions does exist for producers and consumers that would mesh completely in this way, it can be seen that perfect knowledge on the part of all market participants would help them immediately toward achieving equilibrium. The logic employed in Chapter 7 is sufficient to prove that the only price bids and offers made by prospective buyers and sellers are those that they know will not be disappointed and will not involve the sacrifice of more attractive opportunities. Acting, according to "static" assumptions, on the expectation that basic market data will never change, those producers willing to do so will then undertake long-range planning to achieve (at lowest possible cost of production) those outputs that it will pay them to offer to the market at what they know will be the equilibrium price. No other price can prevail, they can be assured, because this would call for the conscious adoption, on the part of some producers or consumers, of plans that they realize must be disappointed. In this way each producer will have constructed the "correct" scale of plant and will have hired the "correct" quantities of other factors necessary to achieve his "correct" share of the "correct" aggregate output. The point is that the long-run equilibrium price for the product is the one able to induce entrepreneurs to initiate long-range plans for the production of exactly that quantity that consumers will be prepared to buy at the same price. Perfect knowledge would make possible the precise calculation of this price, and also the realization that no plans will be made by anyone on the assumption of other prices.

In a subsequent section of this chapter we will proceed with our main purpose—the analysis of the market process in the single-product market when knowledge is *not* perfect. Before this, we will consider two situations where the market for a single product may be in "incomplete" equilibrium. These are model situations where the decisions being made *are* consistent with each other, and *do* mesh, but only on the hypothesis that specific kinds of further decisions (which *might* otherwise be made) are excluded from the models. In other words these two situations are such that they *would* be self-perpetuating *if* certain specified kinds of change are not allowed to occur in the analysis. In themselves these models of "shorter-run" equilibria are purely theoretical constructions, but they will prove helpful in understanding the market process leading to complete, long-run equilibrium.

SHORT-RUN EQUILIBRIUM IN THE SINGLE-PRODUCT MARKET

For this first case, decisions are needed on the part of producers and consumers that should be mutually consistent, on the hypothesis that *no changes shall be made in the size or in the number of plants* where production is carried on. We do not have to inquire therefore into the decisions of producers as to the scale of plant they should employ. For the present problem these decisions are not variables that we seek "equilibrium" values for. Along with the prices and quantities available of all the other products, and of factors of production, they are data that are held unchanged for our analysis, and that form the framework within which our short-run equilibrium situation is to be constructed.

Such a short-run equilibrium requires that producers produce a certain output (each with his given scale of plant) and sell it for a certain price, such that the aggregate output will equal exactly the quantity of product that consumers would want to buy at this price. (There must be of course only a single price for the product if the market is to be in any kind of equilibrium.) The price we seek, then, for the product is the one that will induce producers to produce in aggregate (with given plant size) exactly that output that consumers will buy at the price.

The only opportunity costs of production that are relevant to the short-run model are those incurred for the variable factors used in production. The costs incurred in the past for the plant (including any contractual obligations for the current period incurred for the plant in the past) are irrelevant, as we have seen in the previous chapter, for short-run decisions. It will pay an entrepreneur with a given plant to keep on producing in the short run even though his average revenue is lower than average long-run costs, so long as average revenue is greater than average short-run (variable) costs. With this reservation an entrepreneur will therefore always carry production to the point where the marginal unit produced just adds to revenue an amount in excess of the addition to short-run costs.[2]

For equilibrium, therefore, the following mutually consistent sets of decisions must be made. (1) Each of the given entrepreneurs is producing (in response to the market price of the product) an output whose short-run marginal costs are related to marginal revenues in the manner described. (2) Each consumer is desirous of buying, at the same market price, a quantity such that the aggregate thus demanded is equal to the aggregate output. It will be observed that short-run equilibrium conditions may still be fulfilled even though entrepreneurs outside the industry perceive exceptional profit possibilities in this industry. Moreover, short-run equilibrium may exist even though some entrepreneurs are producing an output such that the price of the product does not help recoup the "fixed" costs incurred in the past in setting up the plant. Clearly, this "equilibrium" might be rapidly disturbed were the hypothetical short-run interdiction on changes in plant size and number to be lifted. These short-run equilibrium conditions define the level of utilization by each entrepreneur of his given plant, the output consumed by each consumer, and the market price.[3]

2. For the special case where entrepreneurs face perfectly elastic demand curves, the best output position will be that where the (rising) short-run marginal cost curve intersects the demand curve. The demand curve indicates for all outputs the (same) marginal (and also average) revenue. We have seen, therefore, that the short-run marginal cost curve becomes part of the supply curve of such an entrepreneur. Such an entrepreneur will thus operate so that his marginal cost equals the market price of his product, as in the diagram. Short-run market equilibrium will require a market price (a) low enough to enable all the entrepreneurs to achieve this position without some of them being left with unsold goods and (b) high enough for the entrepreneurs to achieve this position without resulting in an aggregate output less than what consumers in aggregate would buy at the price.

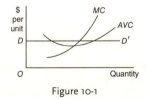

Figure 10-1

3. The reader, as an exercise, may care to convince himself that perfect knowledge would lead to immediate attainment of short-run equilibrium conditions in a market for a single good.

EQUILIBRIUM IN THE SINGLE-PRODUCT
MARKET IN THE VERY SHORT RUN

The second of the hypothetical situations where the market for a single product may be in incomplete equilibrium is often termed the "very short run." In the very short run the hypothesis is made that *no decisions shall be made that should increase the available stock of the product.* All available output is the result of past production decisions. (Thus, we have a situation similar to those analyzed in Chapter 7 where market participants found themselves endowed with non-producible commodities. In the present context, however, we will assume that the producers can make no personal use whatsoever of their product; their past production decisions were made purely with the intention to sell the output in the market.)

The conditions for equilibrium in such a market cannot prescribe, therefore, any limitations for the production decisions of producers, since these decisions are excluded altogether. The only decisions that are permitted, on the present hypothesis (and which must be mutually consistent if equilibrium is to exist), are those of the producers concerning the quantities of output to sell and the price to ask, and those of the consumers concerning the quantities to buy and the prices to offer. We continue to exclude decisions based on pure speculation so that, since producers have no use personally for their product, it is evident that each of them will be willing to sell all available units of product, no matter how low the market price.

It is therefore easy to spell out the conditions for equilibrium in such a case. The product, as always in equilibrium, must be selling at the same price throughout the market. The price, once again, must be such that the quantity of product that consumers, in aggregate, wish to buy at this price is exactly equal to the quantity that producers wish to sell at the price. But we have seen that producers will be willing to sell the entire stock of the product, no matter how low the price. It follows, therefore, that the equilibrium price must be that at which consumers will wish to buy exactly the quantity available. The price must be at a level such that the least eagerly sought-after unit of product that would be bought at the price will just exhaust the entire stock.

For equilibrium to exist in the very short run, it will be observed, it is not necessary that price cover any kind of costs. Moreover, since producers are prepared to sell the entire stock at any price, it follows that the active determinant of what the equilibrium price should be is exclusively the demand situation.[4] The conditions for equilibrium in the very short run define the output bought by each consumer and the market price. It has already been proved in Chapter 7 that in such a market, equilibrium conditions would be immediately fulfilled if all participants in the market possessed perfect knowledge.

ADJUSTMENT TO CHANGE IN A MARKET FOR A SINGLE PRODUCT

The relevance of these situations of incomplete equilibrium for the understanding of the market process (as it takes place in a world without omniscience) may be grasped by considering the following case. Imagine a market for a particular product where the decisions of the various participants are made according to the following schedule. (1) Once every five years, a date is set aside on which all entrepreneurs have, if they wish, the opportunity either (a) to enter the industry by building a plant (for those entrepreneurs who have not been in the industry during the preceding five years); or (b) to build a new plant (for those entrepreneurs who have been in the industry during the preceding five years) in any size they see fit; or (c) to leave the industry altogether (by closing down their plants and having no longer to shoulder any fixed charges upon them). (2) On the first day in each month each owner of a plant decides the daily rate of production for the month. This decision is made in the light of the price of the product expected to rule in the market during the month. Once the decision has been made, it cannot be altered until the following month. The monthly decision determines for the whole month the quantity of factors that shall be employed each day, and provides for a steady daily output that shall be produced each day, *before* the daily buying and selling activity commences, ready for sale to the market. (3) Although during the course of a month a producer has no way of altering the current rate of output until the first of the following month, each producer daily revises his estimation of the current market price for the product. Before the commencement of trading each day, each producer plans the selling offers that he will make during the day, in the light of his current estimate of market conditions. (4) Before each trading day each consumer

---

4. For a diagram illustrating this case, and for some further discussion, the reader is referred to the last portion of the Appendix to Ch. 7, especially to the discussion surrounding Fig. 7-7.

makes his estimate of the market price for the product for that day, and formulates his buying plans for the day accordingly.

Suppose this market is initially in a state of complete long-run equilibrium. Each entrepreneur in the industry is operating with a scale of plant, at a level of utilization, that permits aggregate output to be sold at the equilibrium price. No entrepreneurs in the industry have any reason to offer to sell tomorrow for lower prices than today, nor to demand higher prices. No entrepreneurs have any reason to increase the rate of output for the following month, nor to decrease it. No entrepreneur has any reason, when the date for plant alteration arrives, to do anything except to build the same size plant that he has owned previously. No one presently outside the industry feels any attraction to enter it, when it will be possible to do so. No consumers have any reason to alter their buying plans for the following day. All decisions, therefore, those made by consumers and those made by producers, those made from day to day, those made from month to month, and those made only once in five years, are completely consistent with each other. Into this situation introduce now a sudden, permanent, unexpected increase, occurring one night in the early part of a month, in the intensity of demand for the product (represented graphically by a shift to the right of the entire market demand curve). We must inquire into the effects that this change will generate upon the market activity of all participants, all other relevant factors remaining unchanged.

It is clear, first of all, that the market is no longer in equilibrium. If entrepreneurs go to market on the day immediately following the change in demand with the same selling plans as for the previous days, there will have been by the end of the day many disappointed consumer plans. Consumers will have come to market with plans to purchase greater quantities (at previously ruling prices) than before. The daily output, previously just sufficient to satisfy consumers at the (previous) equilibrium price, is now insufficient. Some consumers will have discovered that they must offer higher prices in order to fulfill their plans. Entrepreneurs will discover that they may expect higher prices and in the succeeding days will make their selling plans on this expectation, refusing to sell for the previous low price.[5]

---

5. In the diagram SS' represents the perfectly inelastic market supply curve for the product (appropriate to the very short run); DD represents the initial market demand curve for the product; $D'D'$ shows the market demand curve after the change. Clearly,

When the first of the following month is at hand, and producers must decide on the rate of output of the next month, their estimates of the product price for the month will have risen from those of the first of the preceding month. Each entrepreneur will realize that whatever the rate of output he had been previously satisfied to maintain, he is now able to improve his position by stepping up the daily output rate for the month. The first unit of the product, which previously just was not worthwhile to add to the daily output, for example, now promises to add more to revenue, should it be produced, than it would add to current costs. The reason why this unit of output had previously been the first submarginal one was that its marginal (short-run) cost just exceeded the addition that it brought about in revenue. Now, however, the entrepreneur can expect a higher price for the product, one that causes the marginal revenue from this unit, and also from some further units as well, to exceed the corresponding short-run marginal costs.[6]

Thus even if the market had achieved, by the end of the first month, "equilibrium" at the new higher price, this is equilibrium only for the very

---

the equilibrium position of the market has shifted, for the very short run, from the position K to the position K'.

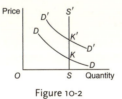

Figure 10-2

6. This may be illustrated diagrammatically for the special case where the entrepreneur faces a perfectly elastic demand curve. With the original average revenue line AR, the position L was the best for the producer. As the product price rises, the AR' line is itself raised. Units to the right of L, previously not worthwhile to produce (because $MC > MR$), have now become worthwhile. The producer's best position has changed from L to L'.

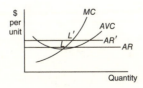

Figure 10-3

short run—until entrepreneurs have the opportunity to step up the rate of output under the new conditions.

When entrepreneurs do increase the daily rate of output, it should be noticed, the aggregate output might be so much greater than that of the previous month that the higher price prevailing at the end of the first month (during which the increase in demand occurred) may be too high. Consumers eager, after the change in demand, to buy the smaller daily output available previously at this higher price are not willing to buy any larger quantity at the same price. Of course, if entrepreneurs had perfect knowledge they would step up output exactly enough for the marginal cost of the output of each producer to fall just short of the corresponding marginal revenue, as determined by the prices aggregate outputs can be sold at to the consumers. In the absence of perfect knowledge we can expect months to go past before entrepreneurs, through the pulls and pushes of market forces, might have completely adjusted their outputs to the new demand situation. When such adjustment has been completed the market will be in equilibrium—but only until the date arrives to review plans for the entire plant for the next five years.

The equilibrium attained in the previous paragraph is, for *two* reasons, only a short-run equilibrium. *First,* entrepreneurs outside the industry who had previously been deterred from entering the industry may eventually find it profitable to do so. Since the price attained in the short run after the increase in demand is higher than before the increase, some of these entrepreneurs may discover that they can do better here with a certain combination of resources than they can do elsewhere. When the opportunity for entry presents itself, the entrepreneurs will build plants and swell the daily supply. *Second,* entrepreneurs who have been producing in this industry are now producing daily outputs with plants that were built years ago on plans that called for only smaller daily outputs. When the opportunity arrives for an alteration in the size of plant, entrepreneurs will certainly expand the scale of plant in order to produce the current larger daily output most economically, *if* they were to plan to continue at this rate of output. But in fact the entrepreneurs will *not* be seeking at this time a scale of plant most suited for the production of this current rate of output. Instead, each entrepreneur seeks to produce most efficiently the output that appears most advantageous under the possibilities opened up by the very opportunity of altering the scale of plant. It is likely that the output most advantageous with the old given plant is not the most advantageous output when the entrepreneur is free to select any plant size he wishes. The most advantageous output from the long-run point of view is that which is, when produced in the most economical scale of plant (for the output), just short of the unit that would make an addition to the variable costs (using this scale of plant) that just exceeds the addition which it makes to revenue. Thus, entrepreneurs will increase the sizes of their plants accordingly.

Once again it may happen that the aggregate daily output that will be produced, in the new scales of plant, will be greater than the quantity that can be sold at what had been the short-run equilibrium price. In this case the market process will lead, during the second five-year period, to a somewhat lower price than had been in effect at the close of the previous five-year period. This will mean that entrepreneurs will find that they are *not* yet perfectly adjusted, since their plans, in this eventuality, must have been made in the mistaken expectation that the old short-run equilibrium price was to continue indefinitely. The situation will thus still not be one of long-run equilibrium, since at the start of the following five-year period entrepreneurs will again alter their plant sizes in order to come closer to their most advantageous production possibilities. In this way the market process will bring about an adjustment in plant size every five years. This process of adjustment will cease only when the industry has once again been restored to long-run equilibrium, under the new demand conditions.

We have in this section been illustrating the adjustment process of a single product market in response to *one* change, with all other relevant factors remaining unchanged. The market model used in this illustration was characterized by a very artificial kind of timetable governing the opportunities to make decisions. In any real world market we will probably expect the various kinds of decisions to be made on a far more flexible schedule, and, especially, we would not expect the decisions of all entrepreneurs to be made simultaneously, as they were in our hypothetical case. Thus, in a realistic market the course of adjustment would be far less even. We would no longer be able to say that, after the occurrence of a particular change, there is a definite span of time during which only decisions relevant to equilibrium in the very short run will be made, followed by a second definite span during which, in addition, decisions affecting equilibrium in the short run will be made—free of long-run decisions until a further definite period of time should have elapsed. Some producers will be altering the rate of output in their plants in response to an increase in demand, while other producers are not free to alter their output at all; still other producers, perhaps, will already be making decisions to increase the scale of plant altogether. Nevertheless, it will still be generally true, even under these conditions, that some effects of a particular change will tend to make themselves felt earlier than others; some effects, perhaps, working themselves out completely only after a very long time. When it is desired to separate analytically these various effects from one another, the mental tools to be used are the different abstractions of incomplete equilibrium that we have been considering.

THE MARKET PROCESS IN A MARKET FOR A SINGLE PRODUCT

The illustration worked out in the preceding section indicates the way the market process exerts pressures on the producers of particular products to make their various levels of decisions consistent with each other and with those of consumers. We will explore this process further in this section, still adhering to our assumption that resource prices (along with all background data) remain unchanged.

If a market is not in equilibrium, we have seen, this must be the result of ignorance by market participants of relevant market information. The market process, as always, performs its functions by impressing upon those making decisions those essential items of knowledge that are sufficient to guide them to make decisions *as if* they possessed the complete knowledge of the underlying facts. Let us assume that the given factor prices are perfectly known, and that both consumers and producers also know the current market price of the product. We can ignore, then, possible price differentials for the product in various areas of the market.

Market disequilibrium, under these assumptions, must mean that the output of the producers is not consistent with the prevailing market price of the product. Producers are in aggregate producing either (a) more than can be sold at the prevailing price, or (b) less than could be sold at the prevailing price, or (c) they may be producing the precise quantity that can just be sold at the prevailing price, but are using methods of production not best suited for production under these price-output conditions.

If producers are producing more than can be sold at the prevailing price, the disappointments of sellers will force them either to cut back output or to offer to sell at a lower price. If producers are producing less than can be sold at the prevailing price, the disappointments of buyers will force them to offer to buy at a higher price. These adjustments are not greatly different from those we became familiar with in Chapter 7.

If producers are producing in aggregate the precise quantity that is just small enough to be sold completely at the prevailing price, but are not using the "correct" production methods for this output, there are several distinct cases to be considered. There will in any event be no *direct* pressure for the price of the product to be changed. Adjustments will take place, initially, on the supply side of the market. The initial absence of full adjustment on the supply side of the market stems, as always, from ignorance of market conditions. Our analysis of the economics of production and costs in earlier chapters suggests the various kinds of ignorance that may be involved. These kinds of ignorance, and the respective kinds of corrective adjustments that will be brought about by market forces, relate closely to the analytical framework within which we have discussed, in the earlier sections of this chapter, the various possibilities of incomplete equilibrium.

An individual producer may find that his own daily rate of output is too large or too small in relation to the product price. He finds that his marginal cost far exceeds or falls far short of his marginal revenue; thus, he would be better off with his margin of output drawn back or advanced to the point where the marginal cost of output is as close as possible to marginal revenue. This situation can have arisen only because of prior ignorance on the part of the producer. When he last had the opportunity to adjust the daily-output volume, he had apparently acted on mistaken assumptions as to the product price to be expected. Since that time market experience has taught him what the product price is, and hence he discovers that he must adjust his output accordingly, at the earliest opportunity. Those entrepreneurs who are most speedily informed of the correct market price are in the position to most rapidly gear their production decisions for the appropriate output volume. The gradual discovery by producers of what the current market conditions really are will then set into motion an adjustment of aggregate output that may in turn generate a series of price adjustments until there is consistency between consumers' and producers' decisions. Market agitation will reflect the impact of the changes in producers' plans in their successive attempts to bring these plans into consistency with the market.

On the other hand, the discovery by an individual producer that his output is too large or too small may reflect decisions made on the basis of incomplete knowledge, not recently, but in the relatively distant past. In other words, the decisions that an entrepreneur has made most recently, with respect to the level of plant utilization and the purchase of variable inputs, may have been made with complete knowledge of all relevant market information. The fact that output volume is too large or too small may be the result of mistaken investment decisions in the distant past, decisions made when market conditions of the then distant future were incorrectly perceived. The scale of plant may be too small or too large in relation to current sale possibilities.[7] The gradual discovery by the different producers, of true market conditions, will lead to a gradual reshuffling of plant sizes. Some entrepreneurs will build larger plants, some smaller, and some will close down their plants altogether. During this process aggregate output will gradually change, and bring in its train gradual movements in the product price and subsequent further adjustments in plant size and rate of output. These long-run market forces will be felt less perceptibly in any one short period, but over the long period will exert overriding influences. So long as complete long-run equilibrium has not been attained, this kind of market agitation will continue. The point is that for production to be completely adjusted both to the tastes and incomes of consumers and to the wishes of producers, decisions must be made at numerous different stages, all of which must be mutually consistent. Lack of consistency in the decisions made at any one level will bring about possible inconsistency at subsequent levels of decision making as well. All this leads to change, as the operation of the market reveals these inconsistencies through the disappointments suffered in the market by decision makers. The entrepreneur who made a complete mistake in entering an industry altogether, for example, will sooner or later discover that his decision to produce at one particular cost of production is altogether inconsistent with the degree of eagerness of consumers to buy his product. His losses will eventually force him to leave the industry.

Thus far we have analyzed the market process in a single product market on the assumption not only that factor prices were constant, but also that consumers' tastes and basic buying attitudes were maintained unchanged throughout the time long-run adjustments were being made. As soon as one relaxes this assumption, market agitation must at once assume far more formidable proportions. Even if we continue the assumption of no change in factor prices and production techniques, and merely allow the attitudes of consumers to change, it is clear that the picture becomes far less simple. In making short-run and long-run decisions, producers must plan not only on the basis of current market data, but also

---

7. Since we are assuming perfect knowledge and forecasting of factor prices, we do not take notice here of the possibility that an entrepreneur discovers his plant to be too large or too small, due purely to the unexpected high or low prices of variable inputs.

on the basis of the expected changes in buyer attitudes for a long time to come. The scope for entrepreneurial activity, based on a superior ability to forecast future conditions in the market, becomes immediately wider. The pressure of market forces will now lead the organization of production to be consistent with the *expectations* of producers and consumers as to future changes in attitudes and tastes. Market disequilibrium will now be the result of (past) imperfect forecasting of (then future) conditions, in addition to imperfect knowledge of the present.

THE MARKET FOR A SINGLE FACTOR OF PRODUCTION

Thus far in this chapter we have been examining one special kind of sub-market—that for a single product—within the market as a whole. We have seen how market forces would manipulate the decisions of producers and consumers in such a sub-market, under specified assumptions with respect to the variability of other market phenomena. Prominent among these restrictive assumptions was our specification that factor prices should not change throughout the analysis. Our purpose in making this obviously artificial assumption was deliberately to illustrate the operation of the market process in a very limited area, as an introduction to the more complicated process to be taken up in the next chapter. In the present section, for similar reasons, we once again consider the market processes operating in a severely limited area, which we insulate from the impact of outside market forces. This time we consider the market for a particular *factor of production*. We will imagine a large number of resource owners endowed by nature with a daily supply of this factor of production. We will assume, for the purposes of the analysis, that the prices of all the products (especially those in whose production the factor is able to cooperate) are given, known, and constant. In addition, since we confine our inquiry to the market for only one factor, we assume that the prices and quantities employed of all other factors of production are given, known, and constant.[8]

Our problem is to understand the nature of the market forces that determine the prices our factor of production is sold at in the market, and

---

8. In this discussion, we will not be making explicit reference to a market for a *produced* factor of production. This case too, however, can be analyzed on the lines developed both in the following discussion, and in the preceding sections.

the quantity of it sold to entrepreneurs and employed in the production of the various products. As before, we will proceed by first spelling out the conditions for equilibrium in this factor market (indicating how these would be achieved were knowledge perfect), and thereafter searching for the market processes that would be set into motion by the absence of equilibrium conditions.

EQUILIBRIUM IN A FACTOR MARKET

For the market for a particular productive factor to be in equilibrium, it is necessary that no resource owner nor any entrepreneur-buyer or prospective buyer of the resource should have any reason to alter his market behavior with respect to the factor. The decisions of the resource owners in aggregate to sell a given quantity of the resource at a given price must mesh completely with the decisions of entrepreneurs to buy the resource. Entrepreneurs must plan to buy currently, at a given price, the precise quantity of the resource that resource owners are planning to sell at that price. Moreover, the long-range plans of entrepreneurs must also call for no change in the quantity of the resource that they will employ. (Since we ignore the possibility of a resource being bought to be stored for future use, we will consider the purchase by an entrepreneur of a resource as reflecting a decision to employ that resource in current production.)

Let us consider the alternatives facing both a resource owner and an entrepreneur-producer when they make their decisions to sell or to buy a resource. For the resource owner the alternatives are relatively clear cut. He finds himself endowed daily with a given quantity of the factor. He can do one of two things with each unit in his factor supply. He can sell it in the factor market, or he can keep it for himself for direct consumption. For example, a man finds that he can supply twelve hours of labor per day. He can choose between selling all or part of this in the labor market, or enjoying the whole time for himself as leisure. A landowner can supply physical space each year to entrepreneurs who may wish to erect plants upon it, or he may if he wishes retain the land for himself as a private garden. At any given market price for the resource, a resource owner will sell a quantity of the factor such that the marginal utility for him of the additional commodities that he can buy through the sale of the last unit of the factor is just higher than the marginal utility for him of the factor unit itself. He will retain for himself that quantity of factor such that the marginal utility for him of a factor unit that he possesses is just higher than the marginal utility for him of the additional commodities that he might have acquired through the sale of one more unit of factor.[9] Of course, in contemplating the sale of a quantity of a resource, a resource owner will seek the highest price obtainable in the market, so far as he knows.

An entrepreneur who is deliberating on the purchase of a quantity of factor faces a rather different set of alternatives. Moreover, he may contemplate such a purchase in the context of decisions on any of several levels, in each of which a separate set of alternatives will be relevant. An entrepreneur knows, on our assumptions, the prices of the various products that he can produce, and he also knows various possible methods of production available to him. In the long run his problem is to decide what branch of production he should enter. In the shorter run he must decide how much of the factor, along with other inputs, he should buy to obtain his current output goals. In the long run he will choose to enter that branch of production where his investment promises him the greatest profits. In making such a decision an entrepreneur commits himself to the purchase of necessary resources, in long-range preparation for future productive activity. The particular combination of resources that he will select will be again one that promises him the greatest net profit

---

9. See Ch. 5, p. 68, n. 1. The analysis of consumer demand developed in Chs. 4 and 5 can be used to examine the decisions of the resource owner. In the diagram any point represents a combination of (1) a laborer's available labor service that he does *not* sell (that is, which he consumes as leisure) and (2) a quantity of a commodity *a*. *OA* represents the greatest quantity of labor that the laborer can sell in a given time period. The line *AB* represents the possible positions that the laborer can take up assuming him to be interested in consuming only the one commodity *a*. The slope of the line *AB* reflects the relative prices of labor and of *a*. The analysis of the quantity of labor that the laborer will sell can then be continued completely parallel to the analysis of the consumer in Ch. 5. (Of course, where institutional conditions make it possible to sell labor only in large units, then, the continuous line *AB* must be replaced by a series of discrete points. In such cases the marginal unit is large. In extreme cases the resource owner may not be able to vary the quantity that he sells; he may be faced with "all-or-nothing" conditions. In this special case, his entire resource endowment is the relevant marginal "unit.")

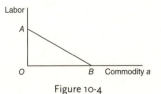

Figure 10-4

advantages. In such a resource combination, planned correctly from the very beginning, *all* the factors that contribute eventually to output will be present (a) in the correct proportions, and (b) in the correct scale. We know, from earlier chapters, what these two conditions involve. They require first of all that the marginal increment of product gained in the long run by the additional expenditure of a given sum of money upon any one factor be approximately equal to the corresponding marginal increment that would be gained by the additional expenditure of the same sum upon each of the complementary factors. They require, moreover, that in the production of any one product, factors be hired up to the point where the value of the marginal increment of product corresponding to the last unit of each factor employed be just greater than the increment in expenditure involved by this unit.[10]

In making long-range plans, therefore, in the light of the known productive possibilities of each of the factors, and of the prices of the factors and the products, entrepreneurs will commit themselves to the purchase of a particular factor, only in sharply defined quantities. For each product produced an entrepreneur will seek to buy a quantity of the factor so that, in cooperation with other factors, he will have erected the scale of plant optimally suited to the future daily production of the most desirable volume of output. This will depend, as we have seen, on the respective marginal increments of product associated with the various factors. Thus, our factor will be purchased by the producer of each product, insofar as his purchase involves long-range preparation for production, so that when expected productive activity is under way, the volume of output and the proportion of the various inputs will fulfill the above conditions for optimality.

In addition, an entrepreneur may contemplate purchase of the factor in making decisions to regulate the current output volume. Here the factor will be one of the variable inputs to be used in cooperation with the fixed plant and equipment. If the original long-range plans were well-laid, the variable factors will be employed in the proportion and on the scale originally envisaged—and therefore again will be fulfilling the optimality conditions. Once again then the employment of our factor will depend upon its efficiency at the margin of employment.

However, as a result of current conditions, the best output that should be maintained with the given plant might be different from that originally

10. See Ch. 9, pp. 215–216, n. 10.

envisaged. In this case it will no longer be true that the variable factors are now to be purchased so that the optimal relationship between their prices and their productive efficiency at the margin are to be achieved. Nevertheless, within the scope of the methods of production possible with the given plant, the entrepreneur will still seek that bundle of variable inputs that will minimize the current costs of the selected output volume. Once again, therefore, a factor will be purchased as part of variable inputs in a quantity such that the marginal increment of product (defined now with reference to the given plant) associated with the purchase of the last unit of it should just exceed its marginal cost to the producer.

We are now in a position to define the conditions for complete equilibrium in our factor market. As usual, the conditions include the requirement of a single price for the factor throughout the market. And, again as usual, it is necessary that the price of the factor be such that the quantity of factor, which resource owners wish to sell in aggregate at the ruling price, is exactly the same as that which entrepreneurs will just be willing to purchase at the price. But the implications of this last requirement for complete equilibrium, which are peculiar to the market for a factor, need to be spelled out.

The equilibrium price for a productive factor (prices of products and of other factors being given) must be such that exactly that quantity of factor is offered for sale (that is, withheld from personal use) as is demanded to be bought. The quantity that resource owners will offer for sale at this price will reflect the fact the marginal utility to the seller of the last unit to be sold of the factor is just lower than that of the additional commodities that he can buy with the increment in revenue derived through sale of his factor unit. In other words the equilibrium price is just high enough to make it worthwhile for the last unit of factor (necessary to complete the equilibrium quantity) to be sold by that seller who is less eager to part with this unit than are the other sellers to part with the units they do sell. (Of course, this marginal seller is also less eager to retain this unit for himself than are the other resource owners to retain all the units for themselves that they do *not* sell at the ruling price.) The quantity that entrepreneurs will seek to buy at the equilibrium price must be exactly the same as this equilibrium quantity. This quantity will be bought by the various producers of each of the various products. For complete equilibrium not only should the current rate of plant utilization be optimally adjusted to the factor prices, but the scale of plant itself also should be so adjusted. The aggregate quantity of the factor that is purchased at the equilibrium price will reflect the fact that the value of marginal increment of product associated with the last unit of the factor purchased by each producer (measured with respect to *long-range* calculations) is just greater than the increment in expenditure required for this factor unit. This must be the case for all producers in all branches of production.

If these conditions are fulfilled, no participant in the factor market has any reason to make plans to alter his activities in this market, all other things remaining unchanged.[11] No resource owner is disappointed in his plans, nor is there any more profitable way he could dispose of his resource endowment. Similarly, no entrepreneur will be disappointed in his plans, nor will he discover any more profitable methods of production. Since his long-range and short-run decisions are mutually consistent with each other and with current market conditions, it follows that any increase or decrease in the quantity bought of the factor will upset the proportions factors are combined in, in a manner that can only decrease efficiency. The conditions for equilibrium define the size of plant used by each producer in the production of each product using the particular factor; they define also the current volume of output for each producer of each product where the factor appears as one of the variable inputs; they define the price the factor is sold at;[12] and they define, for each owner of the resource, the quantity that he will sell.

11. This point occurs, of course, at the intersection of the market demand curve for the factor and the market supply curve of the factor—where these curves, as usual, reflect the amounts of factor that would be respectively asked to be bought and offered for sale at hypothetical *given* factor prices. The analysis in the text explains how *actual* factor prices (like actual commodity prices) emerge from the attitudes reflected in the relevant supply and demand curves.

12. A special case is where the equilibrium price of a resource is zero. Such a resource is a free good that yields its owner no income in the market, and in whose use it is not necessary to economize. Suppose that market participants are endowed with huge tracts of fertile land so large that even the employment of all the complementary resources (such as labor and tools) available to the group cannot bring all the land under cultivation, then clearly no price can be obtained for land; competition among landowners would drive down the price to zero. Whenever, in fact, the quantity of a *specific* factor is so large that a surplus of it remains after combining it with all the other complementary versatile factors worthwhile to apply to the branch of production the first factor is specific to, then the first factor can command no price. As soon as the market demand for the product (to whose production this factor is specific) increases so much that it becomes worthwhile to employ so large a quantity of the complementary factors in its production as to exhaust the entire available supply of the

Once again it is not difficult to see that perfect knowledge on the part of all participants in the factor market would help them immediately toward achieving these equilibrium conditions. With all other prices known, with all possible methods of production known, with the degree to which each resource owner is eager to retain factors for personal use known, each participant would know at what price it would be possible for all of them to adjust their activities so that no disappointments need occur. No entrepreneur would plan production on the assumption that he will have to offer a price for the factor any higher than this equilibrium price. He knows that the lower price is quite sufficiently high to induce the more eager sellers to supply all that entrepreneurs will demand at this lower price. No resource owner, in fact, will waste time asking any higher prices, since he knows that buyers can find all they will want to buy at the lower price. On the other hand, no resource owner will accept a price for the factor any lower than the equilibrium price. He knows that the higher price is quite sufficiently low to attract entrepreneurs to formulate a long-range production plan calling in aggregate for a quantity of factor that is not less than the entire factor quantity that resource owners wish to sell at the higher price.

We notice that, as was the case in our analysis of the market for a single product, it is analytically possible to distinguish cases of *incomplete* "equilibrium" in a factor market as well. It is possible, for example, to set up a model where all decisions to alter the scale of plants are excluded. The only decisions that producers are free to make, then, are those involving alteration of "variable" input proportions employed. In such a model it is possible to talk of "equilibrium" in the factor market, in the sense that the permitted decisions of both resource owners and entrepreneurs are mutually consistent. Within the range of permitted decisions, there will

---

specific factor, the specific factor begins to command a price. This price is a *rent* since the factor is specific; however, as we see, it is governed by the same analysis that we apply to all prices. Continued increases in the demand for the product will force up the price of this factor *more* than the price of the other factors. Even a moderate increase in the price of the other factors may suffice to withdraw additional quantities of them from the other branches of production where they may have been used. But the specific factor is not used elsewhere in the economy; it commands a rent only because all of it is insufficient to satisfy the demand for it in production (when free). The perfect inelasticity of its supply makes its price depend, even more sensitively than that of other resources, on the price of the product. On the relativity of the terms "specific factor" and "rent," see p. 201.

be no disappointed plans in such an equilibrium situation. For such a situation to exist it is necessary that a price for the factor prevail so that the quantity that resource owners wish to sell at the price exactly equals the aggregate quantity that producers will wish to employ at the price, with given plants. This equilibrium price, as before, must be high enough to provide the power to purchase commodities with a marginal utility just higher than that of the last factor unit sold, to its seller; the equilibrium price must also be such as to make the marginal cost of the factor to the producer, just lower than the value of the marginal increment of product derived from the employment of the last factor unit bought.

THE MARKET PROCESS IN A MARKET FOR
A SINGLE FACTOR OF PRODUCTION

In the absence of perfect knowledge we may expect factor sales to be transacted at prices different from the equilibrium price, and production to be carried on in plants calling for employment of the factors in aggregate quantities other than that which would be consistent with an equilibrium price. These buying, selling, and producing activities will result in disappointed plans; the revision of these plans; and a new set of buying, selling, and producing activities. These changes will constitute the agitation characteristic of all markets that have not yet attained equilibrium. In this section we sketch the kind of changes that will be generated by the absence of equilibrium conditions. We will be able to dispense with detailed repetition of patterns of change that we have become familiar with in Chapter 7 and in the earlier sections of this chapter. We will proceed by considering, as an illustration, what happens when a factor market initially in equilibrium is subjected to a sudden change. We retain our assumption of known and constant prices of all products and of all other resources.

A factor market is initially in complete equilibrium. Producers have built plants in the "correct" sizes in the past (so that in aggregate the same number of new plants each year replace an equal number of old ones without any alterations in sizes) such that the annual aggregate quantity of the factor purchased by all producers of all products, in response to the market price of the factor, can be maintained indefinitely if this price continues. Long-range plans of all producers in all industry call for the employment of the factor in each industry to the point where its effectiveness per unit at the margin is just sufficient to justify paying the market price for the last unit purchased. At the same time resource owners are induced by the same market price for the factor to sell exactly the amount sought by producers at the price; and no resource owner finds himself disappointed in his selling plans, nor in any other way under pressure to alter his selling activity. Into this situation a sudden unexpected permanent change in the basic data is introduced—in the form of the invention of a new technique for the production of several products. The relevance of this invention for the market for our factor consists in the fact that as a result of this invention the effectiveness at the margin of our own factor in the production of these products has been sharply increased. Our task is to investigate the consequences of this change for activity in the factor market.

It is clear that the factor market is no longer in equilibrium. We are not assuming perfect knowledge in our model, and therefore, as we have seen, the market prior to the new invention was perfectly adjusted to its absence: nobody had made plans based on the expectation of the invention. The plans of producers thus cannot be expected to be maintained indefinitely without change. Sooner or later somebody producing one of the products that can be produced more efficiently with the new technique will discover this. He will seek, at the earliest opportunity, to replace the older methods of production by the newer one. This will involve a reshuffling of all his variable inputs until he will have achieved (a) what now appears as the most desirable output level (attainable with the existing plant, that, while not planned directly for the new technique, cannot be altered in the short run), and (b) what now appears as the most desirable set of "variable" input proportions. Under our assumptions as to the constancy of other prices, the result will be an increase in the quantity this entrepreneur will seek to buy of our own factor (at least so long as resource owners have not discovered that they may be able to ask a higher price). As knowledge of the new technique spreads, it is clear, the old price for the resource ceases to be an equilibrium price; the aggregate quantity of the factor demanded exceeds the quantity that resource owners are prepared to sell at the price. There will be disappointed plans for at least some producers. These disappointments will gradually lead both producers and resource owners to recognize that higher prices must be offered, and may be confidently asked, for the resource. The immediate impact of the technological discovery has thus been an increase in the quantity of this factor employed, together with a rise in its price. This price rise may be modified by a tendency on the part of producers who cannot use the new technique to replace our factor by substitutes as its price begins to rise.

Eventually, further changes may be expected. When entrepreneurs have the opportunity to revise their long-run plans, they will do so in the light of the new productive technique and the new higher prices for our own factor. For each producer, there will now be a different scale of plant that promises to be the most desirable. A new volume of output and a new set of long-run input proportions will be selected by each producer in each industry. This will again alter the aggregate annual quantity of the factor sought to be purchased at the previously established new price for the factor. This may involve a new adjustment in the market price of the factor. This kind of market agitation will continue for as long as the factor market has not attained complete equilibrium.

TOWARD THE GENERAL MARKET PROCESS

We have in this chapter considered separately two areas within a market system. We first examined the processes that would be generated within the market for a single product, which could be imagined as insulated from the rest of the market. We then examined a similarly insulated market for a single productive resource. The juxtaposition of these two cases should have emphasized the artificiality of the assumptions regarding their "insulation" from the rest of the market. At the same time this juxtaposition should have suggested the direction that the analysis must be extended to if it is to provide a glimpse of the concatenation of decisions running throughout the entire market system. It must have been remarked, for example, that when a new invention increased the marginal effectiveness of one input, with respect to the production of several products, we might have expected (if released from the assumed constancy in product prices) a tendency toward a lowering of the prices of these products, with subsequent further adjustments. We will explore the more general market process in the following chapter.

At this point we merely pause to recognize that our analysis shows the way market forces would operate in *each* limited area of the market, if each of these areas were insulated from the rest and considered in turn. When we drop these "insulating" assumptions, it becomes apparent that for equilibrium to exist in any one area, it is necessary that conditions be fulfilled that relate directly to other areas. Moreover, it becomes apparent that in the absence of equilibrium in any one area, the market forces set into motion will impinge on other areas as well. Agitation in the market, proceeding from an initiating cause in one area, will take the form of ripples of change moving from one area to another and, of course, initiating secondary waves of change having an impact also upon the area the agitation originated in. We turn in the next chapter to this more complex problem.

SUMMARY

Chapter 10 commences the analysis of the way the decisions of both consumers and producers interact in the marketplace to determine the prices of resources and products, the quantities of resources used in each production process, and the quantities of products produced. In this chapter the task is approached by first analyzing the market process as it directly affects a *single product*, and then analyzing the corresponding market process affecting a *single productive factor*.

In the analysis of the single-product market, stable prices for all factors and all other products are assumed to be known. Equilibrium conditions can be spelled out for the market. These define the scale of plant for each producer, the level of utilization of each plant, the output consumed by each consumer, and the product price. Perfect knowledge can be shown to lead to the fulfillment of such a pattern of dovetailing decisions.

By mentally arresting specified types of changes, it is possible to spell out various "incomplete" patterns of equilibrium. In particular it is of interest to work out the pattern of dovetailing decisions that can be achieved with *given* plants (*short-run equilibrium*) and *given* products (equilibrium in the *very short run*). The relevance of these situations of incomplete equilibrium is found in the time sequence of the market processes leading up to *complete* equilibrium. The analysis of these processes makes up the core of the subject under investigation. The thread running through these processes is the consistent revision by producers and consumers of their plans, until all sources of plan incompatibilities among them are removed.

In the analysis of the single-factor market, stable prices for all other factors and for all products are assumed to be known. Equilibrium conditions can be spelled out for the market. These conditions define: the size of plant used by each producer in the production of each product using the particular factor; the current volume of output for each producer of each product in which the factor appears as one of the variable inputs; the price of the factor and the quantity of it sold by each of its owners. Once again perfect knowledge is implied in the fulfillment of these conditions.

Imperfect knowledge implies disappointed plans that will lead to plan revisions on the part of resource owners and producers. These plan revisions, too, may be expected to follow a typical time sequence, with some adjustments being made only after maladjustment has prevailed persistently for a long time.

The principal limitation on the usefulness of the analysis of market processes treated in this chapter arises from the assumed "insulation" of these processes from the full interaction with the rest of the adjustments that will be generated *throughout* the entire market system by any initial maladjustments in the areas under direct examination.

SUGGESTED READINGS

Mises, L. v., *Human Action,* Yale University Press, New Haven, Connecticut, 1949, pp. 324–336.

Wicksteed, P. H., *Common Sense of Political Economy,* 1933. Reprint, Routledge and Kegan Paul Ltd., London, 1949, Bk. 1, Ch. 9.

Wicksell, K., *Lectures on Political Economy,* Routledge and Kegan Paul Ltd., London, 1951, Vol. 1, pp. 196–206.

Machlup, F., *The Economics of Sellers' Competition,* Johns Hopkins University Press, Baltimore, 1952, Chs. 9, 10.

In the present chapter we seek to understand how the competitive market process works in a system where *no* prices are considered as "given" or constant. In such a system the prices of *all* factors, and of *all* products, are variables that take on values determined by the market process itself. For such a system to be in equilibrium, *all* market decisions must mesh completely; the economist cannot be satisfied to seek consistency only among a selected group of decisions against the background of a "given" set of other decisions that remain external to the analysis. When an autonomous change occurs somewhere in the system affecting the fundamental data on whose basis certain decisions are made, the economist must trace the impact of this change upon *all* subsequent decisions. Until now we have been proceeding step by step, confining ourselves primarily to partial analyses. In this chapter we will discuss, after a preliminary foray into one more hypothetically restricted market, the problem of the general market process in a market where both factors and products can be bought and sold at prices freely determined by market forces.

For most of this chapter we will be working with a system organized on the following lines. There are a large number of resource owners. Each resource owner finds himself endowed daily by nature, without cost, with some bundle of resources whose content does not change from day to day. The composition of this bundle differs from one resource owner to another, but each resource appears in the daily endowment of many resource owners. (None of them have monopoly power over any resource.) Each of these resource owners is free either to retain his resources for his own consumption purposes or to sell any quantity of them for what he can get for it. There are also in the system a large number of prospective entrepreneurs who may find it worthwhile to buy resources in the market, convert them into finished products, and sell these products for what they can bring in the market.[1] Finally there are the consumers. (These individuals, in addition to being consumers, are also resource owners, entrepreneurs, or both.) Consumers buy products in the market with incomes that they earn as resource owners or entrepreneurs.

---

1. For the sake of simplicity we continue to refrain from taking explicit notice of intermediate products, the produced means of production.

The fundamental data that must ultimately determine the course of the market process are (a) the daily endowments of resources, and (b) the tastes of consumers. These are assumed to be given and unchanging throughout the analysis unless inquiry is specifically directed toward the consequences of a change in these data. On the one hand, consumer tastes play a role in determining the quantity of resources that will be sold to the market at any given price since, as we saw in the preceding chapter, a unit of a resource will be sold only if its price is high enough to outweigh its marginal utility in consumption to the resource owner. On the other hand, of course, consumer tastes (along with consumer incomes) play a major role in determining the quantity of each of the products that consumers will buy at given prices. The composition and quantity of the resource endowments will determine (along with the tastes of resource owners as consumers) the quantity of the various resources that will be sold to the market at given prices. At the same time the composition and quantity of resource endowments play a major role in the determination of consumer incomes.

The central problem is to understand the way market forces determine the decisions that will be made (a) by each resource owner concerning the sale of each unit of each of the resources in his daily endowment; (b) by each of the prospective entrepreneurs concerning the purchase of the various resources, their organization into various productive complexes, and the choice of products to be produced; and (c) by each of the consumers concerning the purchase of the various available products. These decisions will determine the prices of each of the factors and of each of the products, the quantity of each factor employed, the method of production used for each product, the quantity of each product produced, and the quantity of each of the available products purchased by each consumer. Consistency between all these decisions means that the resulting market phenomena will be maintained indefinitely within alteration. Inconsistency between any sets of decisions will be revealed through disappointments and will be followed by revisions in future decision making. Inconsistencies will thus generate ripples of change affecting wide areas of decision making. Our problem is to understand how the market forces generated by the revelation of these inconsistencies determine subsequent market phenomena. First we take up a preliminary model.

A PRELIMINARY MODEL

In this preliminary analysis we simplify the statement of the problem outlined in the previous section by making a major modification in the institutional framework of the system. For the purposes of the present section, we deal with a system different from that dealt with in the rest of this chapter, in that production can be carried on by a market participant *only with resources that were in his initial endowment,* not with resources bought from others. Resources can be bought only for direct consumption. During the rest of this chapter (after the present preliminary model) we will be dealing with the system, outlined above, where resource owners do sell resources to entrepreneurs who then produce products for sale to consumers. In this section, however, each resource owner, if his resources are not to be left idle, or to be used directly in consumption, must *himself* combine the resources that he possesses, in order to produce products that he must then consume himself or sell to other consumers. This case differs from the hypothetical systems considered in Chapter 10 in that in the present problem the prices of *all* products are determined by the market process that we wish to investigate, with no market decisions imagined to be imposed externally. Our case differs from the multi-commodity case considered in Chapter 7 in that in the present problem, production decisions can and must be made, and these production decisions also must be explained in terms of market forces. Our present case will provide the simplest and most direct introduction to the analysis of the central problem of this chapter, the explanation of the general market system outlined in the previous section.

We turn, then, to consider a system where resource owners (if their resources are not to be used for consumption or to be left idle) must themselves employ their resources to produce goods for their own consumption or for sale to other consumers. Our problem is to understand how market forces in such a system would determine the quantity of each resource consumed directly by each consumer, the quantity of each product produced, the method of its production, and the prices in the market of each resource and each product.

The clue to analysis of such a system consists in its points of similarity with the multi-commodity pure exchange system considered in Chapter 7. There we considered a group of consumers each of whom was endowed each day with a supply of consumer goods. Exchange ensued as each of the market participants sought to convert his initial commodity bundle into the most desirable one obtainable by barter in the market. For each participant this involved giving up units of some commodities in order to acquire units of other commodities. In our present case, also, each participant has an initial endowment that he seeks to convert into the most desirable commodity bundle obtainable. In our present case a participant can convert his initial endowment by sacrificing quantities of resources for a price (a) by sale of resources directly to consumers for use as commodities, and (b) by using the resources to produce products and then selling the products to consumers. These exchange possibilities may arise from *two* causes: *first,* as in Chapter 7, differences in the initial endowments of the different participants, as well as differences in their tastes for the various resources as *commodities,* may create opportunities for mutually profitable exchange of resources between participants for direct use as commodities. *Second,* differences in the initial resource endowments of different participants may result in differences in their ability to produce specific products. This, reinforced by differences in the tastes of the participants for the various *products,* may again create opportunities for mutually profitable exchange of "resources," *in the derivative form of products,* between participants.

The second of these two sources of mutually profitable exchange between market participants, it should be observed, is most illuminatingly interpreted simply as a special case of the first of the two sources. Thus, the whole case studied in this section is seen, too, simply as a special case of the multi-commodity market problem in Chapter 7. This interpretation follows directly as soon as it is realized that a product *is* nothing, in fact, but the whole bundle of resources used to create it. A market participant can thus improve his position by giving up some of his initial bundle of assets (in the form either of (a) the original resources or (b) the product obtained from them) in order to replace the sacrificed assets by other assets (to be bought from other participants either in the form that these assets appeared in initially in their asset bundles, or in the form of derived products) which he prizes more highly.

The complication, which sets our present problem apart from that of Chapter 7, arises, of course, from the presence of production possibilities. It is associated, in particular, with the *versatility* in production of most resources. In a system without production a particular commodity is simply that commodity; but in a system where production is possible, a particular resource may be considered as either that resource (usable, perhaps, in direct consumption), or as part of any one of the possibly numerous products toward whose production the versatile resource may be applied. Our study in Chapters 8 and 9 of the principles of production theory has taught us that this versatility of productive resources imposes upon the producer the necessity to choose among additional series of alternatives.

In the multi-commodity pure exchange market of Chapter 7, a participant made his buying and selling decisions on the following principles. The market prices of any two commodities (say, *A* and *B*) determine the terms on which he may acquire specific quantities of commodity *A*, say, through purchase, for the sacrifice of quantities of commodity *B* through sale. His own subjective scale of values ranks the specific additional quantities of *A* either higher or lower than the quantities of *B* required to be sacrificed. If the quantities of *A* rank the higher, he will seek to sell *B* and buy *A* until, through the law of diminishing utility, the marginal utility of *A* drops, and that of *B* rises sufficiently to make further exchange on market terms no longer desirable. All that the market participant needs to consider, then, are the prices of the commodities and their respective utilities to him at the margin.

In the case we are now considering, the decisions of a resource owner depend upon a number of additional factors. In contemplating the purchase of a specific quantity of product *A* in the market (or the purchase of a specific quantity of resource *C* for direct personal consumption), through the sacrifice by sale of quantities of resource *B* (one of the assets in his own initial endowment), it is not sufficient for a participant to know merely the prices and marginal utilities to himself, of *A* (or *C*), and *B*. The prices, it is still true, of course, determine the quantity of *B* he must sacrifice in order to acquire specific quantities of *A* (or *C*). It is still true, in addition, that the desirability for him of acquiring specific quantities of *A* (or *C*) will depend upon the marginal utility to him of *A* (or *C*).

But in weighing the wisdom of sacrificing the required quantity of *B*, it is now not enough to consider merely its marginal utility to him in direct consumption. He must consider also the additional sacrifices possibly involved in the sale of this quantity of *B*. These potential sacrifices include the difference that this quantity of *B* is able to make (either when used as a single unit, or when used in smaller quantities) in the production of all the various products it is a potential factor for. In considering the sale of the required quantities of resource *B*, the resource owner must consider in turn all the alternative sets of possible ways these quantities of *B* could be turned (in cooperation with other resources, of course) into products. All of these sets of possible ways *B* might be used in production must then be compared with each other. The *most* significant set, among all these alternative sets of possible productive contributions that the quantity of *B* is able to make, will be then the sacrifice involved in withdrawing this quantity of *B* from production. (The significance of any set of productive contributions will of course be measured by whichever the resource owner thinks more preferable: (a) the additional revenues obtainable from the relevant marginal increments of product through sale of the finished products in the market, *or* (b) the differences in the utility for direct consumption that can be derived from the relevant marginal increments of product, through the direct personal enjoyment of the finished products.)

In weighing, therefore, the sacrifice of the quantities of B required by market conditions for the sake of acquiring specific quantities of A, a market participant will rank on his scale of values not only the marginal utilities of the relevant quantities of A and of B, but also this opportunity cost involved in the withdrawal of B from potential production. Only if the specific quantity of A ranks higher on his scale of values than the full sacrifice involved in the sale of B—that is, both higher than the sacrificed consumption of B and also higher than the alternatively sacrificed potential productive possibilities embodied in B—will a resource owner sell B and buy A on the terms available in the market. (Of course, once a resource owner has produced a product, the considerations involved in a decision to sell units of the product in order to buy quantities of other products, or of resources to be used directly in consumption, are no different from those that a participant in a multi-commodity pure exchange market needs to consider.)

We will now consider what conditions have to be fulfilled if our system is to be in equilibrium. The following sets of decisions by market participants will have to be mutually consistent throughout the system: the decisions (a) to sell resources, (b) to produce products, (c) to sell products, (d) to buy resources, and (e) to buy products. In an equilibrium system prices will prevail for each of the resources and products, so that each participant is motivated to make consumption, production, buying, and selling plans, none of which need be disappointed. The quantity of each resource that resource owners wish to sell at this equilibrium resource price will exactly equal the quantity that other participants wish to buy at this price for direct consumption. The quantity of each product that resource owners wish to sell at the equilibrium price will exactly equal the quantity that other participants wish to buy at that price.

Each resource owner will have adjusted his consumption, production, buying, and selling activities completely to these market prices, so that he sees no way of rearranging his activities in any more desirable way. He is producing those products that yield the highest revenue for the expended resources; he is producing each product with a set of input proportions and on a scale that yields the highest aggregate sales revenue obtainable. He can find no way of removing any unit of any of the assets in his initial daily bundle from one disposition to any other, without rendering himself worse off. (1) The marginal utility that he obtains from the last unit of each of his initial resources that he himself consumes directly is just higher than the marginal utility of whatever else he could either: (a) buy with the additional revenue obtainable by the sale of this last unit that he consumes, respectively, of each resource; or (b) buy with the additional revenue obtainable in the market by virtue of the marginal increment of product that these last units, respectively, of each resource could contribute in any branch of production; or (c) enjoy directly as the marginal increment of product that these last units, respectively, of each resource could contribute to any products he might consume himself. (So that were he to consume directly either more or less units of any of the resources in his initial endowment, he would be worse off.) (2) The marginal increment of product derived from a specific quantity of any one of his resources devoted to the production of a particular product possesses, for each of the products to whose production he might allocate this resource, approximately the same market value. (So that were he to switch resources from the production of one product to the production of any other, he would be worse off.) In equilibrium the prices of resources and products each day enable each participant in the market to successfully carry out plans fulfilling these optimal conditions, without disappointment.

As we have been led to expect, it will be observed that the sets of resource and product prices required for equilibrium in such a system must bear strong formal resemblance to the equilibrium set of commodity prices for a multi-commodity pure exchange market. In the pure exchange model a market participant could improve his position by converting some of his assets by exchange into other assets. In the present model a market participant can transform his assets, in addition, by converting them into products and then, if he wishes, converting these products into commodities through exchange. The technologically determined terms upon which a particular participant can convert his resources into products, coupled with the market terms upon which these products can be exchanged for other products, yields sets of "exchange rates" on whose basis the resources of this participant, in effect, are converted into the products produced by a second participant. Going one step further, by taking note of the terms upon which this second participant was able to convert his original resources into *his* products, one notices a set of terms upon which the originally endowed assets of one market participant can be exchanged (either in their original forms or in the form of derived product) for the originally endowed assets of a second participant (again, in either form). By the end of each trading day, in equilibrium, asset ownership will have been rearranged, through production and exchange, so that no further possibilities remain for mutually profitable exchange (in the wider sense that includes production) between any two participants. Observed in this way the equilibrium conditions of prices and production in our present system are seen as reducible in principle to the same conditions that were sufficient for equilibrium in the multi-commodity pure exchange market analyzed in Chapter 7. Just as we saw, in that case, that perfect knowledge on the part of all participants in the market must lead immediately to equilibrium conditions, so also in the present case equilibrium conditions can be seen to follow from perfect knowledge—except that in the present context knowledge must of course include knowledge in detail of all possible methods of combining resources in order to obtain products.

Absence of perfect knowledge must of course lead to a group of decisions that will be far from being mutually consistent. As usual in such a situation, the discovery of this absence of consistency will take the form of disappointments suffered by participants who have formulated plans of market action on the basis of assumptions concerning market conditions that prove to have been mistaken. We may discard the possibility of more than one price emerging for a particular resource or product since we are already familiar with the market movements that will be generated by the eventual discovery of such price discrepancies. Disequilibrium will exist whenever the price of any resource or product results in a greater or smaller aggregate quantity of it asked to be bought, than the aggregate quantity of it desired to be sold. In general, the aggregate quantity of a resource asked to be bought will be, we know from earlier chapters, greater as its relative price in terms of other goods is lower, since more people will then wish to acquire it for consumption, as compared with the alternative consumption and productive opportunities available. The fact that a given price for a resource generates a demand for it in the market that cannot be satisfied at the price is a result of the absence of mutual recognition between (a) those who own the resource and, being less eager sellers than others, are not prepared to sell more of it at the low price; and (b) those who are disappointed in their attempt to buy the resource at the ruling price, and who would have been prepared to offer higher prices had they known that this was necessary. The *first* of these two groups are those for whom either the marginal utility of the last units of their respective supplies of the resource, or the value of the relevant marginal increments of product obtainable from these units, ranks higher than the marginal revenue obtainable through sale of the resource in the market. The *second* of the two groups are in precisely the opposite position. Mutually profitable exchange possibilities thus exist ready to be exploited. As knowledge is spread, members of the second group will offer higher prices for the resource.

Generally, any set of resource and product prices motivates each market participant to transform his initial asset endowment by sacrificing the direct consumption of his resources for the sake of acquiring other commodities either through direct exchange, or through production, or through the combined process of production and subsequent exchange. We have seen that the technological laws governing the various relevant production functions, together with the market prices of resources and products, determine the terms upon which, through these various ways, he can acquire at the margin additional quantities of any particular product by sacrificing other assets. With the terms of technological transformation given, a set of market prices that induces (to take one possibility) too many people to convert the resource A (either by direct exchange, or by production followed possibly by exchange) into the asset B (which may be in the form of a derived product), as compared with the quantity of B desired to convert to A, will result in disappointments. These disappointments will result in a revision downward of the relative price of A, and a revision upward of the relative price of B.

The resulting fluctuations in the price of resources and products are completely homogeneous with those we have discussed earlier, especially in Chapter 7. In the present case, of course, we realize that an alteration in the price of any one resource or product will immediately upset the attractiveness of the opportunities available to its owner through exchange and production involving other resources or products. As knowledge of price changes spreads spasmodically one can expect disappointed plans and consequent plan revisions to be generated in a highly irregular fashion. The direction of adjustments, however, will always be toward the elimination of those disappointments generated at the prior set of prices. Market agitation will proceed in this way initiating changes in consumption and production in a continual tendency away from existing inconsistencies among decisions. Of course, especially with production decisions, the changes prescribed by current disappointment of past plans may not be implemented immediately but may require considerable time. It would be possible, as in the preceding chapter, to spell out analytically the conditions for the achievement of various levels of incomplete "equilibrium."

Any alterations in the basic data of the system will generate the appropriate market forces that will bring about corresponding adjustments in the decisions made by the market participants. Thus, a change in technology will alter the terms on which resources can be converted into products, and also alter the effective terms of "exchange" between the original assets of two producing participants. This will bring about changes in the set of consumption, production, buying, and selling plans of the affected persons, resulting possibly in corresponding pressures toward changes in the sets of resource and product prices. A shift in consumer tastes, or a sudden alteration in the composition of the various initial daily asset endowments, will all alter the terms upon which participants would be eager to convert one asset, directly or indirectly, into another asset. In all these cases, equilibrium can result only after the knowledge of the impact of these changes has been transmitted by the market process to all the participants.

THE PRELIMINARY MODEL AND THE GENERAL MODEL

Once again it will be helpful to focus attention on the differences between the assumptions underlying the preliminary model of the market analyzed in the preceding section, and those that define the more general model of the market which it is our principal purpose to examine. In the preliminary model production could take place only with resources obtained by the producer at the start of each day as part of his resource endowment. Where resources were bought in the market, they were bought for direct consumption as commodities, not for use as inputs in production. The range of production possibilities was thus limited drastically by the composition of each producer's initial asset endowment. It was entirely possible for a unit of a particular resource to be more efficient at the margin in one branch of production than in another and yet to remain employed in the area where its productivity was lower.

No less interesting from an analytical point of view, perhaps, was that there was, in effect, no direct market for resources *as resources*. In calculating his costs of production, the only market values that a producer could use directly in the appraisal of the value of his inputs, were the prices being paid for these resources as *commodities*. (Nevertheless, the market value of a unit of resource would to some degree reflect indirectly its usefulness also as a factor of production, since no owner of a resource would sell a unit of it for a price lower than its worth to him, as reflected in the value of the marginal increment of product that it could bring about.)

The most important implication, however, of the special assumptions of the preliminary model, was that each resource owner necessarily had to be his own entrepreneur. In calculating the worthwhileness of using a particular quantity of a resource in production instead of for consumption, or vice versa, a resource owner had to consider not only the marginal utility of the resource and the price of the resource, but also the prices of the products in whose production the resource could be allocated, and the marginal efficiency in production of the resource. In the preliminary model of the market there was no division of the decision making responsibility possible between resource owner and producer-entrepreneur.

In the more general model of a market system we now turn to, things are different in these respects. Production can be carried on with resources acquired out of the initial asset endowment of any market participant. In the production of any one product a producer is not limited, as in the preliminary model, by the quantity that he possesses of the scarcest of the required complementary factors of production. Generally, there will be little likelihood that some resources will have to be consumed, or left lying idle, or used in branches of production where their effectiveness at the margin is unnecessarily low, merely because any one producer lacks the necessary complementary factors of production.

In the more general market model there will be a genuine market where the various resources will be bought and sold. The price paid for a resource will most probably directly reflect its usefulness to buyers, at the margin, in production rather than in consumption.

Most important of all, in the general market model, it will now be feasible to focus analytical attention upon a distinct and separate entrepreneurial function. In the general market model resources are bought in the market by entrepreneurs who sell "them" (that is, in the form of products) back to the market. We have already seen in earlier chapters that this kind of activity differs sharply from that of the resource owner who, in his capacity of resource owner, simply sells resources to the market; or from that of the consumer who, in his capacity of consumer, simply buys products from the market. A very important implication of the existence of the entrepreneur concerns the terms upon which a resource owner is able to convert his resources into products for his own consumption. In the preliminary model these terms followed from *his knowledge* of the technological laws he is able to operate with, and from his estimates of the prices of the products that he can produce, and those of the products he might wish to buy. In the more general model, the terms on which a resource owner can convert resources into products are yielded directly by two sets of market prices, the prices of the resources that he is able to sell, and the prices of the products that he might wish to buy. In the event that entrepreneurs obtain superior knowledge of technological opportunities and of consumer tastes, the terms of "exchange" available to a resource owner will more faithfully reflect the best available conversion opportunities.

Despite these important differences between our present market model and that discussed in the preceding section, our analysis will place much emphasis on the fundamental *similarities* between the two systems. In both systems resource owners are endowed each day with a bundle of assets, and each seeks to transform his initial endowment, through "exchange," into the most desirable bundle of assets obtainable. (In the present general market model, it is possible for many participants to be able to act as consumers even though they do not receive any daily endowment of assets. Successful entrepreneurial activity may provide them with the income to buy products in the market for their own consumption.) In both systems resources can be transformed into products for one's own consumption by sacrificing quantities of resources and obtaining products. (In the present model this can be done without any act of production on the part of the resource owner himself; he can sell resources to the entrepreneurs and buy back products from entrepreneurs.)

The similarities between the two systems lead, as we shall see, to close formal parallelism in the analysis of market equilibrium conditions (in both systems), as well as in the analysis of market processes set in motion (in both systems) by the non-fulfillment of equilibrium conditions.

GENERAL MARKET EQUILIBRIUM CONDITIONS

The mental construction of a general market in complete equilibrium demonstrates most illuminatingly this fundamental similarity between this market and that of the preliminary model. When one constructs a model of a general market in equilibrium, one realizes that the equilibrium conditions have wiped out that single element in the general market system that is its most important distinguishing feature, as compared with the preliminary model treated earlier in this chapter. In a general market, as we shall see, equilibrium conditions can exist only when there is, in effect, nothing left for entrepreneurs to do.

For a general market to be in equilibrium, it is necessary that all decisions made within the entire system dovetail perfectly with one another. The decisions of the owners of each resource, with respect to selling this resource, must fit in perfectly with the decisions of entrepreneurs with respect to buying this resource. The decisions of consumers, with respect to the purchase of each possible product, must fit in perfectly with the long-run and short-run decisions of entrepreneurs with respect to the production and sale of this product. Of course, the buying, production, and selling decisions of each entrepreneur must show perfect internal consistency (or else he would rapidly find that he must reorganize his plans). Moreover, the decisions of each entrepreneur-producer must be consistent with the decisions of the rest of the market in the sense that he know of no alternative arrangement that in the long run might prove more lucrative from his own overall point of view. There must be no other method of production available to the entrepreneur, involving a difference in product, input proportions, or scale of production that promises greater profits in the long run.

For general equilibrium to prevail, the prices of all resources and products must be precisely at those levels necessary to induce such universal dovetailing of decisions. The price of any resource will be such that the quantity that owners of the resource wish to sell in the aggregate at the price, in each period of time, exactly equals the aggregate quantity that entrepreneurs wish to buy at the price, in order to employ in the execution of their various long-run and short-run production plans. The aggregate quantity desired to be sold is found by totaling, for all owners of the resource, the quantities each of which are (in the light of all other market prices) just large enough for the respective marginal units to rank, each for its relevant resource owner, just lower in subjective importance than the additional purchasing power obtained through its sale in the market. This aggregate quantity must in equilibrium equal exactly that which entrepreneurs wish to buy at the price—an aggregate made up of quantities that (in the light of technological possibilities and all other market prices) are each just large enough for the respective marginal units of resource to yield a value of marginal increment of product that ranks, for each relevant entrepreneur, just higher than the additional expenditure involved in its employment.

The price of any product will be such that the quantity entrepreneurs plan in aggregate to produce and sell in any one period exactly equals the aggregate quantity that consumers wish to buy. The aggregate quantity of a product planned on being produced in any one period is an aggregate made up of quantities of products each of which (in the light of technological possibilities and all other prices) are just large enough for the long-run marginal costs associated with the respective marginal units to rank, for each relevant entrepreneur, just lower than the corresponding marginal revenue. This aggregate quantity must be in equilibrium equal exactly to that which consumers wish to buy at that price—namely, that quantity of the product found by totaling, for all potential consumers, the quantities that (in the light of all market prices) are just large enough for the respective marginal units to rank, each for the relevant consumer, just higher than the sacrifice represented by the additional expenditure required for these marginal units.

Entrepreneurial decisions, for general equilibrium to exist, must in addition satisfy, with respect to each product individually, and with respect to each factor individually, the remaining conditions for equilibrium discussed in Chapter 10. No producer must be producing a product for which his total revenue falls short of his long-run opportunity costs— that is, the total revenue in his branch of production must not fall short of the total revenue he could have obtained by applying the same resources in some different branch of production.[2]

Under these conditions the flow of resources, products, and incomes could be maintained without change through any length of time. Each resource owner, in the light of the set of prices available to him for the sale of various resources, and in the light of the prices of the various products, is able to construct a plan that dovetails perfectly with every other relevant plan being made in the market. Every consumer earns, in his capacity of resource owner, an income that, considering the market prices for the various products, enables him to plan a regular consumption program that, again, dovetails perfectly with every other relevant plan being made in the market. The resources made available by the resource owners for production are being combined in plants of varying size, in varying patterns of input proportions, in the production of various different products—the net result being (a) a stream of output containing the various products in a precise pattern to fit the aggregate buying plans of the consumers,

2. See pp. 231–233, 246–249.

(b) a stream of income to resource owners in a precise amount and pattern of distribution that should make possible the equilibrium set of consumer plans, and (c) an organization of production such that no entrepreneur can discover anything to be done with any group of factors in the system, that might result in the ultimate creation of greater market value than is, in fact, now being created by the group.

An important corollary of these conditions is that no entrepreneurial *profit* can exist in equilibrium. We may define the profit earned by an entrepreneur very broadly for our purposes as the difference between the revenue received through his employment of a group of factors, and the opportunity cost of the factors (that is, the highest revenue being received through the employment of a similar group of factors elsewhere in the economy). If a market is to be pronounced in equilibrium, there can be no such profit. The existence of profit in this sense would mean that those entrepreneurs who are now employing the group of factors "elsewhere" will eventually attempt to take advantage of the opportunities "here" to earn a greater revenue. Equilibrium can only exist when each similar group of factors is earning the same revenue in all areas of the market.

This can be made clearer by recalling that any group of factors suffi-cient for the production of a particular product *is*, for analytical purposes, the product. For equilibrium to exist, there can, of course, be only a single price in the market for each given good or group of goods. In equilib-rium, therefore, there can only be one price for a product, no matter if this product is in its final form, or whether the product is in the form of the group of factors necessary for its production. Consequently, the price that an entrepreneur must pay in equilibrium for his factors of produc-tion cannot be less than the price he receives for his output. This will be true for all entrepreneurs employing a given factor group: each will be paying the same price for the factor group, and each will be producing a product yielding total revenue exactly equal to the cost of the factor group. No entrepreneurial profit or loss can exist.

This absence of entrepreneurial profits most clearly demonstrates the proposition that in equilibrium a general market leaves no room for entrepreneurial activity. It is worthwhile to consider some of the implica-tions of the absence of entrepreneurial profits. The sum of the prices of a group of complementary factors of production will be the same in all employments; and this sum, we have seen, will equal the value of the product of such a group of factors (this value being again the same for all employments). Now this, clearly, is (at least in one respect) exactly what would occur if omniscient resource owners were to produce the products themselves without separate entrepreneurial assistance. In his calculations such an owner of a group of resources would consider them as equivalent in value to the most valuable product that the group is able to yield. In weighing the wisdom of withdrawing a particular bundle of resources from production to consumption (or vice versa), he would balance against its usefulness in consumption, its effectiveness in earning revenue, the latter equal to the value of the final product. In a general market, with production being carried on by entrepreneurs, exactly the same calculations will be made if the market is in equilibrium. The price of a factor group that is just sufficiently high to lure them away from direct consumption by resource owners is precisely the value of the most valuable final product that these resources can produce.

We will soon see, once again, how closely the existence of equilibrium in a market is bound up with perfect knowledge. As usual the mental construction of a market in complete equilibrium is merely a means to an end. Our principal purpose is to understand the market process in the absence of equilibrium conditions. In the general market model, we will find, entrepreneurial activity is the driving force, and the analysis of this activity is the key to the understanding of the entire process. For this reason we place such emphasis on the absence of entrepreneurial profits in equilibrium, and on the absence of opportunities for entrepreneurs to do anything better than is in fact being done. All this is different in a market not in equilibrium.

A GENERAL MARKET IN DISEQUILIBRIUM

Our discussions of conditions in an equilibrium general market make it easy to see what is meant by disequilibrium in such a market. We will continue to work with a market where the basic data are unchanged from period to period. The regular resource endowments continue without alteration; consumer tastes for the various products undergo no change. The only changes are those brought about by the market process itself. In a general market not in a state of equilibrium, market phenomena induce market participants to make plans that are not completely consistent with each other. Clearly, this must be the result of the absence of omniscience on the part of market participants.

In a general market, the absence of equilibrium means that resources are being used in production processes not best adjusted to the existing pattern of product prices. Alternatively, absence of equilibrium means that product prices are not perfectly adjusted to existing production patterns. Put in still another way, the absence of equilibrium means that the prices of resources are not completely adjusted to the prevailing patterns of consumer tastes; or alternatively, that the prices of products are not adjusted to the prevailing pattern of resource availability.

These maladjustments will necessarily make themselves felt sooner or later. In this way, knowledge of these maladjustments will spread and will enforce changes in the plans of market participants. For example, the organization of production may produce "too much" of one commodity and "too little" of a second, in relation to consumer tastes. The producers erred in their estimation of the relative significance to consumers of the two commodities. The result will be that with given prices expected by the producers to prevail for the two commodities, a greater quantity than expected will be asked of the second commodity, while a smaller quantity than expected will be asked of the first commodity. The disappointments of both producers and consumers will alter the relative prices of the two commodities and revise the production plans of the entrepreneurs.

One very important observation is that a state of disequilibrium in a general market expresses itself through the *creation of profit possibilities*. It is especially illuminating to notice the way this market phenomenon focuses attention directly on the real nature of general market disequilibrium. Whenever a market does not fulfill the conditions necessary for equilibrium, it would be possible to transfer a block of resources from one actual employment in the market to some other employment yielding greater market value (that is, greater revenue) than the actual employment. This reflects the fact that the decision actually made, with respect to the allocation of the block of resources, was not completely adjusted to the other decisions being made in the market at the same time. This decision erroneously assumed that no superior opportunity existed anywhere in the market for these resources. In fact, however, a fuller knowledge of the value that consumers place upon this block of resource (possibly in some other form) would have led to a different allocation. Thus, the value placed upon this block of resources by whoever made the "mistaken" decision is less than its value elsewhere in the market. Only imperfect knowledge on the part of those in the market could have permitted the emergence of two "prices" for the same "good." Not only the individual who made the mistaken allocation was in ignorance of the true state of affairs. Everybody else who would have been in the position to take advantage of the price differential, but did not do so, was equally ignorant. In this way, whenever disequilibrium exists in the general market, an opportunity exists to earn entrepreneurial profit by buying where market value is low and selling where value is higher.

DISEQUILIBRIUM IN THE GENERAL MARKET AND ENTREPRENEURIAL OPPORTUNITIES

These considerations reveal the central role that the entrepreneur is able to play in the market process, as well as the relation between the imperfection of knowledge and the existence of a state of disequilibrium. We have discovered that whereas in equilibrium every "good" sells for a single price throughout the market (no matter what the form in which the good may be), in the disequilibrium market more than one price prevails for the same "good" (either when the good is sold in different forms for different prices, or when the same goods sells for different prices). Inconsistency among the decisions of market participants reveals itself in the form of more than one price for the same "good." This is an important discovery, since it links general market analysis of the most complex order with the analysis of the simplest of conceivable markets. We know that in a single-commodity market, for example, equilibrium requires a single price throughout the market. We now know that equilibrium in the general market requires precisely the same condition, somewhat more broadly interpreted. We know, in fact, that *all* disequilibrium in the general market may be interpreted as the absence of this single equilibrium condition.

We recall further, from analysis of the single-commodity market, that the simplest type of entrepreneurial activity is arbitrage—simultaneously buying a commodity where its price is low, and selling it where its price is higher. And we recall that it is precisely this kind of entrepreneurial activity that tends to wipe out these price differentials—converting a market initially in disequilibrium into an equilibrium market. Now we have discovered that *all* entrepreneurial activity, in the most complex of the general markets, reduces analytically to precisely the same kind of arbitrage activity, buying at a lower price to resell at a higher price.

Just as more than one price for a single commodity is possible only because of imperfect knowledge, so also in the general market the existence of more than one price for a "good" is possible only through ignorance. And just as the single-commodity market is brought toward equilibrium by the spread of knowledge and its exploitation by those entrepreneurs who find out first, so also in the general market, the market process operates through the discovery by the more alert entrepreneurs of the existence of these price differentials, and their subsequent exploitation of these opportunities.

All profit opportunities in the general market thus appear as the expression—in the existence of a lower price and a higher price for the same "good"—of a fundamental inconsistency among market decisions. It is the ceaseless search by entrepreneurs for such profit opportunities that prevents the continuation of existing market activities—in other words, it is the search for profits that renders such a market state one of disequilibrium. Those entrepreneurs will be earning profits who discover these price differentials before the others. It is their activity that tends to wipe out these differentials, thus removing the inconsistencies among the decisions being made in the market.

ENTREPRENEURIAL ACTIVITY AND
THE GENERAL MARKET PROCESS

In this section we will discuss the various kinds of market forces that may be set into motion by entrepreneurial activity as a result of particular disequilibrium conditions.

1. Simplest of all will be the market agitation initiated by the discovery of more than one price for the same physical resource, or the same physical product. We have analyzed this already in Chapter 7. Entrepreneurs who find out this price discrepancy will simply buy the product or resource at the low price from those who do not know that any higher price can be obtained for it, and will sell at the higher price to those who do not know that it can be obtained at any lower price. In so doing entrepreneurs are wiping out a lack of coordination between decision makers. Among those who were aware only of the lower price, there were presumably some who might have sold more of the product or resource than they are prepared to sell at the lower price. Similarly, among those who knew only of the higher price, there were presumably some who might have bought a larger quantity had they known of the lower price. Entrepreneurial activity leading to a single intermediate price will remove this lack of coordination.

Of course, in considering a general market, we understand that the adjustment in the prices of the particular resource or product will affect market activity with respect to other products or resources as well. The nature of these secondary adjustments will depend on the particular relationships between the products or the resources. In general, the adjustments will follow the pattern we discuss below in the next few paragraphs.

2. A second possibility for entrepreneurial activity may be created by inconsistencies affecting most directly the decisions being made with respect to two different products. Ignoring the possibility of more than one price for the same physical resource, or the same physical product, there may be an absence of coordination among the production, selling, and buying decisions affecting two different products. This kind of inconsistency has already been noticed in this chapter, and it is, in addition, similar in some respects to cases considered in Chapter 7.

It may be possible, for example, that both consumers and entrepreneurs have each independently misjudged the relative significance that consumers attach to two particular products. As a result of this error consumers have adjusted their buying plans, and producers their production plans, according to the expectation of a price for the one product that is "too high," and a price for the second product that is "too low." Since all concerned make the same error, their price expectations prove initially correct. (We may imagine that the prices of the various resources, too, have become completely adjusted to the entrepreneurial plans constructed according to these expectations.) These production decisions are clearly inconsistent with each other in the light of prevailing consumer tastes. These production decisions would be mutually consistent only if the relative prices of the products would induce each consumer to allocate his income among the various available products in such a way that, in aggregate, consumers wish to buy precisely those quantities of each of the two products that producers have planned to produce. But if the market price of the one product is too high, and the price of the other product too low, the terms of "exchange" between the two products are such that disappointments must necessarily occur. These terms of "exchange" between the two products will in general induce consumers to allocate income so that more of the second product is consumed in place of the first product than would have been the case with "correct" relative prices for the two products.[3] As a result producers of the first product discover that they have produced "too much" of it (that is, they find they cannot sell at the prevailing price all they have produced in expectation of this price); while producers of the second product discover that they have produced too little (that is, they are unable to satisfy all consumer orders made at the ruling price for their product).

3. Where the two products are complementary goods, the direct consequences of the market error may be more complicated than is spelled out in the text.

It should be observed that the inconsistency among production decisions and consumption decisions relevant to the two products implies still further inconsistencies in decisions relevant to the resources allocated to these products. Although we have imagined resource prices to be completely adjusted to the plans of producers, the lack of coordination between the latter plans implicitly makes the decisions regarding the buying and selling of resources also internally inconsistent with each other in the light of consumer tastes. Thus, the adjustments that eventually will be brought about through the discovery of the fundamental inconsistencies in decisions with respect to the products will also exercise an influence upon the resource markets.

It is not difficult to perceive the opportunities for entrepreneurial activity created by these market inconsistencies. The entrepreneur who gathers the earliest information concerning the disappointed plans of the producers of the first product, and the disappointed plans of prospective consumers of the second product, is in a position to gain profits by exploiting his superior knowledge. He will refrain from producing the first product and will expand his output of the second product for which he will be able to ask and obtain a new higher price. In this way (assuming both products to use the same inputs) he will transfer resources from an employment where marginal revenue will be less than marginal cost (since he knows the price of the first product will fall, so that the equality between marginal revenue and marginal cost previously expected with the originally planned output will not be achieved), to an employment where marginal revenue will be greater than marginal cost (after the rise in price for the second product).

Similarly, where the first product has been produced with resources different from those used for the second product, the more alert entrepreneurs will cut down their purchases of the resources used for the first factor and will expand their purchases of the resources used for the second. A tendency is thus caused toward a fall in the prices of the former resources and a rise in the prices of the latter resources. Profits are gained by these nimbler entrepreneurs because they perceive that they can obtain a high price for the second product. They see that resources hitherto thought able to create the greatest market value at the margin when allocated to produce other products (for example, the first product, perhaps) will in fact create the greatest market value when applied at the margin of production of the second product. Continuation of previous plans for the production of the first product must involve losses, they perceive earlier than others, at least on the marginal units produced. Their search for profits and fear of losses induces them to alter their decisions in the pattern described.[4]

Entrepreneurial activity will continue in this fashion for as long as the relevant decisions have not been shaken down into full mutual consistency. Prices of the products, quantities produced of the products, and prices of the resources affected must all be such as to eliminate plan disappointments. In a general market at any one time we may expect numerous groups of products (and these groups containing probably more than two products in each group) that will have the kind of inconsistency discussed here. In all such cases the market will be in agitation set off by entrepreneurial discovery of the profit possibilities thus presented.

3. A third possibility for entrepreneurial activity may be created by inconsistencies in market plans revealed most glaringly in the decisions affecting two different productive resources. We have seen, of course, that imperfection of knowledge in the market for products implies inconsistencies among decisions in the resource markets as well, and we have also seen that the resulting market forces will bring about corresponding changes in the decisions made in the resource markets. But there may be inconsistencies that have their root directly in resource market decisions.

Let us suppose that all resource owners and all entrepreneurs err in their assessment of the relative ease with which two different productive factors can be made available to the market; or that they err in their assessment of the relative usefulness of the two factors in the various branches of production open to the market as a whole. As a result of these errors, all concerned (correctly) expect prices for the resources that are "too high" for the first resource and "too low" for the second resource.

Presented with these market terms upon which the one resource can be substituted for the second, producers in aggregate ask to buy too much of the second resource and too little of the first, in comparison with the quantities of the two resources that their owners (in the light of the market terms upon which they can replace the one resource by the other

---

4. The discussion in these paragraphs illustrates what were described in Ch. 2 as "horizontal relationships" existing among different sub-markets. The reader may work out for himself possible further developments that might follow (working *horizontally*) on the course of events described here. The reader may work out, for example, the consequences for the market prices of products that are used complementarily with one or other of the two products referred to in the text.

in direct consumption) are offering for sale. We may assume that product prices are completely adjusted to the expected and initially realized resource prices, so that no entrepreneur sees any opportunity of improving his position from what he expects to gain by means of his production plans made in the light of the ruling resource and product prices.

Nevertheless, the resource prices are inconsistent with equilibrium conditions. Producers are induced by the relative prices of the two resources to produce definite quantities of various products requiring these resources, with methods of production calling in each case for an input mix with definite proportions of the various available resources. Resource owners are induced by the relative prices to sell definite quantities of the two resources. The aggregate quantity offered for sale of the second resource falls short of what producers are planning to use, while that offered for sale of the first resource is greater than what producers plan to use. The relatively high price of the first resource, as compared with the second, has led producers to plan production with methods substituting more of the second resource for the first, and to plan to produce more of those products requiring relatively heavy inputs of the second resource, and less of those products requiring relatively heavy inputs of the first resource. The relatively high price of the first resource may be inducing resource owners to substitute quantities of the second resource in direct consumption in place of quantities of the first.[5]

Some of the resource owners who have made plans to sell the first resource, and some of the producers who have made production plans calling for employment of the second resource, will find themselves disappointed. This is, of course, the direct result of the inconsistency between the decisions in the resource markets and will set into motion the appropriate corrective market forces. But the inconsistencies directly perceived in the resource market also imply indirect inconsistencies in the decisions made at the level of the product market. Consumers, we assumed, have been making consumption plans fully adjusted to the production plans that entrepreneurs have been making on the basis of *their* expected ability to buy all of each of the two resources that they might wish to buy at the expected prices. Since some of the plans of the producers are

---

5. This will not *necessarily* be the case. For some resources especially, economists have learned to expect a "backward-sloping" supply curve. The high price obtained for the first resource may make it worthwhile for its owners to sell *less* of it, since the smaller quantity sold can command a "sufficient" range of purchasing power.

disappointed, some of the plans of consumers, too, are going to be disappointed (since these latter plans presuppose successful fulfillment of the former). The inconsistent plans of the producers are reflected here in the derived, inconsistent plans of the consumers.

This situation provides opportunity for entrepreneurial profits. As soon as some alert entrepreneur senses what is happening in the market for the two resources, he will immediately offer to buy quantities of the first resource at prices *lower* than the market prices prevailing initially. He will be able to secure these low prices, since resource owners will have been forced by their disappointments to revise downward their estimates of the price of the first resource. The alert entrepreneur will then apply his supply of the first factor to the production of those products that, requiring heavy inputs of the first factor, had been sold in the product market at correspondingly high prices. No consumers, until now, have been disappointed in their plans to buy products requiring heavy inputs of the *first* factor (since we have assumed the existing product prices to be completely adjusted to the output plans of the producers, and no producer who planned to buy the first factor has been disappointed). The price of the products requiring heavy inputs of the first factor, therefore, has no reason to fall. Thus, the alert entrepreneur who discovers the new lower price the first factor can now be obtained at is able to gain profits. Similarly, the discovery by the alert entrepreneur of the new lower price of the first factor (relative to that of the second, especially in view of the higher price that will certainly be charged very shortly for this second factor) may open up for him opportunities for profit through the substitution at the margin of units of the first factor in place of units of the second, in the production of those products using both factors.

These profit possibilities have been made possible by the existing faulty allocation of resources. The "erroneous" market prices for the two resources had guided producers into substituting the second resource for the first in production, and into producing products requiring heavy use of the second resource in place of products requiring heavy use of the first—although, in view of the *real* factors underlying the market, a different pattern of production would have been more efficient. In view of consumer tastes, technological possibilities, and the willingness of resource owners to sell factors, the initially planned production pattern "wasted" the first resource and used the second resource too heavily.

As more and more entrepreneurs move in to exploit the profit possibilities thus created, they set into motion tendencies in price movements that both reflect the improving pattern of resource allocation and render more limited the possibilities for further profits. On the one hand, as entrepreneurs buy more of the first resource, and buy less of the second, they are directly easing the pressures that had been forcing the price of the first resource to fall, and that of the second to rise. At the same time, with the shift from the production of products requiring heavy inputs of the second resource toward products requiring heavy inputs of the first, a tendency is brought about for the price of the former products to rise, and for that of the latter products to fall.

We recognize, especially with respect to entrepreneurial activity set into motion by inconsistencies in the resource markets, that corrective adjustment may take considerable time to be completed. Even alert entrepreneurs may find themselves unable to exploit their earlier knowledge of market conditions, due to past decisions. They may be saddled with plants that cannot easily be converted from the production of one product to another, or from one method of production to another, or from one scale of output to another. What appear to be profits in the long-run view may not be profits in the short-run view (due to the differences in the respective opportunity costs). But eventually market forces will bring about the adjustments outlined above. Of course, in the general market we are dealing with, adjustments of this kind must be expected to bring about alterations in the conditions of related markets as well. These alterations, too, although they are likely to be of a smaller order of magnitude, will bring about adjustments that may be analyzed by one or other of the examples being considered here.

4. A fourth possibility for entrepreneurial activity may exist even where all resource and product prices are completely adjusted to the production and consumption plans that have actually been made. This possibility arises from the fact that these plans may not reflect the opportunities that "really" exist. Producers may be ignorant of particular inventions that might lower their costs; consumers may be ignorant of the way a new product may suit their given tastes.[6] In such cases resources are being used to produce goods that are less valuable than the goods that *could* be

---

6. Clearly, a question of semantics is involved here. If one chooses to define tastes as referring only to those commodities that the consumer *knows*, then by definition a product that is still unknown cannot be described as an unseized consumer "opportunity." Nevertheless, the wider interpretation of "tastes" is in keeping with common usage.

produced with the same resources, if the existing knowledge was fully exploited.[7]

Definite opportunities for entrepreneurial activity arise from circumstances of this kind. Disequilibrium conditions emerge as soon as someone perceives the profit possibilities inherent in the situation. He will then exploit these possibilities by applying the new invention to production (or by introducing the new product to the consumer market). The *innovator* (this term is used to distinguish him from the inventor) will then be able to produce products more cheaply than others, without having to sell these products at a lower price, or he may be able to produce a new product selling for a price greater than its full per-unit costs of production.

The market agitation set in motion in this way will gradually tend to subside as profit opportunities are exploited away. As knowledge of the new production possibilities spreads, the prices of resources, and of products, will adjust until equilibrium is restored, with no further opportunity for profitable entrepreneurial activity.

With respect to all these different kinds of inconsistencies among decisions, and the entrepreneurial activity they give rise to, we must not forget that entrepreneurs may not only gain profits but may also incur losses. In fact, whenever a market is not in equilibrium, some entrepreneurs are clearly forgoing (unintentionally, of course) more desirable opportunities for less desirable ones. Thus, in the broad sense, entrepreneurial loss is always present in a disequilibrium market. Entrepreneurial losses are incurred when producers make "wrong" decisions; that is, whenever they use resources for purposes other than those that the market ranks as most important. Entrepreneurial mistakes are due, of course, to mistaken assessments of market conditions. Even in a market where, like the model we are dealing with, the basic data—resource availability and consumer tastes—do not change, there is ample room for entrepreneurial mistakes. Entrepreneurial mistakes are responsible for any subsequent disappointments in the plans of all market participants. However, the

---

7. Of course, the purist may point out that there are *always* unknown technological possibilities that future generations will discover. From this point of view a market system might be described as always in a state of disequilibrium, with respect to the infinity of knowledge that is beyond human reach. A more workable approach, however, is to define *relevant* technological knowledge as that which *is* possessed by someone in the system. Disequilibrium then exists, with respect to this knowledge, so long as it has not yet been placed at the service of the market.

market contains a built-in device that operates to minimize the likelihood of entrepreneurial mistakes. This device is precisely the fact that such mistakes are inescapably accompanied by losses—that are, by definition, something entrepreneurs seek to avoid.

PARTIAL ANALYSIS AND THE ANALYSIS OF A GENERAL MARKET

From the analysis used in the preceding sections, it will be noticed that although we are dealing with a general market (where all prices and quantities are free to move), the market process in such a market can be envisaged as the picture obtained from superimposing upon one another a number of separate processes characteristic of some one *partial* market not in equilibrium. With respect to the conditions for general market *equilibrium*, this was not the case. Equilibrium in the general market (while of course requiring equilibrium also in each of its distinguishable sub-markets) cannot be considered simply as a quilt made up of discrete patches of partial equilibrium. General market equilibrium implies a definite harmony *between* the various distinguishable sub-markets. But the *process* by which a general market moves, when equilibrium conditions are absent, *may* be considered as a combination of discrete partial processes. In fact, understanding the matter in this way is rather important for an adequate comprehension of the adjustment process in a disequilibrium market.

The essence of any adjustments, of any entrepreneurial activity initiated by disequilibrium conditions, is the making of "corrective" decisions by entrepreneurs in the light of new knowledge of the state of the market. *Two* characteristics of such decisions may be noticed. *First,* such decisions are made "*spasmodically,*" in the sense that the required knowledge is not acquired continuously. *Second,* such decisions each may be considered made with respect to relatively *small* segments of the general market. The first characteristic implies that although disequilibrium conditions are likely to be manifest separately in many distinguishable sub-markets, nevertheless, the entrepreneurial decisions being made in each of these sub-markets are not made *completely* simultaneously. Thus, it is feasible to imagine a general market adjusting itself *step by step*, each step taken in one sub-market bringing about alterations in the data relevant to the conditions for equilibrium in related sub-markets, and thus modifying the subsequent step-by-step process of adjustment. The second characteristic, that decisions are made with regard to small segments of the whole market, is a corollary of the limitations of the human mind, including that of entrepreneurs. An entrepreneur will make decisions affecting prices where he perceives the opportunity for profit. He will operate against the background of other prices that he takes as given and that he does not seek to exploit.

Taken together these two characteristics of entrepreneurial decision making imply that adjustments in a general market will be made one at a time in limited areas of the market, that adjustment in one area will impinge on other areas and will eventually be reflected in the adjustments subsequently made. These subsequent adjustments may of course affect, in turn, still other areas as well as the area where the very first adjustment was itself made. The point is that these intricate webs of adjustments, working in all directions and impinging back again upon areas where these very adjustments had their roots, are woven piecemeal, *not* in any continuous, grand pattern *simultaneously* harmonizing all areas of the market. Appreciation of the complex chains of relationships simultaneously required for a state of general market equilibrium is useful principally in giving an idea of the multitude of separate adjustments set in motion by a state of disequilibrium, and of the power of an entrepreneurial decision in one area of the market to set off intricate and wide-ranging ripples of change felt eventually throughout the market.

TOWARD FURTHER EXTENSIONS OF THE GENERAL MARKET MODEL

Our analysis of the general market has been facilitated by the retention of several simplifying assumptions. Although the model of a general market discussed here has been free of many of the more restrictive assumptions retained in earlier chapters, we are still some distance away from a model that can be applied directly to anything likely to be encountered in a real world. In this section we point briefly to the way our model may be extended to eliminate some of its more glaring simplifications.

One of the more important of our simplifications has been the assumed absence of *monopoly* power throughout the market. In particular, no resource was monopolized, and no monopoly in the production of any one product was assumed. In the next chapter we will explore the implications of the relaxation of this no-monopoly assumption.

A second of our simplifications has been to ignore *intermediate products*. We have been arguing as if the resources endowed by nature to resource owners are directly combined and yield finished products for consumption in a single operation. In a real world we are likely to find that many products can be used not only for consumption but also as factors of production, while other products may be useful only as factors of production.

We have already noticed some of the implications of this in Chapter 2. It is not difficult to perceive that the introduction of intermediate products into the model does not upset the essential logic of its analysis. The principal modification that it would entail is the introduction of new levels for entrepreneurial decision making. Producers producing finished consumer products with produced inputs will use *these* input prices in calculating their costs of production. The producers of these produced inputs will be making decisions with respect to a higher level of factor prices, and so on. Market interrelationships between various levels of production can be analyzed with the same set of logical tools we used in explaining the relationships between factor markets and product markets. The consequences of inconsistencies in the decisions directly affecting the consumer product market will initiate entrepreneurial activity that will eventually affect all the related higher markets, with varying degrees of indirectness.

A more complex problem that has been assumed away thus far in our analysis is that introduced by the *duration* of productive processes. We have been assuming that in a productive process the product emerges simultaneously with the application of the inputs (or, at least, that any duration of production introduced no complications). In any kind of real world the product to be sold is available for sale only at some definite period of time after the productive factors are employed. Thus, every process of production involves *investment* to a lesser or greater extent. Where long-run decisions are made, they will usually involve long-term investments. We will return in an appendix to a brief survey of how the problems necessarily introduced by investment can be incorporated into a general theory of the market process.

The final complication that we will refer to is brought about by dynamic changes in the basic data of the market. Included are changes in the endowments of resources provided to the society by nature—these changes being in the size, composition, and ownership of the endowed resource bundles; also changes in the tastes of consumers. (So far we have assumed away all kinds of these changes, including those that an anthropologist or social psychologist would ascribe to the operation of the market process itself.) However, in earlier chapters we have alluded sufficiently to the effects of changes in the data upon partial markets for it to be apparent how these dynamic changes must be treated in the general market model as well. A change in tastes or resource availability must be treated as something that introduces an immediate set of inconsistencies among decisions otherwise consistent (if the market had previously been in equilibrium); or (if the market had previously not been in equilibrium), as introducing a new set of decisions with respect to which the market process must seek mutual consistency. The speed of adjustment of the market to the new changes will depend on the rapidity with which entrepreneurs gain knowledge of the changes, translated into profit possibilities. The only way, as we have seen in the introductory chapters, to analyze the economic processes of a changing world, is to realize that all action is undertaken with respect to the tastes and available resources relevant to a particular date. All market interrelationships flow from such action. Eventual changes in the basic data will be translated by the market into changing patterns of market action, each pattern traceable to the data of a particular date. Where different sets of relevant market data bring about adjustments with various speeds of reaction, we may expect that at any one time the market process may be a complex set of overlapping programs of action, each set, perhaps, referring to the data of a different date. All this vastly complicates, but does not essentially alter, the analysis developed in this chapter.

SUMMARY

Chapter 11 continues the analysis of the market process until it embraces a system where *no* prices are given or constant. The chapter proceeds in two steps. A market is considered where there are a large number of owners of different resources. Each of these resources can be used to help produce a variety of different products. No prices or quantities of resources or products sold are assumed to be determined externally to the analysis. However, in the first of the two steps, we confine attention to a system limited by the requirement that production be carried on only with resources owned initially by the producer himself; resources can be bought only for consumption. After this preliminary case, in the second of the two steps, a market is analyzed where production may be carried on with the help of purchased factors of production as well.

In the first of the two steps, analysis explains the determination in the market of (a) the quantity of each resource consumed directly by each consumer, (b) the quantity of each product produced, (c) the method of production of each product, and (d) the prices in the market of each resource and product. Analysis proceeds on lines analogous to those followed in Chapter 7, where a multi-commodity pure exchange economy was considered. There a market participant converted his initial commodity bundle into the most desirable possible alternative bundle available through exchange. Here he converts his initial resource bundle into the most desirable possible commodity bundle through production as well as exchange. The principal complication setting the present analysis apart from that of Chapter 7 arises out of the *versatility* of resources in production. Detailed analysis reveals how, in the absence of perfect knowledge, the market process would enforce revisions in these more complicated plans of market participants toward greater consistency between the decisions being made at different points in the economy.

In the second of the two steps, production may be carried on with resources acquired in the market. This alters the character of the market for resources, widens very considerably the scope for production possibilities, and makes possible the emergence of a distinct producer-entrepreneur whose activities promote the spread of relevant market information and the smoothness of the market process.

In this general model of a market system, the conditions for equilibrium can be described in detail, analogous to those that determined the equilibrium position for the preliminary model analyzed in the earlier portion of the chapter. It is easily shown that here again, equilibrium implies complete knowledge throughout the market. Imperfect knowledge, on the other hand, implies disequilibrium, which expresses itself through the creation of *profit possibilities* available to those who discover them first. Detailed analysis reveals the various different kinds of entrepreneurial opportunities that may be offered by a general market in disequilibrium, and the way the exploitation of these opportunities tends to correct the initial inconsistencies existing between the various decisions being made. In this way the market process enforces particular production possibilities, more and more consistent with the underlying data, resource supply, and consumer tastes.

The analysis proceeds on a *step-by-step basis* justified by the nature of the chains of cause and effect relationships involved in the market. An understanding of the more serious complications from which the analysis in this chapter has abstracted will lead to the most useful employment of it in applications to a real world.

SUGGESTED READINGS

Mises, L. v., *Human Action*, Yale University Press, New Haven, Connecticut, 1949, pp. 258–323, 388–394.

Leftwich, R. H., *The Price System and Resource Allocation* (rev. ed.), Holt, Rinehart and Winston, New York, 1960, Ch. 17.

12 MONOPOLY AND COMPETITION
IN THE GENERAL MARKET

We have been examining until now market processes where the relevant market forces operated principally through competitive pressures. We saw how the price that each resource owner obtains for the resources he sells (or the price that each producer obtains for the products he produces and sells) is determined by what he deems necessary to offer the market in order to outstrip his competitors. In the present chapter we consider what can be expected to happen in a general market where the supply of particular resources (or the production of particular products) is concentrated in the hands of single market participants. Most of the cases we will examine are simpler analytically than many we have considered in earlier chapters. Nevertheless, monopoly and related problems should be treated at this stage, because they bring about modifications in the general market model where they are embedded.

In introducing these problems we must be aware of the considerable terminological confusion that surrounds them. The terms "monopoly" and "competition" are used in the literature to denote a number of different market situations. Moreover, economists frequently use these terms quite differently from laymen. These terms have in turn led to numerous further terms and combinations of terms in attempts to distinguish numerous special market situations from one another. We will attempt in this chapter to deal with relatively simple cases specifically relevant to the framework of analysis developed in earlier chapters, and we will try to avoid fruitless terminological disputes. As a result, several of the cases that we will consider possibly will not fall neatly into the terminological pigeonholes that have become popular in the specialist literature on the subject.

THE MONOPOLIZED RESOURCE

Suppose that starting from a given day, in the model of the general market considered in the preceding chapter, a particular resource hitherto present in the endowments of many participants, regularly appears (in the same aggregate quantity as previously) in the initial endowment of only one market participant. How would this affect the various prices, volumes of output, and methods of production on the general market?[1]

The favored resource owner now finds himself in a situation quite different from his previous one. Previously, he dared not ask a price for a quantity of the resource any higher than that asked by his most eager competitor; that is, by that other owner of this resource who was the most eager to sell such a quantity. Now the favored resource owner knows that no matter how high a price he demands for his resource, he need not fear that anyone else will offer it for less. On the other hand, however, he knows that if he raises the price he will be able to sell only a smaller quantity of the resource than can be sold at the lower price.

He knows that although no other resource owner can supply exactly the same resource, there may be many who are willing to supply excellent substitutes for it. He knows, therefore, that the entrepreneurs who buy his resource will continue to do so at higher prices only with full consciousness of the correspondingly increased relative attractiveness of employing substitute resources—or even of entering into altogether different branches of production calling for resources entirely unrelated to the monopolized one. The monopolist-resource-owner is well aware that he faces competition, and that this competition will govern the quantities of the resource that he can expect to sell at higher prices. The resource owner knows that the stronger the competition provided by related resources, the more elastic the demand for his resource will be.

This degree of elasticity of the relevant portions of the demand curve facing the monopolist-resource-owner determines whether or not it will be profitable for him to raise the price. It may not be profitable to raise the price, in which case there will be no changes at all in market activities (as a result of the original concentration of the resource into the endowment of the single market participant).[2] But if it does appear profitable to the monopolist-resource-owner to raise the price of his resource, several further changes and adjustments will be brought about in consequence. These will concern the quantity of the resource bought, the organization

---

1. The reader should compare the discussion in this section with that (on monopoly in the pure exchange economy) in Ch. 7 (see pp. 138–142).

2. Of course, the mere fact of the altered pattern of endowments has altered the initial "incomes" of individuals. We ignore here all consequences that can be ascribed purely to this alteration of "incomes."

of production methods, and, indirectly, product prices and possibly also the prices and employment of other productive factors.

Clearly, the higher price obtained for the resource will mean that only a smaller quantity will be bought. As soon as the price increase is announced, entrepreneurs will revise their short-run and long-run production plans in the light of the new market situation. In the short run, entrepreneurs will now tend to substitute more of other resources in place of the monopolized factor; in the long run (and in some cases even in the short run), entrepreneurs, in addition, will be likely to switch production at the margin from the production of products calling for heavy inputs of the monopolized factor, toward the production of other products. All these changes in plans, involving both the input proportions used in production, and also the scale of production, will result in a smaller aggregate quantity of the monopolized resource being purchased by entrepreneurs at the higher price. In effect, what the monopolist has done is simply to hold a definite quantity of the resource off the market, and then to allow buyers to compete with each other for the remainder. This remainder is bought by the most eager buyers who secure their shares only by offering a price high enough to eliminate the less eager buyers. If the monopolist-resource-owner has correctly gauged entrepreneurial reaction to the price increase, he will find that his total resource sales revenue is greater than before, the increase in revenue per unit derived from the smaller quantity of resource sold, more than offsetting the revenue lost on that quantity of resource that he is unable to sell now at the higher price. (Of course, the monopolist-resource-owner may discover that he has misjudged his market. He may find that his total revenue has shrunk forcing him to lower the price, at least to some degree. Or, on the other hand, the decrease in quantity sold may be so slight that the monopolist might suspect that even greater total revenue is to be obtained at a still higher price.)[3]

With a smaller quantity of this resource being bought and used in production, there will be corresponding consequences with respect to the volume of output available to consumers. If the monopolized resource is one for which, in the production of particular products, no substitute factors are available, these products will show most clearly the effects of the price increase. Sooner or later entrepreneurs will switch from the production of these products to other branches of production. Consumers

3. On the calculations governing the monopolist's best choice of price, see p. 141, n. 14; see also p. 106, n. 7.

will find smaller quantities of these products for sale, probably at higher prices. On the other hand, somewhat larger quantities can be expected to be produced of other products, possibly at somewhat lower prices. Eventually, the market process will have brought about appropriate alterations in the long-range plans of the producers so that a new stable pattern of prices for the other resources will have been established, consistent with the new sets of production and consumption decisions.

The differences between output in the market (in equilibrium) before monopolization of the resource, and output in the market that has achieved equilibrium after monopolization, are results of the fact that a quantity of the monopolized resource remains unsold. The new market as a whole is the poorer by this quantity of factor. It is in the same position it would be in if this quantity of the factor had never been endowed by nature. The concentration of the ownership of the resource into the hands of a single resource owner has deprived the market as a whole of the opportunity to bid for the output that the unsold portion of this resource might have made possible. When the resource was distributed among the endowments of many resource owners, it was never in the interest of any of the resource owners to deprive the market of the output that could be derived from his supply of the factor. The interests of both the resource owner and the consumers were best served by the fullest possible employment of the resource. Now, however, it is in the monopolist's interest to leave a portion of the supply unused, in direct contradiction to the interests of the consumers.[4]

This outcome is not the *necessary* result of the monopolization of the resource. When demand conditions are not favorable to the wishes of the monopolist, he may be forced to offer his entire supply of the resource to the market at the old low price. Any increase in price, he would fear, would result in lower total revenue. In cases such as this no adverse consequences for the market as a whole can be ascribed to the monopolization of the resource.

THE RESOURCE CARTEL

Suppose that a particular resource appears in the nature-endowed factor supplies of resource owners sufficiently few in number for all of them to

---

4. A special case may exist where in the absence of monopoly a resource would have been a free good. Here a monopolist may be able to hold off sufficient quantities of the resource to enable it to command a price. See p. 141, n. 15.

enter into a cartel agreement. Under such an agreement the owners of the resource attempt to earn greater revenue through the elimination of competition among themselves. Each seeks to offer the market less attractive opportunities (that is, to obtain opportunities more advantageous to himself) through the assurance that no other owners of the resource will offer opportunities more attractive to the market than his own.

Such a cartel, in theory, could operate in exactly the same way as the single owner of a monopolized resource. If demand conditions are propitious, the cartel may be able to raise the price of the resource. This higher price, however, will be maintained only if all cartel members refuse to sell for less than the agreed price. This will result in a smaller aggregate quantity of resource sold, leaving some of it unsold in the hands of the owners. A cartel agreement will have to provide for a definite method whereby the sales revenue should be distributed among the cartel members. (Or, to put the same thing the other way around, the agreement must specify clearly the basis on which the loss of revenue attributable to the unsold quantities of the resource is to be borne by the cartel members.)

If the cartel agreement is fulfilled, the group as a whole will gain additional revenue in exactly the same amount as would be gained by a single monopolist-resource-owner. This gain will have been distributed among the members through the arrangement mentioned in the preceding paragraph. The cartel members as a group will have denied the market the output obtainable from the unsold quantity of resource, just as the single monopolist did. In both cases the loss suffered by the market as a whole is the inevitable accompaniment to the additional revenue gained by the monopolist or the cartel.

It is, however, precisely this additional revenue gained through the strict fulfillment of the cartel agreement that makes such an agreement appear exceedingly difficult to set up and maintain. There is a built-in tendency for members of a cartel to break away from it. This can easily be understood. Under the cartel agreement each member, in effect, gives up his supply of the resource to the cartel as a whole; the cartel as a whole holds back a quantity of the resource and is able to sell the remaining quantity at a higher price; the revenue is then distributed among the members. Each member receives in this way more than he would have received if there was no cartel. But (and it is this that makes a cartel agreement precarious) each individual resource owner can probably see that he could obtain even *more* revenue if he remained outside the cartel arrangement and sold *all* his supply of the resource to the market *at the price achieved by the cartel.*

Now it is true that where one or several resource owners refuse to join a cartel, it may still be worthwhile for the remaining resource owners to form a cartel. But these remaining resource owners would now possess, as a group, only an *incomplete monopoly* over the resource. In making their calculations as a group they must now realize that if they force up the price by holding off some of their supply from the market, they must share any resulting gain with outsiders who shoulder none of the necessary cost; namely, the loss of revenue on the unsold portion of the resource supply. With only an incomplete monopoly over the resource, a cartel or a single resource owner holding a large portion of the resource supply must lose all the revenue attributable to the resource supply held off the market (since those outside the cartel are eager to sell all they can at the ruling price). Any price increases can be maintained only if the cartel holds the required quantity off the market. Thus, in calculating the wisdom of pursuing a policy restricting supply, the cartel must offset, against only part of the additional revenue gained through such a policy, the entire loss of revenue on the unsold quantity.[5]

5. This may be illustrated by a diagram. Here DD' represents the market demand curve for the resource. For a monopoly, this line then represents the monopolist's line of average revenue, with MR the corresponding line of marginal revenue. The monopolist's best possibility, assuming he does not wish to use any of the resource for himself, is then to sell the quantity OA at price AB (so that his marginal revenue is zero). His total revenue is then $OA \times AB$. If, however, a cartel has only partial monopoly over the resource, things are different. The line $S_{NC}S'_{NC}$ represents the aggregate supply curve of the resource owners *outside* the cartel. Assuming the DD', $S_{NC}S'_{NC}$ curves are known, the cartel operators may calculate the demand curve that *they* face. At each proposed price they can calculate the quantity that the cartel will be able to sell by subtracting, from the aggregate quantity that the market will buy at the price, the aggregate quantity that the non-cartel suppliers will supply at the price. (Thus, at price OE, the cartel may expect to sell the quantity $EF = GH = EH - EG$.) The line D_cD_c' thus obtained is the demand curve facing the cartel; MR_c then represents the cartel's marginal revenue line. The best decision for the cartel is then to announce a price LM. At this price they can sell the quantity of resource OL yielding the greatest possible revenue $OL \times LM$ (marginal revenue being zero). This revenue is clearly much less than that for the complete monopolist, and will be correspondingly lower as the $S_{NC}S'_{NC}$ line moves to the right.

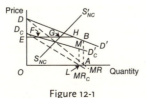

Figure 12-1

Nevertheless, when the number of resource owners is sufficiently small, it may be possible to maintain a collusive price-fixing arrangement. In the literature such cases are frequently called cases of collusive *duopoly* (where there are two sellers) or *oligopoly* ("few" sellers).[6]

RESTRICTION OF SUPPLY: A SPECIAL CASE

A special case of considerable interest may be considered as follows. Consider a resource which is present in the original endowments of a number of resource owners, too large for a stable cartel to be successfully established. Suppose, however, that through some special device (legal, institutional, or other), a group of the resource owners are able to sell their resources to the producers of a particular product (or group of products) *without fear of competition* from the other owners of the resource. In other words the favored group of resource owners, although unable to control the entire supply of the resource to the market generally, has gained complete control over the supply of the resource available to all producers of a particular product or group of products.[7]

In such a situation the favored group of resource owners may act in a way that is in some respects similar to the actions of the resource cartel, but that is in other respects significantly different. Since the owner group faces no competition in its own "preserve," it may (like a cartel) ask a price (within this protected area) without regard to the price being asked by the other resource owners (outside the area). Moreover, although the owner group realizes that the higher the price it asks (within the protected area), the smaller the quantity of the resource that will be bought (in the area); the group is still free to offer (if it wishes) the unsold quantity of resource to buyers outside the area (in competition with all the other resource owners).[8] Thus, it may appear extremely profitable for the group to force

6. A very large literature has emerged dealing in great detail with these cases. Much of the analysis required for these cases depends on postulates that must be imported from outside price theory proper. In this book we do not enter into these problems. For one excellent review of such problems see Machlup, F., *The Economics of Sellers' Competition*, Johns Hopkins University Press, Baltimore, 1952, Parts 5, 6.

7. Strictly speaking, this case is unlikely to be altogether compatible with the definition of a free market system developed in Ch. 2.

8. If the group that has gained the favored control over the supply is not a group of resource owners but a group of entrepreneurs (who admit resource owners as partners in order to supply the "protected area"), then there will of course be no problem of unsold resources. The group will merely admit to partnership only that number of

up the price of its resource to an area where the group can restrict the supply, well above the resource price elsewhere.

The consequences for the market are generally different from those brought about by a cartel with complete or with only incomplete monopoly of the supply of a resource. In the present case no quantity of the resource is kept altogether off the market. What is not sold in the protected area at the high price is sold elsewhere at the lower price. On the other hand, the artificially high price in the protected area must necessarily generate important consequences with respect to production plans and the allocation of resources. Within the protected area the producers will seek to adjust their production plans to the higher price. They will substitute other resources for the "restricted" resource at the margin; they will alter the scale of their output in the light of the new configuration of resource prices. In the long run they may move into other branches of production, outside the protected area.

On the other hand, producers outside the area will find that a larger quantity of the restricted resource is being offered for sale to them at any given price (this quantity including those resources barred from employment in the protected area by the artificially high price). This will result generally in a somewhat lower price than would have prevailed in the absence of all supply restrictions outside the protected area. Producers outside the area will adjust their short-run and long-run plans to this situation. In general, the result will be that the restricted resource is used in the protected area in such a limited degree that the efficiency of the resource at the margin is high so that buyers in this area find it worthwhile to pay the high price; while outside the area the resource is used so freely, in view of its especially low price, that its efficiency at the margin is much lower. The supply restriction, while not denying altogether to the market the output of any quantity of the resource, has succeeded in forcing some quantity of the resource to be used where its efficiency at the margin is lower than in the protected area.

This will be eventually reflected, of course, in the pattern of product prices and the quantities bought of these products. It is observed, once again, that these consequences of the supply restriction result directly from the gain received by the favored group of owners—this gain, in the

---

resource owners necessary to ensure supply of that quantity of resource that maximizes the group's revenue.

present instance, not being offset by any loss of revenue due to any unsold quantity of the resource.[9]

COMBINATIONS OF RESOURCE BUYERS

In the short run it may be possible not only for sellers to combine, but also for all the *buyers* of a particular resource to combine, in this case, for the purpose of forcing *down* the price of the resource. (Alternatively, it is possible that all the supply of the resource is bought by a single entrepreneur, and that in the short run he will be able to exploit this *monopsony* position in order to force down the price.) In the long run, if the price of a versatile resource is very low, there is no *a priori* reason why in the absence of institutional barriers the superior advantages secured by purchase—so cheaply—of the resource should not attract competition from fresh entrepreneurs. (There is thus an important asymmetry in this respect between the buyers' and sellers' sides of the market.) But in the short run the entrepreneurs who buy the resource may feel reasonably secure against outside competition and may seek additional advantage by eliminating competition among themselves.

Such a combination of buyers will be able to offer a low price for the resource without fear that anyone else will offer sellers of the resource a more attractive price. The result will be a lower price for the resource, and a consequently smaller quantity of resource supplied to the market. Buyers of the resource, if they choose to force down the price in this way, will have to adjust their production plans to the availability of only smaller quantities of the resource.[10] The lower resource price may yield short-run advantage to the buyers in their capacity of producers. The other producers of the products that these monopsonist-buyers produce, whose plants

---

9. Some revenue loss may be suffered, of course, due to the lower price the resource must be sold at outside the protected area.

10. This may be illustrated with the help of the diagram. The line *SS'* represents the supply curve of the resource that faces the monopsonist group. Each point on the curve reflects the quantity of resource that the resource owners in aggregate will sell to the monopsonist group if they offer a particular price. The *MC* line then expresses the marginal cost to the buyers' group of advancing purchases of the resource by successive units. The line *MP* reflects the respective increments to revenue that the employment of successive units of the resource is able to afford to the buyers. (The downward slope of this line reflects, among other possible things, the laws of variable proportions.) Clearly, the monopsonist group will do best by offering a price *AB*, so that they will be able to obtain the quantity *OA*. (At higher prices they would be able to secure

and long-range production plans require no inputs of the monopsonized resource, will find themselves at a cost disadvantage.

It is observed, however, that there is a fundamental difference between the previously considered consequences wrought by the monopoly power of a single resource owner, and the consequences of the buyers' combination discussed here. In the monopoly instance, the control over supply (coupled with the existing demand conditions) made it in the interest of the resource owner to hold back from useful employment (in fact to destroy) an available quantity of resource that consumers (through their "agents" the entrepreneurs) would have gladly used (and for which they were willing to pay a price, which, in the absence of monopoly, would have brought all the resource quantity into employment). In the present case of a buyers' combination, on the other hand, the buyers have merely decided to offer, in concert, a price so low that it is worthwhile for resource owners to yield only a smaller quantity of the resource to the market. (Even a resource price established in a competitive market, we observe, is probably able to attract resource owners to yield only a smaller resource quantity than they would be prepared to yield at a still higher price.) Resource owners are not hurt by monopsonistic action on the part of the buyers of resources in the same way the ultimate buyers of resources are hurt by monopolistic action on the part of the sellers of resources.

Nevertheless, in the short run, the combination of buyers will have its effect on consumers. Since we are assuming that the entrepreneurs who are members of the buyers' combination produce their products in competition with other producers, there will not result directly any contraction in product output. Any reduction in output by the members of the buyers' combination, due to the smaller quantity available of the resource

---

greater quantities of the resource.) It should be observed that the selection by a monopsonist of his preferred position does not differ essentially (either diagrammatically or logically) from the selection made by a non-monopsonistic resource buyer. The only difference is that for the latter the supply curve is likely to appear far more elastic (in special cases, even perfectly elastic).

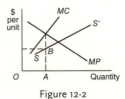

Figure 12-2

that they buy as a group, will be made up by other producers, possibly at somewhat higher prices.

As we have seen, in the long run and, for many resources, even in the short run, even these effects cannot last. Barring institutional restriction upon entry into the ranks of the entrepreneur, the lower costs achieved by the members of the buyers' group will attract competition. If the new entrepreneurs are unable (even by joining the buyers' group) to secure the quantities of the resource they would like (due to the small quantity supplied at the low price even by the buyers' combination), they will offer resource sellers somewhat higher prices in competition with the group. The competition of these new entrepreneurs, bringing about a tendency for the product prices to fall, and for the resource price to rise, will eventually wipe out any profits that the members of the buyers' group had gained.

MONOPOLY IN PRODUCTION

An important monopoly case may arise when an entrepreneur producing a particular product has monopoly control over a resource absolutely essential to its production. We may for simplicity imagine a favored resource owner, the only person in whose resource endowment any of this resource is included, acting as entrepreneur-producer of a product that must include a fixed quantity of the rare resource per unit of product. Since there is no buying and no selling of the monopolized resource itself, the monopoly power conferred upon the favored resource owner can be exploited only in the product market.

The consideration determining his production and pricing policy are similar to those governing the decisions of the monopoly seller of a resource. He is in a position to ask consumers any price he chooses for his product, without fear that anyone else will offer the same product to the market for a lower price. No one else, in fact, can produce the product at all, since no one else is permitted to buy the monopolized factor indispensable for its production.[11] On the other hand, the monopolist-producer knows that he faces the very real competition of other products bidding

---

11. Where it is possible for other resources to be employed as more or less imperfect substitutes for the monopolized resource, certain modifications must be made in the analysis in the text. To the extent that the monopolized resource is superior to the substitute resources, the monopolist-producer may yet be able to exact from the market a monopoly gain. See p. 308, n. 19.

for the consumers' incomes, both the competition of the products that are substitutes in consumption for his own product, and the competition of other products.[12] (All consumer products, of course, are "substitutes" for one another in the attainment of "satisfaction.") He knows, therefore, that the higher the price he asks for his product, the smaller will be the quantity bought by consumers. The keenness of the competition provided in general by all other consumer products will express itself in the elasticity of market demand for the monopolized product. (It is the *market* demand that is relevant to the decisions of the monopolist-producer, since he has to deal with the entire demand of the market for his product. The demand curve that he faces is the demand curve of the entire market.)

A set of factors not considered by the monopolist-seller of a resource complicates the decision of the monopolist-producer. These relate to the costs of production of the monopolist-producer. Like the monopolist-seller of a resource, the monopolist-producer must weigh, against the increased revenue that can be obtained from what he is able to sell at a higher price, the loss in revenue that he suffers due to what, precisely because of this higher price, must remain unsold altogether. But in addition the monopolist-producer must consider the effects of asking a higher product price upon his aggregate and per-unit costs of production. At the higher price he will sell less of the product, will produce less of the product, and will in consequence, in the short run certainly, have lower per-unit costs of production. Thus, offsetting the loss in revenue on potential units of product that will not be sold or produced due to the higher price, the monopolist can weigh (besides the higher revenue on the products produced and sold) the saving in costs of production both on the units of product not produced, and also on the units that are produced (at costs that are lower due to the smaller volume of output).

The deliberations of the monopolist-producer can be conveniently schematized by means of diagrams. In Figures 12-3a, b, and c on the following pages we assume (heroically) that the producer knows (or believes that he knows) both his cost curves and the market demand curve for his product. The diagrams show the short-run average and marginal

---

12. As usual, the elasticity of the market demand curve for the monopolized product reflects the degree to which it faces the competition of other products in general. The chief purpose of the notion of *cross elasticity* of demand discussed on pp. 107 ff, is to measure the degree of competition offered to the monopolized product by any *one* particular product.

cost curves of the monopolist-producer (these costs not including any cost attributable to the use of the monopolized resource). Each of the diagrams reflects a particular (different) demand situation shown by the relevant market demand curve for the product (which is, therefore, also the monopolist-producer's *average revenue* curve). For each average revenue curve the corresponding marginal revenue curve has been drawn. In each diagram the line *BE* marks the absolute upper limit to the volume of output of the product permitted in each period by the available supply of the monopolized resource, no matter how high the product price may be. This maximum output is, for each of the diagrams, the quantity *OB*.

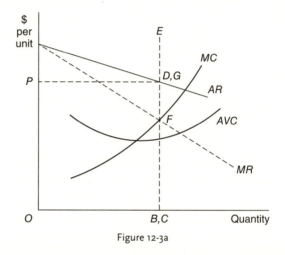

Figure 12-3a

It is clear that in each of the cases shown, the monopolist-resource-owner-producer will seek to produce that quantity at which marginal cost of the other factors required for expanding output just balances the corresponding marginal revenue. This output decision on the part of the resource-owner-producer is completely analogous to what we know to be the optimum decision (*mutatis mutandis*) for an entrepreneur who is a producer but not a resource owner. At any smaller output volume, it is obvious, marginal revenue (derived from the use of the monopolized resource) is greater than marginal cost (of the other required factors). The producer stands to gain, by a unit expansion of output, an addition to revenue that is greater than the required addition to costs of production. (No additional cost would be involved by the increased use of the monopolized resource.) Thus, a smaller output volume would not exhaust all the possibilities open to the monopolist-producer. On the other hand, a greater volume of output (than that at which marginal revenue just balances the marginal cost of expanding output) would also not be the best for the interests of the monopolist. At greater volumes of output, the marginal cost curve is higher than the marginal revenue curve. A unit cutback in production would save the monopolist, at the margin, an amount greater than the corresponding loss in revenue. The best output from the point of view of the monopolist-producer is thus shown on each of the diagrams by the distance OC (to be sold at the price DC), corresponding to the intersection (at F) of the marginal revenue and marginal cost curves.

1. In Figure 12-3a this output happens to coincide exactly with the maximum output (OB) that the monopolist is able to produce with his limited stock of the monopolized resource. In this diagram the demand situation, therefore, is such that it does *not* pay the monopolist-producer to restrict his employment of the resource that he monopolizes. If he holds any quantity of the resource "off the market" (that is, if he refrains from using the whole supply in production), he will be sacrificing, on the units of revenue not produced, a potential revenue that (even after it is reduced by the corresponding saving in costs of production) is not offset by the resulting increased revenue obtained on the units of product that are produced. In this case, demand is sufficiently strong and sufficiently elastic to force the monopolist-producer to use his monopolized resource just as fully as it would have been used in the absence of monopoly. The upper limit to output set by the quantity available of the monopolized factor is fully achieved despite the ability of the monopolist to restrict production.

If, with the same cost and demand structure of Figure 12-3a, the resource (now monopolized) would have been available in a competitive market (in the same aggregate quantity OB), there would have been essentially similar market results in equilibrium. The full quantity of the (now monopolized) resource would have been bought by entrepreneurs at a price, for the fixed quantity of the resource required per unit of product, somewhat less than FD. At this price for the resource, it would just have paid the entrepreneurs to produce the units of product requiring the final units of the (now monopolized) resource. To produce a unit of product they would at this point have been paying the sum FC for the other complementary factors of production (as does now the monopolist-producer also), together with the sum FD (or somewhat less) for the required additional quantity of the (now monopolized) resource. The competitive market would have been in equilibrium. It would just have paid the entrepreneurs to produce an aggregate output of OB: the marginal cost of production (*FC* + *FD*) being exactly covered by the marginal revenue (*DC*) (which is the price that consumers as a whole are willing to pay for the supply *OB*, as seen from the demand curve). Any smaller aggregate volume of output would have sold at a price high enough to leave a profit. Competition would wipe out this profit margin through output expansion up to *OB*.

With the resource monopolized, on the other hand, and with the monopolist-resource-owner himself the producer, the demand pattern in Figure 12-3a brings the same results. The monopolist produces output *OB*, and sells it at price *DC* per unit, paying the sum *FC* for the other factors required for the marginal unit of output, with the difference being the net proceeds that he receives (as resource owner) from the employment of the marginal units of the monopolized resource.

2. In Figure 12-3b the cost curves, and also the limit-to-output line *EB*, are all exactly similar to those in the previous diagram. The demand situation, however, is different. In the present case the market demand curve for the product (the monopolist-producer's average revenue line *AR*) intersects the line denoting the marginal cost of the other factors *to the left* of the line *EB*. This means that if the entire supply of the monopolized resource were to be employed in production, the resulting output volume, in contrast to the preceding case, would be so large that it could be sold only at a price per unit insufficient to cover even the costs of the *other* factors required (for the production of the last possible unit of output). If there were no monopoly of the resource, it is clear that some quantity would remain unused. Competition among sellers of the (now monopolized) resource would force down its price to zero,[13] and entrepreneurs would employ it only up to the point where the additional revenue gained by employing the marginal unit is just greater than the additional costs incurred by the employment of the other factors of production complementary to it. This would result in an aggregate output *OH* (assuming

---

13. Compare, on this point, the discussions on p. 141, n. 15; p. 248, n. 12; and p. 289, n. 4. An example of such a case is where a single producer has sole possession of a piece of technological information that he is able to keep secret. Under competition such information, vital though it might be to a certain branch of production, could command no price. Knowledge of the technological secret could produce, with freely available complementary resources, any desired quantity of product; the distance *OB* would be infinitely great. Monopoly over the secret (conferred institutionally, for example, by patent) would result in the consequences discussed in the text.

that the costs for the monopolist are no different than they would be for a competitive industry as a whole) and a competitive price *GH*.

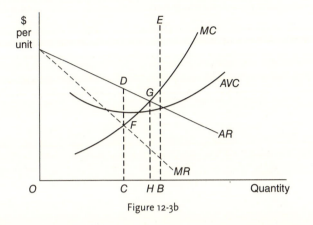

Figure 12-3b

In such a situation it is clearly in the interests of the monopolist-resource-owner-producer to restrict the employment of the monopolized resource so that the volume of output is cut to *OC*. For this output his marginal revenue line intersects his marginal cost line at *F*, with the product selling at a price *CD* per unit. The configuration of demand is such that the interests of the monopolist-producer run counter to those of the consumers generally. Although a sufficient further quantity of the monopolized resource is available to produce the additional quantity of product *CH*, which consumers value *more* highly than the bundle of other complementary factors required, the monopoly position of the resource owner-producer leads him to withhold the required units of the monopolized resource.

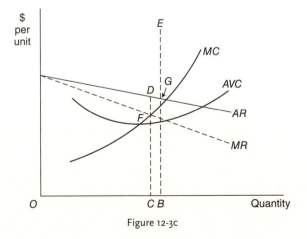

Figure 12-3c

3. In Figure 12-3c we have still another possibility. Here again we have the same cost curves and upper-output-limit line *EB* as before. The market demand curve for the product intersects the line of marginal costs of the other complementary factors to the *right* of the *EB* line (exactly as it did in the case of Figure 12-3a). If the now monopolized resource would not have been monopolized, it would have been fully employed and would have brought a price in the market (again, exactly as in the case of Figure 12-3a). Competitive output would have been *OB*, selling at a competitive price *BG*. However, in the present case (*unlike* the case of Figure 12-3a but like the case of Figure 12-3b), it *would* be in the monopolist's interest to restrict employment of the resource that he monopolizes, and consequently, of course, also the volume of output, below the corresponding levels in a competitive industry.

This is so because at the "competitive" level of output *OB*, the marginal revenue (associated with the monopolist's average revenue line) is *less* than the marginal costs (incurred by the employment of the other resources necessary for the production of the last unit of output). Thus, it would pay the monopolist to restrict output to *OC*, corresponding to the point of intersection of the marginal revenue and marginal cost lines.

The difference between Figures 12-3a and 12-3c thus depends on the relation of marginal revenue to marginal cost, for a volume of output that would exhaust the monopolized resource. If the marginal revenue is not below the marginal cost (of the other required factors), the monopoly position of the resource owner will be innocuous, with no divergency from the price-output pattern that would prevail in a corresponding competitive industry. If marginal revenue falls short of marginal costs at this maximum possible output volume, on the other hand, the monopolist's interest will result in an output restricted below the potential competitive level, with price correspondingly higher.

Figures 12-3a and 12-3c differ from Figure 12-3b in that in the latter case the monopolized resource would be, in a competitive world, a free good. This was expressed in the diagram, we have seen, by the intersection of the market demand curve and the line of marginal costs, to the left of the *EB* line. In this case, as we have seen, it would *always* be in the interest of a monopolist-owner of the resource to restrict its employment. Where the demand for the product is sufficiently strong for the (now monopolized) resource *not* to be a free good (even in a competitive market), then, as we have seen in Figure 12-3a and 12-3c, it *may* be in the interest of the monopolist-producer to restrict output below the level of a corresponding competitive market. In such cases, with a given price the maximum possible output can be sold at (the distance BG in Figures 12-3a and 12-3c), it would be the *elasticity of demand* (at the relevant point G on the market-demand curve) that will determine whether or not the monopolist-producer will attempt to force up the price. As in Chapter 6,[14] the marginal revenue corresponding to any point on a demand curve (such as G) is given by the formula $MR = P + p/\varepsilon$, where p is the height of the point above the quantity axis (such as BG), and ε is the elasticity of the demand curve at the point. Thus, with a given distance BG for the average revenue obtainable by the sale of output volume OB, the corresponding marginal revenue will depend purely on the elasticity of demand (the required marginal revenue being less than BG by the quantity $-BG/\varepsilon$). The more inelastic the demand curve is at the point B (reflecting the weakness of the competition of other products), the greater will be the value of $-BG/\varepsilon$ and, therefore, the lower will be the relevant marginal revenue. For sufficiently low elasticity, marginal revenue will fall short of the relevant marginal costs, and, as we have seen, make it in the monopolist's interest to exploit his monopoly position through output restriction.[15]

THE CONSEQUENCES OF MONOPOLY OUTPUT RESTRICTION

If conditions are favorable, we have seen, it may be possible for a market participant, who is the sole owner of a particular resource, to monopolize the output of a particular product and bring about a price-output pattern for the product different from what would prevail in a competitive situation. In the absence of the particular required constellation of demand and costs, we have seen, the mere fact that the sole control over an essential ingredient in a product gives a particular producer the monopoly of the product's output will not lead to any deviation from what would prevail in the absence of monopoly. The phenomena prevailing in a general market, therefore, where a host of products are produced by the cooperation of a host of different productive factors will not *necessarily* be distorted

14. See p. 106, n. 7. (It will be recalled that for downward-sloping curves, the elasticity is negative.)

15. A monopolist, like any producer, may select one price-output decision as the best that he can achieve with a *given* plant, but may select quite a different plan when he is free to construct an entirely new plant. In the long run a monopolist's cost curves are (like those of all producers) different from those relevant to short-run decisions.

merely because of monopoly control over some of the resources, even if this results in monopoly control over the output of particular products.

Where conditions do favor monopolistic output restriction, the consequences are not difficult to understand. The monopolized resource is employed, and the product produced, in smaller volume than under competition. Complementary factors of production that, in the absence of monopoly, would have been employed in the monopolized industries will seek employment elsewhere. In these other industries their productivity will be lower, and consequently the price that these complementary factors will bring will be correspondingly lower. On the other hand, the output volumes of other products will be increased somewhat due to the transfer of these other productive factors. The owner of the monopolized resource, even after market forces have eliminated all entrepreneurial profits, will still finish with a more desirable income than he would have been able to secure without exploiting his monopoly power. The owners of the other factors will be somewhat worse off, both as a result of the possibly lower prices they may be receiving for their resources, and as a result of the shift of production from the more desirable (monopolized) product to other, somewhat less urgently desired products. These consequences will be affected by the revisions in consumer income allocations induced by these income and price changes, and also by the consequent ripples of change affecting the organization of production.

The greater the number of resources that are monopolized by the same single resource owner, the more powerfully he will be able to distort market activity. Monopoly over many resources, making possible monopoly in the production of many products, will mean correspondingly weaker competition from non-monopolized products. This will provide the monopolist-producer with exceptionally attractive opportunities to gain by raising the prices of his products.

THE MONOPOLIST-PRODUCER AS A RESOURCE BUYER

We have already seen that where a particular entrepreneur or group of entrepreneurs is the only buyer of a particular resource, he or the group *may* be able to obtain a short-run advantage over competitors (who only use other resources) by forcing down the price through restricting their purchases of the resource.[16] We saw that this possibility is by no means

16. See pp. 294–296.

completely analogous, however, to the case where a monopolist-owner of a resource is able to force up its price by holding some of it off the market. The analysis, in the preceding sections, of the effects on the market of monopoly in the production of a particular product (arising from a monopolized resource) makes possible the exploration of a further case involving monopoly on the part of a resource buyer.

Suppose that a producer monopolizes the production of a particular product by virtue of his sole ownership (in his capacity of resource owner) of a resource (say, resource A) essential to its production. Suppose further that the production of the monopolized product calls for the employment of (among other productive factors) a resource (say, resource B) specific to the production of this product. Then it is clear that the monopolist-producer can enjoy complete freedom from competition in buying this specific resource B. No other producer will ever desire to buy this resource, so long as the production of the only product it can be used for is monopolized by the monopolist-owner of resource A. The monopolist-producer will adjust his purchases of the specific resource B, as we have seen in a previous section, so that the marginal revenue that he can derive from the last unit purchased of it is just higher than the increase in costs necessitated by its purchase. In the present case the producer will be able to rely on the low price that he thus secures, not only for the short run, but also for the long run. So long as he monopolizes production, he will be the only buyer of resource B who purchases it at a lower price (but for this reason being able to buy only a smaller quantity of the resource) than would prevail in a competitive market.

Under certain conditions the position of the monopolist-producer as sole buyer of the specific resource B may bring about results that seem analogous to what the monopolist-seller of a resource is able to do. In the

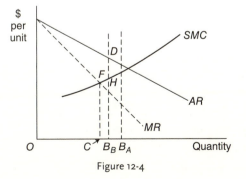

Figure 12-4

diagram, OB_A represents the upper limit to the volume of output obtainable from the supply of the monopolized resource A (obtainable; that is, if all other inputs, including the specific resource B, were plentiful). On the other hand, OB_B represents the limit to volume of output obtainable with the *actual* supply of the specific resource B. The market demand curve for the product (the monopolist-producer's average revenue curve) and the corresponding marginal revenue line are also shown on the diagram. The cost line shows, for each successive unit of output, the increment in costs of production attributable to all the quantities of resources required for its production *except resource A and resource B*.

If the resource A were not monopolized, the situation would then be as follows (assuming other things to be unchanged). Output would be produced by competing entrepreneurs in the aggregate volume OB_B, this quantity being sold at the price $B_B D$. Since this aggregate output requires all the available supply of resource B, but not all the available supply of resource A, the latter resource (if specific to the production of this product) would be a free good. Competition between sellers of resource A would force down the price to zero. Resource B would command the price DH in the resource market. Since, however, resource A is monopolized by the producer, it can be in his interest to restrict output to the quantity OC (corresponding to the intersection at F of the marginal cost line and the marginal revenue lines).

Such a restriction of output means that the producer will be employing less of the specific resource B than is in fact available. Competition between the various owners of this resource will therefore force down its price close to zero (assuming the owners of resource B do not form a cartel). The monopoly position of the producer, gained from his control of resource A, has thus made it possible for him to cut back output, and hence the employment of resource B to a point where the latter resource has a zero price. His monopoly position, as in cases considered earlier, has made it in his interest to deny consumers the output obtainable from quantities of the resource which he monopolizes (even though consumers value additional units of product more highly than the cost of other required productive factors); but in addition this *same* interest of the producer has implicitly required that he deny consumers the output obtainable from a quantity of resource B which he does *not* monopolize. Since both A and B are specific and essential to the product, any restriction of the supply of A allocated to production, implies also a corresponding "waste" of some of B. The monopoly position of the owner of resource A, coupled with the specificity of resource B, together have robbed owners of B of any income they might have been able to obtain in the market through the sale of their endowments of resource B, and also robbed consumers in general of the quantity CB_B of output, for whose production they would have been prepared to pay.[17]

FURTHER REMARKS ON MONOPOLIZED PRODUCTS

Until now we have considered the possibility of the monopolization of production, and consequent restriction of output, only as the result of the sole control by a producer of a resource essential to the production of a particular product. All the consequences for market phenomena that we were able to deduce as resulting from such a monopoly of production sprang thus from the favored position of a producer, not in his capacity of entrepreneur, but *as an owner of resources*. The monopoly gain obtained by a monopolist-producer who has successfully exploited his position is thus not a kind of entrepreneurial profit, but a kind of gain that may be extracted from the market by a monopolist-seller of a resource. Where no monopoly of any single resource exists, there is, in the absence of institutional barriers, no *a priori* reason why any one producer-entrepreneur should find himself in a favored position concerning any particular branch of production.

There may be cases of monopoly in production where the existence of a monopolized resource may not be immediately perceived. It may happen that a number of producers are competing with each other in the output and sale of a particular product, and yet each of the producers feels that *his* product commands the loyalty of at least some of his customers. Each producer feels confident that even if he were openly to raise the price of his product a little higher than the prices charged by his competitors, not all of his customers would switch to the products of his competitors. Clearly such a situation must mean simply that each of these producers is producing a product that is *not* exactly the same as the products of the other producers in the group—at any rate from the point of view of consumers (which is all that matters). There may be numerous factors capable of differentiating the product of one producer from closely similar products produced by other producers, in the eyes of consumers. The packaging, the color, the location of production, the name a product is

17. Compare with Mises, L. v., *Human Action*, Yale University Press, New Haven, Connecticut, 1949, pp. 380–381.

marketed under—these and similar factors may make two products "different" from one another to consumers, even though an outsider might pronounce them "the same."

While each of the producers may be producing a product that, in this sense, is "unique," they are, of course, still competitors with each other. We have seen that a producer of any product experiences the competition of producers of other products; certainly a producer will feel the competition of producers whose products differ only slightly from his own. On the other hand, in the strict sense of the term, the sole producer of a product, no matter how slightly it is different from others, may still be called a monopolist of his product *if* he has sole control over a resource that is responsible for the uniqueness of his product. (If he does *not* possess sole control over any such resource, then there is no reason why any uniqueness that he imparts to his product should not be achieved by other producers, too, if this proves profitable.)[18] But there may well be monopolized resources that make possible the product differentiation, and these may not always be immediately perceived, and may sometimes be the result of institutional barriers.

A catchy trade name, for example, may be such a resource that could be monopolized as a result of appropriate laws. A special location of production, "superior" in the eyes of some customers to alternative locations, may be another such monopolized resource.[19] The good name acquired by a particular producer through past activities may be yet another such resource (one which, in the nature of things, is monopolized, at any rate in the short run). These may not be immediately recognized as being resources, so that the source of a monopoly in the production of a differentiated product may not be immediately perceived as resulting from

18. In the price theory literature these cases have acquired the name *monopolistic competition*. In this (very voluminous) literature the existence of a *resource* monopoly (as foundation for the restriction of output) has not been emphasized. Within the framework of discussion adopted for the present chapter the cases labeled "monopolistic competition" differ or do not differ from bona fide monopoly cases insofar as they do or do not involve resource monopoly.

19. These resources, it is noticed, confer an *advantage* over the similar, but *"inferior"* resources, used by the other producers. The monopolized resources, in these cases, are "indispensable" only with respect to the advantage which they confer. For an excellent discussion of this point see Bain, J. S., *Pricing, Distribution and Employment* (rev. ed.), Holt Inc., New York, 1953, p. 195.

a resource monopoly. But from the point of view of pure theory, it is clear, *anything* that contributes toward making a product superior in any way, from the point of view of consumers, is a factor of production.

As far as the impact upon the market exerted by the uniqueness of such a differentiated product is concerned, the relevant analysis is no different from the analysis of the activities of all monopolist-producers. We have seen that the monopoly of production, which is the result of sole control over an essential resource, may or may not lead to monopolistic restriction of output below the competitive level. Where there are a number of producers each producing a product that he is able to differentiate from the others by virtue of a resource that he monopolizes, each of them will certainly produce an output where marginal revenue is just balanced by the marginal cost of all resources except the monopolized one. This may or may not call for monopolistic restriction of output. The less important the differences between products, the less likely it will be, other things being the same, that a producer will stand to gain by monopolistic restriction of output. Even where the difference between two products is considerable, the higher price obtained for the superior product of course simply may reflect its relative superiority in the eyes of the public, rather than be the result of monopolistic restriction of its supply.

So far from resulting in monopolistic exploitation of the market, the various methods whereby producers differentiate their products, moreover, sometimes may be simply the very *means with which they compete* with one another. We know that the essence of the competitive market process is that each participant seeks to obtain more desirable opportunities for himself through offering the market opportunities superior to those available elsewhere. Entrepreneurs with superior knowledge of the availability of resources and of the demand for various products can earn profits by offering consumers better and cheaper products than other entrepreneurs less well-informed about market conditions. The attempt to offer to sell a given product at a lower price is only one of the dimensions competitive market activity may proceed along (although it is, admittedly, the dimension analyzed most thoroughly in the literature).[20] Entrepreneurs

---

20. The traditional emphasis on price competition seems partly due to the fact that in the analysis of the "very short run" (the market where no further production is possible), it is through price competition that the market does, in fact, achieve results.

will compete with each other, in addition, as we have seen, in the selection of which product to produce—and this includes of course the selection of quality (or qualities), which packaging to use, which location to produce at, which name to assign the product, and so on. Thus, if (*without* any monopoly of a resource) an entrepreneur is the only one among a group of producers of a product who chooses to package the product in a particular way, this simply means that other entrepreneurs believe they can compete more effectively by other means. Just as we know that, until equilibrium has been attained, different entrepreneurs may be asking different *prices* in the market for the same product, so also may they be offering different *varieties* of the product to the market in their attempts to most successfully cater to the wishes of consumers.

THE SINGLE PRODUCER WITHOUT MONOPOLY

The remarks in the preceding sections should help, in addition, in explaining the case where a particular product happens to be produced by only one producer who does *not* control the supply of any of the resources required (either by technology or by institutional conditions) for his product. Such a producer, it is clear, may be the only producer in his "industry," but certainly does not monopolize production. His situation is usually described as one in which he faces *potential competition*. The situation might be one, for example, where all other entrepreneurs happened to believe that this particular product could be produced only at a loss, so that only one entrepreneur undertook the risk of building and equipping a plant for the production of this product. The single producer may know that it is perhaps within his power in the short run to restrict output, and to raise the price that he asks for his product, without fear that his customers will turn to another source of supply for this same product at a lower price. On the other hand, he also knows that there is nothing to stop the eventual emergence of competing producers of this product, and that a restriction of his own long-run capacity in order to secure higher prices will certainly invite the competition of other producers eager to sell the additional units of output for whose production consumers are prepared to pay. If the single producer is intent on avoiding long-run losses as well as on securing short-run supernormal gain, he will avoid a restrictive price-output policy.

A special case of considerable theoretical (and practical) interest arises where a particular product happens to be produced by only one producer as a result of the economies of large-scale production. If the long-run average cost curve for a particular product is declining throughout its relevant extension, the competition of entrepreneurs will eventually bring about the emergence of bigger and bigger producers. The industry will not be in equilibrium with a large number of small producers. Whatever the price of the product may be, a firm that has been satisfied to produce with a plant designed for a small output volume will realize that it could do even better with a bigger scale of plant. In the long run, therefore, competition between producers will force them to seek a bigger output volume. The bigger the scale of plant, the lower the price a producer can afford to sell the product at. Producers will therefore seek to offer consumers lower prices than others are offering through continual increases in the scale of their operations. On the other hand, of course, if bigger producers are to do well enough in the industry to wish to stay there, the aggregate output must not be larger than that which can be sold at a price high enough to cover costs of production.[21] Thus, in the long run the competition among producers will force out of the industry a sufficient number of producers so that those remaining can cover their costs. Eventually, it is conceivable that a single producer may be able to produce the entire supply of the product at so low a cost and therefore at so low a price, that it pays no one else to remain in the industry.

A tendency toward the emergence of big-scale production will certainly evolve in such an industry. So long as this is the result of competition, it is clear this tendency operates consistently with the tenor of the competitive market process, in general, to force entrepreneurs to organize production as efficiently as possible. On the other hand, it is also clear that where only one or only a very small number of larger producers are left as a result of this competitive process, a cutback in production may be tempted (if demand conditions are propitious) in order to achieve greater gains. As we have seen, such a single producer may be in a position to do this during the short run. A producer with a specialized large-scale plant, which would require much capital and time to duplicate, does in fact monopolize a resource essential to the production of his product. However, it is important to recognize that he monopolizes this resource only *from a short-run viewpoint*. In the long run, anyone who believes he

21. This assumes that the market demand curve for the product, at least for large outputs, does slope downward. Considering the analysis of Ch. 5, this assumption is eminently reasonable. Economies of scale will boost industry output to the point where the demand curve, in fact, does slope downward.

can do better in this industry than anywhere else can raise all the necessary capital and buy all the productive factors required to erect another plant large enough to secure all the economies of big-scale production. (If the first single producer has been using a scale of plant that has *not* yet exhausted all possible economies of scale, then in the long run it will certainly pay other entrepreneurs to continue the competitive process whereby ever bigger and bigger plants emerge. Moreover, if we momentarily relax our habitual *ceteris paribus* assumptions just sufficiently to consider the impact of a progressing technology, it is clear that in the long run competing entrepreneurs will be able to set up newer, more efficient plants than those of the existing "short-run monopolist.")

Thus, while a single large producer might be tempted to underutilize his plant (in other words to deny consumers the output obtainable from a resource that he monopolizes in the short run—even though consumers are willing to pay the additional costs of the other required factors), he would know that in the long run this would only attract other entrepreneurs into the industry who will be able to produce as least as cheaply as he himself can. Potential competition may thus effectively bar even short-run restriction of output by the single producer.

SOME REMARKS ON THE MODEL OF "PURE" OR "PERFECT" COMPETITION

Thus far in this book very little explicit mention has been made of a model very much used by writers on price theory; namely, the model of a "perfectly" (or "purely") competitive economy. In this model it is assumed, in addition to the general assumptions that set up a market system, that there are so many buyers and sellers of each resource and product that *no one buyer or seller is able by himself to influence market prices,* and also that there is nothing preventing any market participant from entering into the production of any product he chooses. (Many writers also include the further condition of *perfect knowledge,* especially where they refer to the *perfect* competition model.) Although models based on these assumptions have played a very important part in the development of price theory in this century, and despite the considerable pedagogical usefulness of such models, they do not contribute significantly to an understanding of the market *process.* Analysis of perfectly competitive models is usually confined almost exclusively to the *state* of competitive equilibrium. (In fact it has frequently been pointed out that rather serious logical problems arise when an attempt is made to find out how a purely competitive industry can ever conceivably *attain* a state of equilibrium from any other initial position.)[22]

One implication of perfectly competitive models is of particular importance in connection with the discussions of the preceding sections. Implied in the definition of a perfectly competitive industry is the condition that each seller of a resource or of a product faces a perfectly elastic demand curve for what he sells, and also that each buyer of a resource or of a product faces a perfectly elastic supply curve of what he buys. (Sometimes perfectly competitive conditions are *defined* in these terms.) These conditions reflect the assumptions that no seller can raise the price (even slightly) no matter how he may restrict the quantity that he offers the market, and also that he will not lower the price no matter how much he offers to sell to the market; and that no buyer can lower the price no matter how little he buys, and also that he will not raise the price no matter how much he seeks to buy. It follows from these perfect-elasticity assumptions that to any seller under perfect competition, marginal revenue is equal, for all possible sales quantities, to his average revenue (which is of course the market price of what he sells).[23] Similarly, to any buyer under perfect competition, marginal cost is for all possible quantities purchased equal to average cost (which is simply the market price of what he buys). Now, since every seller of a product will always seek (with or without perfect competition) to sell a quantity for which his marginal revenue just balances his marginal cost of production, it follows that in perfect competition, equilibrium requires that for all producers output be such that marginal cost of production just balances product price. And similarly since every buyer of a resource seeks to employ just enough for the increment in revenue obtainable through the employment of a marginal unit of it to be just balanced by its marginal cost to him, it follows that in perfect competition, equilibrium requires that for all producers output, and the proportions of inputs, be such that for each resource the additional revenue obtained from the marginal unit be just balanced by the resource price.

As a result of the attention paid to the model of perfect competition, a special significance has frequently thus come to be attached to the

22. In addition, it has frequently been complained, the term pure (or perfect) "competition" is a misnomer, since it requires conditions that prevent individual market participants from engaging in any of those activities usually understood by the verb "to compete."

23. See pp. 105–106.

equality for a producer both (a) of marginal cost of production and product price, and (b) of additional revenue derived from the marginal unit of each resource and resource price. Any excess in the price of a product over its marginal cost of production (or any excess in the revenue obtained from the marginal unit of a resource, over the price of the resource) being a departure from perfectly competitive conditions, is immediately associated with monopolistic or monopsonistic control. Thus the possibility of a producer being faced with demand curves and supply curves of less than perfect elasticity (and thus leading to a volume of output where product price is greater than its marginal cost of production, and the price of a resource less than the additional revenue obtained through the employment of a marginal unit of it) is described as monopolistic deviation from the standards of a perfectly competitive market.

It should be emphasized that such conditions (while certainly inconsistent with the assumptions of a perfectly competitive economy) *need* not be accompanied by the monopoly of any one resource and are consequently *different* from conditions involving deliberate restriction of output through denying to the market the use of an available resource. The monopolistic restriction of output that we found to be a possible consequence of monopoly control of a resource should therefore *not* be considered as the case symmetrically opposite to the *perfect* competitive model.[24] Rather, monopolistic restriction of output resulting from sole control over a resource should be seen as analytically counterposed to the situation in a "competitive" market[25] where competition means simply the freedom for a person to produce anything that he chooses (*without* the assumption that when any one product is produced, it is in fact produced by a very large number of "atomistic" producers).

When attention is focused exclusively on the state of equilibrium, a significant difference may appear between the performance of a market model where each participant faces only perfectly elastic supply and

24. In the context of the "perfect-competition" models, and hence also of the monopolistic-competition literature, the polar opposite to perfect competition is provided by the case of the single producer in an industry that (a) does not permit entry of new producers and (b) is not faced with the competition of close substitutes.

25. The term *free competition* sometimes has been used to denote closely similar models (but also has been used to cover other cases). See Scitovsky, T., *Welfare and Competition*, George Allen & Unwin, Ltd., London, 1952, Ch. 15; and also Machlup, F., *The Economics of Sellers' Competition*, Johns Hopkins University Press, Baltimore, 1952, p. 104.

demand curves, and the performance of market models where these curves ("monopolistically") have some slope. But when, as in this book, the focus of interest is in the market process (*leading* to equilibrium, possibly), then the significant distinction is the one emphasized in this chapter; namely, whether or not market conditions make it worthwhile for the monopolist-resource-owner-producer to deny to consumers a quantity of output (one of the resources for which the producer himself has available, and the remaining resources for which consumers are willing to pay for). Certainly the idea should be avoided that the assumptions that characterize the perfect competition market are in any sense "normal" or "standard" for a market economy.

MONOPOLISTIC PRICE DISCRIMINATION

Finally, we consider the possibility that the existence of monopoly control over supply may lead to the emergence of more than one price for a particular good. Under competition, we have seen, such a state of affairs must be intrinsically unstable. Should two competing sellers charge different prices for the same good, buyers will cease buying (as soon as they discover the true state of affairs) from the higher priced seller. Of course where a seller is able to sell at prices considerably below those of his competitors, he may be in a position to demand different prices for his product from different buyers. But, with no monopoly over required resources, competition between sellers will eventually enable them all to sell for the same low prices. For this reason the analysis of *price discrimination*—the sale of the same product by a seller to different buyers at different prices—is usually confined to monopoly situations.

Under certain conditions it may be feasible for, and in the interest of, a monopolist-seller (either of a resource or of a product) to sell to some buyers at prices lower than those that he obtains from other sellers. For this to be *possible,* the seller must feel sure that the buyers from whom he demands the higher prices are not able to buy the good from the other buyers to whom he is selling for lower prices. Clearly if this condition is not fulfilled, it will pay the latter group of buyers to buy at the low prices and then resell to the first group of buyers at prices below those demanded by the monopolist-seller. For price discrimination to be *worthwhile* an additional condition is that net proceeds with discrimination be higher than without. This condition, it will be seen shortly, depends on the respective conditions of demand within each of the groups of buyers it is possible to discriminate among.

Suppose that a monopolist-seller knows that those who buy from him (or who might buy at low enough prices) fall naturally into two separate groups between which no resale of the good (which he sells) is technically feasible.[26] Suppose further that he has available a given quantity (q) for sale, and, pondering on how to secure the greatest possible revenue from its sale, is considering asking a price that is the highest price the entire quantity can be sold at (without discrimination and without holding any units entirely off the market). At this price, the seller knows, the first group of buyers (group A) will buy altogether a quantity q_a, and the second group (group B) will buy quantity q_b, $(q_a + q_b = q)$. Now, the respective demand conditions in group A and group B may be such that the marginal revenue derived from the last unit sold to group A is less than the marginal revenue that would be obtained through the sale of an additional unit to group B. In this case it is in the seller's interest to sell (at a higher price) a quantity $(q_a - 1)$ units to group A (rather than q_a) and a quantity $(q_b + 1)$ units at a lower price to group B (rather than q_b), since he would gain a greater increment in revenue from the latter than he would have to sacrifice in group A. The demand situation within each of the two groups, A and B, is such that the $(q_b + 1)$th unit is valued more highly by group B (as measured by the sums that the group as a whole is prepared to pay respectively for q_b units and for $(q_b + 1)$ units) than the (q_a)th unit is valued by group A (as measured by the sums that the group as a whole is prepared to pay respectively for $(q_a - 1)$ units and for q_a units). So long, then, as a given aggregate sales volume is distributed among the two groups in such a way that a significant discrepancy exists between the marginal revenues associated with the last units sold in each group, an opportunity exists for profitable price discrimination. By exploiting the division between the two buyer groups, the seller may take advantage of the greater eagerness of some of the buyers to buy in the one group at the same time as he taps the revenue obtainable from the large number of potential buyers in the second group who are prepared to buy only at low prices. The seller will have exhausted all opportunities for further profitable price discrimination when he has adjusted prices in the two groups so that marginal revenues are the same for both groups.[27]

26. A standard textbook example is provided by the market for electric power.

27. The point made in the text is frequently expressed alternatively by saying that discrimination will be worthwhile where the aggregate demand curves of the two (or more) sectors of the market have respectively different elasticities at a given price.

Where discrimination in the price of a *product* is possible in this way, the monopolist-producer will determine his optimum output accordingly. As always, he will seek to adjust his output to the point where his marginal revenue is just balanced by his marginal cost. The marginal revenue relevant to the case where discrimination is possible is of course the additional revenue obtained through a unit of expansion of total output when output (both before and after the proposed expansion) is distributed between the groups by means of the different prices asked so that the marginal revenues of the quantities sold in each of the groups are equal to one another.

By discriminating in this way between the two groups, the monopolist-producer may be able to profitably employ *all* of the resource that he monopolizes, even though, without price discrimination, it might have been in his interest to raise the overall product price through monopolistic output restriction. Price discrimination enables the monopolist-producer to gain at least some of the additional revenue resulting from a higher price, without having to sacrifice *all* the revenue that he would have to lose (without discrimination) on the units that cannot be sold at the high price. The price-discriminating seller is able to sell the units that cannot be sold at the higher price to a group in which they can be sold at a lower price.

Where price discrimination is practiced, those charged the higher price are being deprived of part of the *consumers' surplus*[28] that they might have enjoyed in a market without discrimination. Without discrimination those buyers most eager to buy would not have had to pay a price any higher than the price paid by the least eager buyer. Now the division of the market into buying groups forces the buyers in each group to pay a price no lower than that paid by the least eager buyer *within the group*. The segregation of the more eager buyers into one group thus forces them all to pay prices higher than would have been paid when less eager buyers were in their market as well. Of course, each of the buyers, even those paying the highest prices, consider themselves better off by buying than by refraining from buying (or else they would not be buying); nevertheless the division of the market has enabled the monopolist-seller

---

Since $MR = p + p/\varepsilon$, it follows that where the sector demand curves have different elasticities for a given value of p, the respective marginal revenues will not be the same.

28. See p. 118.

to prevent them from gaining an even greater advantage from their purchases.[29]

A special case where this can be achieved almost completely is sometimes termed *perfect price discrimination*. Perfect price discrimination is possible where the seller divides buyers from each other so completely that each of the buyer's "groups" consists of only one buyer.[30] By dealing with each buyer individually, a seller conceivably might charge (assuming he possesses complete knowledge of each buyer's eagerness to buy) each buyer a price so high that *all* consumers' surplus is wiped out for all buyers. Where a number of buyers are included in a group of buyers, even where they are all very eager buyers, the most eager still gain *some* consumer surplus, since they pay a price no higher than is sufficiently low to induce the least eager in the group to buy. When the size of a "group" dwindles to one buyer, however, it may be possible for the seller to extract from each buyer the highest price that he is prepared ever to pay for each unit bought. (This implies, of course, that a different price will be extracted from a buyer for each of the units that he buys.) The seller can achieve this by offering a given quantity to a buyer and demanding a price for the whole quantity (the price being what the seller believes will just leave no consumer surplus), with no option to the buyer of purchasing any smaller quantity at a proportional price. (The seller will determine the sizes of the lots he will offer to the various buyers, in this all-or-nothing fashion, in the way that will maximize his own net proceeds.)

Analysis analogous to that presented in this section can be developed to deal with the conditions price discrimination might be practiced under by a *buyer*.[31] In the absence of institutional divisions between different groups of sellers, however, it is doubtful whether monopsonistic price discrimination could be maintained for any length of time.

SUMMARY

This chapter has examined the modifications in the general market process that are introduced as a result of the concentration of the supply of

29. For a situation where *each* of the buyers is better off with price discrimination than without it, see Mises, L. v., *Human Action*, Yale University Press, New Haven, Connecticut, 1949, p. 387.

30. The standard textbook example of this possibility is a physician selling medical services to his patients.

31. See Robinson, J., *The Economics of Imperfect Competition*, The Macmillan Co., London, 1933, pp. 224–228.

particular resources (or the production of particular products) in the hands of single market participants.

When the entire natural endowment of a particular resource is concentrated in the hands of one owner, it may or may not be profitable for him to force up the price by restricting supply (depending on the elasticity of demand for the resource). Where the monopolist finds it worthwhile to hold some of the resource off the market, corresponding changes are brought about in the methods and volume of production affecting the availability of goods to consumers. Where a resource is exclusively owned by a group of owners able to act in concert, they too may conspire to force up the resource price by restricting supply. (Several variants of resource cartel possibilities can be analyzed.) However, such cartels may face serious problems of enforcing the respective cartel agreements. Where all the *buyers* of a resource combine, they may be able to exert short-run effects on prices and production.

Where the sole owner of a resource chooses not to sell any of it to other producers, but establishes himself as the sole producer of a product for whose production the resource is essential, he can employ his monopoly power in the product market. Detailed analysis shows the conditions under which he will be able to profit by using his monopoly power to raise the product price through *output* restrictions. Further analysis explains how his favored position may also have an impact upon the markets for the other resources required for the production of the exclusively produced product.

In a market where there are numerous, slightly differentiated competing products, it may not always be immediately apparent whether or not some of the resources are monopolized.

The analysis also clarifies the existence and impact of the sole producer in situations where he does *not* have monopoly power, as defined in this chapter. In such cases market activity is carried on under the influence of *potential competition*. A special case typical of this kind of situation is where the economies of large-scale production result in only one producer or a very small number of producers.

The absence of monopoly power, as defined in this chapter, does *not* imply that each buyer of any good or service faces a perfectly elastic supply curve, nor that each seller faces a perfectly elastic demand curve. These latter conditions *are* usually required for much discussed models of "perfect competition." The idea should be avoided that such models are in any sense "normal."

One particular possible result of monopoly control is that more than one price may emerge for a particular good, even in equilibrium. Such possibilities are investigated by the techniques of the theory of monopolistic *price discrimination.*

SUGGESTED READINGS

Mises, L. v., *Human Action,* Yale University Press, New Haven, Connecticut, pp. 354–388.

Hayek, F. A., "The Meaning of Competition," in *Individualism and Economic Order,* Routledge and Kegan Paul Ltd., London, 1949.

Machlup, F., *The Economics of Sellers' Competition,* Johns Hopkins University Press, Baltimore, 1952, Ch. 4.

13 THE PRICE SYSTEM AND THE ALLOCATION OF RESOURCES

Most of this book has been concerned, "positively," with the operation and mechanics of a free enterprise system and the market process. We have discussed the process by which the market determines (a) the prices and quantities produced of each possible product, (b) the prices and quantities employed of each of the available resources, (c) the particular group of resources used for the production of each of the products produced, and (d) the income secured in the market by each of the consumers and the particular group of products each consumer spends his income on. In Chapter 3, as part of our overall preliminary survey of a market economy, it was noted that such a system can (like so many other things) be viewed not only positively but also *normatively*. That is, a market system can be examined not only in order to discover chains of cause and effect, which may exist under such a system, but also in order to judge the degree of success with which the system *achieves specified goals*. In the present chapter we return to such an appraisal.

We have seen that each market participant takes part in the market process only because he believes that he can in this way achieve his own goals more fully than by acting completely on his own. In Chapter 3 we saw further that each of the participants is concerned that the system *coordinate* the activities of all the participants. A participant will specialize in repairing other people's automobile engines only if he can rely on the market system to ensure that other people will bake *his* bread, build *his* home, and produce *his* clothes. The more efficiently such coordination is achieved, the more fully each of the participants will be able to fulfill his own goals through the market. Coordination, we found, must involve (a) the *priority system* according to which the wishes of consumers are successively satisfied, (b) the *method of production* employed for the production of each of the products produced, and (c) the means by which the several contributions of different individuals, who have cooperated jointly in a single productive process, can be separated for the purpose of *assigning incomes* corresponding in some way to individual productive contribution.

In the market system, we found, it is through the assignment of market prices to resources and products that these coordinating functions are fulfilled. In the present chapter, within the framework of such a price-coordinating system, we appraise the market system as a means to achieve the appropriate allocation of the available resources, as judged from the point of view of the market participants. Market participants, in general, will wish to know how faithfully the market process impresses upon the organization of production the pattern that "efficiency" requires, *as measured with reference to the very price system* upon whose coordinating properties the market participants are relying.

THE POSSIBLE LEVELS OF "WELFARE" APPRAISAL

Inquiries into the allocative efficiency of an economic system usually are termed "welfare economics." (This term goes back to a time when economists uncritically believed it possible to talk meaningfully about the "total welfare" of a group of individuals. Since then it has come to be used to cover discussions of the efficiency of a social apparatus in which "efficiency" is far more carefully defined.) It should be stressed that inquiries into the allocative efficiency of a market system can be attempted at *two* levels, and that it is only one of these that primarily concerns us here.

The *first* kind of welfare inquiry assumes *all* the relevant data are *known*, in principle, to the inquiring economist as well as to the market participants. The initial problem for the economist is to devise "optimum" patterns of productive utilization of the known quantities of all resources, and of distribution of the resulting products among participants with known tastes. A market system will then be appraised as to whether its freedom from ignorance enables it to attain such an optimum-allocation pattern of activities. With full knowledge of all relevant data assumed, the market position that is set up for appraisal on this level of inquiry is the position of full *equilibrium*. The *conditions that spell out an equilibrium position* for a market economy (endowed with a given initial set of factor endowments and with participants of given tastes) are appraised and compared for their consistency with the *conditions for optimality.* We do not consider this kind of welfare inquiry in this chapter.[1]

The *second* kind of welfare inquiry we *are* concerned with proceeds from the assumption that each of the participants is to a large extent *ignorant*

---

1. This first kind of welfare inquiry presents an essentially mathematical problem. The general results of this kind of welfare inquiry usually lead to the conclusion that the so-called "welfare conditions" for optimality, with some reservations, are fulfilled by the equilibrium conditions for an economy where "perfect competition" prevails in all industries.

of the body of information that includes all the "data" of the market. The initial position assumed for the market is thus a state of *dis*equilibrium. Initially, the market is understood to be making numerous "errors"; the initial decisions of the various participants are to a large extent *un*coordinated with one another. The market process brings alterations in these decisions. The process may be appraised as to the efficiency with which, employing the limited scraps of information scattered among the participants, it discovers and corrects the initial errors and failures in coordination. In this second kind of appraisal, it is the market *process* that is being judged rather than the *state* of equilibrium the process leads toward. In many respects this second kind of inquiry is the one that market participants may be expected to be the most interested in. After all, in a changing world, a state of market equilibrium, as we have seen, is hardly an attainable goal. The precise degree in which the state of market equilibrium deviates from the conditions of optimality is therefore likely to appear a distinctly academic question. On the other hand, participants will be most interested in knowing the *direction* the market process moves in; they are vitally concerned with the efficiency whereby *existing mis*allocations are discovered and removed, and with the faithfulness and speed whereby the market process tends to adjust market activities to changes in the basic data. (Of course, participants would hardly be concerned with the efficiency of a market process unless they also knew that the final state of equilibrium the process tended toward was also at least *reasonably* efficient from the point of view of the *first* of the two kinds of welfare inquiry mentioned in this section.) It is the normative examination of the market *process* that concerns us in this chapter.

MISALLOCATION OF A RESOURCE IN A MARKET SYSTEM

First of all, we should fix in our minds precisely what is implied in the statement that a resource has been misallocated in a market system. A unit of a particular resource, let us say, has been employed together with quantities of other productive factors in the production of a particular product. The employment of this unit of factor in this way has deprived consumers of the productive contributions that it might have rendered in an alternative employment. On the other hand, consumers under the existing arrangement, are enabled to enjoy the productive contribution that the unit of factor is making in its present employment. In a market system there is a market value placed upon each of the various *foregone* productive contributions that might have been rendered elsewhere by the factor, and there is also a market value placed upon the productive contribution that the factor actually does render. If the market value of any one of the foregone productive contributions is greater than the value of the actual contribution of the unit of factor, then we say that this unit is being employed in the "wrong" use. Measuring "usefulness" by market value of productive contribution (since we are conducting our examination of the market system in terms of its own "guide lines"), it is evident that the unit of factor is being employed less usefully than is possible.

The market value of a productive contribution is an objective magnitude determined jointly (a) by the physical increment of product attributable to the employment of the unit of factor, and (b) by the market value of a unit of the product. The physical increment of product attributable to the factor depends upon the technological laws of production and upon the quantities of other factors the unit of the first factor is to cooperate with in production. The price of a product depends, as we know, on the willingness of buyers to buy, and of producers to produce and sell, the particular product. The difference between the market values of the different possible productive contributions that a unit of factor may be able to make may thus be due to the different degrees of physical productivity of the factor in the various proposed processes of production and/or to the different conditions of market supply and demand for the relevant products. Misallocation of a resource may thus be due to its employment in a productive process where its potential physical productivity is not being exploited to the full, and/or to its employment in the production of a product that the market pronounces less important ("importance" being measured, once again, by market price) than another potential product.

Our statement of the meaning of the term "misallocated resource" refers to *any given* state of affairs (insofar as concerns other market phenomena). We do not here speak primarily of a resource that is not being employed as it would be under conditions of equilibrium. A resource is misallocated if it is in the "wrong" place in terms of *actual* market prices and with respect to a state of the economy *as it is*. Our task is to examine the effectiveness of the market process in detecting and eliminating this kind of "waste." This is waste (a normative word) because, under the *current* conditions of the market, a resource is being used in an employment that the market declares to be less important than an alternative available employment.

IMPERFECT KNOWLEDGE, THE SOURCE
OF RESOURCE MISALLOCATION

The discussions in Chapters 7, 10, and 11 concerning the market process commencing from a state of disequilibrium clarified the reasons for any resource being misallocated in a competitive market economy. A resource may be misallocated only as a direct result of the *imperfection of the knowledge* of market participants. If knowledge of all relevant data were possessed by all participants, no perverse discrepancy could exist between the market value of the productive contribution of a factor in its actual employment and the value of its potential contribution elsewhere. With perfect knowledge the price of the unit of factor would be the same in all areas of the market; differences in the technological efficiency of the factor in different uses, and in the desirability to consumers of the different products, would be fully reflected in the prices and output volumes of the various different products. No room would be left for a perverse difference between the market values of actual and potential productive contributions.

But we proceed here from a position where all the available information is initially widely scattered in the form of scraps of knowledge possessed by individual participants. Resources will be misallocated as a result of this incomplete knowledge. A resource may be employed in a less important manner because the entrepreneur is unaware of the more important employments possible, or because those who are aware of the more important possible employments do not know of the availability of the resource. In the first case, the entrepreneur using the resource in the less important employment may be unaware of the greater technological productivity of the resource in other branches of production, and/or of the higher prices obtainable in the market for the other products. In the second case, the entrepreneurs who are unaware of the more important productive contribution that such a resource can make elsewhere may mistakenly believe that the price of the resource is too high to make its use worthwhile in these more important employments.

In general, then, the misallocation of a resource can be equated with widespread (if uneven) ignorance of the gaps in pertinent information. Some market participants may know all about one piece of information (for example, the availability of the resource); others may know all about a second piece of information (for example, the value of the contribution that the resource could render). But because nobody simultaneously knows *both* these pieces of information, nobody is aware of any possibility of improving the existing allocation of resources. An appraisal of the efficiency of the market process therefore involves an appraisal of the way the market process disseminates these missing links of information necessary for the discovery of superior opportunities for the allocation of resources. In the case of the changing economy, the basic data (concerning resource availability and productivity, and consumer tastes) are free to change. The efficiency of the market process in this case is again a question of its ability to transmit to the relevant decision makers those pieces of new information necessary for the "correct" allocation of resources in terms of the new conditions.

It should be apparent by now that the answer to an inquiry into the efficiency of the market process is embedded in the very description and analysis of the process itself. In the following sections we will merely make explicit what has already been implied in the earlier chapters.[2]

PRICES, PROFITS, AND THE REALLOCATION OF RESOURCES

The market process, as we have seen, is kept in motion by entrepreneurial activity. Entrepreneurial activity is undertaken to gain profits and therefore, of course, avoid losses. The discussions in earlier chapters concerning the circumstances where opportunities for profit exist, and where entrepreneurial activity may be undertaken, are sufficient to indicate that these circumstances *are precisely those where resources are misallocated.* Thus, the general proposition emerges that the market process itself tends to correct existing misallocations of resources—in fact the essence of the process is inseparable from the tendency toward such corrective activity.

On the level of the inquiry made in this chapter, this proposition has a definite meaning which must not be confused with other propositions possible at other levels of inquiry. This proposition asserts there are market forces operating upon the price system that *tend to remove all internal inconsistencies* within the system. In other words, prices are under the pressure of forces tending to ensure that, *as measured by prices,* no resource should be used except where the value of its productive contribution is highest. This merely restates the proposition, developed in previous chapters, that the market process tends to achieve the *dovetailing* of the numerous decisions being made. The process commences with an initial absence of such consistency among decisions. The process itself is

2. See especially pp. 41–46 and pp. 270–281.

the agitation whereby decisions are rendered consistent. This agitation is the continual reshuffling of resources from one employment to another; the process does not cease so long as complete consistency had not been achieved.

The key point is that the misallocation of a resource implies the existence of an unexploited opportunity for profit. A profit opportunity exists wherever a given resource or a given product can be bought in the market at one price and sold again for a higher price. We have seen that the more general kind of profit possibility—where a producer sells his product for a sum exceeding his costs of production—also can be viewed as being created by the existence of two prices for the "same" economic good. In such cases the producer bought resources for one sum and resold them (as a finished product) for a greater sum. A possibility for profit exists wherever there is a price discrepancy, even if its existence is unknown. The price an entrepreneur pays for any resource reflects the highest value placed by other entrepreneurs upon the productive contributions they believe the resource can render at the relevant margins—at least insofar as they are aware of the current price of the resource. If other entrepreneurs believed they could derive a higher market value from the productive contribution of an additional unit of the resource, their competition would tend to force up its price to this point. On the other hand, the price the entrepreneur obtains for his product, together with the technological productivity of the resource, will determine the value that *he* should place upon the productive contribution of the resource. If an opportunity for profit exists, due to a discrepancy in price between the product and the required resources, it follows that unless someone perceives and seizes this opportunity, a misallocation of resources will inevitably occur. A block of resources capable of rendering, in one use, a productive contribution with a high market value (evident in the price that could be obtained in the market for their product in this use) will be employed in other uses only if the market value placed on their productive contribution at the margin is lower (as evidenced by the price that the block of resources can be secured at). The discovery of a profit opportunity amounts thus to the discovery of a situation where, from the normative viewpoint, resources are being misallocated. The grasping of a profit opportunity amounts, by the same token, to a step in the direction of correcting such misallocation.

Prices and the opportunities for profits that they may present play a *dual* role in the market process whereby resource misallocation is corrected. First, a price discrepancy *exposes* an existing misallocation of resources.

The perception of an opportunity for profit is thus the discovery of such misallocation. (This, of course, is not surprising, considering the fact that we are *defining* the correctness or incorrectness of allocation in terms of existing prices.) *Second,* a price discrepancy *promotes* corrective action. A price discrepancy means a chance to make profits. By definition entrepreneurs seek profits; thus, the very situation that symptomizes the need for a correction creates the forces capable of inducing such action. Moreover, and this is of fundamental importance, the entrepreneurial search for profits implies a *search for situations where resources are misallocated.* The price system not only announces the existence of incorrect employments of resources and makes it worthwhile to correct them; it makes it worthwhile to *ferret out* such cases that may exist. (It is, of course, an aspect of this function of the price system that induces entrepreneurs to constantly seek out new products, new patterns of consumer tastes, new resources, or new techniques of production.)

THE ENTREPRENEUR AND RESOURCE ALLOCATION

Thus, any appraisal concerning the efficiency of the market process in detecting and ironing out existing "waste" in resource employment is reduced to an appraisal of the ability of entrepreneurs to detect and seize profit opportunities. If those who are financially able and willing to accept the risks of entrepreneurship are competent to their task, they will attain a high degree of success in pouncing upon even the smallest profit opportunities. They will familiarize themselves with current prices in all parts of the market, for all kinds of resources and products. Specialists among them will concentrate, perhaps, on maintaining complete awareness of all price movements relating to certain limited kinds of productive activity. The ceaseless activity of such entrepreneurs will tend to keep the opportunities for profit relatively small and very short lived. This, as we know, is merely a different way of saying that their activity will prevent resources from being grossly misallocated, and that whatever cases of misallocation do emerge will be of only temporary duration.

On the other hand, if entrepreneurs are not adept in discovering price discrepancies, these discrepancies may conceivably persist for some time, and may even reach considerable proportions. *Entrepreneurial errors* may be fully as "wasteful," from the normative point of view of allocative economics, as corrective entrepreneurial activity is "beneficial." When an entrepreneur makes losses, at the same time he has also wasted resources in employments less valuable than others open to them.

The price-profit system *rewards* the successful entrepreneur—the one who corrects existing cases of resource misallocation—and *penalizes* the unsuccessful ones. In the long run, the market process itself thus attracts only those most able and competent to direct the future course of the process. After all, the efficiency of the market process in detecting waste can only be judged against the background of alternative possibilities. Since some entrepreneurs may be incompetent, and since profit incentives are as attractive to the competent entrepreneur as to the others, it will be the competent and successful entrepreneurs who will tend to stay in business. If the best entrepreneurial talent is insufficient to remove all misallocation, even with the inducement of the profit motive, then the remaining misallocation must simply be undetectable.

The entrepreneur, as noted before, does not have to know *all* the information concerning a misallocated resource. It is sufficient for him to detect a price discrepancy. Changes in consumer demand, the availability of resources, and the technologies of different branches of production will probably create numerous cases where the allocation of resources is inadequate. The entrepreneur need not discover the exact nature of these changes in order to perform corrective action. All that he needs to know are the relevant price changes that have occurred. If he becomes aware of price changes in the product markets before these are reflected, correspondingly, in the resource markets, he will be able to make profits and contribute toward the correction of an otherwise inadequate pattern of resource employment. In fact, this is one of the chief advantages of a price system as a means of communicating knowledge (for the purpose of a more correct allocation of resources), namely, that it conveys only that part of relevant information essential for corrective action.

RESOURCE MOBILITY AND THE ALLOCATION PATTERN

Until now our discussion has implicitly assumed perfect *mobility* of all resources. In other words we have argued as if every resource owner will respond immediately to the offer of a higher price, and that all that is needed for a profit-seeking entrepreneur to succeed in luring away resources from a "wrong" employment to the correct one is to offer slightly higher prices than are being offered by the other (less well-informed) entrepreneurs. In a purely formal sense this assumption is irreproachable, but needs some interpretation and caution when the analysis is applied to real world situations.

It may happen that a resource owner cannot transfer the sale of his resource endowment from one branch of production to another without incurring costs. Such costs may be either psychological or pecuniary in nature (or both). A laborer may feel an attachment to his job, friends, and surroundings that is sufficiently strong to prevent his changing jobs for a small increase in pay. Some resource owners may prefer that the services of their resources go into one branch of production rather than into another. Again, the different location of two entrepreneurs competing for the services of a given block of resources may involve out-of-pocket expenditures on the part of the resource owner desiring to take advantage of a more attractive price offer. All these may be grouped together as costs of transferring resources. These costs have the effect of reducing the mobility of resources, and of delaying the adjustments that would otherwise be secured by the market process.

Insofar as these costs express the personal tastes of resource owners, or reflect, say, the direct employment of other resources physically necessary to effect resource transfers, it is misleading to say that these costs interfere with the correct allocation of resources. These costs may be no less real, and no less "deserving" of being considered in the pattern of resource allocation, than any other kinds of cost. A system which directs labor to a more productive employment for one less productive, but that altogether ignores the costs of transporting the laborers from the one location to another would clearly be inefficient. Similarly, any other costs of moving, insofar as they can influence prices, must be considered in the appraisal of the allocational efficiency of a price system.

Any inquiry into a real world concerning the efficiency of its allocation pattern must bear these considerations in mind. Especially if the normative standards of the inquiring economist lead him to measure efficiency against a yardstick that does not consider certain of these costs of transferring resources, he must be prepared to find the market process delayed in the execution of its allocative functions. It may happen, in addition, that from the long-run point of view, such costs of transfer may be less formidable than in the short run. (In the long view, it might not be more difficult to make friends in a new location than in an old location; in the long view, it might not cost more to furnish a home in a new location than to refurnish a home in the old location; and so on.)[3] In this case the market process will secure results (in respect to advancing toward a more correct

3. From a wider point of view, the long run increases mobility in the sense that young members of a labor force, for example, can begin their careers in places strange to their parents far more easily than their parents themselves could have changed location.

allocation of resources), slowly but surely, if the conditions that call for a correction in resource allocation are sufficiently permanent in character.

MONOPOLY AS AN OBSTACLE TO CORRECT RESOURCE ALLOCATION

A genuine obstacle to the ability of the market process to secure the correct allocation of resources is the monopolization of resources. We have seen in the preceding chapter that where a resource has been endowed only to one market participant, he may be able to exact monopoly prices from the market for the sale of the resource itself, or he may be able, by monopolizing the production of products that require the monopolized resource as a factor of production, to exact monopoly prices for the products. In such cases the monopolist's control over the resource enables him to defy the market process. He serves his own interests best by refusing to allow his resource to be combined with other resources where, together, they can make their most valuable productive contribution to the market (as measured by the prices of the other resources and the price of the product from which the monopolist is able to bar them).

Whereas in the absence of monopoly power, entrepreneurial activity tends to manipulate the allocation of resources so as to lead toward the elimination of profit, the monopolist-producer may be able to secure a permanent gain in the form of an excess of sales revenue over costs of production, which is immune from erosion through the efforts of other entrepreneurs.

ARTIFICIAL OBSTACLES TO CORRECT RESOURCE ALLOCATION

Besides monopoly power (which may be endowed by nature), there may be numerous *artificial* obstacles to the process working toward correct resource allocation. Although such obstacles are ruled out of a pure market system by definition,[4] arbitrary controls may easily be grafted on to a market system. (Most present-day "capitalist" economies, in fact, consist of market systems where a greater or smaller volume of obstacles have been imposed for various reasons.) From the point of view of the market system itself, all such arbitrary controls are "obstacles" that "interfere" with the normal operation of the market process. Such controls hamper the allocative functions of the market system. (From the point of view of policy, therefore, the advantages expected to follow from the imposition

4. See pp. 14–15.

of any controls upon the market system must be compared with the consequent loss in allocative efficiency.)[5]

Market participants may band together (for example, through appropriate extensions of governmental power) to circumscribe the range within which each participant can exercise free choice in the market. A very general form that such circumscriptions may assume is that of imposed restrictions upon price movements. Minimum (or maximum) prices may be declared for particular products (or for products sold to particular consumers), or for particular resources (or for the resources when sold to producers of specified products). If the free market prices do not conflict with the imposed price floors (ceilings), then, of course, the restrictions are innocuous and, indeed, superfluous. But where the price that would have emerged on the free market is prohibited, the restrictions tend to interdict the market from allocating resources in the optimum manner with respect to the given availability of resources, the given tastes of consumers, and the given distribution of knowledge concerning these data. Exchanges that might have taken place at lower (higher) prices are prohibited. Quantities of output that might have been produced and sold at lower (higher) prices remain unproduced; the resources that might have been employed in more important uses must seek employment in the production of other, less important products. Resources that might have been employed at lower prices (or at higher prices) remain idle, with either a consequent direct loss of potential output (output for which consumers are prepared to pay), or a consequent loss of efficiency because of the use of inferior substitutes or substitutes needed urgently for other purposes.

In addition, hindrance of the market process may consist of artificial obstacles to resource mobility (for example, immigration laws). Or there may be institutional grants of monopoly power (for example, patent laws). Or there may be an infinity of different patterns of taxes and subsidies that might bring about an allocation of resources different from what would result from the unhampered market process. Clearly, each such possibility must be analyzed on its own merits. The general tools of analysis developed in earlier chapters must be applied to the special restrictions

---

5. Of course, a society might attempt to alter the consequences of a free market system, not by hampering the free market, but by redistributing at the start of each day the initial natural endowments of the market participants. This would change the data, but might permit the market process to continue without obstacle. Not all natural endowments, of course, can be transferred.

imposed in each case. In each case the restrictions will then affect in some way the resulting complex of productive organization, incomes, and resource employment.

These interferences with the market mechanism may prevent it from *revealing* existing misallocations of resources (as when the market is prevented from allowing the "true" prices of resources or of products to emerge), or they may prevent the exploitation and *correction* of such misallocations as are discovered (as when the mobility of resources is restricted, or when competition is artificially curbed, or when special taxes or other sanctions are imposed on profits, or when inefficient producers are subsidized).

A market economy, even the purest of pure, can never be a utopia. So long as scarcity is the fundamental fact of economic life, the participants in the market must resign themselves to limited consumption. Participants are endowed with only limited, periodic initial resource endowments. They may be able to convert these endowments in the market, through exchange and/or production, into more highly desired income streams. However successful they may be in their attempts to do this, they can still imagine income streams that they would prize even more highly but that are beyond their reach. All that a market can do is to provide the framework within which participants may squeeze the utmost out of their initial endowments through a system of social competitive cooperation and division of labor. Even if such a process were carried through to its ultimate possibilities, nobody would necessarily be guaranteed against unhappiness or even hunger. All that participants would be guaranteed against would be waste. But, as we have seen, the market process cannot be carried to its utmost possibilities. All that the market can offer to its participants, therefore, is a *process* that is ceaselessly at work *tending* to prevent waste from being perpetuated and from being carried too far. This is certainly no guarantee against dissatisfaction, but it is at the same time of tremendous value when the extent and complexity of the required processes are considered. Interference with the webs of forces that are woven through the market process limits the attempts of participants to coordinate their activities through an engine of remarkable efficiency—the market. The analysis of the market process can clarify the costs involved through such interference, making it possible for market participants to decide, through the political process, upon the extent to which they are willing to lay aside their engine of efficiency for the sake of special purposes of possibly overriding importance.

SUMMARY

This chapter appraises the degree of coordination among the decisions made individually by market participants that can be achieved by a price system. The appraisal undertaken here deals with the degree of success achieved by the market in detecting and correcting existing "errors."

A unit of resource is said to be *misallocated* if the market value of the actual productive contribution falls short of the market value of some alternative productive contribution that it *could* be making elsewhere in the economy. A unit of resource can be misallocated only as a result of the *imperfect knowledge* of some market participants. An appraisal of the efficiency of the market process therefore involves the appraisal of the way it detects gaps in available knowledge, and the way it proceeds to fill these gaps. The key point with respect to the market process is that the misallocation of a unit of a resource (together with the antecedent imperfection of knowledge) implies the *existence of an unexploited opportunity for profit*. Price discrepancies *expose* misallocation in the form of profit opportunities. Further prices *promote* corrective activity by attracting entrepreneurs to seize these opportunities. The entrepreneurial search for profit implies a *search* for the consequences of previously imperfect knowledge and an attempt to correct them.

Rapidity in this process of correcting existing misallocations requires resource *mobility*. An obstacle to the process may be monopoly control of certain resources. Numerous *artificial obstacles* may conceivably be introduced into an economy that may hamper this market process. Control of prices is the most direct kind of obstacle of this group. The analysis of the market process throws light on the costs involved in attempts to interfere in such ways with the market process.

SUGGESTED READINGS

Hayek, F. A., "The Use of Knowledge in Society," *American Economic Review,* September, 1945, reprinted in *Individualism and Economic Order,* Routledge and Kegan Paul Ltd., London, 1949.

Baumol, W. J., *Economic Theory and Operations Analysis,* Prentice-Hall Inc., Englewood Cliffs, New Jersey, Ch. 13.

This book has outlined the process by which decisions of individual market participants interact and are brought into mutual coordination. Through the price system, the owners of resources are attracted to sell their respective resources to entrepreneurs whose production plans are designed to dovetail with the consumption plans being made by consumers. The presentation of the analysis, thus far, implied that the masses of decisions involved in the process of plan-interaction were made solely with reference to a *single short period* of time. Resource owners were viewed as deciding each day on the quantity of the day's resource endowments to offer for sale and the prices to ask. Consumers were viewed as deciding each day on the best pattern of income allocation to seek to achieve. Entrepreneurs were seen as deciding each day on what to produce, and what particular combination of resources to employ for the production of a given product. The market process was seen as bringing about revisions, each day, in the plans being made *for that day* as compared with those made for the preceding day.

Once the nature of the market process is understood, it becomes possible to extend the analysis explicitly to cover the interaction of plans made (at any one time) for any number of future time periods. A consumer may make plans for the allocation of his income, not merely the income for the current week, but also the incomes of any number of future weeks. In the summer he may make plans to buy sports clothes now, and at the same time he may plan to set aside enough of his annual income to buy winter clothes several months later. Resource owners may plan to sell some of their currently endowed resources now and next year to sell a different quantity out of the resources they expect to be endowed with next year. In each of these examples a *single* unified plan is made to cover a number of periods of time. A decision within each of these plans, with respect to any *one* of the periods, is a *part* of the whole multi-period plan—the decision made for one period *fits in* with the decisions made for the other periods. (This is of course completely analogous to the situation with respect to a plan made for only a single period, say a particular month. Plans for the quantity of food to be bought this month are coordinated with, and fit into, plans made to buy clothing during the same month.)

In reality, of course, *all* planning is multi-period planning in the sense that the component parts of *any* plan are related to one another in some sort of *time sequence*. One does not plan, in any one month, to buy or consume both food and clothing *perfectly* simultaneously. Even plans made for only the next half-hour specify the sequence of activities. However, it has been convenient to ignore this aspect of plans thus far in this book. The discussion assumed that within each period activities were being planned for, the sequence of activities was of no importance—precisely as if the length of the time period were compressed into a single moment in time. In this appendix we consider in barest outline the consequences, for the analysis of the market process, of the relaxation of this assumption. We wish to take notice of the kinds of alternatives facing the individual resource owner-consumer who plans for several successive periods of time. We wish to explore the consequences of the interaction, in the market, of the plans of numerous such individuals. In addition, we will consider the consequences of the fact that production planning too, involves planning for a number of successive periods in the future. In particular, we will notice the *market* consequences of multi-period production planning.

MULTI-PERIOD DECISIONS IN THE PURE EXCHANGE ECONOMY

The analysis of individual multi-period plans and of the interaction in the market of numerous individual plans of this kind can be demonstrated most simply by the case of the pure exchange economy discussed in Chapter 7. It will be recalled that in such an economy each of the participants finds himself endowed each day with some bundle of endowed commodities which he is free to consume himself or to exchange in the market for other commodities. No production is possible in such an economy: consumption is restricted to the commodities in one's own endowment, or to the commodities obtained by exchange from the endowments of others.

In Chapter 7, each of the participants was viewed as coming to market each day with a plan of action—for buying and for selling—based on his own scale of values on the one hand, and on the market prices that he expects to prevail for each of the commodities on the other hand. Such a plan of action was viewed as incorporating no provision of any kind, however, for future "days." No commodities were saved for future consumption nor were any other opportunities seized for the transformation of one's current endowment into means of future consumption. The scales of values, and the market prices, upon which the marketing plans of any one day were based, referred exclusively to commodities endowed on that day.

As soon as multi-period plans are considered, a whole new series of possibilities becomes relevant. Until now a plan has called for the sacrifice of a quantity of one commodity by sale today, for the sake of the acquisition by purchase on the same day of a quantity of another commodity. A multi-period plan, however, may call for, in addition, the sacrifice of a quantity of one commodity out of the endowment of one particular day, for the sake of the acquisition, *on some other day*, of a quantity of another (or for that matter the same) commodity. Where numerous market participants are in touch with one another, and are aware of the multi-period plans that each is seeking to implement, opportunities are likely to present themselves for mutually profitable *intertemporal exchanges*. The terms upon which such exchanges will be effected will depend on the degree of coordination that the intertemporal market has secured between the different plans.

Even in a Crusoe economy, and even on the assumptions that no possibilities for production exist, opportunities for intertemporal allocation may be opened up through *storage*. We may assume that the storage, for the sake of tomorrow's consumption, of a commodity acquired out of today's endowment calls for no sacrifice other than today's consumption of the stored commodity. (In this way we may justify the treatment of storage in an economy without production.) A decision to store a commodity for the future implies the acceptance of the sacrifice of current consumption for the sake of future consumption. In a market economy several additional opportunities are likely to exist for the sacrifice of present for future consumption. A market participant, for example, may sacrifice a commodity today by sale in order to acquire for tomorrow's consumption a commodity that will appear in tomorrow's endowment of a second participant. And of course such opportunities may exist for "intertemporal transfer between *any* two "days."

THE INTERTEMPORAL MARKET

Clearly, the existence of such opportunities for intertemporal exchanges arises from the differences that exist between the scales of values of the different market participants, in respect to the order in which the pleasures of prospective consumption on different dates are ranked today. Smith gives a dozen oranges today to Robinson in return for the latter's promise to return fifteen oranges on the next day. On Smith's scale the oranges of today rank lower than the oranges of tomorrow; on Robinson's scale the order is reversed. The divergence between the degrees of *time preference* of Smith and Robinson have thus created the conditions for intertemporal exchange.

The emergence of intertemporal exchanges of this kind is accompanied by *intertemporal terms of exchange*. In the single-period market discussed in Chapter 7, there were market prices for each of the commodities exchanged. These prices represented the terms upon which a participant could transform a given quantity of one commodity into a different commodity by exchange. In the multi-period market, quite analogously, intertemporal exchanges yield rates of exchange according to which given commodities of one date can be transformed by exchange in the market into commodities (either the same commodities or different ones) *of a different date.* If Smith gives up 100 oranges today in exchange for Robinson's promise to return 110 oranges a year hence, this 10% "orange-rate of interest" represents the relevant terms of intertemporal exchange. In a monetary economy, of course, intertemporal exchanges need not be on a barter basis. Instead of Smith obtaining a promise of oranges next year in direct exchange for oranges today, he may accept a promise of money for next year and then buy oranges next year when the promise is redeemed. (Or again, he may accept money *now* from Robinson for his sacrificed oranges, and then, in a separate transaction, lend this money for a year to Jones, and buy oranges next year when the loan is repaid.) Under these conditions, terms of intertemporal exchange will be represented most clearly by the money rate of interest, taken in conjunction with the current prices of the various commodities, and with their expected prices for the various relevant future dates.

If a market where intertemporal exchanges are taking place is to be in equilibrium, the multi-period plans of all the participants must "fit in" with one another. The terms of intertemporal exchange must be such that for each planned sacrifice of a quantity of commodity of date *a*, for the acquisition of a commodity of date *b*, some other participant should have been induced to plan the same exchange in reverse. If, as a result of imperfect knowledge of each other's desires, rates of intertemporal exchange are any different from the equilibrium pattern, some participants coming to market, at the end of a trading day, will have been disappointed in their attempts to accomplish intertemporal exchanges; and they will, in making plans for entering into such exchanges on the following day, revise their estimates of the market intertemporal rates of exchange. For equilibrium to exist in the intertemporal market, it is clear, a very precise relationship will be required between (a) the current price of each commodity, (b) the prices that each of the various participants expect to prevail for the various commodities on each of the future dates, and (c) the various money rates of interest prevailing on loans of various maturities.

Of course, just as in the single period case considered in Chapter 7, an intertemporal market may be expected, in general, to be in *dis*equilibrium. Changes in time preference from one day to the next will alter the plans being made and will (on top of all the other changes in the data that tend to keep a market in disequilibrium) complicate the market forces of adjustment that are set into motion by the disequilibrium existing in the market on any one trading day. The intertemporal market, moreover, is subject to complications that are of especial relevance to multi-period decisions. Such decisions, we have seen, depend in an extremely sensitive way upon the *expectations* that participants hold concerning the prices of the various commodities on different future dates. (Intertemporal exchanges may clearly arise merely as a consequence of divergent price expectations on the part of various market participants.) The *uncertainty* and the *risk* necessarily attached to expectations are likely to color the plans being made on any one day, and, in particular, the revisions in plans that will be made as the result of previously disappointed plans. Within the framework of this book, all that can be done is merely to point to these complications without any thorough further examination of them.

SPECULATION AS AN ASPECT OF INTERTEMPORAL MARKETS

The possibilities of intertemporal exchanges outlined thus far indicate the role that *speculation* can play in a pure exchange economy. Suppose there is reason to believe that during some particular future time period the endowments of market participants will contain relatively few oranges (as compared with the endowments of other periods of time). Then many participants would gladly sacrifice the consumption of some oranges during other periods for the sake of oranges during the scarce period. Complete adjustment by the market to achieve this particular allocation of oranges over time would call for the storage of oranges from other periods up to the scarce period. A market that has achieved equilibrium with respect to these expectations and tastes would have adjusted the current price of oranges, the money rate of interest, and the expected future prices of oranges into a very particular pattern. This particular pattern would be such that exactly the "right" quantity of oranges is purchased in the market by speculators during each period to be held in storage for the future scarce period. With this particular pattern prevailing, no two market participants can discover any alteration in their multi-period plans that might leave them both in a preferred position.

Where an intertemporal market has *not* achieved equilibrium with respect to current expectations and tastes (for consumption in the various periods), "arbitrage" opportunities exist which the more alert potential speculators may exploit. Where for example a particular market participant has discovered, *before* the other participants have become alerted to this possibility, the likelihood of a future scarcity of oranges, he will be able to earn speculative profits by exploiting his superior knowledge of future conditions. He will be able to buy oranges today at cheap prices (or, alternatively, to buy cheaply the *promise* of oranges to be delivered in the future) and to sell them for high prices in the future scarce period. By exploiting his superior knowledge in this way he is at the same time reallocating oranges over time, from consumption during periods where the marginal significance of an orange is low, to consumption during a period where the marginal significance of an orange (as ranked by consumers *today*) is higher.

As market participants compete with each other for these speculative profits, the market is brought closer toward equilibrium and further opportunities for such profits become more and more difficult to obtain. In this way entrepreneurial activity succeeds in bringing coordination into the mass of individual intertemporal plans, incorporating their decisions to consume, save, lend, and borrow. All these market repercussions would take place, as we have seen, even in an economy where production is impossible. Where opportunities for production do exist (as they did in the cases studied in Chapters 10 and 11), these kinds of intertemporal exchange (and the resulting opportunities for speculative activity) are no less relevant. In a production economy, however, the necessity and the opportunities also exist to make additional intertemporal decisions; we now turn to these.

MULTI-PERIOD DECISIONS OF PRODUCERS

In an economy where production is possible, market participants find themselves endowed with productive resources. It is possible for the entrepreneur to buy resources, allow them to combine and yield output, and then to sell the output in the product market. A fundamental feature of any decision to produce in the real world is that any decision to produce represents at the same time *a decision to effect an intertemporal transfer of assets.* Since every production process takes time, it follows that every decision to produce is a decision *to sacrifice inputs now for the sake of output later.* This aspect of production was not stressed in the treatment of production in Chapters 8, 9, and later chapters. In these chapters, where attention was focused on other aspects of production, a production decision was treated as if any difference in date between the application of resources and the yield of products could be ignored as of no consequence. We must now outline, or at least point to, the major implications for market theory that arise from taking notice of such time differences. These implications, taken in conjunction with the widened possibilities that exist within a production economy for those intertemporal decisions that we have already noticed for the pure exchange economy (with their application being widened now to cover also decisions concerning *resources* as well as consumer goods), provide the temporal framework within which a market system operates.

In the multi-period production economy, in fact, *each* decision— whether concerning the sale or purchase of a resource, the production of consumer products, or the sale or purchase of consumer products—has a time dimension. Each resource owner must make an allocation over time with respect to the sale of the services of his resource (insofar, that is, as he is able to store his resource endowment over time). Every utilization of a resource for a particular process of production involves an opportunity cost that reflects, not only the potential contribution to other processes of production that this resource might make *now,* but also any such contribution which it might make *at other times.* (Thus, even the employment of a completely specific resource may involve an opportunity cost insofar as its use today precludes its use in the same employment in the future.) Every process of production, as we have seen, reflects an intertemporal transfer, sacrificing current inputs in favor of future output. Every decision to buy or to sell consumer products involves, of course, the very same kinds of intertemporal decisions we considered in the preceding sections.

Now, the time dimension attached to the decisions concerning the sale or purchase of resources or of products introduces no essential complications beyond the analysis referred to in the preceding sections. For equilibrium to prevail there must be certain relationships between the current prices and the expected future prices of the respective items, and, of course, the relevant rates of interest. These will spell out the terms upon which present resources or products can be directly transferred into specified future ones. The agitation of the market will be continually adjusting these intertemporal terms of exchange so long as they perversely encourage unrealizable plans on the part of market participants. But the inherence in every production decision of a temporal aspect does introduce complications not previously encountered.

These complications have to do principally with the necessity faced by each would-be producer to choose between production processes absorbing *different lengths of time*. This, in turn, is closely related to the problem of which particular *capital goods* will be employed for the production of given consumer goods. Let us first consider the production of a given consumer good, say a chair, by a would-be producer who finds only *naturally endowed* resources available in the market. Any of several methods of production might be employed. Each of them requires the use of productive resources; in each of them the producer finds himself, after the elapse of some time interval shorter than the length of the entire process, in command of *intermediate goods*. If, for example, he attempts to fashion a seat, with his bare hands, out of a tree, an uncompleted process of production will have yielded perhaps the pieces of wood to be somehow contrived later on into the chair. If, on the other hand, he first contrives tools to construct the chair with, an uncompleted process of production might yield only a hammer or a saw. *In both cases the intermediate products are steps toward the final product.* In selecting the particular method of production to adopt, a would-be producer is at the same time selecting the particular form the intermediate goods should take.

THE PLACE OF CAPITAL GOODS IN PRODUCTION

Observing a cross section of a particular process of production prior to its completion, then, one encounters intermediate products. Such products constitute *capital goods*. Looking *backward*, one realizes that the production of such capital goods has already *absorbed time*. In fact, it may be possible to know of some alternative process of production that might have yielded already, in the time already absorbed, at least some quantity of the final product. (Thus, during the time in which the carpenter's tools have been constructed, it might have been possible to fashion one crude chair without tools.) Looking *ahead,* one realizes that the past production of these capital goods will *save future time* in the attainment of the final output aimed at. Assuming that the producer selected wisely the capital good that he has produced, it follows that he is temporally closer to the attainment of his own output goal than he would have been otherwise. In fact, of course, it was precisely this prospect—of being closer to the final goal—that justified the intertemporal transfer of assets represented by the production of the intermediate product. In producing the intermediate products, the producer sacrificed the inputs of an earlier date (inputs that he might have been able to utilize for earlier consumption) for the sake of the intermediate product of today. He did so only because of the prospect of the superior position he is *now* placed in as a prospective producer, by virtue of his command of the intermediate product.

Now, in a market economy, it is not necessary for the producer of a final consumer product to have himself produced the capital goods he uses in his production process. He may buy them from other producers for definite prices. These prices, like all others in the market, will reflect on the one hand their usefulness to *users of the capital goods* (as expressed in the *demand* side of the market); and on the other hand will reflect (in the conditions of *supply*) the sums required by the *producers of the capital goods* to have made it worth their while to devote *their* resources to the production of these goods rather than others. Demand conditions for capital goods will thus reflect the relatively greater *nearness* in time to the final production goal, which command of these goods confers. Supply conditions for capital goods will reflect in turn, among other costs of production, the sacrifice of *time* that went into their production. Whatever the money rate of interest that is currently prevailing, and which helps determine the terms of intertemporal exchange, it will be reflected in the price of the capital good, as compared with the prices of the inputs used in its production. Ultimately, of course, such capital goods will be produced only in the quantities that will be demanded by the producers of final products; that is, only in the quantities justified by the superior achievements of producers using these goods and by the prices of the final products themselves.

Where, for the sake of simplicity, two different capital goods can be produced out of the *same* inputs, but require respectively different periods of time for their production, definite market forces will influence the decision as to which of the two should be produced. The more time consuming of the two goods will involve the greater sacrifice in terms of *postponement*. The producer of the capital goods could clearly benefit from his efforts *sooner* by producing the other good. Or, if this producer has *borrowed* the required inputs (or purchased them with borrowed money), and produces the more time consuming of the two capital goods, he will have to compensate the lenders for the additional postponement that *they* accept, by paying interest for the longer period. This additional sacrifice clearly will be justified only by the correspondingly higher price obtainable for this capital good in the market. And such a higher price will clearly only be obtainable as a result of the correspondingly superior productivity of the more time-consuming capital good.

If the relative superiority in production of this capital good (whose production absorbed more time) is *very* outstanding, it may conceivably offer an opportunity for intertemporal transfer of assets that is superior to any obtainable elsewhere in the market. In this case the inputs originally invested in the capital good have yielded a greater return in value of final product than could have been obtained by investing the value of the inputs elsewhere over the same period. The existence of such an opportunity clearly will result in market agitation that will operate toward lowering the price of the final product, and raising the prices of the inputs and of the money rate of interest, until the opportunity for intertemporal transfer of assets is no more profitable by this means than by other means.

The market process tends to determine in this way, not only the rates of interest, the prices and quantities of resources used, and the prices and quantities of products produced, but also the *time structure of production*. The time structure of production refers to the lengths of the processes of production that are necessary to make up final products. A cross section of a production economy at any one time reveals a mass of capital goods, each of them an intermediate product leading toward some final output. The makeup of this mass of capital goods, the degree to which they represent greater or smaller investments of past time, is a reflection of the earlier operation of the market process. The greater the degree that market participants have in the past been prepared to sacrifice earlier for later consumption, the "deeper" will be the time structure of the existing capital stock of the economy. The continued operation of the market process will now determine (a) how this *existing* stock of capital goods will be used for further production (that is, for the production of what products each of the capital goods will be employed), (b) whether the stock of capital goods will be added to, merely replaced as they wear away, or permitted to depreciate without replacement—and (simultaneously with the determination of the quantity, if any, of new capital goods to be produced), (c) the *particular* capital goods to be produced and especially the *time structure* of these goods (that is, the lengths of time to be taken for these goods to be produced, and the planned lengths of time for which these goods will be used severally in further processes of production in the future). The analysis of the way the market process determines these matters comprises the body of the *theory of capital,* a branch of price theory where the temporal aspects of the market are of the essence.

SUGGESTED READINGS

Mises, L. v., *Human Action,* Yale University Press, New Haven, Connecticut, 1949, Chs. 18, 19.

Stackelberg, H. v., *The Theory of the Market Economy,* Oxford University Press, New York, 1952, Bk. 2–Ch. 6, Bk. 3–Ch. 3, Bk. 5–Ch. 3.

Malanos, G., *Intermediate Economic Theory,* J. B. Lippincott Co., Philadelphia, 1962, Chs. 4, 12, 13, 14.

Conard, J. W., *An Introduction to the Theory of Interest,* University of California Press, Berkeley, California, 1959, Ch. 8.

Henderson, J. M., and R. E. Quandt, *Microeconomic Theory,* McGraw-Hill Book Co., Inc., New York, 1958, Ch. 8.

INDEX

abstractness aspect, economic theory, 8–11

allocation efficiency: overview, 334; as economic problem, 35–37, 322–23; imperfect knowledge effects, 325–26; obstacles to, 331–33; and profit opportunities, 326–29; resource misallocation defined, 323–24; and resource mobility, 329–31

autarkic economy, defined, 2

automobile market example, market system structure, 22–23

average revenue relationship, market demand elasticity, 104–6

Ayers, C. E., xii*n*3

buyer's surplus, defined, 118

capital factor category, production activity, 161–62

capital goods, production activity, 207–13, 342–44

cardinal utility approach, 62–64, 71*n*3

cartels, resource, 289–92

centrally controlled economy, defined, 2

choice category, human action, 5–7

compensation element, in coordination problem, 40–41, 43–44

complementarity characteristic, production factors, 162, 163

complementary goods, 107–8, 110–11

complementary related goods, 55–56

consumer activity: dynamic nature, 108–11; from resource owners, 43–44, 68*n*1; role in market system model, 16–17, 19–23, 41–42. *See also* *specific topics, e.g.,* demand analysis,

individual; general market *entries;* income allocation

consumers-only model, competition element: overview, 113–15, 142–46; graphic representations, 147–52; imperfect knowledge conditions, 120–25, 132–38; monopoly effects, 138–42; multi-period market, 336–37; multiple-commodity market, 125–38; perfect knowledge conditions, 116–20, 130–31; resource-constrained model compared, 257–59, 261–62; single-commodity market, 115–25, 147–52

coordination problem: overview, 46–47, 321–22; elements of, 38–41; solution processes, 41–46. *See also* allocation efficiency

cross elasticity, 107–8

demand analysis, individual: elasticity measures, 96–97, 100–101; graphic representation, 85–88; static nature, 88–90

demand analysis, market: overview, 92–94, 111–12; elasticity measures, 96–101; entrepreneurial perspectives, 101–7; graphic representation, 94–96; revenue relationships, 103–7

demand forces, theoretical foundation, 48–51. *See also* consumer *entries;* income allocation; marginal utility

diamonds example, marginal utility, 57–58

diminishing marginal utility, 52–55, 70, 109–10, 120, 202

347

189–94; and monopolized resources, 304; price effects, 222–25; and profits, 269–70; proportions change representation, 175–76; and resource misallocation, 323–24; scale change representation, 175–78; variable proportions mapping, 180–89; variable proportions problem, 178–80. *See also* single-factor market model; single-product market model

production-constrained market model, 256–66. *See also* general market *entries*

profits: as coordination solution, 41–43, 44–46; in general market model, 269–70, 271–73, 278–80; from misallocated resources, 326–29; as production motive, 159–60

proportions change representation, factors of production, 175–76

purpose category, human action, 5–6

quantity utility approach, 62–64

related goods, marginal utility, 55–57
relative character of utility, 61
rent, costs compared, 201
resource owners, role in market system model, 17–18, 19–23. *See also* general market *entries*; production *entries*
returns to scale, 176–78
revenue relationships, demand elasticity, 103–7
Rothbard, Murray, xii–xiii

scale change representation, factors of production, 175–78
seller's surplus, defined, 118
shirt examples, diminishing marginal utility, 54–55, 64, 69
short-run costs, 206–7, 210–18, 223

single-commodity market, consumers-only model: graphic representations, 147–52; imperfect knowledge conditions, 120–25, 272–73; perfect knowledge conditions, 115–20

single-factor market model: overview, 243–44, 253–54; adjustment processes, 250–53; assumptions, 243–44; equilibrium conditions, 244–50

single-product market model: overview, 252–54; adjustment processes, 235–42, 252–53; assumptions, 228–29, 231–32, 242–43; long-run equilibrium price, 229–31; short-run equilibrium price, 232–35

specialization and efficiency, 38, 40–41, 158–59

specificity characteristic, production factors, 163–64, 207–10

speculation, 18–19, 339–40

steel market example, market system structure, 22–23

substitutability characteristic, production factors, 162–63, 170–75

substitutes/substitution: cross elasticity, 107–8; in general market model, 277–78; monopolized resources, 287–88; related goods, 56–57. *See also* complementary goods; income allocation

supply forces. *See* production *entries*
surface, production, defined, 167

taxicab firm example, opportunity costs, 198–200
time element. *See* multi-period market
toothpaste example, demand elasticity, 103
total revenue relationship, demand elasticity, 104
total utility, 63–64

This book is set in Scala and Scala Sans, created by the
Dutch designer Martin Majoor in the 1990s.

Printed on paper that is acid-free and meets the
requirements of the American National Standard for
Permanence of Paper for Printed Library Materials,
z39.48-1992. ∞

Book design by Richard Hendel, Chapel Hill, North Carolina
Typography by Newgen, Austin, Texas
Printed and bound by Malloy, Inc., Ann Arbor, Michigan